The refugee question
in mid-Victorian politics

T0381817

The refugee question
in mid-Victorian Politics

BERNARD PORTER
Senior Lecturer in History, University of Hull

CAMBRIDGE UNIVERSITY PRESS
CAMBRIDGE
LONDON · NEW YORK · MELBOURNE

CAMBRIDGE UNIVERSITY PRESS
Cambridge, New York, Melbourne, Madrid, Cape Town, Singapore, São Paulo, Delhi

Cambridge University Press
The Edinburgh Building, Cambridge CB2 8RU, UK

Published in the United States of America by Cambridge University Press, New York

www.cambridge.org
Information on this title: www.cambridge.org/9780521226387

First published 1979
This digitally printed version 2008

A catalogue record for this publication is available from the British Library

Library of Congress Cataloguing in Publication data
Porter, Bernard
The refugee question in mid-Victorian politics
Bibliography: p.
Includes index
1. Great Britain – Politics and government – 1837–1901
2. Refugees, Political – Great Britain – History
3. Great Britain – Social conditions – 19th century
I. Title
DA550.P6   325'.21'0941   78–73947

ISBN 978-0-521-22638-7 hardback
ISBN 978-0-521-08815-2 paperback

For
Zoë, Ben and Kate

Contents

Illustrations

Acknowledgments

This book is based to a very large extent on manuscript materials in public and private collections. I am glad therefore to acknowledge the help given to me by the guardians of those collections: in particular by Sir Robin Mackworth-Young and Miss Jane Langton in the Royal Archives at Windsor; Miss Margaret Cash in the Hampshire Record Office; Miss J. W. Thompson of the Newcastle Central Library; Mr H. G. Pearson, Departmental Record Officer at the Home Office; and by the staffs of the Public Record Office, the British Library, and the Royal Commission on Historical Manuscripts. For their assistance in other ways I must record my grateful thanks to Mrs Valerie Masterman, Assistant Departmental Record Officer at New Scotland Yard; Mr David Holland, who helped me in connexion with the Spencer Walpole papers; Dr David Sumner, who advised me on a very ancient medical matter; Dr J. J. Tobias and Dr Roger Bullen, who gave me some useful hints on matters historical; and Dr Derek Beales, whose comments on my manuscript were helpful in many ways. I owe probably the greatest debt to the Librarian and staff of my own university library, and to the British Academy, a grant from whose 'Small Grants Research Fund in the Humanities' enabled me to glean most of my material. The University of Hull provided other monies, and time to write up my research in its present form in the guise of a term's leave of absence.

Certain materials from private archives have been consulted, and are reproduced, by permission of their owners, for which I am grateful. Letters in the Royal Archives are reproduced with the gracious permission of Her Majesty the Queen. Items from the Cowen Collection are included by permission of the County Archivist, Tyne and Wear County Council. Permission to quote from the Palmerston papers has been kindly granted by the Trustees of the Broadlands Archives Trust and the Royal Commission on Historical Manuscripts. The Clarendon and Malmesbury papers were consulted and quoted with the permission of the present Earl of Clarendon and of Lord FitzHarris. One 'closed' government file was consulted by special permission of the Home Office, who have also approved the passages in the book which are based on it.

I cannot say that the dedicatees of this book, my children, have helped its progress: but they have often hindered delightfully. My wife Deirdre has sheltered me from the worst effects of their disruptive activities, at a difficult time, and in other ways has helped the book more than she knows. For the defects in it, and also its considerable limitations, I am alone responsible.

Cottingham,
July 1978

BERNARD PORTER

Abbreviations

B.L.Add.Ms.	British Library Additional Manuscript
Clar. P.	Clarendon Papers
Cowl.P.	Cowley Papers
FO	Foreign Office
HO	Home Office
Malm.P.	Malmesbury Papers
MEPO	Metropolitan Police
Palm.P.	Palmerston Papers
PD	Parliamentary Debates ('Hansard') [e.g. 3PD 48 c. 1760 = Parliamentary Debates, third series, volume 48, column 1760]
PP	Parliamentary Papers
PRO	Public Record Office
QVL	*Queen Victoria's Letters*
RA	Royal Archives
TWAD	Tyne and Wear Archives Department

I

Introductory: Asylum

From time to time during the nineteenth century, whenever for some reason or other the bubbling cauldron of continental European politics could no longer contain them, little bands of political exiles were found crossing the English Channel or the North Sea to Britain, to rest and recuperate – or maybe to continue their struggles – in an environment which was politically more tranquil, and more safe. They were called refugees: but the term covered a multitude of situations. Some of them were exiles by decree – *'proscrits'*. Others were deposed kings and royalists, or the remnants of failed revolutionary armies, or escapees from prisons abroad. A few of them were refugees more by choice: men who had chosen to live elsewhere rather than obey régimes they disagreed with, or who anticipated that harm would come to them if they stayed, and so fled before the need arose. Some of the exiles came to Britain *via* other European countries like Belgium or Switzerland which had appeared safe refuges at first, but were not strong enough to remain safe for long, in the lee of powerful winds from bullying neighbours. Some of them stayed in Britain only for a while before they moved on again across the wider water to America, though these tended to be the defeatists among them, who had given up their old national ambitions, and now wanted only to settle down. By and large the ones who stayed in Britain were the more politically active ones, who chose Britain rather than America because it was closer to where their hearts still lay; and most of them regarded their exile as only temporary, although for some it could last for decades, and might not end before their death.

When it did end it was either this way, or by their voluntary repatriation; never by decree of the British authorities, who from 1823 right through the nineteenth century did not expel a single refugee from Britain, or prohibit a single one of them from coming in. Britain consequently was the most dependable of all European asylums, for everybody. For most Britons this was a source of considerable national pride. 'I can well conceive', said the Conservative Lord Malmesbury in the middle of the century, 'the pleasure and happiness of a refugee, hunted from his native land, on approaching the shores of England, and the joy with which he first catches sight of them; but they are not greater than the pleasure and happiness every Englishman feels in knowing that his country affords the refugee a home and safety.'[1] We shall see that it was not always regarded so pleasurably by either party. Nevertheless her policy of asylum remained an inviolate feature of Britain's national life, one of her most distinctive freedoms, during nearly the whole of Victoria's reign, and a little way before and beyond. It is this policy and its vicissitudes during the middle years of the nineteenth century – not the lives and activities of the refugees themselves – which it is this book's principal task to describe and explain.

Britain was not unique in affording asylum at this time to refugees. Most other European nations did so too; and some did more for them, and could at times boast larger colonies of them, than Britain. Very often Britain was a refugee's last choice rather than his first, and he would stay in France or Switzerland if he could. What was however distinctive about Britain's policy of asylum was that it was entirely undiscriminating. Continental countries by and large were selective about whom they took in: if they accepted republicans they would not accept monarchists; if they welcomed Poles they might not welcome Italians. Britain took in anyone: men whose causes she disliked and feared as well as those she sympathised with; republicans and socialists as well as liberals, autocrats as well as constitutionalists, men who wished her no good as well as those who worshipped her for taking them; even firebrands and madmen and murderers. 'We do not enquire', wrote a member of Parliament in 1858, 'whether they be democrats or aristocrats, French Italian or Austrian, Buonapartist or legitimist. We only know them to be friendless, homeless, and miserable.'[2] At Holland House, which was a favourite haunt of many of the more prominent refugees, Henry Greville in 1857 was amused to notice 'people of all sorts, of all nations and of every hue of politics . . . To-day, for example, M. de Maupas, who was Préfet de Police when the coup d'état was made, met in Lady Holland's Salon M. Duvergier d'Hausanne, whom he arrested!'[3] At different times – occasionally at one and the same time – Britain could give homes to men as wide apart in their political allegiances as Louis Philippe, Louis Napoleon and Louis Blanc: which would have been a combustible chemistry anywhere else in Europe. Nor was her policy of asylum a respecter of rank or reputation: 'From the despotic ruler of sixty millions', wrote an Italian in 1845, 'to the starving organ-grinder and broom-girl, the land of refuge is equally open to all. As at the famous Carnival of Venice, dethroned kings, disgraced viziers, and bankrupt financiers, may be seen jostling each other in the London

---

[1] 3 PD 119 c. 675 (5 April 1852).
[2] Sir Arthur Hallam Elton, *The Case Against the Late Ministry Plainly Stated* (1858), p. 5.
[3] Countess of Strafford (ed.), *Leaves from the Diary of Henry Greville*, 3rd series (1904), p. 27.

streets.'[4] It was this entire lack of discrimination which made Britain, if not the refugees' first choice of a home, the safest of their last resorts.

Like all the best British freedoms, this policy of asylum was maintained, not by law, but by the absence of laws. This too was unusual. Most sovereign societies in the present and in the past have felt justified in exerting some kind of special control over who comes into them from outside: over immigration, and over the activities of outsiders living in them. Britain at this time did not. She never abrogated the *residual* right of legislating against aliens if she felt it to be necessary. In 1793 she *had* felt it to be necessary, and had enacted then a law to regulate them and to allow her government to expel them which, with modifications, remained in force until 1826.[5] In 1848 another similar Alien Bill was enacted for two years (though it was never implemented against anyone).[6] But these Acts were considered to be justified only by very extraordinary circumstances, and in 'normal' times it was not thought proper that governments should have any powers at all to exclude or expel aliens, except under extradition treaties for crimes committed abroad. Consequently from 1826 until 1848, and again from 1850 to 1905, there was nothing on the statute book to enable the executive to prevent aliens from coming and staying in Britain as they liked. (There always remained the technical possibility, maintained by some constitutional lawyers, that ministers of the Crown could expel aliens by royal prerogative, without legislative sanction: but it was a case which was disputed, and was never likely to be tested for the constitutional fuss it might cause.)[7] This freedom of entry applied to all foreigners, whether refugees or not, and for whatever reason they desired entry. That they were free to come in did not mean that once they were in they were free to do anything they liked. While they were in England they were subject, of course, to the same laws as Britons. Beyond this they were subjected also to certain civil disabilities: things which Britons could do which they could not, unless they became naturalised, which until 1844 was a difficult and expensive process;[8] and sometimes not even then. Before 1870 an alien could not hold any place or trust or emolument under

[4] 'Anglomane' (Anthony Gallenga), 'Foscolo and English hospitality', in *Fraser's Magazine*, vol. 31 (1845), p. 402.

[5] *An act for establishing regulations respecting aliens arriving in this kingdom, or resident therein, in certain cases*: 33 Geo. III c. 4.

[6] *An act to authorise for one year, and to the end of the then next session of Parliament, the removal of aliens from the realm*: 11 & 12 Vict. c. 20; and see *Return, showing the number of aliens who may have been directed . . . to depart the realm*: PP (1850) xxxiii p. 227; and *vide infra*, p. 86 fn. 113.

[7] 'An Alien' (William Empson), 'On the Alien Bill', in *Edinburgh Review*, vol. 42 (1825), pp. 101ff.; and see Lord Grenville in the House of Lords, 21 December 1792: Cobbett's *Parliamentary History of England*, vol. 30, cc. 156–7.

[8] In 1818 it was discovered that an ancient act of the Scottish parliament still entitled any foreigner who bought £80 of stock in the Bank of Scotland to become a naturalised Scot, and consequently, since the Act of Union, a naturalised Briton. This loophole was speedily closed: see 1PD 38 cc. 1266ff.

the Crown, or hold land unless he took out letters patent of denization, and even then he could not inherit land or transmit it to any of his children born before his denization. These disabilities were claimed by one M.P. in 1843 to be 'more rigid, more inhospitable, than those of any other civilized country in the world',[9] although the property qualification was frequently evaded.[10] In 1870 they were greatly ameliorated.[11] Even before 1870, however, aliens were absolutely tolerated as *visitors*, which made Britain in this sense one of the *most* hospitable countries of Europe. As well as the same laws as Britons they were subject to the same processes of law, with the added privilege, until 1870, of being able to be tried by a 'mixed' jury of half foreigners if they so elected. They could not be prevented from coming in to Britain, or expelled for doing anything in Britain. After 1836 they did not even have to notify anyone they had come or were there.[12] For the best part of the nineteenth century, therefore, the British government deliberately denied itself any control over immigration, and appeared indeed for the most part to take no interest in it.

So far as the mass of immigrants was concerned, there seemed to be good material reasons for this. The main one was that foreign immigration appeared to do no harm, and it was very much against the spirit of nineteenth-century Britain to regulate things which were harmless. Foreigners in Britain were just not numerous enough, for example, to present any great social problems which were not easily and locally resolvable. The 1851 Census reported 50,289 foreigners in England and Wales, in a total population of nearly 18 millions, which was a percentage of only 0.28. They were greatly outnumbered by the 520,000 Irish in England and Wales, who *did* present social problems, and by 130,000 Scots. In London the percentage of foreigners was far higher at 1.08 (25,500 out of 2,362,000), but there were still many more from Ireland (108,000), Scotland (30,000) and from the English and Welsh provinces (723,000).[13] The number of foreigners in England and Wales increased steadily thereafter: to 84,090 in 1861, 100,638 in 1871, and 118,031 in 1881;[14] but before the massive Jewish influx of the 1890s they were

---

[9] 3PD 67 c. 429 (Hutt, 8 March 1843).

[10] See 3PD 199 c. 1132 (Clarendon, 3 March 1870).

[11] 33 Vict. c. 14, clause 2.

[12] Technically they were still supposed to, but in 1843 this stipulation was reported to be 'very generally disregarded by Foreigners, and . . . never enforced by the authorities': *Report from the Select Committee on the laws affecting aliens*, PP (1843) v, pp. ix, xii.

It should perhaps be made clear that these general statements, and other similar ones in the course of this book, apply only to the British mainland, and not to Ireland, which for most of the century was subject to different laws and practices.

[13] *1851 Census Report*, vol. II, pp. ciii, cclxxxviii.

[14] *1861 Census Report*, vol. II, p. lxxv; *1871 Census Report*, vol. III, p. 1; and *Report from the Select Committee on emigration and immigration (Foreigners)*, PP (1888) xi, p. 252. In 1823 there were reported to be 25,000 aliens in Britain: 2PD 10, c. 1340 (23 March 1824).

insignificant by the side of other minority groups. Even these figures did not accurately reflect the number of foreigners *settled* in Britain: nearly a fifth of them were classified in the Census reports as 'seamen', and many of the others may have been on short visits only. Those who did come to settle did not generally come in as cheap labour, and so were not resented for that, or not half so much as the Irish. Many of them worked at very specialist occupations which were their acknowledged preserves, and so competed with scarcely anyone: Italian organ-grinders and fine craftsmen, Swiss confectioners and pastrycooks, French language teachers, German bandsmen, merchants, bakers and clockmakers.[15] The rest could be absorbed easily and unobtrusively into the British labour force. And when they did compete with natives, it was felt (though not perhaps by the natives they were in direct competition with) that this might not be such a bad thing anyway. A Select Committee Report in 1843 summarised the prevailing orthodoxy:

that it is desirable for every people to encourage the settlement of foreigners among them, since by such means they will be practically instructed in what it most concerns them to know, and enabled to avail themselves of whatever foreign sagacity, ingenuity, or experience may have produced in art and science which is most perfect.[16]

If foreigners were going to compete with Englishmen, said a Liberal politician in the same year, then they would compete with them anyway whether they were in England or outside: so was it not better that they should compete with them in England, where they could teach them their tricks?[17] An oft-cited illustration of this, which touched the refugee question too, was the immigration in the seventeenth century of the French Huguenots; bringing with them (as Henry Brougham told the House of Commons in 1816) 'their wealth, where they had any, and . . . what, perhaps, was more valuable, their industry and skill, which they poured into our lap'. In this case and in others, 'The asylum which our humanity granted they amply repaid.'[18] Free migration, in fact, was a very simple and obvious corollary of free trade, and its benefits as indisputable.

This was all very well for the main body of foreign immigrants, who had come to Britain to work. It did not, however, seem quite so applicable to the nineteenth-century brand of political refugee, who had come there for quite other reasons. For them it could not be argued so convincingly that their presence in Britain was positively and materially advantageous

[15] See *1861 Census Report*, vol. II, pp. lxxx–lxxxix.
[16] *Report from the Select Committee on the laws affecting aliens*, PP (1843) v, p. iv.
[17] 3PD 67 c. 433 (Hutt, 8 March 1843).
[18] 1PD 33 c. 437 (10 May 1816). Cf. Sir James Mackintosh in the same debate (c. 475): 'They came here to exercise industry and to seek fortune. They contributed to the national wealth or enjoyment, while they augmented their own fortune.'

to the national interest. Most of them were good for little else than politicking, or fighting, or labouring, or teaching their languages to Englishmen, or perhaps a little tasteful literary activity, or taking charity. There were exceptions. The *Art Journal* catalogue to the Great Exhibition of 1851 claimed that 'recent events abroad' had brought to Britain a number of superior foreign silver-workers, who 'by this fusion of adventitious aid with English energy, perseverance, and capital' had greatly stimulated a previously rather inferior craft in Britain.[19] But from the refugee immigrations of the nineteenth century there was never anything like the same economic return as from earlier immigrations, because the immigrants were not, in the same kind of way as the Huguenots, persecuted minorities with special skills. Most of them were too interested in politics anyway, and in returning, to want to stay in Britain long enough to stimulate its industry. Some of them did set up shop in Britain, a few of them in highly original ways: as when some of the French exiles in 1850 tried to set up a factory in Bradford to take the soap out of dirty soapy water and re-cycle it.[20] Neither this, nor any other refugee business enterprise, was notably successful. It needed very little acquaintance with the new breed of exile in the nineteenth century to know that they would not ever be particularly useful to Britain: though it could still be argued, and was,[21] that any legislation directed at them would automatically discourage others from coming, who might be more so.

As well as not being of any positive benefit to Britain, the presence of the refugees could be an irritant. Many of them were poor, and were found begging and occasionally stealing and swindling to stay alive. More seriously, we shall see that their political activities could involve Britain in all kinds of diplomatic difficulties with her continental neighbours who, when plots were hatched on her soil of rebellions in Italy, for example, or assassinations in France, tended to regard it as an unfriendly act of Britain's to harbour them. They might also be considered a threat to Britain's domestic security and tranquillity, if enough of the more desperate ones got together with the bloodier of Britain's own Chartists, and distracted an unpredictable proletariat from its loyalties. For most of the nineteenth century there might be thought to be ample cause for tension between the refugees and the governing class in Britain. To the latter the refugees brought very little measurable benefit with them, except to enhance its pride that it was able to put up so well with the inconvenience of having them.

[19] *The Art Journal Illustrated Catalogue of the Industry of all Nations* (1851; facsimile edn. New York, 1970), p. 57.
[20] Alvin R. Calman, *Ledru-Rollin après 1848 et les proscrits français en Angleterre* (Paris, 1921), pp. 129–31; Marcel Dessal, *Un Revolutionnaire Jacobin: Charles Delescluze* (Paris, 1952), p. 195n.
[21] E.g. 1PD 33, c. 479 (Mackintosh, 10 May 1816).

When arguments from self-interest failed, as they did with the refugees, the justification most frequently offered by members of the governing class for putting up with them was that it was required by 'principle'. Freedom of entry was not one of the leading canons of nineteenth-century liberalism: freedom of speech and the press and religion and conscience were talked about more, and fought for harder. But it was an important principle all the same, and was felt to be important enough to make all kinds of unpleasant side-effects worth suffering for its sake. 'We cannot', said *The Times*, which was by no means disposed to love many of those who took advantage of the refuge Britain offered,

prevent this metropolis from being even what Rome was described by its satirists, the sink of the human race. We cannot save our public thoroughfares from the floods of vice poured in by neighbouring States. For better, for worse, we have long been wedded to liberty, and we take it with all its evils for the sake of its manifold blessings.[22]

The future 13th Earl of Derby told Parliament in 1822 that 'the creed which he had imbibed with his mother's milk, was this – that to the distressed and persecuted of all the world, England was the land of protection'.[23] It was a proud claim, and amply (though unevenly) justified by past history. It was one of those things which made Britons feel superior to foreigners: it was in fact a very direct proof of their superiority, that their institutions were solid and secure enough to bear strains which less enlightened nations felt they had to persecute out of existence. It was another virtue to brag and bluster about: 'Every civilised people on the face of the earth', said *The Times* again, 'must be fully aware that this country is the asylum of nations, and that it will defend the asylum to the last ounce of its treasure, and the last drop of its blood. There is no point whatever on which we are prouder and more resolute.'[24] That it was attended by so many inconveniences, of course, made it the more noble, and the better to brag about. It was on principle, one of the glorious principles of her free constitution, that Britain was supposed to remain so constant in the refuge she afforded not only to fugitives she approved of, but also to those she did not; even to those who gave her little thanks for the privilege, little credit for her tolerance, and little quiet in return for her protection of them.

Proud declarations to this effect were, in their way, true and justified. But as the following chapters will show, they did give a slightly distorted impression of the whole-heartedness of some British governments' commitment to the principle of political asylum, as they did too of the real

[22] *The Times*, 19 January 1858, p. 8.
[23] 2PD 7, c. 823 (5 June 1822).
[24] *The Times*, 28 February 1853, p. 4.

hospitality the British people accorded to the refugees who sought its
protection. Neither was quite so pure and simple and grand as it was made
to seem. The refugees themselves suspected this, and they were not
altogether wrong. Despite the impression of resilience which was given by
Britain's acceptance of them, the presence in England of these wild foreign
revolutionaries was in fact, and from the point of view of those who
governed the country, a strain. There were times when it was thought to
be too much of a strain, and when consequently the policy of asylum was
at risk. That it survived for as long as it did, and in the form it did, was not
for want of opposition both outside Britain and within. To a great extent it
was due to luck, and to a great deal of vigilance and effort on the part of its
friends; and also, as we shall see, to the fact that the British ruling classes,
who would have clipped the refugees' wings if they could, were not
always able in the nineteenth century to have their own way. While it
survived, therefore, it was against not inconsiderable odds. But it did
survive, and without any very great harm being done thereby to the fabric
of British society, which in the last analysis says a great deal about the
strengths of that society, and vindicates those who at the time were most
confident of those strengths. Despite all the pressures, and for all the
annoyance they caused, it is a prime fact that between 1823 and 1906 no
refugee who came to Britain was ever denied entry, or expelled;[25] or
necessitated any very drastic revision of Britain's free institutions. In this
matter the Victorians were able to keep an almost clean slate: cleaner than
any of their European contemporaries, and a good deal cleaner than their
posterity in Britain in the following century.

It was a notable achievement; and it calls for an explanation. Just how was
it that the refugees could be so well tolerated in England at this time, by a
governing class which had so little cause to love them? Ultimately of
course this is not a question which can be answered solely by reference to
the refugees themselves and the controversies which surrounded them.
The policy of asylum did not stand on its own in the nineteenth century.
Insofar as British attitudes and actions towards the refugees were tolerant,
they were part and parcel of a broader pattern of toleration in contemporary Britain; and inasmuch as there were tensions and conflicts over
them, these were aspects of broader tensions and conflicts in Victorian
society. The part can only be understood in the context of the whole; and
so any convincing and complete and ultimately satisfying explanation of
this phenomenon of toleration of the refugees must depend greatly upon

---

[25] The last expulsion under the old Alien Act (Count Bettera in 1823) was referred to by Peel
in the House of Commons on 23 March 1824: 2PD 10 c. 1339. No one was expelled under
the 1848 Act. The Act of 1905 was implemented immediately: see J. A. Garrard, *The
English and Immigration 1880–1910* (1971), p. 107.

an analysis of Victorian society as a whole – or even of 'society' as a whole. These are large questions, which a study of this nature is intrinsically unfitted to tackle. To embark upon them would be like a book on horse breeding launching into an explanation of DNA. The general discussion, if it were not to be so attenuated as to be tendentious, would very soon overwhelm and engulf the particular subject matter of the book. For this reason no such discussion will be attempted here, and no ultimate explanation of the phenomenon of asylum will be offered.

Nevertheless there is still much interesting and unexplored ground to be covered on the way to that ultimate explanation, which may justify a journey which stops short of it. In the first place, although an empirical study of the refugee question will not take us all the way there it will take us very near it: if it cannot tell us why the refugees *were* tolerated it may be able to tell us why they were *able* to be tolerated – which will not be so very far off. In the second place, it may shed a little light beyond itself. If the part cannot be understood except in the context of the whole, neither can the whole be fully comprehended except by reference to its parts; and it may be that a detailed examination of this particular small aspect of Victorian culture will have implications for the general historical context which are significant, and even surprising. From a study of the ways in which the Victorians reacted to the presence of the refugees among them, it is possible to learn far more than about the Victorians' attitudes to the refugees and their causes. There is something to be learnt, for example – even if it is only to confirm what was known before – about how they regarded themselves and their own society; about their notions of 'freedom' and their practise of it; about the new political attitude of 'liberalism' at a crucial stage in its gestation; about Victorian politics and the forces beneath it; about the relationship, and the tensions, between governors and governed; about the relationship too between Victorian English society and the continent's; about the practices of nineteenth-century diplomacy; and about the workings of the minds of some of the nineteenth century's leading statesmen, including that of the third Viscount Palmerston. This is not a bad return on just a little intellectual capital, and it must be this book's main justification.

Asylum of course had been a political tradition in Britain for many years before the nineteenth century. In its Victorian – and most uncompromising – form it went back to 1826, when as we have seen the British government finally, after the Napoleonic fever was over, abrogated its power to ban aliens. That was when the seed was sown: but it was not the most crucial time for the policy of asylum. That time came after the revolutions (and reactions) of 1848, when there appeared the first serious pressures on it, to have it uprooted. Those pressures continued forcefully for about a decade, and then fell back again. The 1850s thus saw a kind of battle over the question of the refugees, which was decided in the latter's favour. Once that battle was won there were no more serious pressures from any quarter at all to have the policy revoked, for twenty years at least. Consequently it was the 1850s which really mattered for the refugees and the policy of asylum in Britain: when that policy survived the first severe frost which threatened it, and grew from a sapling into a tree. It was also incontrovertibly the most exciting time. Quite suddenly, and uniquely, the refugee question irrupted on to the centre of the British political stage. As the result of it, an emperor was bombed, a government fell, a war was threatened, and a famous state prosecution was dramatically lost. All this explains why this book will concentrate so intensively (though not exclusively) upon the 1850s, out of all the years that the refugees lived and worked and even conspired in Britain.[26]

For Britain afterwards the question of the refugees never regained the prominence it had briefly in the 1850s; and yet several of the broad issues it raised then were never finally disposed of, and indeed are still with us today. To what extent, for example, is a country which harbours conspirators responsible for the outcome of their conspiracies abroad? This was the issue raised in the 1850s for France and Austria by the activities of Mazzini and Orsini in England against them, and it is an issue between Britain and Ireland, and Israel and her neighbours, today. Another dilemma which we shall see the 'refugee question' posed in the 1850s was the familiar liberal one, of whether threats to liberalism can always be countered by liberal means, or whether in self-defence liberalism must sometimes betray itself: which again is a matter of urgency today. The 'refugee question' in the nineteenth century also provoked discussion about 'conspiracy' itself, whether it was ever truly effective on its own: whether healthy societies really could be 'subverted' by minorities, or only sick societies which deserved to be. These are all enduring problems. If the solutions to them in the 1850s (at least so far as Britain was concerned) were different from what they generally are today, the questions were the same: which suggests that what follows may not be merely (though of course it is mainly) an academic exercise, but may possibly father some thoughts for our own time.

What those thoughts should be, however, it is not the place of this book to say. Here we are concerned exclusively with the past. The following chapter will deal with the refugees themselves in the nineteenth century, as background to the rest. It is based upon a range of sources which is restricted by my own linguistic deficiencies, and consequently should not

---

[26] As well as the left-wing refugees – socialists, democrats, republicans, liberals – who are the principal focus of this book, there were some right-wingers, who however, as they very rarely posed the kinds of problems to the British government the others posed, were not essentially part of the 'refugee question', and so will be generally ignored.

be taken as more than an introductory sketch. Chapter 3 will deal with the attitudes of foreign powers towards the refugees and towards Britain for harbouring them; and the remainder of the book with attitudes and policies in Britain.

2

The Refugees

It is almost a sociological commonplace that the attitudes of an indigenous towards an immigrant population – or of any distinguishable group of people towards another – need have little to do with the reality of the relationship between them. Fears which are genuine and widespread may nevertheless be imaginary; threats which communities of men are supposed to pose to other communities may be illusory. That the refugees in Britain in the mid nineteenth century were tolerated, therefore, is no sure indication that they were in fact tolerable; nor, if they can be shown to have been tolerable, will that on its own be a sufficient explanation of why they were tolerated. Tolerance, like bigotry, can have other than entirely rational roots: some of which will be explored in a later chapter. Nevertheless it may be instructive first to determine the extent to which this particular toleration was consistent with objective reality: the degree to which the refugees, by the ways they lived and by their actions, really did merit their reputation amongst the British. If the reality turns out to be the same as the image, it will not explain the latter, but it will at least render it more easily explicable. This must be the justification for a digression at this point into the situation of the refugees themselves: who they were, where and how they lived, and what they did.

There are different kinds of refugees. There are short- and long-term refugees; exiles by edict or by choice; fugitives from religious persecution, or racial, or political. The refugees who came to Britain in the middle of the nineteenth century were distinguishable from other waves of refugees at other times by being mostly political refugees. They were men, that is, who had been exiled (or had exiled themselves) because of political activities they had taken part in or political attitudes they had revealed. Very few of them were exiles on account of their religion, like the Huguenots, or their class, like many of the refugees from the French revolution, or their race, like the Russian Jews at the end of the century. This meant in the first place that there were fewer of them, because a man's politics is more a matter of choice than his religion or class or race, and usually he will think twice before choosing to take a political attitude which might lead to his exile. It might mean also that those who did come were more likely eventually to return to their own countries, or if they stayed then to remain 'refugees', and not merge into the rather different category of 'immigrant' or 'settler'. Because most of them had by deliberate choice defied an established government on the continent, it followed too that they would be likely to remain defiant, and actively so, during their time in exile: more so than those whose offences had been more passive (like Jews for being Jewish), and whose overt interest in politics was less. And lastly, it meant that the flow of them into Britain, and the character and composition of the refugee community there at any one time, was likely to be affected greatly by political happenings on the continent: which largely determined how many of them there were, where they were from, and how long they stayed.

The refugee community in Britain was always a mixture of nationalities, but with different elements preponderating at different times. In the 1820s and thirties it comprised mainly Italians, fleeing from the after-effects of the Risorgimento's early failures in Naples and Piedmont in 1820–1 and then in the central Italian provinces in 1831. Many of the Italians were high-born and distinguished literary men in their own countries, whose reputations had gone before them to Britain. We shall see that this was a great help to some of them in exile, as was the colour of their political beliefs, which tended at this time to be moderate and constitutional and 'respectable'. The most famous of the Italians, Giuseppe Mazzini, arrived in London in January 1837 and stayed there intermittently for thirty years, becoming progressively less 'respectable' as he lingered.[1] Hard on the heels of the Italians came the Poles, who came to England in groups after the savage suppression of their revolution by the Russians in 1831: which set off what was the biggest and saddest political emigration of these years, of many thousands of men across Germany to various destinations in western Europe – most of them to Paris in the first place, but a good number (680 in 1838) to London. Many of the Poles were as high-born as the Italians, but not so literary. Many of them were also more radical. The most distinguished of them was probably Stanislaus Worcell, who arrived in April 1834 and died in exile in 1857. Of all the refugee nationalities in Britain in the nineteenth century the Poles were the most numerous, the poorest, the most intractable and, as it turned out, the most permanent.[2] For a while they and the Italians, together with a few

---

[1] See Margaret C. W. Wicks, *The Italian Exiles in London, 1816–1848* (1937); Harry W. Rudman, *Italian Nationalism and English Letters* (1940); Toni Cerutti, *Antonio Gallenga* (1974); E. R. Vincent, *Gabriele Rossetti in England* (Oxford, 1936).

[2] See Günther Weber, *Die Polnische Emigration im neunzehnten Jahrhundert* (Essen, 1937); Peter Brock, 'Joseph Cowen and the Polish Exiles', in *Slavonic and East European Review*, vol. 32 (1953–4); 'The Polish Revolutionary Commune in London', in *ibid.*, vol. 35 (1956); 'Polish Democrats and English Radicals 1832–62', in *Journal of Modern History*, vol. 25 (1953);

Spaniards, were the only substantial groups of refugees in Britain. Then in the forties they were joined by some others: some French socialists, and some Germans who had been living in Paris but had got involved in the Blanquist rising of 1839 and so had to leave. They were not very numerous but were notably 'advanced' in their opinions: men like Karl Schapper, Heinrich Bauer and Joseph Moll.

This was the mixture until 1848. The events of that year and the next in Europe upset it utterly. Democrats and republicans in England rushed to join their national revolutions on the continent, to be replaced in exile (though not in the same quarters) by deposed kings and courtiers. If they could not reach their own national struggles, as the Poles could not, then many of the old refugees turned to France to help with hers: which gave the Poles thereafter the reputation of being rather indiscriminate revolutionaries, professional trouble-seekers who would man anybody's barricades if they could not build their own. The Germans also were more often found in Paris than in Frankfort. As the ships sailed out of England with their complements of eager revolutionaries, so others sailed in with the losers of the day: Louis Philippe, who landed at Dover under the name of Mr Smith; Guizot; Princess Lieven; Metternich; and others. But this was a very temporary exchange. Soon the European reaction set in; and if not all the reactionaries managed to get back to their old positions – not Louis Philippe, for example, who died in exile in 1850 – yet most of the revolutionaries did, and found themselves in England again before very long. By the early 1850s they were nearly all back in their old haunts and their old ways; and with new friends, who had a marked effect on the composition of the refugee community thereafter.

The arrivals of this period – the new refugee vintage of the early 1850s – included some famous men. Among them was Karl Marx, who had visited England before, to see his friend Engels who was in business there, but first came as an exile in August 1849, and stayed there until his death in 1883. Marx subsequently became by far the most distinguished of Britain's refugees, but he was not so during his lifetime. More famous then were Louis Blanc, Alexandre Ledru-Rollin, Victor Hugo, Louis Kossuth, Alexander Herzen and Felice Orsini, all of whom arrived in 1849 or the early fifties. Ledru-Rollin, Kossuth and Mazzini were the best-known among their English contemporaries. As well as these new and notable individual faces, the early 1850s saw a considerable and significant change in the national balance and political character of the refugee community. For the first time Germans and Frenchmen made up a large proportion of it: 1,300 Germans, according to counts made by the British authorities in

'Zeno Świętosławski. . .', in *American Slavic and East European Review*, vol. 13 (1954); 'Polish Socialists in early Victorian London', in *Polish Review*, vol. 6 (1961).

1. The best known of the refugees in England in the 1850s: Mazzini, Kossuth and Ledru-Rollin, pictured by the *Illustrated London News*.

1852, and 4,500 Frenchmen.[3] The French numbers were helped along by the deportations ordered by Louis Napoleon after his *coup d'état* of December 1851; a year or so later they had dropped to about 1,000.[4] Another new nationality was the Hungarians, in flight from the suppression by Austrian and Russian troops of their national revolution in 1849, who took a long time to arrive while British diplomacy sought to get them extricated from Turkey where they were trapped, but who finally came in several boatloads in 1851. Some of these were straightaway re-directed to America, but many stayed, and merged (or so it seemed to the English, for whom the difference between two sets of 'Slavs' was too subtle to perceive) with the Poles. (Some of them in fact probably *were* the ubiquitous Poles.) The Poles themselves had recently had their numbers swollen greatly by compatriots coming out of Paris, which was always a more popular refuge for them than London, partly because they were generously assisted there by the French government, but which by the 1850s was becoming too hot for some of them. Together with the Hungarians they were reckoned to number 2,500 in March 1853, which made them the largest refugee nationality at that time.[5]

These changes made a considerable difference to the composition of the refugee community in Britain. In the first place it was bigger now: probably bigger than at any other time between 1820 and 1880. How big it was exactly is impossible to say. The police at the time tried to count them, but there was no way of doing so properly. They could not be counted as they came in. The police tried to count them where they lived, by means of street surveys in likely areas, and inquiries among publicans.[6] The figures they arrived at at different times varied wildly, and can in reality have been scarcely better than guesses.[7] Those guesses put the number throughout the country at 4,380 in March 1853, by which time it was already on the decline.[8] Shortly after the French *coup d'état* it may have touched 7,000.[9]

---

[3] Police reports (Sanders), 4 March and 14 October 1852: PRO MEPO 2/43 and HO 45/4547A.

[4] Police report (Sanders), 19 March 1853: PRO HO 45/4816.

[5] *Ibid., loc. cit.*

[6] *People's Paper*, 26 March 1853, p. 26. In 1852 the authorities in Jersey tried to conduct a proper census of Frenchmen living there, but were met by opposition from refugees fearing that this was a prelude to expulsion: see Love to Walpole, 30 September 1852, in PRO HO 45/4013; and Police report, 28 September 1852, in PRO HO 45/4547A.

[7] There is no way of knowing, for example, whether they included *assimilés*, or the families of refugees, or even perhaps a few stray non-refugee foreigners.

[8] Police report of 19 March 1853: PRO HO 45/4816; to which is appended a note, that 'There is reason to believe that nearly 3,000 French have returned to France, some of them included in the Amnesty.'

[9] Or even more, if the estimates of 4,500 French, 1,300 Germans and over 2,000 Poles are anywhere near the truth, and allowing for a few hundred Italians and others.

Everything points to this being the peak of refugee immigration between 1820 and 1880. For example, well-informed sources put the numbers of *Poles* in England in the 1830s and 1840s at between 350 and 700, which was much lower than in the 1850s: see 3PD 55 c. 1221

This is likely to have been its peak. But as well as being more numerous than at other times, the refugee community in the 1850s was also more radical. Simple constitutionalists like the early Italians, those Liberal counts and poets who had struggled in gentlemanly ways for national freedom from foreign yokes, were now in a minority, and *passé*. They were overshadowed by less refined and more violent men: republicans, democrats, socialists, 'reds'. And thirdly: the refugee community of the 1850s contained now a larger number of men from nearby friendly countries, with whose governments the British government was, as we shall see, not anxious to quarrel on their behalf. These developments gave the refugees of the 1850s a particular potency, which helps account for the special prominence of the refugee question in British politics in those years.

Towards the end of the 1850s that potency diminished a little. Many of the refugees left. Most of those who left went to the United States – about 1,500 of them secretly assisted by British government money.[10] Others went back to their homelands, as continental governments gained in confidence sufficiently to offer amnesties to at least the lesser fry. Austria started pardoning Italian and Hungarian exiles as early as 1856.[11] In 1859 Louis Napoleon offered an amnesty to political refugees which some of them (like Ledru-Rollin) were excluded from, and others (like Louis Blanc) rejected, but some accepted.[12] In 1861 a Prussian amnesty took away many of the Germans. To set against this a shipload of 66 Neapolitans arrived in 1859, released from the dungeons of the notorious King 'Bomba' after one of Gladstone's earliest moral crusades:[13] but no other large groups. Those who returned to their homes were probably the more 'moderate' ones, by and large satisfied with the new constitutional shifts which transformed Europe in the 1860s, like the emancipation and unification of Italy under Liberal Piedmont, and the Austrian *Ausgleich* of 1867 which gave Hungary a measure of self-government. Those who had to remain in exile became more and more disheartened, both by the departure of their comrades-in-arms and by what *they* saw as the effective consolidation of the reaction abroad. This did not necessarily render them less dangerous: some of them it made more so, as desperation drove them to more violent methods. The others, who had finer scruples, waited and faded. Most of the refugees who lived in Britain in the 1860s had been there

(3 August 1840) and 3PD 101 c. 437 (23 August 1848). Before 1848 there were more alternative refuges to Britain than afterwards. And after about 1853 amnesties and embarkations to the United States diminished the numbers, and little happened on the continent to augment them very dramatically – until the anti-Jewish pogroms of the last two decades of the century. [10] *Infra*, pp. 160–1.
[11] Austrian amnesties are mentioned from the spring of 1856 in dispatches from Vienna, in PRO FO 7/485–6, 488–92 *passim*.
[12] Alvin R. Calman, *Ledru-Rollin après 1848 et les proscrits français en Angleterre* (Paris, 1921), pp. 190–2.   [13] Rudman, *op. cit.*, pp. 254–7, 263–5.

for some time already. Many of them were quite comfortably settled now in their exile, and isolated from political developments in their homelands, where new generations of radicals had pushed them from the fronts of their compatriots' minds. So the refugee community in Britain was diminishing, and ageing, and carrying rather less of a sting than it once had. But it was by no means moribund. Occasionally excitements abroad set its heart pumping again: in Italy at the beginning of the sixties, and during the Polish insurrection of 1863, which before it was crushed cheered the Polish contingent enormously and had many of them clamouring to join in. Among the socialists fraternal activity was buzzing, and gave birth to the First International, which was chiefly a London refugee-based affair, in 1864. There were some comings and goings, though not in large numbers until the early 1870s, when quite a sudden influx of international socialists from the Paris commune of 1871 for a time revived memories, and for the British establishment some of the fears and problems, of the early fifties. And during the 1860s, and then at an accelerated pace during the seventies and eighties, there was a steady influx of Russian exiles into Britain – including Bakunin in 1861, Nechaev in 1870, Kropotkin in 1876, and Stepniak in 1883 – who by the end of our period came to dominate at least the public image of the refugee community in Britain.

This broadly was the pattern of refugee immigration into Britain until the 1880s, when the arrival of thousands of Jews fleeing from pogroms in Russia and Eastern Europe transformed its character fundamentally. Throughout these sixty years from 1820 to 1880 its complexion changed frequently, with only the unfortunate Poles providing a consistent element. It was never a very large community. Four thousand men, or even seven thousand, were not a flood of people, and scarcely bore comparison with the numbers of refugees who had come to Britain in Napoleonic times, who were said to number 40,000 in 1792;[14] or with the Jewish immigration of the 1880s and 1890s which may have reached 120,000 by 1900.[15] Their small numbers were an important factor affecting their relationship with their hosts. But so too were certain other things about them, and the ways they lived.

More than half of the refugees when they arrived made for London, and spent the greater part of their exile there. The poorer ones usually landed up around Soho and in the rookery of dirty little streets east of what is today Charing Cross Road, or in large, overcrowded houses found for them in the East End. The better-off, or those with prosperous patrons, after a spell perhaps in the houses of compatriots or English sympathisers, lived like ordinary middle-class Englishmen scattered about the respect-

[14] W. Cunningham, *Alien Immigrants to England* (1897), p. 259.
[15] See J. .A. Garrard, *The English and Immigration* (1971), Appendix I.

able suburbs. London was an almost irresistible magnet for the refugees, although a few of them for special reasons studiously avoided it – like Kropotkin, for example, who when he first came made for Edinburgh to give the slip to the 'spies of the Russian embassy' who he suspected 'would soon have been at my heels' in the metropolis.[16] Another powerful magnet in the early 1850s for the French and a few Poles was the island of Jersey, where the prevalence of the French language and a kind of French culture softened their exile, and whose proximity to the French coast made it an ideal centre for propaganda operations, and even for military operations if an opportunity ever came. Altogether about 100 refugees lived in Jersey in the early 1850s, including most notoriously the novelist Victor Hugo. Other parts of Britain had their little refugee communities too: the police census of 1853 estimated that 1,900 lived outside London.[17] They were drawn to the provinces usually by offers of employment, or of relief from committees set up to help certain special groups of them, like 262 Hungarians and Poles who arrived in Liverpool from Constantinople on 28 February 1851, and then were scattered thinly all over the country to help their chances of finding work.[18] But London was always the active political centre of the immigration, with Jersey furnishing, for a short time, a kind of encampment beneath the walls for some of the wilder ones.

For very few of the exiles did London (or Jersey) provide more than the barest refuge. Most of those who recorded their impressions of their exile looked back on it as a dismal time, and although some of them may have exaggerated their sufferings to emphasise the sacrifices they had made for their causes, there was much about a London exile to depress them. Recollections of their reception in England may have reflected more the spirit with which they approached the country than the objective reality. Most of them remembered docking in fog, although in at least one case it seems likely to have been imagined.[19] To most of them London appeared a cold, dirty, unwelcoming place, as to a homesick continental it was likely to do.[20] Possibly their expectations before they came were pitched too high; in any event they often felt greatly let down. The pitfalls that awaited

---

[16] P. Kropotkin, *Memoirs of a Revolutionist* (2nd. edn., 1906), p. 353.

[17] Police report of 19 March 1853: PRO HO 45/4816.

[18] See issues of *The Refugee Circular* in Cowen Papers, Tyne and Wear Archives Department (TWAD), 634/A26 *et passim*. Their final distribution was as follows: Sheffield 31, London 16, Leeds 14, Halifax 13, Bradford 12, Manchester 11, Glasgow 8, Padiham, Newcastle and Rochdale 7 each, Burnley 6, Huddersfield, Keighley, Paisley, Oldham, Preston and Shelton 4 each; St. Helens, Barrhead, Sunderland and Dundee 3 each; Birstal, Holmfirth, Bingley, Todmorden, Leicester, Northampton, Shields, Bleydon, Royton and Nottingham 2 each; Gateshead one. The balance of 54 went to Paris (13) or the United States, or perhaps were lost. [19] E. H. Carr, *The Romantic Exiles* (1968 edn.), p. 107.

[20] See 'Miss A. M. Birkbeck' (Sándor Mednyánszky), 'Daguerreotype of an Exile's fate', in *Sharpe's London Magazine*, n.s. vol. IV (1853), p. 91; and [Otto von Wenckstern], 'Lost in London', in *Household Words*, vol. III no. 68 (1851), pp. 372–8.

the more obscure of them, especially when they first arrived, will have done nothing to lift their depression. They were easy prey to all kinds of petty exploitation: most often from some of their own countrymen, who played on their needs, their ignorance and their responsiveness to a familiar dialect to provide them, until they got wiser, with dirty rooms at inflated rents, and English money at grossly deflated exchange-rates.[21] For those who had no friends already in England, or who had not found them yet, their first days in the country could be cruel. There were exceptions: like the 262 Hungarians (and Poles) who docked in Liverpool in February 1851, and who by all accounts were well looked after by their English champions when they arrived: fêted and embraced in the streets, and repeatedly invited, as a local newspaper put it, 'to partake of the fruits of John Barleycorn, to which they appear to be very partial', and which was reported to have given rise to 'some very exciting scenes . . . in several parts of the town on Thursday evening'.[22] Even for those lucky ones however, things did not necessarily stay so cheerful for very long: six months afterwards, and despite all the efforts of their English friends to spread the load, fewer than half of them had managed to find jobs which brought them a living wage;[23] and for those hundreds of others whose arrival had not been so celebrated as the Hungarians', the situation will have been much worse.

Many of them remained poor and out of work for quite long periods. In March 1852 the Metropolitan Police reckoned that, of the 1,970 refugees they counted in London then, 'two-thirds . . . are in straitened circumstances'.[24] Their privations, like much Victorian poverty, were hidden from the eyes of all but the very inquisitive, but they were real enough. 'Only those who have wandered through Patmos', wrote a contributor to Charles Dickens' *Household Words* in 1853, 'who have watched the gates of the London Docks at early morning when the chance labourers apply for work, who have sat in night coffee-houses, and explored dark arches, can know what awful shifts some of these poor refugees, friendless, foodless, houseless, are often put to.' *Household Words* claimed that, to their honour, they starved in silence, and did not 'beg, nor rob, nor extort':[25] but some of them did. The London police courts saw a lot of the underside of refugee life in England in the middle of the nineteenth century: fraudulent beggars brought in by the officers of the Mendicity Society; pathetic thieves

---

[21] See von Wenckstern, *art. cit.*, p. 373; and *The Times*, 3 May 1849 p. 7, reporting the trial of two German boarding-house keepers for defrauding their compatriots by giving too little sterling in exchange for foreign currency.

[22] *Liverpool Journal*, 8 March 1851, in Cowen Papers, TWAD 634/A20.

[23] See *The Refugee Circular*, 16 August 1851, in *ibid.*, A87.

[24] Police Report, 4 March 1852: PRO MEPO 2/43.

[25] [George A. Sala], 'Perfidious Patmos', in *Household Words*, vol. vii no. 155 (12 March 1853), p. 29.

brought in by the police, like one Pedro Vacheo, a Spanish refugee who in 1855 was caught taking a bottle of catsup from a shop because, as he was heard to mutter as he left the court, 'he must thieve or starve';[26] or like the several Poles who stole umbrellas and hats from the house of Lord Dudley Stuart, who was their benefactor.[27] If they did not thieve or beg, the poorer refugees lived off charity, which was generally organised by the better-off refugees and their English friends, but was never enough, and very rarely distributed to the satisfaction of them all. The worst off were always probably the Poles, and especially the more radical and less aristocratic Poles, against whom a political test was applied by their main relieving agency, the Literary Association of the Friends of Poland, and who got very little joy, as we shall see, when they turned to their democratic friends in England for the relief the bourgeoisie denied them.[28] Charity in any case was not what many of the refugees wanted most: 'could you not help us,' wrote one of them to a Radical newspaper in 1852, 'to something better than money – to work? It is sad for us to remain in unwilling idleness, it is wearisome for us to do nothing all the day long; for we are accustomed to labour, even to hard labour, and we should like to work and deal with you, that we may know you, and love you, and obtain a free and honest living for our wives and children.'[29] Work, however, could be difficult to come by, especially for refugees who spoke little or no English, had no useful skills, and were regarded with jealousy by native English workers and with suspicion by their masters.[30] 'They had made every effort to obtain food by their labour', Viscount Sandon told the House of Commons in 1838;

on railroads and public works, Colonels and others of high rank might be found working as common labourers, but being strangers, speaking a strange language . . . the majority were left to wander starving about the streets. In the police reports accounts would be found of Poles taken in the act of sleeping under our porticos and at our hall doors and such other places of shelter as chance threw in their way.[31]

Starved of charity, and denied gainful employment, many of the refugees sank rapidly and anonymously into the bog of destitution which underlay English society in the mid nineteenth century. 'They barely exist. They are scantily supplied with food; they are poorly clad. Far from their homes, and severed from the friends they love, in addition to all their other ills, they are dragging out a most wretched existence.'[32] This, commented

---

[26] *The Times*, 26 July 1855, p. 11.
[27] A Pole named Racibuski was convicted of this offence twice: see *The Times*, 26 March 1851 p. 8, and 17 January 1852, p. 7. On crime among the refugees, *vide infra*, p. 43 fn. 125.
[28] *Infra*, p. 83.   [29] *Star of Freedom*, 4 September 1852, p. 58.
[30] See Leo A. Loubère, *Louis Blanc* (Evanston, Ill., 1961), p. 146; [Frederic Marshall], 'Alien Laws', in *Blackwood's Edinburgh Magazine*, vol. 116 (1874), p. 450.
[31] 3PD 44 c. 731 (27 July 1838).
[32] *People's Paper*, 12 March 1853, p. 3; and cf. *The Times*, 5 March 1853, p. 5: 'This wretched class of beings live for the most part in squalid poverty.'

bitterly the English republican Harney, was the full extent of the freedom
England offered to the persecuted of other nations: 'The exile is free to land
upon our shores, and free to perish of hunger beneath our inclement
skies.'[33]

It was not always so bad for them. After the big influx of the early 1850s,
for example, there were fewer reports of refugee destitution. Most of them
will eventually have come to terms with their new situation, one way or
another: some of them by passing on to America, where a living was
reputed to be more easy to come by;[34] others by being absorbed into the
British labour market. The east Europeans were the most difficult to place,
because of the language barrier, but most of those found jobs eventually.
Some of them had special skills which could always be used: like tailoring,
cabinet making, bookbinding, or watchmaking. For the others, a few
sympathetic employers could usually be found willing to apprentice them
to new trades, if their living meanwhile was found for them out of another
pocket: which is what happened in the end to most of the 1851 Hungarians, who by the summer of 1851, if they could not support themselves
yet, had at least been put on the road towards doing so.[35] A few refugees
found they could make a living from occupations related to their main
revolutionary interests: like the Pole Zeno Świętosławski, who set up as a
printer of refugee literature in Jersey,[36] and Karl Marx, who eventually
found a market for his political writings in an American newspaper. The
rest became labourers.[37] Things were generally better too for the more
prominent exiles, the 'chiefs': some of whom came with enough money to
see them through the difficult early years; most of whom thereafter
managed to eke out a moderate existence, usually by writing or teaching;
and very few of whom had to endure for long the privations of the Soho
slums. The French and the Italians had the advantage of speaking languages that well-bred English men and women wanted to learn, and many
of them became language tutors, at least for a time. Some of the early
Italian exiles came to do very well for themselves in the English literary

---

[33] *Star of Freedom*, 18 September 1852, p. 88.
[34] But see the *Refugee Circular*, 10 May 1851 (Cowen Papers, TWAD 634/A31), containing
letters from Polish emigrants in America telling their compatriots of the bad conditions
there, and advising them not to join them.
[35] See *Refugee Circular*, 16 August 1851, pp. 34–9, in *ibid.*, A87.
[36] Peter Brock, 'A Polish "Proscrit" in Jersey', in *Bulletin of the Société Jersiaise*, vol. XVI no. 2.
[37] A survey among the Polish refugees compiled in 1858 by the Literary Association of the
Friends of Poland managed to account for the occupations of 308 of them, out of 760
believed by the Association to be in England. Of those 308, 127 were labourers. The next
largest group was 76 slipper and shoe makers; followed by 23 teachers, 15 clerks, 10 tailors,
6 surgeons (including a dentist and a vet), 6 carpenters, 5 clergymen, 5 printers, 5
shopkeepers, 4 designers, 4 confectioners, 3 painters, 3 cooks, 2 engineers, 2 sugar bakers, 2
saddlers, 2 umbrella makers, 2 hairdressers, a schoolmaster, a lithographer, a baker, a
gardener, a soap maker and an artificial flower maker. *Annual Report of the Council of the
Literary Association of the Friends of Poland*, 1858, pp. 8–9.

and academic worlds: like Antonio Gallenga and Gabriele Rossetti, who
both became professors, and Antonio Panizzi, who was a professor, and
then principal Librarian of the British Museum, and eventually was
knighted.[38] But the Italians were exceptional. Most of the other leading
refugees led quite middle-class lives in respectable suburbs; sometimes
very English lives, like Louis Blanc:[39] probably because it was difficult to
reproduce continental lives in suburban London. Few of them lived
ostentatiously well. But most of the leading refugees had friends and
exploitable talents enough to live moderately.

Yet physical privation was not the only way in which a refugee in
England could be made to suffer, or feel he was. Alexander Herzen felt
very keenly the lack of *moral* succour he found there: 'The life here', he
wrote, 'like the air here, is bad for the weak, for the frail, for one who seeks
a prop outside himself, for one who seeks welcome, sympathy, attention;
the moral lungs here must be as strong as the physical lungs, whose task it
is to separate oxygen from the smoky fog.'[40] For himself, life in England
appeared 'as dull as the life of worms in a cheese'.[41] The feeling that they
were neglected, cold-shouldered, unduly and unfeelingly ignored was a
widespread one amongst the refugees, and added to their *ennui*. We shall
see that, except for the early Italians and a few others, they *were* widely
neglected by their hosts: more so probably than they had reason to expect.
But a certain degree of neglect was an inevitable concomitant of their
situation, in a different world from their own, a world where they *were* less
worth attending to, and far away from the places where they had been
attended to, more even than was comfortable, all the time. Hungarian
Hamlets became insignificant bit-parts on the English stage, or nothing at
all: the sudden fall from notoriety to obscurity was dispiriting.

As well as this, many of the refugees were predisposed to find England a
very uncongenial refuge anyway. They disliked her for all the normal
reasons that foreigners dislike England: the reserve of her people, the
dirtiness of her cities, the dampness of her climate and the blandness of her
cuisine.

The Frenchman [wrote Herzen, who probably exaggerated] cannot forgive the
English, in the first place, for not speaking French; in the second, for not under-
standing him when he calls Charing Cross Sharan-Kro, or Leicester Square,
Lessesstair-Skooar. Then his stomach cannot digest the English dinners consisting

---

[38] M. C. W. Wicks, *op. cit.*, chs. 5 and 6; E. R. Vincent, *op. cit.*, Toni Cerutti, *op. cit.*

[39] 'Sur le mur des gravures anglaises. Au milieu, un guéridon anglais, chargé de livres reliés à
l'anglais et symétriquement rangés à l'anglais. Quelques chaises et un canapé, le tout garni
de petites housses blanches en broderie anglaises. Ajoutez à cela un tapis anglais, des
rideaux anglais et un rayon de soleil anglais. Vous êtes, comme moi, chez Louis Blanc,
esquire.' Charles Hugo, *Les Hommes de l'exil* (Paris, 1875), p. 330.

[40] Alexander Herzen, *My Past and Thoughts* (1968 edn.), vol. III, p. 1025.

[41] Quoted in Monica Partridge, 'Alexander Herzen and the English press', in *Slavonic and East
European Review*, vol. 36 (1957–8), p. 470.

of two huge pieces of meat and fish, instead of five little helpings of various ragouts, fritures, salamis and so on. Then he can never resign himself to the 'slavery' of restaurants being closed on Sundays, and the people being *bored to the glory of God* . . . Then the whole *habitus*, all that is good and bad in the Englishman, is detestable to the Frenchman.[42]

To this was added, for the socialists, a distaste for the materialism of her culture.[43] Charles Hugo had a special hatred of London:

la ville noire, sans ciel et sans fin . . . une immense ville sans grandeur . . . Trois millions d'inhabitants qui vont, viennent, courent, circulent, spéculent, fourmillent et ne vivent pas . . . Ces trois millions d'êtres effarés n'ont qu'un but, l'argent . . . On respire du charbon et on avale de la suie . . . la richesse est monstreuse et la misère est stupide . . . Sodome de la bank-note, Gomorrhe du coton

and where (it is surprising to read a refugee complain) there was scarcely a policeman or a soldier to be seen to brighten it up.[44] Charles Hugo's positive dislike of England was more intense than most refugees', but others shared it, and some of them broadcast it amongst their hosts. Friedrich Engels' *Condition of the Working Class in England in 1844* is the best-known of a number of criticisms of English life and institutions penned at the time by foreign residents (though Engels was not technically a refugee when he wrote it). Others were Marx's letters to the *New York Daily Tribune* in the fifties and sixties; Ledru-Rollin's book *La Décadence d'Angleterre,* published in French and English barely a year after he came to England, and widely resented;[45] and Félix Pyat's public letter to Queen Victoria in 1855, which accused her of sacrificing her chastity for the sake of the French alliance – which was meant metaphorically, but was not the kind of metaphor the Victorian public appreciated.[46] That there was not more of this sort of thing was due to the fact that most of the refugees were not interested enough in British affairs to want to make an issue of them; or frightened that if they did, their hosts might turn on them.

For Englishmen this tried their sympathy sorely. If only out of 'gratitude' to England for receiving them when no one else would the refugees, they felt, should have thought and written better of her. But it was natural in a way that they should not. They were exiles, not settlers. The only reason they found themselves among the English was that the English let them be there, and other European countries, which they would have preferred, did not. That fact alone should not have been

---

[42] Herzen, *op. cit.,* p. 1058.

[43] See Th. Karcher, 'L'Exposition de Londres', in *La Voix du Proscrit,* vol. II (1851), pp. 89–93.

[44] Charles Hugo, *op. cit.,* pp. 324–6.

[45] *La Décadence* was widely reviewed: see for example *Fraser's Magazine,* vol. 42 (July 1850) pp. 74–85; *Blackwood's Magazine,* vol. 68 (August 1850) pp. 160–73; *Punch,* vol. 18 (July 1850) p. 234; and see Lyndhurst's comments on its 'atrocious libels' in 3PD 115 c. 624 (27 March 1851).　　[46] *Vide infra,* p. 165.

expected to warm them to England. Even the asylum she granted them was, as we shall see, distrusted by many, who suspected (with some cause) that she would deliver them back to their oppressors if she could. They had not been *attracted* to England by anything English; nor did they intend to stay there longer than they needed. Consequently there was little reason why they should love the English, or need to cultivate their approval. They suffered England merely; just as England merely suffered them. Between the two communities it was a curious, unloving relationship.

For these reasons too very few of the refugees, with the exception of the early Italians, even after years of residence in England made or tried to make close English friends. Not intending to make their homes in England they felt no need for them. Not being interested in English things, they had no particular desire for them. Englishmen had to come to *them*. Some did, and friendships did grow up between Englishmen and refugees. But nearly always it was through the former's interest in the refugees' national politics, and very rarely the other way around: between Poles and English Polonophiles, rather than between Englishmen and Polish Anglophiles. In order to know them Englishmen had to come into the refugees' own worlds: there was no meeting-place in the Englishman's. And even those Englishmen who did get to know some of the refugees usually knew them far less well than the refugees' own people did. The refugees' social life was nearly always passed exclusively amongst others of their own nationalities, or fellow-refugees of other nationalities. So far as they could they kept apart and aloof: separated from English life and culture, and with their own little cultures wrapped closely around them for support in a foreign environment.

Those little cultures could be observed any day of the week around Soho Square and Leicester Square and the Seven Dials, where most of the poorest of the refugees lived, and where the rest of them usually came for company. There they had their own streets, their own clubs, their own shops, their own cafés; and their own conversation, whose continental political obsessions probably as much as anything else kept them apart from the *indigènes*. To George Sala of *Household Words*, who insisted he was not caricaturing them, their nightly gatherings in their cafés appeared alien and exotic:

> . . . hooded, tasselled and braided garments of unheard of fashion; hats of shapes to make you wonder to what a stage the art of squeezability had arrived; trousers with unnumbered plaits; boots made as boots were never made before; finger and thumb-rings of fantastic fashion; marvellous gestures, Babel-like tongues; voices anything but (Englishly) human; the smoke as of a thousand brick-kilns; the clatter as of a thousand spoons . . . [47]

[47] [George A. Sala], *art. cit.*, p. 27.

When they celebrated, too, it was in ways of their own. Anniversaries of past revolutions were made the occasions for vast banquets, hundreds or even a thousand of them and their British sympathisers feasting at a single sitting, with republican banners and Phrygian caps and all the other familiar symbols of their faith above and around them, and toasts and speeches from their leaders, following on one after the other, going long into the night.[48] More occasionally, when one of their number died in exile, they would treat him, and themselves, to funerals such as the English never provided except for royalty and national heroes: with long processions, and flags and banners, and stirring declamatory orations at the graveside: defiant and dramatic assertions of the resilience of their causes even through death.[49]

These latter were almost the only occasions on which the London public, unless they ventured into their areas, saw the refugees *en masse*. Usually their congregations were more private, and less colourful. The centre of emigré life in London in the nineteenth century was the political club, which the English were very seldom allowed into. This was always a refugee's main and vital link with his homeland and his cause. There were dozens of them: meeting for the most part in smoky rooms above cafés, or school-rooms for the poor:

A lamp hung from the low ceiling . . . between two Phrygian caps was a . . . banner, with the inscription – *Second anniversaire de la révolution du 24 Fevrier*. But the banner was torn or twisted, so that one had to guess part of the words. Ragged, full of stains, and adorned with withered laurels, the whole trophy had a painfully unpleasing effect . . . The room had a damp and musty smell when we entered it. Gradually it filled. There were about fifteen ladies, and sixty or seventy men . . . They were all wild-looking and negligently dressed. There were some fine heads amongst them, however, and hardly one commonplace or inexpressive countenance . . . They were all frightfully determined physiognomies.[50]

There followed customarily a lecture, or a discussion, which more often than not would turn into a row. What struck contemporaries most about the clubs was how schismatic they were. There were attempts made to unite and co-ordinate their efforts, under the aegis of a succession of transient internationalist revolutionary organisations culminating in the First International of 1864. The most successful before 1864 was probably the non-socialist *Comité Démocratique Européen Central*, founded in 1850 by Mazzini, Ledru-Rollin, Arnold Ruge and Albert Darasz, which did not last

[48] E.g. *Reynolds's Newspaper*, 9 March 1851, p. 14, reporting a French republican banquet for 600, plus an audience of onlookers in the gallery.
[49] E.g. *ibid*., 26 April 1857, p. 6, reporting the funeral of M. Rougée, with an estimated crowd of 10,000 following the coffin and making a procession half a mile long.
[50] Frederick Hardman, 'The London Diary of a German Authoress', in *Blackwood's Magazine*, vol. 70 (August 1851), p. 214.

beyond 1853, but whose leaders continued to co-operate thereafter.[51] Socialists were keener internationalists, but initially less successful. A secret 'Universal League of Revolutionary Communists', founded in April 1850 by Marx and Engels with the French Blanquists and the English Chartist Harney, sounded fiery, but probably did not leave the drawing board.[52] In 1856 an 'International Association' was founded 'to propagate and organise international solidarity and to form a centre where the laws of the new social order could be studied, propagated and put into practice'; it embraced Polish, French, German and British socialists, and was active until 1859, but then folded.[53] Other manifestations of refugee solidarity were shorter-lived. Generally the refugees could not agree even within their national groups. It was perhaps inevitable that they should not, with so many different varieties of freedom being struggled for – the Germans, for example, striving towards social democracy while many of the Poles were still far behind struggling to make themselves a *nation*; and with the way ahead, in those reactionary times, so dim as to defy a clear, bright solution. There was ample scope for real differences of revolutionary principle, which Alexander Herzen, who himself had rather a low view of most of the other refugees, and especially the French, believed to be compounded by personal jealousies and ambitions, and exacerbated and embittered by exile, and poverty, and the London air – 'damp, smoke-laden, never warmed by the sun'.[54]

Consequently dissension proliferated. One of the earliest Italian exiles commented on how his countrymen, wherever they were, seemed possessed of a spirit of 'discordia calunniatrice'; which was manifested throughout the 1840s and 1850s.[55] The Poles were split between the old conservative and aristocratic adherents of Prince Adam Czartoryski, and the newer socialist followers of Stanislaus Worcell, until the latter died in 1857 and the radicals crumbled into smaller cliques.[56] The French in the 1850s divided themselves between Ledru-Rollin's *Société de la Révolution*, Louis Blanc's *Union Socialiste*, and then Félix Pyat's *Commune révolutionnaire* – which last Herzen regarded as identical in its aims to Louis Blanc's *Union*, and only started because Pyat felt himself too big to serve under Blanc.[57] An English policeman observed in 1852 what a 'very curious sight' it was 'to see the uproar that exists at all times' at meetings of the French refugees, 'the words *Canaille, Voleur, Brigand, Coquin,* Jean-foutre' being 'continu-

[51] See Calman, *op. cit*, pp. 95ff; A. Müller-Lehning, 'The International Association (1855–9)', in *International Review for Social History*, vol. III (Leiden, 1938), p. 201; A. R. Schoyen, *The Chartist Challenge* (1958), p. 212.   [52] Müller-Lehning, *art. cit.*, p. 199.
[53] *Ibid.*, pp. 213–35.   [54] Herzen, *op. cit.*, pp. 1052, 1139.   [55] Wicks, *op. cit.*, p. 98.
[56] Peter Brock, 'Polish Democrats and English Radicals 1832–62', in *Journal of Modern History*, vol. 25 (1953).
[57] Calman, *op. cit.*, pp. 135–9; Marcel Dessal, *Un Révolutionnaire Jacobin: Charles Delescluze 1807–1871* (Paris, 1952), p. 190; Herzen, *op. cit.*, p. 1055.

ally used in speaking of each other'.[58] Likewise the Germans – probably the least disciplined of them all – were forever quarrelling over whether they should try for revolution now or wait for the time to ripen: 'tearing each other to pieces', observed again the uncharitable Herzen, 'with indefatigable frenzy, unsparing of family secrets or the most criminal accusations'.[59] There were frequent and insalubrious quarrels too over money. The French *Société fraternelle des démocrates-socialistes à Londres*, which was supposed to be strictly philanthropic and apolitical, was racked with dissension between 1852 and 1854 over the question of how funds secured from Paris should be distributed amongst the refugees.[60] In November 1850 rival groups of Poles – 'Hungarian Poles' and 'Baden Poles' (according to where they had last fought) – had to be restrained by the police from setting on each other at a public meeting over the question of money.[61] Refugee leaders were constantly having to deny accusations that they were pocketing monies intended for the refugees' relief: the Hungarian Pulszky, for example, in 1851; Kossuth himself in 1853; and Herzen in the 1860s.[62] Whatever the refugees might have had in common with one another, doctrine and money together saw that they remained divided.

Even if they could have agreed on these two things there still remained, to undermine the fraternity which otherwise might have prevailed, suspicions that some amongst them might be spies and agents-provocateurs, planted by foreign police in their midst to watch and compromise their activities. Sometimes the suspicions themselves may have been planted by foreign police against innocents to foment discord. Konrad Schramm, who was surely not a spy, was incensed by an incident at a meeting at Highbury Barn in February 1851, when

I, and a friend of mine, were assaulted in an incredible manner. A set of individuals, whom I will refrain from qualifying, raised against us the cry of 'spy, spy'; a numerous mob rushed upon us, and after having undergone a series of insults, we were obliged to leave the place without being able to obtain even a hearing.[63]

Likewise a woman calling herself the Baroness von Beck, who died

---

[58] Police report (Sanders), italics in original, 14 October 1852: PRO HO 45/4547A; and cf. police report of 2 March 1853, reporting the departure of Caussidière to America 'because he finds that the Democrats are continually quarrelling together without coming to any serious resolutions': Clarendon Papers, Bodleian Library, Oxford (Clar. P.), c. 2 f. 475.

[59] Herzen, *op. cit.*, pp. 1155–6. The ideological quarrel between Marx and Willich is described in Heinrich Gemkow *et al.*, *Karl Marx: A Biography* (Dresden, 1968) pp. 198–9; Robert Payne, *Marx* (1968), p. 243; and (most reliably) David McLellan, *Karl Marx, His Life and Thought* (1976 edn.), pp. 246ff. It was enlivened by malicious gossip about Marx's relations with Helene Demuth, the family's companion/maid, whom he got pregnant in 1850 (McLellan, pp. 271–3).

[60] Calman, *op. cit.*, pp. 140–8.   [61] *The Times*, 22 November 1850, p. 5.

[62] See *ibid.*, 4 August 1853, p. 7 (report of the case of Derra de Meroda v. Dawson etc., at Warwick Assizes); police report of 26 March 1853, in PRO HO 45/4816; Herzen, *op. cit.*, pp. 1342–8.   [63] *Friend of the People*, 15 March 1851, p. 107.

suddenly and sensationally as she was being tried for fraud in Birmingham in August 1851, was widely supposed to be an Austrian spy, although she probably was not.[64] In some cases there may have been an element of mild paranoia in it; or some of the refugees might have liked to imagine that they had spies set on them, like Dostoevsky's Stepan Trofimovitch in *The Possessed*, in order to inflate their sense of their own importance. Exile could have this sort of effect on a man. But genuine spies there certainly were amongst the refugees. A notorious one called Huber managed to infiltrate the French *Union Républicaine* in the late 1850s.[65] The British police discovered two by the name of Sullivan amongst the Jersey refugees in the pay of the French government in 1852.[66] Another one, called Ranet or Ravet, tried to implicate Ledru-Rollin in a spurious assassination conspiracy in March 1857, which Ledru-Rollin immediately revealed to the police and press to clear himself.[67] In 1851 a British ambassador discovered that an Austrian regiment in northern Germany, in order to 'prove' that some of its Hungarian troops were being incited to desert by refugees in London, had sent an agent-provocateur among them to persuade them to do just this; with the result that an unwitting exile named Pataki was enticed back to Germany, where he was arrested.[68] These were some who were found out; undoubtedly there were many more. How effective these foreign police spies were in their main function of providing intelligence of refugee activities in England is not certain. For their part the British authorities, as we shall see, regarded their reports, when they were forwarded to them through the Foreign Office, as untrustworthy. They were effective, however, in creating an atmosphere of suspicion in the refugee communities in England: which knew that there were spies among them,

[64] The Baroness von Beck was the authoress of *Personal Adventures of a Lady during the late War of Independence in Hungary* (1850). Her trial, for fraud, is reported in *The Times*, 2 September 1851, p. 6. She died in an ante-room of the Court just before the trial opened, which did not however prevent the prosecution from putting its case against her before the proceedings were stopped. They claimed that her title was fraudulent, and that she was in fact a spy in the joint pay of the Austrian and British police. The *Northern Star* (13 September pp. 4–5) and *Reynolds's Newspaper* (7 September p. 6) both accepted that this was so. After her death her secretary Constant Derra de Meroda went to enormous lengths to clear her name: publishing pamphlets exonerating her (C. Derra de Meroda, *A Refutation of the Charge of Imposition and Fraud, recently made at the Police Court of Birmingham, against the Baroness von Beck. . .* [1851]; [Anon.], *The Persecution and Death of the Baroness von Beck, at Birmingham, in August 1851. . .* [1852]); petitioning the House of Lords (3PD 121 cc. 1275–88 [28 May 1852]); suing the police for malicious prosecution at Warwick Assizes (*The Times*, 29 July 1852, pp. 6–7); and then when that failed appealing to the Court of Queen's Bench for a new trial (*The Times*, 8 November 1852, p. 8; 20 January 1853, p. 7): which decided for him in August 1853 (*The Times*, 4 August 1853, p. 7).   [65] Calman, *op. cit.*, p. 136.
[66] Police reports of 10 August and 19 September 1852: PRO HO 45/4547A.
[67] Calman, *op. cit.*, pp. 174–5; Howard C. Payne, *The Police State of Louis Napoleon Bonaparte 1851–1860* (Seattle, Wash., 1966), p. 151. On French police spies in general, see H. C. Payne and H. Grosshans, 'The Exiled Revolutionaries and the French political police in the 1850s', in *American Historical Review*, vol. 68 (1963).
[68] See Granville to Brunnow, 15 January 1852: PRO FO 65/416.

but could not be sure who they were, and whom, therefore, they could trust.

For these reasons the meetings of the refugees were often less than fraternal, and much valuable revolutionary energy was dissipated in battles amongst themselves. Occasionally the battles could be bloody. In 1850 the Germans Konrad Schramm and August Willich crossed to Belgium to settle a point of revolutionary doctrine with pistols.[69] Emmanuel Barthélemy, who was one of the most violent of the French exiles – 'maigre, chétif, pâle, taciturne', as Victor Hugo described him, 'une espèce de gamin tragique'[70] – appeared out of the shadows of the political underworld twice in English courts for killing; once in 1853 for the manslaughter of a fellow refugee in a duel at Egham, for which he was given a very light prison sentence by a lenient judge who allowed for his ignorance of English ways;[71] the second time for the apparently senseless (and apolitical) murder of two Englishmen in Warren Street, for which he was publicly hanged in January 1855 – and eventually found his way in effigy to Madame Tussaud's Chamber of Horrors.[72] In April 1856 an Italian refugee named Foschini stabbed four other Italians in a café in Rupert Street, probably under the impression that they were spies, and then disappeared into thin air.[73] In October 1857 a mutilated body in a carpet bag was fished out of the Thames under Waterloo Bridge, which was later surmised, though never confirmed, to be that of the French victim of another political murder.[74] Such incidents did not reflect the way the refugees generally conducted their debates. Usually the violence was merely verbal. But it was often there, very close to the surface: a product, perhaps, of the special frustrations of emigré life.

Nevertheless the refugees were not always arguing amongst themselves. Between quarrels they found time too for more significant political activities, directed outwards, against the governments they had fled from. In the main these activities were literary and didactic. All the different groups of refugees produced occasional manifestoes (of which *The Communist Manifesto* was one), sometimes directed against other groups of refugees, and consequently part and parcel of their internecine feuding; but more often aimed at rallying support against their common enemies.

---

[69] Robert Payne, *op. cit.*, p. 244.   [70] Quoted in Charles Hugo, *op. cit.*, p. 30.
[71] *Ibid.*, pp. 31–8; *The Times*, 22 March 1853, p. 7.
[72] *The Times*, 9 December 1854, p. 10; 5 January 1855, p. 9; 11 January 1855, p. 9; 17 January 1855, p. 10; 23 January 1855, p. 8; Charles Hugo, *op. cit.*, pp. 38–42.
[73] *The Times*, 18 April 1856, p. 9; 19 April 1856, p. 12; 23 April 1856, p. 7; 24 April 1856, p. 9; 29 April 1856, p. 5; 1 May 1856, p. 12; G. J. Holyoake, *Sixty Years of an Agitator's Life* (1892), vol. II, pp. 40–1. Holyoake's account of this (as of most things) is not to be relied on.
[74] *Annual Register*, 1857, Chronicle pp. 194–7; *Reynolds's Newspaper*, 11 October 1857, p. 11; 3PD 148 cc. 946–7 (8 February 1858).

These manifestoes were published as broadsheets, or pamphlets, or in English Radical newspapers, or in the refugees' own newspapers. Of the latter there were several right through the nineteenth century, printed in London or Jersey in the emigrés' own languages, and meant for circulation amongst themselves, and also for distribution in their countries of origin, if ways could be found to smuggle them in. They proliferated in the 1850s, though most of them were short-lived. The most important were probably *Le Proscrit*, edited by Ledru-Rollin and Charles Delescluze, which ran (under different names) from the summer of 1850 to the end of 1851; *L'Homme*, which was published in the Channel Islands from 1853 to 1856; and the two papers Alexander Herzen produced for the Russians and Poles, *Poliarnaia Zvezda* ('Polar Star') which appeared occasionally between 1855 and 1861, and *Kolokol* ('The Bell'), which came out more regularly from 1857 to 1867.[75] These emigré newspapers provided, as well as news of emigré happenings, and of their national causes abroad, vehicles for debate and propaganda. In all these ways – in their newspapers, in manifestoes and pamphlets, and also in speeches and orations at political meetings or banquets or over the coffins of dead compatriots – the more active refugees carried on, as their main political trade, a voluminous war of words against their continental enemies.

They attacked on a number of fronts. Most common were straight denunciations of the misdeeds of their foes, of which Victor Hugo's pamphlet *Napoléon le Petit*, published in London in 1852, was the most celebrated, but by no means alone in the genre. Others went back over recent history, retailing their own recent adventures (like Orsini's *The Austrian Dungeons in Italy*, published in 1856), or the revolutionary achievements of the past – especially of 1848 – and how they had been betrayed: like Mazzini's *Republic and Royalty in Italy* (1850).[76] Sometimes the propaganda was more constructive and forward-looking, arguing the merits of different kinds of revolutionary alternative systems of government to the tyrants': possibly ineffectively, because controversially.[77] Occasionally there were published practical exhortations to action, which, as we shall see, irritated the tyrants most of all: calls to the people to take arms against them; appeals to armies to mutiny; and incitements to tyran-

---

[75] *Le Proscrit* became *Le Voix du Proscrit* in the autumn, then (for a single issue) *Le Peuple*. *L'Homme* was edited by Charles Ribeyrolles. During the same period the Germans had the *Deutscher Londoner Zeitung* and then *Das Volk*, and the Italians had *Italia del Popolo*.

[76] Other examples are the Baroness von Beck's *Personal Adventures . . .*, cited *supra* (p. 29 fn. 64); Orsini's *Memoirs and Adventures* (1857: the sequel to *Austrian Dungeons*); Louis Blanc's *1848: Historical Revelations* (1858); and Mazzini's *The Late Genoese Insurrection Defended* (1857).

[77] The most famous example is the *Communist Manifesto* of Marx and Engels, but there were many other more ephemeral ones: like Blanc's pamphlet *La République une et indivisible* (1851); and *Au parti républicain*, published in 1855 by Mazzini, Ledru-Rollin and Kossuth.

nicide.[78] Most of this was very likely more significant in maintaining the morale of the exiles, than for any direct effect it had abroad (though this was disputed): but much of it did find its way to the continent, and was found circulating among the democratic underground there – *Napoléon le Petit*, for example, appears to have been smuggled in some numbers into France from Jersey, sometimes, with deliberate irony, hidden in plaster busts of *le Petit* himself;[79] and proclamations signed by Mazzini and Kossuth were always turning up in Italy and Austria. The outraged reactions of the continental emperors when they *were* found in their territories must, if they knew of them, have pleased the refugees, and relieved their sense of impotence.

As they were in England the refugees also addressed themselves to Englishmen to help them further their causes, though with less hope of success. 'They must be aware', said *The Times* in November 1856, 'how small are the effects of this pertinacious propaganda, how narrow is the circle which their preachings influence, how wide is the opinion that they are fanatical disturbers of the public peace, unworthy of the attention of any serious man'.[80] Most of the refugees had in fact few illusions about what they could do among the English, and some, like Herzen, deliberately refrained from pressing their causes on them: 'It is not for us to litigate in the court of our enemies, who judge by other principles, by laws which we do not recognise.'[81] Nevertheless there was a little missionary work carried on amongst them, in the correspondence columns of all ranks of newspapers, which were fairly generous in the space they gave to them; or in public speeches such as those delivered by Kossuth and Worcell up and down the country in 1855 and 1856 to try to turn the Crimean War to the advantage of east European nationalities.[82] Such preaching rarely reached beyond the converted, who could do little themselves for the refugees, and were too few and too distant from the centres of power to put any significant pressure on those who could. The latter, though very occasionally they might have sympathised with some of the refugees' aims, were too great political realists to allow their policies to be swayed by them, and in any event were generally, throughout the whole of this period, wedded to certain concepts like 'the European Balance' which were directly inimical to them.[83] An exception may have been Italy,

---

[78] E.g. the Hungarian proclamation in PRO HO 45/3720; and Félix Pyat's *Lettre au Parlement et à la Presse* (1858).

[79] See Léon Deries, 'Policiers et Douaniers contre Victor Hugo', in *Grande Revue*, vol. LXXXV, 25 June 1914.   [80] *The Times*, 14 November 1856, p. 8.

[81] Herzen, *op. cit.*, p. 1026.

[82] A small band of Roumanians in England also lobbied British politicians and tried to win public support for their cause: see Radu R. N. Florescu, *The Struggle against Russia in the Roumanian Principalities* (Monachii, 1962), ch. 10; and N. Iorga, *A History of Anglo-Roumanian Relations* (Bucharest, 1931), p. 90.   [83] *Infra*, p. 139.

a number of whose exiles did manage to penetrate socially and sympathetically very high in the British governing hierarchy, and may well have influenced policy.[84] The Italians – the earlier generations of them, who worked much harder to cultivate the approval and the acceptance of the British establishment than any of the other groups of refugees – were the only ones in a position to do so.

All this activity, if it was not all entirely above board, was at least open. When the refugees turned to more practical means of furthering their political aims, it was usually less so. Direct action took a number of forms. Occasionally it could be merely desperate, and pathetic: as when a poor sick Hungarian called Johann Lhotsky was found breaking the windows of a hotel where Metternich was staying in April 1848, and calling him names: for which a London magistrate had not the heart even to fine him.[85] Usually the actions they took were better conceived, and more effective. Much effort was put into raising money for revolutionary ends. A common device was to issue bonds or banknotes and sell them among the refugees and their sympathisers, to be redeemable when their revolutions succeeded. Mazzini was involved in such a scheme in 1850–1, and Kossuth in 1861.[86] More direct action still was usually clandestine. Consequently it never was, and is not now, easy to extricate the truth about it from the fog of rumours which surrounded the question of the refugees' 'conspiracies' in Britain. The middle years of the nineteenth century were full of attempted revolutions and assassinations on the continent. Many of them involved or were supposed to involve men who at some time or another had lived in Britain. Whether it was in Britain that they devised their plots could only rarely be established for certain. If revolts and assassinations *were* plotted in Britain, then it was usually in groups small enough to maintain secrecy, then and thereafter. Consequently there was always room for doubt about the rôle of the refugee community in most of these conspiracies, and even about whether some of them really existed at all, which as we shall see furnished strong ground for dissension between the British and continental governments. Nevertheless in some cases there was very strong circumstantial evidence connecting *attentats* in Europe

[84] In 1855 several very high-ranking British statesmen, including Palmerston and Gladstone, were induced by Panizzi to conspire to release some Neapolitan prisoners: see Rudman, *op. cit.*, pp. 205–6; and G. B. Henderson, *Crimean War Diplomacy and other Historical Essays* (Glasgow, 1947), pp. 238–41.
[85] *The Times*, 27 April 1848, p. 7. Later on, in June, Lhotsky was in trouble again for sending a threatening letter to Metternich, and again let off: *The Times*, 13 June 1848, p. 7. A short biography of Lhotsky appears in W. E. Houghton (ed.), *Wellesley Index of Victorian Periodicals*, vol. II (1972), pp. 984–5.
[86] There are copies of such banknotes in the Cowen Papers, TWAD 634/A153 and A161: the latter issued by the Poles. A batch of French bonds was seized at Ostend in July 1853: see Walewski to Clarendon, 16 July 1853: PRO FO 27/989. For the Mazzini notes of 1851, see PRO HO 45/3720; on Kossuth's 1861 banknotes, *vide infra*, p. 202.

2. Revolutionary
   banknotes issued by
   Italian and Polish
   exiles in the early
   1850s.

with groups of exiles in London: strongest of all in the case of the Orsini assassination attempt of 14 January 1858, in which eight innocents were killed and 150 injured by bombs meant for the French emperor, and in which it was shown beyond a doubt that most of the participants had lived recently in England, and that the bombs had been made there.[87] There were other fragments too which came to light of evidence strongly suggesting murderous conspiracies going on in England, not all of which were carried out, and some of which never had a hope of succeeding, but which revealed a dark underside of some of the refugees' activities.

It is inherently unlikely anyway that there was not a certain amount of 'conspiring' in England in the mid nineteenth century. 'It is in the very nature of things', as the *Daily News* pointed out in 1855, 'that exiles should be ever scheming to effect a triumphant return to their native land'.[88] For those refugees who had been nurtured in the 'conspiratorial' tradition derived from Babeuf and Buonarroti, and associated at that time with Blanqui, it was a normal way of revolutionary life. Even for the more moderate of them 'conspiring' in some form was almost a necessary activity, if they were to retain their sense of political potency. During the early years of their exile at least, most of them did not and could not regard it as a kind of retirement or vacation, an interlude in the game when action for the moment was suspended. To have done so would have been a dereliction of duty, and a concession to their enemies. Though they were away from the theatres of their revolutionary activities, they saw themselves as active revolutionaries still, helping on their causes from abroad, not content merely to propagandise or to sit and wait for better times to come. What they did to help on their causes they usually did and arranged to do in secret, to avoid forewarning their enemies, or risking encounters with the British authorities, or just out of habit; and in combination, for effectiveness. In the context of the time, this was enough to define a 'conspiracy'.[89] Sometimes the secret combinations in which they conspired were linked with underground movements abroad, like the *Marianne* in France, the Italian *Carbonari*, and the *Bund der Gerechten* in Germany: which to those people who inclined to the theory that all the world's troubles derived from the activities of international secret societies gave them a sinister smell.[90] At other times their plots were implemented –

---

[87] See Michael St John Packe, *The Bombs of Orsini* (1957); and *infra*, ch. 6.

[88] *Daily News*, 11 October 1855, p. 4.

[89] In the Cowen Papers (TWAD 634/A189) there are letters written in invisible ink which Cowen agreed to carry to and from the continent on his business trips. The secret messages were written between the lines of conventionally-written letters, with a mixture of 'kali ferrohydrocyanici and Agna destilatta'; then revealed by painting over them with a solution of 'Coperas and Accid Oxalique'. Unfortunately for the historian the effect of the latter concoction was to make the letters too brittle to handle, and they are now impossible to decipher.

[90] See J. M. Roberts, *The Mythology of the Secret Societies* (1972).

if they were implemented at all – by themselves in clandestine crossings to the continent, or by agents sent over for the purpose. Very occasionally the end they had in view was a full-scale invasion of the continent simultaneous with a rising there: like a plot which was revealed to the British government in Jersey in 1852 for a fleet of small boats to sail on Bayonne when a signal was given in Paris. (It never happened, because the signal never came.)[91] More often the conspiracies involved smaller numbers of refugees taking key political centres by stealth, as preludes to popular risings: like the abortive Milan revolt of 1853.[92] Other conspiracies, like Orsini's, were directed at the lives of kings and emperors. All these things were plotted by groups of refugees in England. Often the plotting was mere idle talk, and in all there was far more conspiracy than there was action. But some action there undoubtedly was, with European régimes as its target, and England's asylum the soil in which it was cultivated.[93]

In fact few refugees denied that this was so. What was denied was that the *leaders* of the refugees were involved: in particular in the 1850s Mazzini, Ledru-Rollin and Kossuth. This was, as we shall see, what much of the controversy between the British and continental governments over the refugees then was about. What made continental governments so eager to implicate these men in 'conspiracies' was partly a genuine belief that they *were* implicated; but also an anxiety to implicate them anyway, because they were more dangerous to them politically than the lesser emigrés. If possible they would have liked to implicate them in the worst kinds of conspiracy, like conspiracy to assassinate, because this was a thing the British government would have to take notice of. This kind of possible motivation made the accusations which foreign governments made against the refugee leaders suspect. There was rarely any solid evidence to back them up: inevitably, perhaps, in the nature of the case. If they were careful not to be caught red-handed, and if those who were caught red-handed were loyal to them, then the leaders' complicity was likely to be difficult to prove except circumstantially: by reference to suspicious comings and goings, furtive meetings, a nod and a wink, and other such shadows. Even the refugee 'chiefs' themselves might not have been fully in the know about each other's more clandestine activities. Herzen was sure that Mazzini and Ledru-Rollin 'did their utmost to make revolutionary attempts every two or three months, Mazzini by risings, Ledru-Rollin by the despatch of agents', but not Kossuth, who in Herzen's eyes was wiser.[94] Mazzini's part in the 1853 Milan uprising, and in other conspiracies, is scarcely disputable. But Herzen may have been wrong about

---

[91] See police report of 14 August 1852, in PRO HO 45/4547A.
[92] Packe, *op. cit.*, pp. 130–2.
[93] The 'conspiracies' of the French exiles are discussed in Howard C. Payne and H. Grosshans, *art. cit.*   [94] Herzen, *op. cit.*, p. 1041.

Ledru-Rollin, who is acquitted of conspiracy by the main authority on this stage of his career;[95] and about Kossuth, who may have been more of a conspirator than Herzen knew.[96] No real evidence ever came to light implicating any of the leaders in the wilder assassination attempts, like the Orsini plot, which continental governments tried to pin on Mazzini but could not. They may have been involved, but succeeded marvellously in covering their tracks. In any event they were not inactive. At the very least they made contingency plans. In all kinds of ways they tried so far as they could to direct resistance on the continent. Occasionally they initiated, and more often gave approval to, direct conspiratorial actions. And they may have done more.

Whatever they did do, the leaders and the main bodies of the refugees went to very great lengths to persuade the British authorities that it was very little. They knew that there were likely to be certain limitations imposed on their activities in England: if anything they tended to have exaggerated notions of the limits that would be set; and they did what they could to give the impression – which may or may not have been a 'cover' – that they were working comfortably within these limits. When a new society with the challenging name of 'the German Agitation Union of London' was founded in August 1851, it took great pains to emphasise to the British that it would 'make use only of means of agitation within the limits of the laws of England,' and it added that 'to prevent misconception, or wilful misrepresentation, the society declares that it has no pretension whatever to be a secret Government of Germany'.[97] Another gathering of Germans in the same year – aware perhaps of the presence in it of an informer, who dutifully reported all this back to the London Police Commissioners – decided not to exclude non-refugees, expressly in order to reassure the British authorities: 'It was ridiculous', said one member, ' . . . to expect that their meetings would be approved of, if they chose to act in a mysterious manner, and to make their meetings a conclave.' For the same reason 'It was decided to exclude Dr Marx and Engels, knowing them to be violent and intriguing men.'[98] Engels, for his part, also tried to persuade Marx to do nothing provocative.[99] If they were violent and intriguing men then, Marx and Engels became less so later, for ideological reasons which were probably too subtle for the British authorities to understand; and in their turn did what they could to reassure their hosts that they were as

---

[95] Calman, op. cit., ch. 11.

[96] In 1851 he was reported to be setting up a school in London to teach Hungarian officers military engineering (Reynolds's Newspaper, 7 December 1851, p.8), and in 1853 to be drilling an invading army (Police report of 5 March 1853: PRO HO 45/4816) and manufacturing war-rockets at a factory in Rotherhithe (infra, p. 145 and fn. 75).

[97] Reynolds's Newspaper, 24 August 1851, p. 14.

[98] Police report of 5 August 1851: PRO HO 45/3518.   [99] Robert Payne, op. cit., p. 263.

innocent of conspiracy as the rest: in 1871, for example, obliging the Home Office by sending copies of the International's papers to it.[100] The French refugees were if anything more cautious: at least in front of informers. Any of them at their meetings who got particularly worked up and violent was immediately disowned by the more responsible ones, and 'excused, from his being excited with drink'. 'They state', reported one informer, 'that no one can blame them so long as they conform to the Laws of the Country of whom they receive hospitality.;[101] At a meeting in 1852 Caussidière and Ribeyrolles, again possibly for police consumption, launched into fulsome panegyrics of the British government, assuring their compatriots that the latter would not annoy them 'unless they were foolish enough to violate the laws of England'. The refugees, they informed whoever might be listening, were not fomenting revolutions, but merely waiting for them to happen; 'they would never be the cause of any Revolution abroad, but if one took place, they would rally under the Republican flag': and who could blame them for that?[102] The internationalist *Comité Démocratique Européen Central* made similar disclaimers.[103] Ledru-Rollin went to considerable lengths to avoid any suspicion that he might be involved in direct action: unmasking *agents-provocateurs* to the British police, as we have seen; and in 1855 journeying to Edinburgh to be far away from London when Louis Napoleon visited, in case anything was tried against the French emperor and he, Ledru-Rollin, falsely implicated.[104] The Jersey contingent of refugees was different: wilder, and a good deal less cautious; but even in Jersey there were those who were worried about the effect their intemperance might have on the British government, and tried to restrain the wilder ones, or to brand them as *provocateurs*.[105]

The reason for this very studied cultivation of a moderate 'image' was their fear that, if they revealed themselves as too violent, they might be removed. For most of the leading refugees, Britain was far too valuable a refuge – so conveniently close as it was to the objects of their ambition – to want to imperil needlessly; and also, it was thought, too precarious a one to take chances with. Very few of the refugees reposed enough confidence in British institutions to believe that the asylum they were granted under them was entirely secure and inviolable. Much of this uncertainty could be attributed to habits of thinking nurtured in more suspicious political environments, which they found it hard to shake off in Britain's freer air. They were used to more arbitrary ways of government, and could not altogether credit the degree of security which a constitutional government afforded them. These suspicions were very likely encouraged by their English Chartist friends, who had good reason to believe that if you

[100] *Ibid.*, pp. 426–8.   [101] Police report of 1 November 1851: PRO HO 45/3518.
[102] Police report of 25 January 1852: PRO HO 45/4302.   [103] Calman, *op. cit.*, p. 103.
[104] *Ibid.*, p. 179.   [105] See police report of 27 September 1852: PRO HO 45/4013.

scratched them the British authorities themselves very often turned out in fact to be fairly arbitrary underneath. Nevertheless, some of the notions the refugees had about their situation under existing English law were fundamentally wrong. Many of them were under the impression that they could be 'deported', which they could not in any likely circumstances: Herzen, for example, thought so, and also Ledru-Rollin.[106] Most of them also seemed to have an exaggerated idea of the effectiveness and severity of the other laws which could be marshalled against them in England, and to believe that it would not take much to induce the British authorities to make those laws even more severe. Consequently every attack by foreign governments on Britain for her asylum policy was watched by the refugees apprehensively, lest the citadel be surrendered by a governing class which was, after all, not so different from or better than the continental governments it hobnobbed with. 'Ay', wrote a French refugee to *The Times* in 1858, 'we know perfectly well the ruling classes would be delighted to expulse that venomous band . . . from these free (of course) shores' if they could.[107] Throughout the 1850s they were reported to live in daily fear that at any moment, on the slightest pretext, the British government might bring in a law to enable it to 'give all the Refugees up to France'.[108] Hence the diligence with which the most responsible of them tried as far as they could to shed their reputation 'of being turbulent people, opposed to all reasonable measures', which, claimed Caussidière in 1852, was 'a name we do not deserve'.[109] That was what they wanted the authorities to believe.

The same reasoning, the fear of being thrown out if they overstepped some very vaguely-perceived mark they believed had been set by the British authorities, also lay behind their obvious and studied avoidance during most of the period, and especially in the 1850s, of any kind of involvement in British domestic politics: this, and the fact that most of them found it difficult anyway to get interested in British politics, except insofar as they directly affected themselves. There were a few significant exceptions to this rule. In the first place some of the Italians could hardly help being dragged into British religious politics: sharing as they did with English protestants a common antipathy to the papacy (or to its incumbent), and only too eager to seize on this to make common cause with their hosts, and maybe even a little money too.[110] This was (except of course to

---

[106] Herzen, *op. cit.*, p. 1121; Calman, *op. cit.*, pp. 185–6.

[107] *The Times*, 2 February 1858, p. 12.

[108] Police report of 16 September 1852: PRO HO 45/4547A. At the time of Louis Napoleon's visit to England in 1855 Clarendon reported to Cowley: 'I was glad to hear from Mayne that all the leaders such as Ledru Rollin L. Blanc & V. Hugo are most anxious to keep the *Rouges* quiet as they are sure that if an attentat was made an Alien Bill wd. be passed next day & it wd. be fatal to their *prospects*, they think, to be ejected from Engd.' Clarendon to Cowley (private), 6 April 1855: Cowley papers (Cowl. P.), PRO FO 519/171 ff.304–5.

[109] Police report of 27 September 1852: PRO HO 45/4013.   [110] *Infra*, p. 107.

English and Irish catholics) an unprovocative kind of interference; little odium could attach to the refugees for bolstering the prejudices of nearly every class of Englishmen in their own domestic quarrel with the Roman church – and so it did them no harm. What could do them harm, and what therefore was avoided rather more, was any dabbling by them in English secular revolutionary politics: with Chartism and the working-class radical movements which came after it. From time to time there were rumours of such dabbling – reports that the refugees were out subverting the lower classes of England: but very rarely was there any solid cause to believe them, except perhaps in Jersey, where the French refugees shared a common language with the inhabitants, and where therefore the constant complaints of a nervous governor-general against their 'disseminating amongst the lower orders of the people their doctrine of socialism and communism'[111] may have had some substance. On the mainland, however, the only significant example of a refugee involving himself in British radical politics was the Pole, Major Beniowski, who was a member of a Chartist association and was supposed to have helped organise the Newport rising of 1839: and his involvement was probably exaggerated at the time.[112] Otherwise the Chartists got very little help from their foreign friends: far less than they gave to them. As ever in these cases contacts between them, which the authorities sometimes regarded with apprehension, were in fact nearly always about matters of concern to the refugees, on behalf of foreign causes the Chartists happened to sympathise with, and very seldom to do with matters British.

We have seen that there was really very little reason why the refugees should have been particularly interested in British politics, as they were not in Britain by choice, did not intend to remain there, and were more than most people preoccupied with other politics. By their allies in England, however, it was sometimes regretted that the traffic of sympathy and aid between them was so one-way. 'We could wish', said the republican *Star of Freedom* in August 1852,

that the residence among us of these our brother workers from other lands were not altogether useless to our own people. We think that, without ceasing to labour for the re-establishment of liberty in their own countries, it would neither be unwise nor unprofitable for them to lend us their aid in the truly holy work of regenerating the British people.[113]

[111] Love to Home Office, 19 October 1853: PRO HO 45/4816. Cf. Love to Jolliffe, 19 August and 4 November 1852: PRO HO 45/4547A; Love to Palmerston, 3 December 1853: PRO HO 45/4816; Love to Grey, 4 and 7 August 1855: PRO HO 45/6188; Love to Cowper, 12 August 1855: PRO HO 45/6188. For rumours of subversion on the mainland, *vide infra*, pp. 85–8, 130.
[112] Henry Weisser, *British Working-Class Movements and Europe 1815–48* (Manchester, 1975), pp. 101–3.   [113] *Star of Freedom*, 7 August 1852, p. 4.

More often, however, Chartists regarded their aloofness as politic: because it gave the government less excuse to act against them. 'We deem it a duty to state emphatically', said the *Red Republican* in 1850, when some politicians were claiming otherwise,

that between the British Democrats and the 'foreign'[114] refugees, there is not, nor has there ever been, any connexion. The sympathies of our friends are sufficiently indicated by their broadly-avowed principles, but as regard any intervention in our politics, or any association with our political parties, there is none whatever; and consequently no grounds for the application of the Alien Act to them[115]

– an assurance which Government ministers, from their own sources of information, could and did confirm.[116]

If the refugees took little active part in British domestic politics in the mid nineteenth century, however, still by their mere presence they may have had some impact. The Chartist and socialist leaders who met them will inevitably have been influenced in some way or other by them, as for example Harney and Ernest Jones were by Marx and Engels.[117] As a whole the Chartist body was made less parochial, more internationalist-minded by the refugees, chiefly through the agency of the 'Fraternal Democrats', a vigorous organisation founded in 1846 on the joint initiative of British Chartists and mainly German and Polish refugees to propagate the principle of the fraternity of all peoples.[118] The refugees made Chartists aware of the coincidence of their own interests and struggles with those of workers abroad, and the identity of their common capitalist enemy. Marx and Engels' *Communist Manifesto* was serialised in Harney's *Red Republican* in November 1850. As the century wore on the British working-class movements became increasingly permeated by continental developments in socialist thought, which may have been helped on by the physical presence of some of the leading continental socialist thinkers in England. As well as 'internationalising' the home-grown working-class movement, therefore, the refugees may have helped radicalise it. G. J. Holyoake was

[114] Harney, who edited the *Red Republican*, believed that the word 'foreigner' should be abolished, since the cause of workingmen everywhere in the world was identical. See Müller-Lehning, *art. cit.*, p. 196.

[115] *Red Republican*, 29 June 1850, p. 13. Cf. the *Star of Freedom*, 21 August 1852 p. 4, which on this occasion *commended* the exiles for 'wisely' keeping aloof from British politics.

[116] *Infra*, p. 130. See also the *Globe*, 10 February 1852, p. 2: 'No one who recollects the spring of 1849 can pretend that M. Louis Blanc and M. Mazzini have ever thrown themselves into English politics with half the zest that distinguished the Kings and Princes of the Bourbon family, and the Prime Ministers of France and Austria.'

[117] Weisser, *op. cit.*, p. 145.

[118] *Ibid.* pp. 134–50; Müller-Lehning, *art. cit.*, p. 196; Th. Rothstein, *From Chartism to Labourism* (1929), pp. 128–32 and Part III ch. 2; A. R. Schoyen, *op. cit.*, pp. 135–41. During the operation of the 1848 Alien Act its foreign members were shed, in order 'to avoid giving unprincipled enemies. . . any handle against our persecuted brethren' – *Democratic Review*, vol. I (1849), pp. 203–4.

sure they had some effect, claiming (rather imprecisely) that they 'extended freedom' by their teaching 'and exalted it by their example'.[119] W. J. Linton considered their value in spreading republican principles in England to be invaluable – 'were it only by example'.[120] The *People's Paper* was a little more specific:

Freedom is infectious. Example is catching. The Refugees are scattered all over our manufacturing towns – they have learned the English tongue – they work in our workshops, side by side with our workmen – they converse with their new comrades – unpretending preachers of Social Right and Political Justice – compulsory, but glorious apostles, who, like the scattered congregations of old, fled to the four winds, but each created a new colony of truth, more numerous than the parent commonwealth; these men are inoculating the British working world; and their presence is dangerous to the destroyers of its rights.[121]

It may have been so. But there was an element of wishful thinking in those who said it was so (or of alarmism in those who said it was so from the other side). The attitude of many of the refugees themselves towards the British working men they were supposed to be 'inoculating' was more often one of exasperation, that they remained so impervious to their 'example', and so loyal to their own home-grown varieties of radicalism.[122] If the presence of the refugees in Britain did have an effect on British radicalism it was chiefly to make it more internationalist, more aware of its place in a Europe-wide movement of progressivism; and also sometimes, as we shall see, to provide *foci* for demonstrations of discontent. It probably did not influence it much otherwise, ideologically or in any other way, and certainly the refugees themselves seemed very little concerned to try to influence it, beyond getting it to interest itself in *them*. It may be that the *People's Paper* spoke truer than it intended, and that the main propaganda effect of the refugees among the British was not to infect, but to inoculate against infection.

Neither did the refugees make any other kind of direct significant impact on British society. Just occasionally they might give rise to an identifiable and distinctive 'social problem' – when a shipload of them landed at a port and asked for relief, for example, and so became (as the Clerk of the Dover Petty Sessions complained to the Home Secretary in 1849) 'a great burthen on the rates of the town':[123] but generally that problem soon dissolved as the refugees moved on and dispersed and were looked after by their own communities. Then again, very occasionally

[119] Holyoake, *op. cit.*, vol. II p. 258.   [120] *Northern Star*, 5 April 1851, p. 1.
[121] *People's Paper*, 26 February 1853, p. 4.   [122] See Weisser, *op. cit.*, p. 145.
[123] Clerk of Dover Petty Sessions to Grey, 18 July 1849: PRO HO 45/2963. Cf. Mayor of Harwich to Home Office, 21 February 1834: PRO FO 64/198; letter from 'The Governors and Directors of the Poor' in the Parish of St James Westminster to Home Office, 27 May 1851: PRO HO 45/3518; Clerk of Justices at Dover to Granville, 16 May 1872: PRO HO 45/9303/11335.

there was trouble where the refugees lived, if they were concentrated and unruly enough to provoke resentment: as the Italians in Holborn did, for example, amongst their Irish neighbours, who tended not to appreciate the political reasons behind their hostility to the Pope, and were found engaged in little religious wars on the streets with them on more than one occasion.[124] This kind of communal tension too was rare. Nor do refugees seem to have been noticeably more criminal than others, although there were, as we have seen, some celebrated murders by one or two of them; and on a lower level of delinquency the 'fraudulent mendicant', who was usually a Pole making a living by pretending he was a captain or a count, was a common figure in the police courts.[125] Otherwise the refugees were just too few to give rise to any identifiable social problems among the British, or even to be much noticed; and judicious enough not to want to be. Most of them lay very low indeed.

[124] See police report of 12 July 1853: PRO HO 45/4816; *The Times*, 26 September 1853, p. 11; and Sheridan Gilley, 'The Garibaldi Riots of 1862', in *Historical Journal* vol. 16 (1973), p. 700. (The 'Garibaldi riots' themselves were between Irish and English supporters of Garibaldi, rather than Irish and Italians.)

[125] The refugees do not appear to have had any particular reputation for crime, nor to have deserved one. Nevertheless they contributed their share. Their most common offence was begging, although many mendicants who claimed to be refugees in fact were not. There was clearly a certain fund of sympathy for refugee causes in England, which could easily be exploited by impostors to their own advantage. At the trial of a German student for this offence in 1851 it was said that in his pockets were found letters 'in ridicule of the English people for the easiness with which they were duped by foreign adventurers passing themselves off as refugees and victims of despotic tyranny': *The Times*, 17 September 1851 p. 7. One of these 'adventurers', a man styling himself 'Colonel Count Sarcie Dumbicki', was reported to do very well for himself out of it, living 'in the best style' in between his frequent prison sentences: see *The Times*, 29 May 1849 p. 8; 2 June 1849 p. 7; 23 August 1850 p. 7; 8 January 1851 p. 7. The most outrageous was an 'Alexander Borromeo', who when he was charged with fraud in 1858 gave a brilliant speech in his own defence on the sufferings of his native Italy, but later turned out to be an Irishman (and a bigamist): *The Times*, 21 May 1858, p. 11. Most of these imposters obtained money under the guise of subscriptions for foreign liberal causes; some used subtler ploys, like one 28-year-old 'Count Waszkowski' who married a 42-year-old English heiress and then swindled her, which prompted *The Times* in a leading article on 3 December 1857 (p. 8) to issue a general warning to 'our fair countrywomen' to resist if they could the charms of these plausible rogues. There were therefore almost as many false refugees in the police courts at this time as real ones: but there were some of the latter, charged usually with begging, or petty larceny, and not in general treated any the more leniently for their special circumstances (one Sussex magistrate on the contrary regarded a refugee's offence as 'aggravated by the circumstance that the prisoner was a foreigner receiving hospitality and protection from this country, and who therefore ought to have been the last person to break its laws': *The Times*, 17 March 1853, p. 7). No refugees were charged with any more serious types of crime, except for the murderers Barthélemy (*supra*, p. 30), and Luigi Baranelli, who was hanged in April 1855: *The Times*, 1 May 1855, p. 9.
　　Although refugees in particular were not notorious for crime, foreigners in general may have been. In 1858 the Lord Mayor of London regarded 'the vast influx of foreigners of bad character into London' as 'so alarming a nuisance' as to require a change in the Alien laws: *The Times*, 23 April 1858, p. 11.

If this were a book about refugees *per se*, much more could be written about the life they lived in England in the nineteenth century, their activities and attitudes, and about the material and psychological impact their exile had on them. As minority groups go they made up a special and in many ways peculiar one, whose modes of adaptation to its surroundings would be well worth exploring, and to some extent have been explored, by others.[126] Our purpose, however, is limited to discovering how they appeared to and affected the society they found themselves amongst; and enough has been said to show that, from their side, the refugees did virtually nothing directly to disturb the stability and the tranquillity of the country they lived in. They had little impact on its society, and interfered overtly in its politics hardly at all. This was because their particular function gave them no need or wish to interfere, and because they were unreasonably afraid of being expelled if they did. This of course did not ensure that they would not be *suspected* of interfering, or of endangering the stability of the realm in some other way. The refugees did not do much, but they did do enough, to give rise to apprehension if the British were inclined to be apprehensive. They consorted in Britain with subversives; they published in Britain subversive propaganda, most of which had continental targets but some of which – like *The Communist Manifesto* – could be seen to have implications for Britain too. Even if they had done nothing at all they might still not have been tolerated. Tolerability by itself does not guarantee toleration. Sometimes certain activities and doctrines can be regarded as so intrinsically obnoxious as to be proscribed whatever the effects of them might be. And opinions as to the effectiveness of activities and doctrines anyway may depend less upon observed fact, than on the preconceptions of those doing the observing. Consequently more is needed than this, to show how the refugees were regarded in England, and why. Nevertheless this much can be said about them, from our knowledge of how they lived and what they did in England: that their activities in themselves were unlikely to *force* upon the British the idea that they were dangerous to them. That inference was by no means ruled out of court, but it was a less natural one than it would have been if, for example, Kossuth had been a Chartist, or Marx had stumped the country preaching socialism to audiences of English workers. The natural apathy of most of them towards British society, and the studied avoidance by the rest of them of British politics, distanced them from their hosts, and helped them be tolerated.

What did not help them be tolerated were their activities directed against *other* countries, which some of them tried to play down for the same reason that they played down their involvement in British politics, but less

[126] Especially by E. H. Carr, *op. cit.*

convincingly. The real effect of these activities on those other countries is difficult to measure. Even where it could be determined for certain what those activities were, their effect was not always straightforward. Orsini's plot, for example, failed in its main aim, which was to kill Napoleon III: yet it was bloodily effective in that it did kill other people, and it may possibly have been effective on another level, by helping to persuade Napoleon of the justice of Orsini's cause.[127] Of other kinds of refugee activity the effects are more difficult to establish. The effect especially of their didactic activities was controversial at the time, and conclusions about it depended (and depend) less on empirical facts than on opinions about the power of propaganda and of conspiracies in general to subvert. What is not in doubt, however, is that by continental governments, which did tend to believe in the power of conspiracies to subvert, these activities were thought to be effective: which led them to resent strongly the fact that Britain allowed them. This resentment they made felt in Britain: with the result that the refugee community, though it meant and did little harm directly to its hosts, was an embarrassment to them during much of the nineteenth century, and particularly in the 1850s.

[127] Louis Napoleon is said to have been moved by Orsini's letters to him before his execution to achieve for Italy her independence and unification a dozen years later.

3

The View from Abroad

If the refugees made any showing in British public affairs in the mid nineteenth century, as we shall see they did, it was not because of what they did directly to the British. Rather it was the indirect effect of things they did – or intended to do, or were thought to intend to do – to people outside. They were a diplomatic problem rather than a domestic political one. If they had no interest in subverting the British government they had a very strong interest in subverting continental governments, which, because their subversion was carried on from Britain, might threaten relations between her and her neighbours. This could be serious, or not, depending upon whether Britain required her relations with those neighbours to be friendly, or not.

The reasons why continental governments might resent Britain's harbouring of fugitives are not difficult to guess. Those fugitives in general intended them harm, and the forces of legitimacy in Europe were fearful of the harm they might do them. By and large they were right to fear them. Most continental régimes between the defeat of the first Napoleon and the fall of the third were basically insecure polities, never free from the threat of internal revolution, and consequently never able to relax their vigilance against revolutionaries. Britain was the European power least affected by the succession of revolutionary attempts which broke out all over the continent after 1820, but even in Britain the possibility of revolution was not ruled out, until perhaps the most serious and dramatic revolutionary outbreak in 1848 had passed, and left her unscathed. For other European countries it was always a very proximate danger, even during the periods of most apparent stability, like the 1850s, when no repeat of 1848 happened, but when nevertheless it was constantly predicted that it might. Many of the revolutions were successful: a few permanently (like Belgium's in 1830), most of them for just a few brief intoxicating months until they were finally crushed by superior force. Sometimes they could only be crushed with help from outside, and all in all they were only contained with difficulty. As well as revolutions these years were filled also with sporadic risings and assassination attempts, some of the latter successful; and by rumours and reports of others which were plotted but never carried out. All of these events justified and gave credence to a feeling among continental rulers, though they might not admit to it, of vulnerability in the face of subversion.

There were two explanations for this vulnerability current at the time. The liberal explanation, which we shall see was widely held in Britain and has generally been preferred by historians since, was that continental régimes were vulnerable because they were felt to be oppressive. The forms of authority which pertained on the continent were somehow out of phase with the natural and just order of things; were *imposed* on that order, so that the dominant and growing aspirations of the time, be they nationalism or liberalism or capitalism or whatever, were allowed insufficient expression under them, and felt restricted and repressed by them. Consequently protest was natural, and if it was not to be appeased could only be contained by means of more repression. This conclusion, though it may have been consistent with the evidence, was not derived from an empirical study of the evidence but from an essentially deductive theory or model of revolutions in general, which held that they, and all kinds of political 'extremism' (like democracy or socialism) were provoked by, and could only hope to flourish in, situations in which more moderate demands were unreasonably withheld. It followed that if any particular régime was vulnerable to revolutionary subversion it was because it was in some way defective. The explanation for revolutions and revolutionary feeling lay in popular grievances, indigenous causes, grass roots. The best prevention was the concession of moderate liberal institutions, which would then act as a kind of safety-valve, preventing dissatisfaction from overflowing into socialism and violence. That was one view.

It was not the view, however, of those who spoke for most continental régimes in Europe in the 1840s and 1850s. In their opinion the government they provided was good and just, and acceptable to their peoples. It was only threatened by minorities of evil men, whose power derived, not from the justice or popularity of their causes, nor (as the liberals would say) from the depth of real discontent they could exploit, but from their organisational strength and the unscrupulousness of the methods they were prepared to use. This conservative view of revolution was no more empirically-derived than was the liberal one. It too was based on a theoretical 'model'. That model saw political extremism, not as an unnatural excrescence which could be eliminated by kindness and moderation, but as an ever-present threat, which concessions would only encourage to press harder and further: like floodgates being opened. Where liberals looked to popular grievances to explain revolutions this conservative theory looked to external agencies, subversives, professional revolutionaries, conspirators. To the conservatives, revolutions were the work of clever and plausible agitators, working on the minds of the impressionable but otherwise contented masses, in close secret, and with their clandestine activities ultimately organised and concerted by the Secret Societies: those sinister and even possibly diabolical revolutionary agencies which had been at the root of all the trouble of the past, and, organised now on a trans-European scale, were seeking to plunge the continent into ruin again.[1] The fundamental conflict in Europe was between established, legitimate government on the one hand, and on the other a secret and insidious conspiracy of darkness working to subvert it.

What the liberals, therefore, saw as the expression of a natural develop-ment which should be allowed freedom to grow, continental conserva-tives regarded as a disease, which had to be cut out of the body politic before it spread and killed it. Hence the repression, which was a kind of surgery. Hence also the conservatives' fear of those microbes which escaped beyond the scope of their surgeons' knives, but which might still infect the body from without. It followed in fact from this conspiracy theory of revolution that exiles were as much to be feared as anyone. Exile might successfully separate them from the scenes of their revolutionary ambitions: but it did not separate them from the European conspiracy which had its cells in, for example, Berne and Brussels as well as in Milan and Madrid, and which in the 1850s was widely thought to have its central ganglion, its chief directorate, in London, where it could exist 'au grand jour' with less fear of being smoked out.'Sur le continent,' wrote the French propagandist Charles de Bussy in 1858, 'elle rampe et se cache comme un serpent; en Angleterre, elle se montre, et chacal affamé, rugit . . . c'est de Londres qu'elle envoie ses émissaires sur le monde . . . Hyènes cherchant des proies.'[2] Believing as they did both in the intrinsic potency of 'conspiracy', and also in the ultimate direction of all revolutionary and even liberal conspiracies from a central source, continental conservatives tended both to fear and to suspect the refugees in England more than they otherwise would have done, and more (as we shall see) than English liberals did. Whenever in the 1850s an *émeute* or *attentat* was discovered on the continent it was immediately laid at the door of this 'conspiracy': not necessarily because there was evidence pointing this way, but because it was assumed that this was where all such outbreaks had their origins. And because the 'conspiracy' was directed from London, by the refugee 'chiefs' there, that was where the main blame had to lie. 'England', wrote the British ambassador from Vienna in 1853, 'is looked upon as the focus, from which, not only every revolutionary movement in other countries is propagated but murder & mutiny fomented & encouraged. This feeling is

[1] See J. M. Roberts, *The Mythology of the Secret Societies* (1972).
[2] Charles de Bussy, *Les Conspirateurs en Angleterre, 1848–1858: Etude Historique* (Paris, 1858), pp. 2, 35.

intense & generally spread through the population.'[3] The same feeling was reported from Paris – 'Tout cela vient de Londres'; and from St Petersburg and Berlin.[4] It was regarded as a natural deduction to make: 'Is it necessary,' asked rhetorically a French pamphlet inspired by the Emperor himself in 1858, '. . . to prove evidence?'[5] To disbelieve it without direct proof of the connexion was as perverse (or as naïve) as to disbelieve the connexion between a tree and a shoot until the ground between were dug up. On the continent revolutionary deeds were being done; in London revolutionary deeds were being devised: the relationship was transparent. In London itself, and also in Jersey and the other substantial centres of refugee activity in Britain, continental police spies imbued with the same assumptions wrote and sent back to the continent reports confirming the connexion; assuming, because it was natural, always the worst: that if two refugees met and talked secretly together they were plotting; that if they plotted and then something happened on the continent what happened was a result of that plot . . . and so on. The picture was complete, and consistent. Peace and order and legitimacy in Europe would be assured, were it not for the sanguinary conspiracies of a few political madmen. Those conspiracies did not originate on the continent.

They are all born in the bosom of those revolutionary associations . . . which raise murder to a doctrine and a duty – which fanaticise the minds that they have corrupted – which arm the insensate whom they have fanaticised – which send forth assassins with their way-bill, and which thence wait, under the tolerance of English hospitality, for the result of those nefarious machinations.[6]

For this reason the activities of the refugees in England, and the policy of the British government in granting asylum to them, came to take on in the 1850s an immense importance. Count Buol told Prince Leiningen in 1853 that for the whole of the continent it was '*a question of life and death – to be or not to be*' – no less.[7] Hence the strength of their feeling.

By some continentals, unable to understand otherwise how Britain could allow such monstrous harm to be done under her aegis, it was suspected that she did it purposely, *in order* to subvert or ruin them. 'On more than one occasion', reported the British ambassador to Russia in 1851, 'it has been intimated or insinuated in my hearing, that England, secure in her own position, is probably not sorry to hold in her hands an

---

[3] Westmorland to Russell (private), 21 February 1853: Clar. P., c. 1, ff. 4–6.
[4] Cowley to Malmesbury (private), 27 September 1852: Malmesbury Papers, Hampshire Record Office (Malm. P.), 9M73/1852/2; Seymour to Clarendon no. 161, 5 April 1853: PRO FO 65/426; Bloomfield to Clarendon (private), 8 April 1853: Clar. P. c. 1, ff. 494–5.
[5] [L.E.A. de la Gueronnière], *The Emperor Napoleon III and England* (1858), p. 18. On the imperial inspiration of this pamphlet, see Natalie Isser, *The Second Empire and the Press* (The Hague, 1974), p. 42.   [6] [Gueronnière], *op. cit.*, p. 10.
[7] Prince Leiningen to Queen Victoria, 1 March 1853: Royal Archives (RA) I29/14. Translation in Aberdeen Papers, BL. Add. Ms. 43047, ff. 7–9.

engine which might readily be directed against the tranquillity of neighbouring states.'[8] Ambassadors elsewhere echoed this intelligence.[9] King
Leopold of the Belgians wrote to his niece Queen Victoria in 1858 that
'The notion exists that England keeps as it were on purpose, the worst
subjects of all countries to let them loose over Europe, whenever it
becomes more quiet.'[10] In the same year a French pamphleteer expressed it
as the common opinion in France, that the refugees 'ne sont que des
instruments dans leurs mains pour les lancer à défaut de soldats dont ils
manquent, sur les gouvernements du continent'.[11] This suspicion, though
it was unfounded, was not unnatural. Britain's gradual but resolute ex-
periments with political and economic liberalism from the 1830s onwards
were not altogether understood on the continent. British liberals saw
themselves as something less than revolutionaries, and indeed often
regarded their liberalism as a bulwark against violent revolution. By some
continentals, however, from whose political vantage-point it was sometimes difficult to distinguish between the different kinds of radicalism they
could descry on the very distant horizon, it was presumed that they had
gone over to the devil. To dislike of Britain's political institutions, and also
perhaps of her state religion, was wedded the impression that she was
endeavouring to foist them on other powers, to revolutionise the continent by stealth. In a way she was, though not in the way the continentals
suspected. Although British authorities would have liked to see the continent liberalised, did what they could to encourage the process, and
believed in their more optimistic moments that liberalism would come to
the continent regardless, they did not wish to see her ruined by democrats
and socialists. This was a distinction, however, which many continentals
failed to see or to credit. From their ideological point of view it was natural
to distrust Britain's intentions and motives. The image grew up in the
1850s of a new *Albion perfide*: an England which, for nefarious purposes of
her own, was giving succour and encouragement to the continent's tormentors, not out of impartiality, but because she favoured or wished to use
them.

This by and large was the reaction of those on the continent who
understood Britain least. By those who knew her better she was given
more credit. To Louis Napoleon, for example, who was a refugee himself
in Britain on more than one occasion, and was never as Anglophobe as the

[8] Seymour to Palmerston no. 35, 14 October 1851: PRO FO 65/395.
[9] E.g. Forbes (Dresden) to Palmerston, 23 April 1851: copy in PRO HO 45/3518; Howard
(Berlin) to Palmerston, 19 December 1851: RA I 27/18; Westmorland (Vienna) to Russell
(private), 21 February 1853: Clar. P. c. 1 ff. 4–6.
[10] King Leopold to Queen Victoria, 12 February 1858: RA Y81/39.
[11] Albert Savignac, *Attitude et Conduite de l'Angleterre envers la France et les autres nations* (Paris,
1858), p. 17, quoted in A. R. Calman, *Ledru-Rollin après 1848 et les proscrits français en
Angleterre* (Paris, 1921), p. 187.

majority of his own ministers, Britain's unfortunate policy was more a matter of ignorance than of malevolence. The English failed, as he told his old friend Lord Malmesbury in 1853, to 'make sufficient allowance for the Revolution of 1848, which prostrated the country and was felt by all Frenchmen to be only the forerunner of the Reign of Terror prepared for 1852 by Mazzini, Louis Blanc, &c.' For Englishmen, 'who had never seen a drop of blood shed, and read of 1688 as a romance', it was difficult to understand the peril to which the continent was put by the activities of the refugees; and this accounted for their tolerance of them.[12]

Even if it were accepted, however, that Britain's policy was not meant maliciously, still it was universally taken to be wrong: because it was unneighbourly, inconsistent with friendly diplomatic relations, and contrary to what was called 'the law of nations'. The 'law of nations' at this time was a vague and speculative concept, comprising little more than a body of principles and procedures agreed amongst some nations on a few matters, and the mere opinions of some more or less ancient authorities (Vattel, Pufendorf, Grotius) on most others. Consequently it was frequently controversial and easily ignored. Nevertheless it was cited by continental powers to give their charges against Britain, or any other harbourer of revolutionaries, the appearance of legal weight. It was supposed to give sanction to the idea of asylum, but also to require, as the Russian Foreign Minister Brunnow told the British ambassador in 1852, 'that people in amity should not conspire against each other' in such a way as to 'prejudice their tranquillity, their dignity, their honour'.[13] That the 'conspiracies' complained of did not directly implicate the British authorities, or (usually) British nationals, was irrelevant. The British government was responsible to other nations for everything done within its sway which might affect them, including things done by aliens (who while they lived in Britain might be regarded technically as British 'subjects' anyway). This latter point was never in dispute. It, and also the substance of this whole question, were tacitly conceded by Britain's own Foreign Enlistment Acts of 1819 and 1870,[14] which forbade 'any person whatever' equipping ships or recruiting soldiers in Britain for use against friendly foreign states. This admitted the principle. For those who regarded conspiracies to subvert and assassinate as every bit as dangerous as the fitting out of frigates – possibly more so because less easily spotted – it was no step at all to outlawing this kind of activity too. If Britain did not have the means to, then she should arm herself with them. This was her plain duty, on simple grounds of international morality.

[12] Lord Malmesbury, *Memoirs of an Ex-Minister* (1885 edn.), p. 299 (Diary for 20 March 1853).
[13] Memorandum by Brunnow, enclosed in Seymour to Granville no. 47, 4 February 1852: PRO FO 65/407 and PP (1852) liv pp. 85–9.
[14] 59 Geo. III c. 69; 33 & 34 Vict. c. 90.

So the case for the continentals rested. As long as England was used as a refuge by foreign revolutionaries who still harboured hostile designs against the governments which had been the cause of their exile, there was material there for continental resentment against her. But by itself this was not sufficient. During most of the nineteenth century England was the home of significant numbers of political refugees. Not all of that time, however, was she castigated for being so. In the 1830s and 1840s, for example, though the protection she afforded to fugitive Italians and Poles and Germans may have been widely resented in Europe, that resentment was never intense enough to cause serious trouble between them, or to provoke more than two or three official complaints from foreign governments, and those of the politest kind. There were very mild representations, for example, from France and Russia in 1836 and from Austria in 1844, but nothing to cause even the smallest of diplomatic ripples.[15] Much more often at this time the complaints went the other way: from the British government to France in particular, for foisting her destitute refugees on English coastal towns which had the means neither to support them nor to 'keep them in order'.[16] France was made to feel the guilty party for sending them, not Britain for receiving them: 'A nation in friendly relations with another', wrote the Chancellor of the Exchequer to Palmerston in 1838, 'would never constitute the dominions of its ally a kind of penal settlement to which the criminal or the ill constituted are to

[15] Lord Durham (St Petersburg) communicated to Palmerston on 21 May 1836 a request from Count Nesselrode that Britain prevent Polish refugees forming 'confederations' hostile to Russia (PRO FO 65/224); on 18 November the same year Lord Granville (Paris) transmitted an injunction from Count Molé that the British government 'watch and endeavour to counteract' refugee schemes directed against 'social order' in Europe (PRO FO 27/526); early in January 1844 the Austrian ambassador in London requested from Lord Aberdeen information concerning the whereabouts and activities of Mazzini (PRO FO 7/319); and in March 1848 Nesselrode through his ambassador Brunnow expressed the hope that Britain 'surveillera de prés' the Polish refugees' 'machinations et leurs intrigues' in London, in the common interest of both powers (PRO FO 65/357). No other formal protestations were made to Britain before 1850, although the comment which the British ambassador in Paris confided to his diary in April 1845, that he was 'tormented with demands for information respecting the guilt of Mazzini' (F. A. Wellesley, ed., *The Diary and Correspondence of. . .First Lord Cowley 1790–1846* [n.d.], p. 302), suggests that there may have been informal pressures.

[16] Phillips (Home Office) to Backhouse (Foreign Office), 21 February 1834, transmitting a petition from the Mayor of Harwich (PRO FO 64/198), which in the event was never passed on to the continent because Palmerston could see no real ground for complaint (see Backhouse to Phillips, 24 February 1834, in *ibid.*, *loc. cit.*, and also Foreign Office to Treasury, 17 August 1835: PRO FO 27/514). In 1835, however, representations were made to France protesting against this practice (see Palmerston to Granville no. 60, 19 September 1835: PRO FO 27/498); and thereafter: see Aston to Palmerston no. 70, 12 September 1836: PRO FO 27/524; Palmerston to Granville no. 17, 20 January 1837: PRO FO 146/180; Palmerston to Granville no. 55, 2 February 1838: PRO FO 27/555; and Palmerston to Granville no. 37, 22 January 1839: PRO FO 27/573. In the end the French government promised to discontinue the practice: see Molé to Granville, 20 February 1839: PRO FO 27/580.

be transported. England has not acted on any principle so objectionable & unsocial.'[17] And the harm that the refugees might do from their 'penal settlement' to the continent, far from being an embarrassment to Britain was used in the 1830s as an argument against the continent: to prove, as Palmerston wrote to Granville in 1836, 'how unwise it was for Foreign Governments to send such persons here'.[18] Throughout the 1830s and 1840s the refugees were hardly an issue in British diplomacy; and on the very few occasions when they became so, it was generally on Britain's initiative, and with Britain having the moral advantage.

There were a number of reasons for this. One may have been that Britain in the 1830s and forties was not the only haven for political refugees, and others which were closer to those powers which felt threatened by their activities tended consequently to draw the bulk of their fire. Throughout the 1840s, for example, there were far more Poles in Paris than in London, and assisted far more generously, and therefore provocatively to the Russians, by the French government than the English Poles were by the British. There were also probably more Italians in France than in England, and certainly more Germans and Spaniards. The really hot diplomatic rows which broke out during this period over refugees were all between countries with adjacent land frontiers on which refugees amassed more ominously than they could amass against anyone in Dover or Harwich: between France and Spain, for example, over the Carlists collected on the French slopes of the Pyrenees; between Switzerland and her neighbours, and between Belgium and hers. By comparison with these Britain was a very secondary threat. Another reason for the comparative lack of animus against her may have been that anyway Britain was not felt to be particularly obstructive on the question of the refugees. She could not (after 1826 and before 1848) prevent their coming, or expel them; nor was she particularly well-fitted even to watch them properly: but this was always made abundantly clear, and perfectly understood and accepted on the continent.[19] What she could do, however, she never refused to do: which was to pass on to the continent any information which might come to her hands about refugee activities and intrigues which seemed to pose a threat to her allies. In 1836 the British ambassador in Paris assured the French Foreign Minister of this: that His Majesty's Government 'would most readily communicate to the French Government any Information which it could obtain as to the Designs of this Directing Committee of Refugees [discovered by the Sardinian government to be based in London]

[17] Spring-Rice to Palmerston, 31 January 1838: PRO FO 27/570.
[18] Palmerston to Granville no. 211, 25 November 1836: PRO FO 27/518.
[19] E.g. Granville to Palmerston no. 27, 23 January 1837 (PRO FO 27/538): 'Count Molé replied that he was perfectly aware of the Position of Foreigners in England, and that the Govt. had not the Power of removing them from the Country, or controuling their proceedings within it.'

against the Peace and Tranquillity of neighbouring Governments'.[20] If little seems actually to have been communicated it is less likely to have been because of British government reluctance than because they had little to communicate. On the sole very famous occasion when they were directly asked to find out about refugee conspiracies they obliged by authorising Mazzini's private mail to be secretly opened and communicating its contents to the Italian authorities.[21] With such co-operation, though it caused a storm in England and had repercussions long afterwards, no continental government could possibly find fault. This was the position in the 1840s. During the following decade, however, things changed. The refugee question for the first time became a serious issue between Britain and her allies. The biggest and most celebrated row was in 1858, after the ex-refugee Orsini's attempt on the life of Napoleon III at the beginning of that year. But this was not an isolated event. It was foreshadowed by two only marginally less serious refugee crises earlier in the 1850s, which themselves, because they were never fully resolved, contributed cumulatively to the gravity of the 1858 one.

It was the aftermath of the 1848 revolutions which first pushed the refugee question to the front of Britain's diplomatic stage in the 1850s. When those revolutions were put down (or in the case of the French, metamorphosed into something else), thousands of defeated revolutionaries found themselves in England: a more numerous and also a *fresher* collection of refugees probably than England had had to accommodate for fifty years before. This was not all. As well as more of them, they were by and large more hopeful than refugees had been before; and the reactionary authorities they had fled from correspondingly more fearful. Although the revolutionary movement of 1848–9 was in the end comprehensively defeated, for a few years afterwards hardly anyone in Europe felt sure that the defeat was final, the game won (or lost) quite yet. Viewing the 'state of the continent' from England towards the end of 1851 Lord John Russell still felt that it was 'such as to cause much anxiety', and that during the following year things could go either way: it may, he advised the Queen, 'see the triumph of democracy; it may see the triumph of absolutism'.[22] In France, what was called 'le spectre rouge' haunted the official mind for a long time after 1848,[23] and was used to justify Louis

---

[20] Granville to Palmerston, after no. 363, 18 November 1836: PRO FO 27/526.
[21] F. B. Smith, 'British Post Office Espionage, 1844', in *Historical Studies* (Melbourne), vol. 14 no. 54 (1970).
[22] Russell to Queen Victoria, 3 November 1851: RA A79/95.
[23] See Howard C. Payne and H. Grosshans, 'The Exiled Revolutionaries and the French Political Police in the 1850s', in *American Historical Review*, vol. 68 (1963); Howard C. Payne, *The Police State of Louis Napoleon Bonaparte 1851–1860* (Seattle, Wash. 1966); and Normanby to Palmerston no. 79, 31 March 1851 (PRO FO 27/899), reporting the French government's daily expectation of 'the meditated general rising.'

Napoleon's *coup d'état* of December 1851, which was supposed to be a pre-emptive counter-revolution. 'They are, one and all, trembling on their thrones', said the *Morning Advertiser* in 1853; '. . . That an explosion is at hand, much more fearful than any which has been witnessed since the outbreak of the French Revolution, no one can doubt.'[24] Revolutionaries in London and in exile elsewhere probably indeed were more optimistically active at this time than at others. It was about then that many of their clubs and societies were founded, including the *Comité Démocratique Européen Central*, which, however significant or effective it might really have been as a revolutionary agency, assumed frightening proportions in the eyes of the continental autocrats.[25] After the early 1850s the revolutionaries appear to have become a little less hopeful: after the reaction in France, for example, was overwhelmingly confirmed by plebiscite, which lessened for a while the likelihood of new broadly-based (or broadly-supported) revolutions breaking out. We shall see that this, and other distractions (like the Holy Places), took the spotlight a little away from the 'refugee question' for a time. But the fact that the prospect of *revolution* had receded did not guarantee security for the continental rulers, against more narrowly-based attempts, by a dozen or just three or four men in secret, to *assassinate* in order to create anarchy from which the revolutionary cause might benefit; indeed, as other ways of rebellion were frustrated these became more likely: so that the pressure was never relaxed more than a little. The 1850s were a particularly nervous time for legitimists, with the traumatic memory of 1848 still fresh in their minds, and the instigators of 1848 still staring evilly at them from out of their lairs in England.

There was something else, too: another legacy from 1848 which affected very materially the way the continentals felt about the refugees and Britain's policy towards them. For a few years before 1848 Britain's fundamental attitude on questions of law and order and subversion and revolution had been suspect to some continental conservatives, in view especially of the aid – open and clandestine – which British Liberal governments in the 1840s had afforded to movements for political change in Greece and Portugal and elsewhere. For these conservatives 1848 served to confirm their suspicions. Britain's diplomatic stance during the year of revolutions, which was certainly not one of full-hearted support for the forces of reaction, was widely interpreted on the continent as being on the revolutionaries' side: or at the very least, 'not opposed to them to the extent we were entitled to expect'.[26] Charles de Bussy charged ten years

---

[24] *Morning Advertiser*, 23 February 1853, p. 4.

[25] Walewski insisted on translating this 'the Central Society of Demagogues' (Walewski to Palmerston, 29 October 1851: FO 27/917 and PP (1852) liv, pp. 49–50).

[26] Westmorland to Clarendon (private), 13 March 1853: Clar. P., c. 1 ff. 54–7.

later that during 1848 'Pas un révolte n'éclata en Europe, pas une conspira-
tion ne s'ourdit, sans la complicité audacieuse et criminelle des agents
anglais.'[27] To this was added evidence of sympathy in high places in
England for continental revolutionaries, some of which was false – British
ministers often had to issue denials of press reports of interviews they were
supposed to have had with prominent exiles[28] – but much of which, as we
shall see, was true, and damaging to the continentals' trust in Britain's
impartiality. The worst offender, though he was in fact a good deal less
sympathetic to foreign revolutionaries than many of his contemporaries,
was Lord Palmerston, whom Princess Lieven described once as 'l'homme
le plus universellement et le plus cordialement haï en Europe'.[29] Palmerston did a great deal to irritate continental rulers, particularly during his last
two years as foreign secretary; not least by his constant lecturing to them
on the virtue and expediency of liberal concessions.[30] To those who
suspected Britain's liberal designs anyway this bolstered up their suspicions; as did Palmerston's provocatively impenitent apology to Austria
after one of her generals had been set on by a mob in London in 1850,[31] and
his services to the Hungarian leader Kossuth: first securing his release from
Turkey, against the wishes of Austria and Russia who wanted him surrendered to them; and then doing all he could to identify himself with the
popular welcome Kossuth got when he arrived in England in September
1851.[32] The tone of what we shall see was at this time a particularly
xenophobic press, and xenophobic largely on political grounds, completed the picture. From the continentals' vantage point in the early 1850s
the fact of Britain's positive antagonism towards them appeared crystal-
clear. Soon after Palmerston's temporary fall from power in December
1851, her ambassador in Vienna reported to a new Tory Foreign Secretary
how for his part Prince Schwarzenberg, the Austrian Prime Minister,
wished more than anything to be friends with Britain:

but he is always recurring to the many acts of hostility & injuries which his
Country has recd., & he fancies is still receiving from England & Englishmen. He
recurs[?] to the case of Genl. Haynau, to the Piedmontese War, to the release of

---

[27] C. de Bussy, *op. cit.*, p. 178.
[28] E.g. Palmerston to Normanby, after no. 121, 23 February 1850: PRO FO 27/862.
[29] Princess Lieven to Aberdeen, 26 July 1852, in E. Jones Parry (ed.), *The Correspondence of Lord Aberdeen and Princess Lieven 1832–1854*, vol. II (1939), p. 632.
[30] *Infra*, p. 131.
[31] PRO HO 45/3340 contains police reports and copies of correspondence with the Austrian government on this affair. There is also much about it in Palmerston's correspondence with the Queen: see Palmerston Papers (Palm. P.), RC/F/466–8 and RC/FF/17; Brian Connell, *Regina v. Palmerston* (1962), pp. 126–8; and *The Letters of Queen Victoria* (*QVL*), *1837–1861* (1907), vol. II, pp. 319–22.
[32] See Dénes A. Jánossy, *Great Britain and Kossuth* (Budapest, 1937), chs. 14–15; *QVL 1837–1861*, vol. II, pp. 392–400; Charles C. F. Greville, *A Journal of the Reigns of King George IV, King William IV and Queen Victoria* (1896–8 edn.), vol. VI, pp. 420–5.

Kossuth & all its consequences, to the language of Mazzini, & to the excitement constantly kept up by the public press.[33]

All this was supposed to reveal a deliberate campaign of hostility towards the continent, of which Britain's refugee policy was a part. Britain was widely seen, in a way she never had been seen before, as in league with the refugees she harboured and in sympathy with their deeds: fair quarry therefore for the resentment of those who stood for peace and legitimacy against the death and disorder the revolutionaries wished upon them.

Nevertheless, it took a little time initially for the dispute between Britain and the continent over the refugee question to get under way. Until about the end of 1850 the brunt of the pressure over refugees was born by Switzerland and Belgium still, with Britain, ironically, using her diplomatic offices mainly to persuade them to give in to it.[34] When they did give in many of the refugees they expelled concentrated in England, which consequently thereafter became the continental powers' chief target. It was in 1850 – which also saw the lapse of the 1848 Alien Act, which might have been a deterrent before – that the refugees in London regrouped, formed their different national associations and their *Comité Central*, and began to take initiatives again: most notoriously the 'Loan' floated by Mazzini in the summer to finance his new revolution in Italy. During the course of 1850 the British Foreign Office received a few routine notifications from foreign governments of suspicious gatherings revealed by their police spies among the refugees in London, but nothing which seemed to require any action or even reply.[35] Then at the very end of the year came a representation from France which voiced a more general unease, and a definite request, though politely put, that in view of the 'progress of the Mazzini Loan' and the 'excitement kept up by the organisation of Revolutionary Committees' in London, the British Government'

should take means of shewing they discouraged that which was exciting such unpleasant feelings in all who are anxious that Europe should not again be exposed to the Miseries and confusion which had so generally & lamentably characterised the year 1848, from which many Countries were but just recovering.[36]

Continental unease at the activities of the refugees increased during the

[33] Westmorland to Malmesbury (private), 2 March 1852: Malm. P. 9M73/1852/1.
[34] See Ann G. Imlah, *Britain and Switzerland 1845–60* (1966), p. 70 *et passim*; and with regard to Belgium, see Clarendon to Cowley (private), 21 October 1853: Cowl. P., PRO FO 519/169 ff. 1012–4.
[35] E.g. Montherot to Palmerston, 30 January 1850: PRO FO 27/884; Westmorland to Palmerston no. 191, 24 May 1850: PRO FO 64/317 (this despatch covered a Memorandum from Manteuffel on republican clubs in England, based on a Prussian police report, which R. Payne, *Marx*, pp. 234–40, takes rather less critically than it deserves); Koller to Palmerston, 23 July and 7 November 1850: PRO FO 7/384.
[36] Normanby to Palmerston no. 430, 30 December 1850: PRO FO 27/876.

following year, especially as there approached the Great Industrial Exhibition planned to open on 1 May in Hyde Park: which the continental rulers, who could not have dared allow such a concourse of working people and foreigners in their own countries so soon after 1848, considered to be insanely foolhardy, and where it was widely rumoured that the expected European revolution was planned to be fired: 'there is an universal terror', reported the British minister in Dresden, 'respecting the Great Exhibition & the Plots probably concerting there':[37] which terror was reported to grip the Russian and Austrian authorities also.[38] That event in the outcome passed over peacefully, but for the continental governments it did not rule out the probability of some kind of serious revolutionary attempt soon.[39] Nor did it appease the irritation they were beginning to feel at Palmerston's repeated refusals to do anything to help them in this matter. By October 1851 they were expressing themselves more forcibly as to what Baroche, French Minister of the Interior, called 'the disastrous effects of the permissive encouragement which the state of the law in England gave to the worst designs of the Confederatic Revolutionists', which was aggravated, in Baroche's view, by Palmerston's conduct towards Kossuth when he landed in England that month.[40] It was shortly after this that the French Government presented to Britain (on 29 October) a long memorandum retailing the intelligence it had about the activities of the refugees, with a covering despatch which made it clear – politely still, but firmly – that France expected Britain to do something to stop them.[41]

By itself the French note was not too serious a matter. But it came to appear so when it was followed up six weeks later by remonstrances from all the other great military powers of Europe, and some lesser ones, couched in terms so similar as clearly to indicate collusion between them,[42] and perhaps with France as well: which was an ominous combination, threatening (as Hamilton Seymour, Britain's minister in St Petersburg, pointed out) 'very evil consequences'.[43] This latter batch of complaints too was less polite in tone than the French, and contained for the first time explicit demands, and implicit threats if those demands were not met of reprisals against, for example, British travellers on the continent.[44] This was the first of the major confrontations which took place between Britain

[37] Forbes (Dresden) to Palmerston no. 52, 23 April 1851: copy in PRO HO 45/3518.
[38] See Bloomfield to Palmerston no. 39, 19 February 1851: PRO FO 65/391; Magenis to Palmerston no. 65, 5 April 1851: PRO FO 7/389.
[39] This was apparently confirmed for the Prussian government by the inquiries of its police agents sent over to help the British police (*infra*, p. 152) during the course of the Exhibition: see Bloomfield to Palmerston no. 30, 14 August 1851: PRO FO 64/332.
[40] Normanby to Palmerston no. 279, 6 October 1851: PRO FO 27/903.
[41] Walewski to Palmerston, 29 October 1851: printed in PP (1852) liv, pp. 49–50.
[42] *Ibid.*, pp. 60–71.
[43] Seymour to Palmerston no. 143, 22 December 1851: PRO FO 65/396.
[44] Buol to Palmerston, 9 December 1851: PP (1852) liv, pp. 60–3.

and the continent over the refugee question in the 1850s. Its menace was defused a little when in January France denied that she was acting conjointly with the other powers,[45] and when Prussia withdrew from it,[46] leaving behind an altogether less menacing configuration. It was also eased by the dismissal from his post in December of the arch-irritant Palmerston: for other reasons, but continental rulers suspected, and were mollified by the suspicion, that his bad conduct over Kossuth had had something to do with it.[47] Now he had gone, said the *Morning Chronicle,* 'we shall, it is to be hoped, hear no more complaints of our harbouring refugees'.[48] Nevertheless the question for the complainants was by no means settled yet: certainly not by the official British reply given by Palmerston's successor Lord Granville on it,[49] whose vague assurances the continental powers wanted to see translated into action before they would credit them.[50] On the continent the sense of grievance still simmered, especially in Austria, which never allowed Britain to forget it;[51] and in France, whence the *proscription* which followed Louis Napoleon's *coup* of 2nd December 1851 added to the numbers of French malcontents in London and Jersey – and hence to the problem. Jersey in fact during 1852 started to become the particular object of the French authorities' fears, because of its proximity to France and the propagandist and conspiratorial activities there of Félix Pyat, Victor Hugo and a hundred or so more of the most lively *proscrits.*[52] It required only one new revolutionary *attentat* on the continent to set the whole refugee question blazing again; and in February 1853 there were two of them: an abortive rising in Milan on the 6th, which accomplished nothing beyond the stabbing to death of a few guards, and in which Mazzini, until recently living in London, was deeply implicated; and then on the 18th an attempt on the life of the Austrian emperor on the ramparts of Vienna by a Hungarian with a knife, which had no clear connexion with the London revolutionaries but which nearly every conti-

---

[45] See Granville to Jerringham no. 23, 20 January 1852: *ibid,* pp. 74–5.

[46] See Howard to Granville no. 2, 30 December 1851: *ibid.* pp. 71–2; and Bunsen to Russell, 30 December 1851: Russell Papers PRO 30/22/9Jii f. 186. Prussia however continued to complain about the activities of the Fraternal Democrats in London – e.g. Bunsen to Malmesbury 20 February and 5 May 1852: PRO FO 64/348; to the dismay of the British government – see Malmesbury to Bloomfield (private), 18 May 1852: Malm. P. 9M73/1/4; until the summer, when the Prussian authorities appeared satisfied by a reassuring report from the British police – Bloomfield to Malmesbury (private), 4 June 1852: Malm. P. 9M73/1852/1.

[47] Which was in fact so. See Greville, *op. cit.,* vol. VI, p. 435.

[48] *Morning Chronicle,* 5 February 1852, p. 4.   [49] *Infra,* p. 149.

[50] See Brunnow to Granville, 23 February 1852: printed in PP (1852) liv, p. 85.

[51] Austria never fully accepted Granville's circular despatch as an adequate reply to her complaints; on the other hand Malmesbury felt confident enough to write to Bloomfield on 18 March 1852 'that all our wrangles with Austria are terminated': Malmesbury, *op. cit.,* p. 252; and Bloomfield Papers, PRO FO 356/31.

[52] Léon Deries, 'Policiers et Douaniers contre Victor Hugo', in *Grande Revue,* vol. LXXXV (1914).

nental conservative – 'without investigation' – was prepared to believe did.[53] Immediately the diplomatic temperature rose.

The response of the continental powers to these events was even more violent than in December 1851, and the diplomatic crisis it provoked for Britain if anything more perilous. 'The general feeling which is raised agt. us, not only here but in the whole of Germany is stronger than you can have any idea of', reported the British ambassador in Vienna, Lord Westmorland, who had to be given a police guard to protect his house from the mob.[54] From Bavaria, where it was reported to be dangerous for Englishmen to be seen in the streets, the British minister was moved to ask his superiors for a 'conditional leave of absence' in case his residence there proved 'intolerable'.[55] From elsewhere in Europe the reaction was reported to be the same: abnormally violent and menacing.[56] More disturbing were rumours that these menaces might soon take a practical form: that Austria was 'knocking at every door in Europe in order to get up a League agst us',[57] which might lead to British visitors and imports being banned from the continent, or much worse: the Foreign Secretary Lord Clarendon at the beginning of March retailed to Lord Westmorland in Vienna a report 'that there is a project now under consideration for excluding us from the continent – moreover that we are known to be in a defenceless state and that the time is now come for putting us down as a nuisance'.[58] As in 1851–2 nothing came of it all. Europe did not ever combine offensively against Britain, chiefly because France and Prussia, again, though they made it clear informally that they were in agreement with Austria over the refugee question,[59] for extraneous reasons of their own refrained from formally siding with her;[60] and in April the fuss died down, with Austria again the last to tire of it. While it lasted, however, it gave many British statesmen and diplomats a whiff of a war they all dreaded. And although it soon blew over, it could not be said that the matter was ever in any way *resolved*: so that it remained in the background to poison relations between Britain and her neighbours, and

---

[53] Hodges to Clarendon no. 7, 4 March 1853: PRO FO 33/137; and cf. Westmorland to Aberdeen, 18 February 1853: Aberdeen Papers, BL. Add. Ms. 43429, f.98; Westmorland to Russell no. 66, 18 February 1853: PRO FO 7/416; Cowley to Clarendon no. 118, 4 March 1853: PRO FO 27/964.

[54] Westmorland to Clarendon (private), 27 February 1853: Clar. P. c. 1 ff. 9–10; and Malmesbury, *op. cit.*, p. 295 (Diary for February– March 1853).

[55] Milbanke to Clarendon (private), 3 March 1853: Clar. P. c. 2 ff. 295–6, and RA I29/15.

[56] E.g. Bloomfield to Clarendon no. 87, 25 February 1853: PRO FO 64/353.

[57] Clarendon to Westmorland (private), 23 March 1853: Clar. P. c. 125 pp. 144–9.

[58] Clarendon to Westmorland (private), 2 March 1853: Clar. P. c. 125 pp. 32–6.

[59] See Bloomfield to Russell no. 71, 19 February 1853: PRO FO 64/353; Bloomfield to Clarendon no. 109, 19 March 1853: PRO FO 64/354 and RA I29/24; and Cowley to Clarendon (private), 3 March 1853: Clar. P. c. 5 ff. 65–7.

[60] See Bloomfield to Clarendon no. 109, 19 March 1853: PRO FO 64/354; Cowley to Clarendon (private), 3 March 1853: Clar. P. c. 5 ff. 65–7.

always threatened to erupt again into the foreground, in a more dangerous guise than before: this time, perhaps, with France or Prussia less willing to restrain themselves. 'I am inclined to fear', wrote Seymour from St Petersburg to Lord Clarendon in April 1853, ' . . . that this actual cessation of demands may prove rather a lull than a settled calm, while the question . . . may become the more embarrassing as it affords a ground upon which, under altered circumstances, France may be found taking up a position alongside of the Northern Powers.'[61]

For a few years after 1853 those circumstances never arose, and the refugee question remained quiescent. It remained quiescent in the first place because other more urgent diplomatic priorities made it important on all sides that this problem should not be allowed to ruffle some very fragile diplomatic edifices, especially the active Crimean alliance between Britain and France and the more passive one between Britain and Austria; secondly because the British authorities, possibly with this in mind, were as we shall see rather more attentive and responsive to continental demands than before, though quietly and unobtrusively;[62] and also because the refugee community itself in London seemed to lose some of its edge,[63] and so had come to appear less of a problem to its continental enemies. This, however, was not to say that all refugee activity ceased, or that the lives of European rulers were at last safe from would-be assassins: if anything assassination became slightly more popular as a political method as other revolutionary hopes receded, and Napoleon III, for example, still feared it when he no longer felt he had anything to apprehend from other forms of resistance.[64] In March 1854 Duke Charles III of Parma was stabbed to death in the street by his groom with a file sharpened to a point; in 1855 there were two attempts on the life of Napoleon, one (on 28 April) by an Italian, Pianori, who had been a refugee in London; and in the summer of 1857 another plot against the emperor's life (the Tibaldi conspiracy) was discovered before it could come to anything, and by a French court of law attributed – though on tenuous evidence – to Mazzini and Ledru-Rollin in London.[65] This last *complot*, together with French police reports of a debate on the subject of 'regicide' which had taken place in a London public house in November 1857, and about which more was made than it merited,[66] revived for a short time all the old resentments against Britain on the continent; mainly in France, but also elsewhere, awakening old fears once more of a European combination

[61] Seymour to Clarendon no. 173, 9 April 1853: PRO FO 65/426.
[62] *Infra*, pp. 160–8.   [63] *Supra*, pp. 17–18.
[64] See G. Harris to Malmesbury, 2 September 1852, in Malmesbury, *op. cit.*, p. 263.
[65] For the Tibaldi plot, see *The Times* July 4 (p. 10), 13 (p. 9), 24 (p. 9) and 31 (p. 10).
[66] See Cowley to Clarendon (private), 15 November 1857: Clar. P. c. 75 ff. 532–3, communicating a French complaint about this; and Clarendon's reply, 17 November 1857: Clar. P. c. 140 pp. 238–9 – that the motion on regicide was a very abstract one, and defeated.

against Britain. Hamilton Seymour, who was Britain's ambassador in Vienna at this time, believed that this was a certainty. 'Sooner or later', he wrote privately to Clarendon in July 1857, 'the necessity of breaking up a Gang of Revolutionists who make England the Laboratory for their plans will make a bond of union among the Continental states against us which Russia – or France – our enemy . . . of the day – will turn to good account.'[67]

Seymour was the one among Britain's front-line ambassadors who was most obsessed by the refugee question, and he had been trumpeting such warnings for years, so that they might not have been taken as seriously as he would have liked by his superiors. But when on 14th January 1858 Orsini's bombs went off in the rue Lepelletier, fatally to many and so nearly fatally to the emperor himself, it looked as though the moment he had warned of might at last have come. Orsini's was the bloodiest and therefore the most shocking of all the *attentats* of the 1850s; and it took very little time to prove, what was of course assumed from the beginning,[68] that Orsini and his collaborators had lived in England recently, had in all probability plotted the thing there, and had had their bombs manufactured there: all of which was a damning indictment of Britain's policy, against which very few of the defences and excuses she might use, and had used in the past, could carry much conviction. The diplomatic onslaught on Britain which followed the Orsini plot was the strongest and bitterest of them all. From Paris Walewski, the French Foreign Minister, spearheaded the attack with a famous despatch bristling with righteous indignation: 'Ought . . . the right of asylum to protect such a state of things? Is hospitality due to assassins? Ought the English legislation to contribute to favour their designs and their plans, and can it continue to shelter persons who, by their flagrant acts, place themselves beyond the pale of common right and under the ban of humanity?'[69] The French press, Anglophobe politicians and, most ominously, the French military weighed in with less temperate articles, speeches and addresses.[70] Other powers looked set to join in: with Austria and Russia, who had been the most uncompromising complainants before but had never had France's support all the way, now no doubt happy to see her in the van.[71] Persigny, the French ambassador, believed it meant war;[72] and at that moment, as Lord Malmesbury wrote

[67] Seymour to Clarendon (private), 21 July 1857: Clar. P. c. 76 ff. 350–1.
[68] See Cowley to Clarendon (private), 15 January 1858: Cowl. P., PRO FO 519/223 ff. 37–8; Seymour to Clarendon no. 50, 18 January 1858: PRO FO 7/538.
[69] Walewski to Persigny, 20 January 1858: printed in PP (1857–8) lx, p. 116.
[70] See *Annual Register*, 1858, pp. 32, 221.
[71] See Seymour to Clarendon no. 50, 18 January 1858: PRO 7/538; Seymour to Clarendon (private), 20 January 1858: Clar. P. c. 85 ff. 368–9; Bloomfield to Clarendon no. 45, 20 January 1858: PRO FO 64/456; Wodehouse to Clarendon (private), 23 January 1858: Clar. P. c. 86 ff. 114–16.
[72] R. W. Seton-Watson, *Britain in Europe 1789–1914* (1937), p. 377.

in his diary, 'when our resources are taxed at the utmost to reconquer India, we are not in a position to have war with anyone'.[73] This was the most perilous refugee crisis of them all; to which, as we shall see, the British government had at last to make some effort to respond, openly, constructively and conciliatorily.

The seriousness of the refugee question for Britain arose out of the peculiar fact that it was an issue which had a direct bearing on, and was directly affected by, the internal political and social institutions of both sides: where those institutions touched and jarred. This was highly unusual. Relations between European states in the nineteenth century generally had very little to do with each other's domestic arrangements. That is not to say that foreign policies were not chiefly determined by national interests which might be very firmly rooted in those arrangements: only that in pursuit of those interests nations generally had regard only for the external attitudes of other states, and not for their internal constitutions. (This was often true in the twentieth century too, and could be illustrated for example by the Nazi–Soviet Pact and the Chinese–American rapprochement.) Sometimes alliances and alignments between European countries may have been related to similarities and sympathies between their respective internal policies, so that autocracies naturally inclined towards each other, and republics tended to take opposite sides to monarchies: but it did not need to be so. Nations generally took other nations as they found them, not allowing differences over their domestic arrangements to affect relations between them, so long as the internal interests of one did not conflict with the external policies of another. If a man wishes to buy bread from a baker it will not generally matter to him greatly, or affect his purchase, that the baker fiddles his tax returns or beats his wife. If he fiddles or beats his customers, of course, or if his financial activities lead to his bankruptcy, or his treatment of his wife leads her to lock him out of the bakery, or burn it down, then that is another matter. In those cases his domestic activities are spilling over into and affecting his external relations. Until they do, however, the two things can be kept separate. In nineteenth century diplomacy too, domestic and external policies were regarded separately, because the one did not generally affect the other: except at one or two points. The refugee question was one of those points.

Refugees were refugees because of the domestic policies of the states they had fled or escaped or been expelled from. Britain gave refuge to them because her domestic policy allowed her to, and because that policy differed from the continent's. Continental governments complained of this because of the harm they believed the refugees could do to them domestically. We shall see that Britain resented their complaints because

[73] Malmesbury, *op. cit.*, p. 415 (Diary for 1 February).

she saw them as assaults on her domestic institutions. The whole difference, therefore, arose out of the internal, constitutional differences between Britain and the continent. Those differences were probably greater
in the 1850s than at almost any other time in the century. Britain was
dynamic and liberal, the continent static and repressive; Britain in
Gladstone's words 'advancing' while on the continent there was 'a down-
ward and backward movement'.[74] On other occasions during the mid-
nineteenth century these differences produced misunderstandings, suspicion and disapproval between them, but usually no material conflict. Here,
however, they rubbed against each other abrasively. This fundamental
divergence was at the root of Britain's disagreements with the continent
over the refugee question, which meant that it governed, quite ineluctably,
the attitudes the two sides took up on it. For this reason too the refugee
question was almost the sole diplomatic issue of the time on which the
continental powers were bound to have an identity of interest together,
and on which Britain's interest was bound to be apart from them, against
them, and to all intents and purposes alone.

This was what lent the refugee issue its most menacing aspect. It was just
the kind of question which might provide the spark to what Clarendon
called 'a war of opinion in Europe':[75] a confrontation of ideologies, between
liberalism and reaction. The Austrian Foreign Minister Buol in 1853 saw
it as fundamental. Britain had to ask herself, he told Prince Leiningen,

> whether it is for the interest and is the intention of England for the future to take up
> a position wholly separate and isolated from the Continent and, so to speak, *apart
> from the European Community*. For, according to my firm conviction, nothing less
> than this is at issue. This state of things will in a short time be brought about by the
> force of circumstances . . . *A continental system will form itself.*[76]

If such a system did form, and a confrontation along these lines developed,
no power could choose its own side or its allies. These were predetermined
by the political situation of the continent. Ranged against her, in a new and
wider Holy Alliance, Britain would find all the great military powers of
Europe; and no one, save little Piedmont, perhaps, and Belgium if she
dared, and the hope of a few malcontent Hungarians and Poles, on her
side.[77] This was the eventuality the British Foreign Office dreaded most in
all the world.

Even if it did not come to that, however, the fact that the refugee
question set Britain so clearly apart from the rest of Europe could be

---

[74] 3PD 148 c. 1819 (19 February 1858).
[75] Clarendon to Westmorland (private), 2 March 1853: Clar. P. c. 125 pp. 32–6.
[76] Prince Leiningen to Queen Victoria, 1 March 1853: RA I29/14; translation in Aberdeen
Papers, BL. Add. Ms. 43047, ff. 7–9.
[77] 'America, Belgium, Piedmont, and the patriots and insurgents of every land are our only
real friends and cordial allies, in the present position of the courts of Europe' – W. R. Greg
in *North British Review*, vol. 18 (1853), p. 343.

damaging in lesser ways. It was a handicap her foreign ministers took with them everywhere; a deadweight issue which could not be shed, and which could only harm her foreign relations, for no tangible benefit in exchange. To Britain's foreign-policy makers, as we shall see, the refugees meant nothing; yet at any time, and outside anyone's control but their own, by a foolish or wicked action abroad or even by an outspoken speech in England one of them might endanger a critical and fragile alliance,[78] or provide a pretext which could be used by a malevolent enemy to seduce and detach her friends from her: as Russia was suspected of doing throughout the 1850s.[79] The refugees acted as a diplomatic repellant: always antagonising, never attracting any continental party worth attracting; an issue which worked naturally to draw the continent together against Britain. To Seymour it appeared 'monstrous' that the foreign relations of Britain should in this way be 'at the mercy of a band of foreigners':[80] but this was how it was.

For Britain therefore the refugee question could prove a particularly irritating diplomatic burden, likely at critical times to interfere with other priorities which to Britain were far more vital, and always to Britain's disadvantage. How significant it was in this rôle, however – how serious the damage done or likely to be done – must be a matter for doubt. On the refugee question the continental powers believed they had good reason to complain of Britain's conduct, and solid grounds for complaint too: a good case in 'international law'. Diplomatic attitudes and policies, however, are very rarely solely governed by the merits of cases, and were not in this instance. If they had been, then Prussia and France would have gone much further than they did with Austria and Russia, with whose viewpoint on the refugee question they agreed almost entirely. They did not do so because, just as for Britain the refugee question could interfere with others of her diplomatic priorities, so for continental governments other priorities could have a bearing on the stand they took over the refugee question. For if it was true that the great powers of the continent had a common interest together against Britain on the refugee question, so was it also the case that the continental powers had few *other* interests in common against Britain, and that during the nineteenth century, as at other times, ideological affinities and differences were very seldom allowed to become the final arbiters of alliances and alignments between nations, where other national interests obtruded. Just as Russia may have

[78] E.g. the concern felt by Clarendon in 1854 at the effect of Kossuth's speeches on relations with Austria – Clarendon to Westmorland (private), 7 June 1854: Clar. P. c. 129 p. 34; and Wodehouse's concern at the effect of the Orsini affair on the Anglo-French alliance – Wodehouse to Clarendon (private), 23 January 1858: Clar. P. c. 86 ff. 114–16.
[79] E.g. Cowley to Clarendon (private), 6 February 1858: Cowl. P., PRO FO 519/223 pp. 85–8: 'Russia is profiting by the Refugee question to play her games.'
[80] Seymour to Clarendon no. 85, 27 January 1858: PRO FO 7/539.

exploited the refugee question in the 1850s to try to open up rifts in the alliances forming against her then, so did Prussia exploit it in another way, and to the opposite effect: by ostentatiously abstaining from common continental anti-British fronts in order to ingratiate herself with Britain at the expense of France or Austria, and to detach herself from the other Northern Courts, all probably as part of her current challenge to Austria for dominance in Germany.[81] In January 1852 the Prussian King told Victoria that another motive for his country's conciliatory attitude over the refugee question was to prevent a French alliance with the Northern Courts which could only drive Britain into 'an alliance with North America and aggressive revolution',[82] which would be of no service at all to the cause of reaction. It may have weighed with other powers too that to force Britain into this rôle could only serve the revolutionaries' ends.[83] France also on more than one occasion forbore to press home an advantage over Britain on the refugee question in order to preserve an alliance between them which other diplomatic priorities made desirable, and out of recognition of the British government's (and especially Palmerston's) friendliness towards her parvenu régime.[84] That France's diplomatic attitudes on the refugee question were not solely related to the justice of her complaints is indicated by the fact that, whereas in April 1855, when she had good cause to berate Britain for Pianori's *attentat*, she did not, in August 1857 after the Tibaldi *complot*, when she had less cause for complaint, she did. It all depended on the general diplomatic context.

Consequently the seriousness for Britain of the attacks made on her by continental countries for harbouring refugees depended partly on the degree of activity among the refugees, and the degree to which those countries felt threatened by them; but also on extraneous factors, embracing the whole pattern of intra-European diplomatic relationships at any one time. For this reason the refugee question, serious though it sometimes appeared (particularly in the winter of 1851–2, the spring of 1853 and at the beginning of 1858), never did manage to overshadow all other European questions in the 1850s. It was never more than an assertive and sometimes discordant counterpoint to other melodies, other main issues of European diplomacy, on none of which was Britain so ineluctably isolated as on this refugee question. It was this fact which in the end prevented a war in Europe on this issue, between the massed forces of reaction on the one hand, and on the other the one powerful but lonely representative of liberal enlightenment.

---

[81] *Supra*, pp. 59, 60, and see Bloomfield to Clarendon no. 95, 7 March 1853: PRO FO 64/354.
[82] King of Prussia to Queen Victoria, January 1852?: RA I27/24.
[83] See Clarendon to Bloomfield (private), 5 April 1853: Bloomfield Papers, PRO FO 356/31.
[84] Palmerston may have counted on this. The *Morning Post*, which was greatly influenced by him, in March 1853 was quite certain that France would keep clear of the 'League' it believed Austria was trying to form against Britain at this time: 2 March 1853, p. 5.

4

'Public Opinion'

Continental conservatives, at a loss otherwise to understand why Britons should suffer the presence of the refugees among them, assumed that they must like and sympathise with them. That, however, was not the impression of many of the refugees themselves. Alexander Herzen found England 'an alien and inimical country that did not conceal that it maintained its right of asylum for the sake of its own self-respect, and not for the sake of those who sought it'.[1] Ledru-Rollin, who held that his particular section of refugees was owed something for the misfortunes it had had to suffer, claimed that instead it had been greeted in England only with insults.[2] Such feelings were not untypical.[3] They were corroborated by *The Times*, which considered it a point in Britain's favour that although the refugees were allowed to live there, it was 'with no sympathy from the people among whom they dwell, with nothing to flatter their vanity or their ambition'.[4] *The Times* was not always consistent, and on other occasions it was found regretting that 'all classes of the country' were so free with their friendship towards them.[5] The refugees' own impression of their hosts' coldness towards them might have been an unfair one, coloured perhaps by the climate (with which Herzen was obsessed), or by the loss of the limelight to which many of them, as major actors in foreign settings, had been accustomed. Nevertheless it was broadly true that, during most of the nineteenth century, their reception was less warm than they sometimes expected, and Britain's charity towards them not so tangible as they would have liked. This was a matter for some regret and shame, too, for their English friends.

It was not always so. It was not so, for example, for a short time in the 1820s and 1830s, when the first waves of post-Napoleonic exiles, chiefly Italians and Poles, were greeted in England by a clamour of enthusiastic

[1] Alexander Herzen, *My Past and Thoughts* (1968 edn.), vol. III, p. 1052.
[2] A. A. Ledru-Rollin, *The Decline of England* (1850), vol. I, p. 3.
[3] E.g. 'Miss A. M. Birkbeck' [Sándor Mednyánszky], 'Daguerreotype of an Exile's fate', in *Sharpe's London Magazine*, n.s., vol. IV (1853); [Otto von Wenckstern], 'Lost in London', in *Household Words*, vol. III no. 68 (1851).
[4] *The Times*, 5 March 1853, p. 5.   [5] *Ibid.*, 19 September 1850, p. 4.

sympathy which seemed universal: fêted by the working classes, dined by the middle classes, and lionised by the Whig aristocracy.[6] It was on the crest of this wave that the old defences against alien immigrants were finally demolished, in 1826;[7] and that the House of Commons even saw its way to granting public money to relieve some of them, in 1834.[8] This unusual enthusiasm for them may have had something to do with the types of refugees they were. Certainly they were easier for liberal-minded Britons to like than were earlier or later ones. The Italians and Poles who came over in the 1820s and thirties were no Jacobins, nor were they – or were not yet widely known to be – socialists. Consequently there was no need for them to be feared, as had been those earlier generations of refugees – 'educated in . . . all the horrors of the French revolution'[9] – whom Canning in 1818 had characterised as 'a set of malignant spirits . . . hovering about . . . to rekindle the flames of war'.[10] Between 1792 and 1820 scarcely anyone in Parliament had objected to this way of describing them, even among those who most objected to the laws which were enacted against them. After 1820 there were many who did. What 'crimes' were they guilty of? asked John Cam Hobhouse in 1822 of Sir Robert Peel, who had called them criminals; their only 'crime' was 'the longing of the expatriated friends of liberty to overthrow their tyrants at home'.[11] Quite suddenly the refugees came to have champions. They were seen, not as wild-eyed extremists, but as romantic nationalists of the most respectable kind, fighting against the clearest kind of tyranny, which was the tyranny of a foreign oppressor, and wishing for no more than that their own countries should become more like Britain. They were the stuff of which good Liberal causes were made: well-born 'honourable and high-minded men',[12] 'glorious martyrs in the cause of universal liberty', struggling to establish in their own countries 'a liberty founded . . . upon a kingly basis, and a constitutional government'; and not 'by secret conspiracies and fell means', but in an 'open' and 'manly' way:[13] 'models of their kind', parodied Canning, who considered that all this was a little over-done, 'more angels than men, heroes of the noblest order, and patriots of the purest water'.[14] Their sufferings in exile seemed the more poignant for their gentility: what distressed Lord Sandon most of all in 1838, when he moved in Parliament to have their relief grant increased, was the sight of 'Colonels and others of high rank . . . working as common labourers'.[15] (Later on it came to be remarked, sceptically, how many of the Poles

[6] See M. C. W. Wicks, *The Italian Exiles in London 1816–1848* (1937); and Harry Rudman, *Italian Nationalism and English Letters* (1940).
[7] 2PD 15, cc. 498–502 (20 April 1826).   [8] 3PD 22, cc. 651–63 (25 March 1834).
[9] 1PD 38, c. 821 (Sergeant Copley, 19 May 1818).   [10] *Ibid.*, c. 907 (22 May 1818).
[11] 2PD 7, c. 1442 (1 July 1822).   [12] 3PD 44, c. 730 (Sandon, 27 July 1838).
[13] 2PD 7, c. 820 (Denman, 5 June 1822).   [14] 2PD 11, c. 133 (2 April 1824).
[15] *Vide supra*, p. 21.

claimed to be high-ranking, as if their whole population consisted of colonels and counts: but for the present such uncharitable suspicions were suppressed.) To nearly all the classes represented in Parliament in the 1820s and 1830s these men were admirable, and they were said to be popular with the masses too.[16] For a brief while, therefore, the public 'image' of the alien refugee in Britain ceased to be that of the old bloodthirsty Jacobin shudderingly remembered from the 1790s, and became instead that of a nobler breed of men, brave aristocratic freedom-fighters shining vividly in the glory of their recent exploits in Italy and Poland, against foes who were an English Liberal's foes also.

The Italians retained much of this widespread sympathy at least until the 1840s. (Later, in the 1850s, it flared up again in support of the victims of the dreadful King 'Bomba' when they were released and came to England.) The Italians had certain advantages over other exiles: that their cause was so reasonable, and their enemies – like 'Bomba' and the pope – so horrid; that their homeland was so familiar to the better classes of Englishmen, from their grand tours and the classics; and that their language was so mellifluous, and so indispensable a part of the educational baggage of ladies and gentlemen of culture and refinement – which for a start gave them a need for tutors, which offered ready employment to many of the exiles, from which could develop amongst their pupils a deeper Italophilia, and sometimes a love too of Italians, many of whom married English maidens. It helped also that so many of the Italian refugees were well-bred, and respectable, and well-lettered: which augmented their reputations, and may have added to the horror of their persecution (for to many it must have seemed so much more terrible that poets should be persecuted than ordinary men of less sensitivity) – and hence to the attraction of their cause.[17] Their literary facility – in Italian, and frequently also in English – ensured too that their cause was well-sung. And they made it easier for themselves to be accepted in England by the way some of them accepted the English so warmly. Many of them became British subjects, or married English wives; a few became pillars of the British establishment;[18] some cultivated very close friendships with prominent Englishmen;[19] more of them expressed Anglophile views. This section of the Italian refugees, although in a way they themselves became less refugee-like as they did so, created a strong link between British 'society' and the Italian cause, which redounded to the advantage of those other Italians dedicated to pursuing that cause more actively. This link was sustained by a succession of

[16] E.g. Sinclair in the House of Commons, 25 March 1834: 3PD 22, c. 654.
[17] Gladstone was much moved by a story that the Neapolitan authorities, learning that the political prisoners in their dungeons got some solace from the singing of a nightingale outside, had it killed.   [18] *Supra*, p. 23.
[19] The Italians' English friendships are described in Wicks, *op. cit.*, and Rudman, *op. cit.*, as well as in the memoirs and biographies of the more prominent Italians.

dramatic events and brave men coming out of Italy in the middle of the
nineteenth century, which periodically buoyed up interest in the refugees'
cause. For the Italian exiles, support in Britain was always spread much
more widely than for others – from aristocratic Whigs to almost the
reddest of revolutionaries; from Lord Holland to the Chartist William
Linton and to Swinburne, who affected to worship the assassin Orsini.[20] It
was more resilient than most, surviving even Mazzini's later excesses, and
the Orsini affair. And it survived for longer, and more continuously, than
'causes' can usually be maintained, by the depth of its roots in British
society, and the regularity with which it could be fed by events in Italy.

The Italians in particular, therefore, were intrinsically more sympathetic
types of refugees than were other types which had gone before. That they
were received so warmly, however, also owed something to the dominant
political mood of Britain at the time: which after about 1820 began to relax
from the fearful, repressive Toryism of the Napoleonic age into something milder and more tolerant. The French revolution and revolutionary
wars had not only blackened the image of the refugee; they had also, until
Waterloo and for a few years afterwards, set back the English reforming
tradition, by seducing it into or associating it with French excesses, and so
stiffening resistance to it. The periodical renewals of the Alien Act during
those years, therefore, reflected not only the contemporary image of the
refugee, but also the weakness of the forces of those who might on more
general grounds of constitutional propriety be expected to resist such a
measure: whose voices were still heard in Parliament,[21] but ineffectively. It
was only in the 1820s that middle-class reformism in England began to
recover its feet and some of its vitality, and gave birth to the tradition
which became known as liberalism. A little confidence seeped back into
the middle classes, as memories and fears of events in France receded.
'Good Heavens!', exclaimed John Cam Hobhouse during one of the Alien
Bill debates, 'is this country, is the English House of Commons, are the
people of England always to be governed by their fears? . . . It is time to
have done talking of the French revolution.'[22] Was it not extraordinary,
commented another in 1824, that such a Bill should be requested now,
'when our situation was prosperous – when every man was contented –
when all domestic differences had subsided'?[23] This feeling that the country
was safe enough now not to require such measures was by no means
universal yet amongst the upper and middle classes: but it was growing. It
was at this time too that the idea began to be aired and acted upon, that if

[20] Rudman, *op. cit.*, p. 124.
[21] There were lengthy Alien Bill debates in 1816 (1PD 33), 1818 (1PD 38) and 1820 (2PD 2).
The largest minorities against the Bills were 48 in 1816, 37 in 1818 and 63 in 1820. The most
active parliamentary campaigners against the Alien laws were Sir James Mackintosh, Sir
Samuel Romilly and John Cam Hobhouse.
[22] 2PD 2, c. 406 (12 July 1820).   [23] 2PD 11, c. 141 (Tierney, 2 April 1824).

there were still elements in the country which appeared subversive of order and stability, perhaps they were better reformed out of existence than repressed. The most famous manifestation of this new doctrine was the Parliamentary Reform Act of 1832. Another smaller one was the repeal of the old Alien Act, which was finally conceded by a Tory government in 1826 with no resistance at all from Parliament, and scarcely any discussion.[24]

What was thus so casually dismantled in 1826 was a system of national defence against alien subversion which had stood for more than thirty years. It was a highly significant decision, and requires more to explain it, perhaps, than the mere combination at this time of a more tolerable brand of alien with a more tolerant brand of Briton. Britons anyway were not so tolerant in other directions as they appeared to be in this. They were for example notoriously *in*tolerant of foreigners: which might generally have been expected to put them against those foreigners who sought refuge among them, but in fact did not, because at this time their xenophobia was strongly coloured by political prejudices, and was directed particularly against the political régimes of the continent. Being against Russian and Austrian absolutism set them also against laws which might be construed as acting in the absolutists' interests: as the Alien Act was supposed to. This in fact was the main burden of the complaints against that Act which were voiced at the time: that it had been introduced, as one M.P. put it in 1818, 'not . . . for the purpose of protecting these realms from danger, but for the purpose of assisting tyrants, and upholding continental despotism'.[25] Some even claimed that it had been drawn up by the autocrats: 'hatched and fostered', said Sir Robert Wilson in 1822, 'in the sanguinary and bigoted despotisms of the continent'.[26] Hobhouse's objection was that it was

part of the new European system of general police . . . part of that system which is to make Great Britain an accomplice in the conspiracy against the liberties of mankind, and is to degrade our English minister for the home department into a mere runner for the continental cabinets.[27]

Subserviency to foreigners, and to despotic systems of government: these two distinct elements combined to form a compelling indictment of the Alien Laws, which also redounded to the more positive advantage of the refugees themselves. Debates on the Alien Acts in the 1820s concentrated to a large extent on the misdeeds of the particular régimes from which the refugees had fled, especially those of the 'impiously miscalled . . . Holy alliance':[28] which was bound automatically to augment the stock of the

[24] 2PD 15, cc. 498–502 (20 April 1826). Technically what was done was to replace the 1824 Alien Act, which was about to lapse, with a new 'Act for the Registration of Aliens' (7 Geo IV c. 54), which contained none of the former's powers of exclusion.
[25] 1PD 38, c. 737 (Lambton, 15 May 1818).   [26] 2PD 7, c. 818 (5 June 1822).
[27] 2PD 2, c. 407 (12 July 1820).   [28] 2PD 10, c. 1356 (Hobhouse, 23 March 1824).

enemies of those régimes who were in Britain. Without this kind of public feeling it is difficult to imagine the Poles in particular being so generally welcomed and supported as they were in the 1830s, when it can hardly be coincidental that popular hostility against their main enemies, 'the barbarians and ruffians of Russia', was at one of its peaks.[29] To a very great extent sympathy for the refugees was merely the reverse side of a much more genuinely felt antipathy towards their tormentors.

This particular concatenation of circumstances sustained the refugees – served to remove the chief obstacle to their exile in Britain and then to nourish a few of them – until about 1840. Thereafter things began to change. Russophobia in Britain appears to have waned.[30] The refugees themselves lost some of their glitter: the Italians probably least of all, but the Poles certainly and considerably. Polonophilia was likely to be difficult to sustain anyway, lacking as it did any really deep roots in England outside of simple Russophobia. By comparison with Italy, for example, Poland was a mystery, far away, off the grand tour route, dark and damp and with no known cultural tradition, apart from Chopin, to take a hold on cultivated Englishmen's imaginations. Its language was one there was little point in learning, and anyway not the kind to trip easily off fashionable ladies' tongues. Likewise it was rarer and more difficult for Poles to learn English, and consequently harder for them to find work, and to communicate directly with their hosts. It soon became clear too that the Polish refugees had more 'extremists' among them, one or two of whom engaged themselves actively in English radical politics, and that they tended to be not so flatteringly appreciative of British institutions. They did not put the same effort as the Italians into enlisting the sympathies of the British establishment, and, apart from the Cracow rising of 1846 and the revolt of 1863, they did not have the same succession of adventures and brave deeds coming out of Poland to sustain them. Consequently the Poles found, as did most other refugee groups after them, that once the laurels they had brought with them faded, they could expect very little positive support from the English middle and upper classes.

To some extent this was compensated for by the support they had from working-class radicals, who in the 1840s forged strong links with the more democratic of them : with those Poles who believed that their struggle was an international class struggle rather than a narrowly national one, and so was part and parcel of English democracy's struggle for a more equitable society. It was this section which produced those Polish revolutionaries who were found at every European barricade in 1848, in aid of the general continental upheaval which was to bring Polish liberty in its train; and which produced also the handful of Poles who joined Chartist groups in

[29] 3PD 22, c. 656 (O'Connell, 25 March 1834); and see J. H. Gleason, *The Genesis of Russophobia in Great Britain* (1950).   [30] *Ibid.*, ch. 10.

England.[31] For the same reasons that the upper and middle classes disapproved of them, working-class radical leaders like George William Harney and Ernest Jones vigorously championed them. 'It has been levelled as a reproach against the Poles', wrote Harney after 1848,

that wherever a barricade was erected, thereon was to be found one of that nation, though it might be even in a country which had no connexion with Poland. That reproach is the greatest glory of the sons of Sarmatia; for what can be more glorious than to risk life and limb for the triumph of justice, even though amongst 'a foreign people'?[32]

Possibly the fact that the democratic Poles were so disapproved of by the respectable classes made them more attractive to Chartists, who later, for example, came to resent the way the middle classes came to expropriate to themselves their hero Kossuth.[33] The Poles were their own, and no one else's. For whatever reason (and most of the reasons will have been political and genuine), the connexion between the democratic Poles and the Chartist leadership was always close. Co-operation between them, and with the Germans also, reached a peak with the formation of the Society of Fraternal Democrats in 1846.[34] Throughout that and the following decade democratic refugees, who were spurned and neglected by others, had constant and active champions among the more internationalist of the leaders of the British working-class movement: though the extent to which international class-consciousness permeated the Chartist *ranks* was always doubtful.

So far as the more dominant classes of British society were concerned, however, the late 1820s and the 1830s saw the refugees' popularity reach its peak. The combination of special factors which had given rise to the dismantling of the Alien laws in 1826, and the Polish subsidy in 1834, did not occur again. The latter came very quickly to be regretted by the body of men who had granted it, so that after 1840 it was left to just a small core of vigilant Polonophiles like Lord Dudley Stuart to remind an increasingly forgetful House of Commons of the Poles' virtues, and to defend a diminishing grant from the onslaughts of champions of retrenchment like John Bright.[35] The lapse of the Alien Act was not regretted so much, because nothing had happened since its repeal to give cause for regret: but it may be that if it had been left to the 1840s to repeal it, it would not have

---

[31] Henry Weisser, *British Working-class Movements and Europe 1815–48* (Manchester, 1975), ch. 4; Peter Brock, 'Polish Democrats and English Radicals 1832–62', in *Journal of Modern History*, vol. 25 (1953).   [32] *Red Republican*, 13 July 1850, pp. 24–5.

[33] *Reynolds's Newspaper*, 2 November 1851, p. 8, and 29 May 1853, p. 8; Dénes A. Jánossy, *Great Britain and Kossuth* (Budapest, 1937), pp. 94–5.   [34] *Supra*, p. 41.

[35] 3PD 101, cc. 437–8 (23 August 1848): 'John Bull was considered a great milch cow for everybody to draw from.' If the vote were turned down, said Bright, 'there was no doubt these persons would seek a living by employment'.

been done. The positive enthusiasm which had lighted the refugees' path in the 1820s and 1830s had a short life, and by the middle of the century had been dimmed for several years. In the 1850s the situation for them was entirely different.

In the 1850s the refugees still had English supporters: but they were now by and large very small and specialist groups of men. The socialists among the exiles, especially the Poles, Germans and Hungarians, had Harney and Jones and other English democrats for friends, and the democratic weekly press for a regular champion.[36] To look after the more 'respectable' Poles – the Czartoryski or 'aristo' faction – there was the M.P. Lord Dudley Stuart, who was almost a full-time Polonophile, and his Literary Association of the Friends of Poland, whose Council included an impressive list of noble titles and some M.P.s, but no one really prominent in public affairs.[37] The Italians had a much broader spread of active sympathisers, from the Chartists W. J. Linton and G. J. Holyoake (who claimed to have tested Orsini's bombs for him)[38] to Liberals like David Masson, William Ashurst and James Stansfeld. Helping them more occasionally the Italians also had some of the most distinguished members of Victorian society: especially prominent literary figures like Coleridge, the Carlyles, Browning, Dickens and Swinburne, and some famous politicians like Gladstone and Lord John Russell.[39] Some Liberals made a regular practice of welcoming all nationalities of refugees into their homes, so long as they were clean and famous: like Lord and Lady Holland, who had been doing it since the 1820s. The more famous and attractive a refugee was, the more Liberal doors opened to him. New arrivals tended to get more sympathetic attention than old residents, especially when their arrival was prefaced by a popular *cause célèbre* like the affair of the Hungarians trapped in Turkey at the beginning of the fifties, and the scandal of King Bomba's dungeons at the end. The French refugees seemed to have far fewer champions than most, for all kinds of reasons: endemic Francophobia, their own chauvinism, their politics, their unsoldierly, unpoetic, unromantic image. But none of the refugee nationalities lacked English supporters somewhere.

What was missing, after the 1820s and thirties, was any general enthusiasm for them: a real warmth towards them among the mass of the

[36] Also Harney's short-lived *Democratic Review* (June 1849–September 1850), which was more than half given over to foreign affairs.
[37] Stuart died in November 1854. His place as President of the Literary Association was taken by the Marquis of Breadalbane until 1857, and then by the 4th Marquis Townshend – distinguished names both, but undistinguished bearers of them. Townshend was a distant relative of Stuart's. See *Annual Reports of the Literary Association of the Friends of Poland*, 1855 and 1858.   [38] G. J. Holyoake, *Sixty Years of an Agitator's Life* (1892), vol. II ch. 60.
[39] Wicks, *op. cit.*, and Rudman, *op. cit.*, *passim*.

British people. Occasionally there were signs of downright hostility. The English democrat Harney told his followers in 1852 how he had 'shuddered to hear of well authenticated instances of personal, disgusting insult offered to the most unhappy of these unfortunate men, – instances of mob brutality, which, though not going beyond words, recall the memory of those hideous days when "George the Third was king", and loyal ruffians burnt Paine in effigy, and consigned Priestly's house to the flames'.[40] Possibly the stories he had heard had their origin in the Great Exhibition scare of the previous year,[41] which may have sent some John Bulls alien-baiting. There were insults too from some members of the higher and middle orders of society: like one correspondent to *The Times* in 1849 to whom they appeared as 'scum and refuse', 'filth' and (less plainly) 'intramural deposit';[42] or like the Earl of Eglinton, who in the House of Lords in the same year accused the Poles of being mostly syphilitic – which was a slander, and for which he was chasteningly rebuked by a government spokesman who knew better.[43] Many people resented the refugees' mendicity, especially that of the Poles, who (said *The Times* in 1850) had had ample time – nineteen years – 'to adapt themselves to their new situation, and to turn their energies to the less brilliant but equally honourable career of private industry . . . The man who in this busy hive of industry can find no employment after such a time is unworthy of compassion.'[44] 'The Englishman', commented Herzen later, 'has no special love for foreigners, still less for exiles, whom he regards as guilty of poverty, a vice he does not forgive.'[45] If there was a danger that they might fall on the rates, for example of the ports they landed in, they might provoke a flurry of invective from alarmed ratepayers like those of Liverpool who accused the Hungarians who disembarked there in 1851 of being perpetual cadgers, 'a burden upon the public, permanent recipients of charity, incapable and unwilling to earn their bread', preferring 'a degrading and miserable indolence and dependence to manly industry and self-reliance'.[46] 'It would be well', a 'man of wealth' was reported as saying in March 1851, 'to force them on board ship, take them away, and sink them in the Atlantic.'[47] To be compelled to contribute to the relief of a group of able-bodied men, especially of foreigners, was likely to bring out the worst feelings in most middle-class Victorians. Luckily for the refugees it did not happen very often. But there were other things about them too

[40] *Star of Freedom*, 18 September 1852, p. 88. [41] *Infra*, p. 86.
[42] *The Times*, 28 November 1849, p. 8.
[43] 3PD 103, cc. 949–52 (19 March 1849); 3PD 104, cc. 55, 135 (30 March and 2 April 1849).
[44] *The Times*, 28 October 1850, p. 4. [45] Herzen, *op. cit.*, vol. III p. 1112.
[46] Broadsheet of March 1851 issued by the Polish–Hungarian Central Refugee Committee, Liverpool: Cowen Papers, TWAD 634/A22; and *vide supra*, p. 42.
[47] Handbill of March 1851 issued by *idem*: Cowen Papers, TWAD 634/A21.

which did not endear them to some Englishmen. Many, who had read for example Ledru-Rollin's *Décadence d'Angleterre*, were offended by their ingratitude, by the way in which in return for all England had done for them 'they decry our institutions, vilify our character, and endeavour to embroil us with the rest of the world'.[48] Others, less rationally, may have been put against the refugees by their appearance – especially the beards which some of them sported, which the smooth-chinned Englishmen of that time were supposed to associate with 'dirt, revolution, immorality, poverty, atheism, and non-payment of rent';[49] or by the lurid activities of the Barthélemys, the Foschinis and the Orsinis.

Usually when the refugees were disliked, however, it was for their politics: for their political beliefs, and also their political methods. Their political beliefs were probably not understood very well, but by those who knew anything about them at all it was known that they had a different flavour from those of the earlier refugees. Republicans, democrats and socialists, which is what most of them were, were not likely to be much loved by the British middle and upper classes, Liberal or Conservative, who were none of these things. Of course there had been foreign republicans and socialists to be found among the refugees in Britain before: yet until the middle of the century they were always less in the public eye than were the Liberal counts and poets, and consequently not likely to give the émigrés too muddy a name amongst respectable people. In the 1840s the balance began to shift, and consequently the 'image' of the refugee too. Again, after the 1840s there were still some who conformed closely to the older type, and who by discriminating men were given proper credit for it: like the Italian victims of King 'Bomba', for example, who arrived in England in 1859, and whom *The Times* made a special point of distinguishing from the others for commendation.[50] Yet amongst the wave of fugitives which accompanied the European reactions of the 1850s there were fewer of this ilk, and more republicans and democrats – most of them French – whose aims were emancipation, not simply from foreign tyrants, but from tyrannous social orders, among which many of them included Britain, and said so. Unlike most of the old Italians and Poles, the French refugees especially were, all of them – even the tamest of them, the followers of Ledru-Rollin – too wild for polite English society, and professed opinions which middle-class Englishmen could not take so lightly as (for example) Polish constitutionalism, but feared themselves. The Earl of Arundel in 1848 called them 'wild and anti-social';[51] to a writer to *The Times* in 1849 they appeared 'hellish';[52] and even *The Economist*, which on the whole was on the refugee's side, found it could not abide 'his

[48] *The Times*, 9 February 1852, p. 4.   [49] *Household Words*, vol. x (1859), p. 1.
[50] *The Times*, 9 March 1859, p. 11.   [51] 3PD 98, c. 581 (1 May 1848).
[52] *The Times*, 23 November 1849, p. 8.

brutal doctrines and his sanguinary plans'.[53] Those of a liberal disposition were scarcely less disapproving than Tories, because of the harm the extremists did to the reputation of more reasonable causes: 'Those who are anxious to witness the political progress of the Continental nations', said the Peelite *Morning Chronicle* in 1851, 'can have little sympathy with the associated Republicans', whose 'intrigues and . . . exploits have served most effectually to discredit the popular cause.'[54] The more radical *Weekly Dispatch* condemned them for trying to hurry things on too quickly: 'it is useless to attempt to gather the pear until it be ripe'.[55] They all disliked too the ways the refugees (and now the Italians especially) were supposed to implement their plans. Lord Derby in 1858 told of how Englishmen could always be counted on to sympathise with a gallant loser, whatever side he was on (and by definition the refugees were all of them losers). But he had to be gallant: fighting 'fairly and in the open field' for his cause, and not resorting 'to the base and vile means of assassination' which, everyone in Parliament at that time and the whole of the press agreed, all Englishmen deprecated.[56] 'As a moral and religious people', said the historian A. W. Kinglake, and as 'a people used to bracing exercise and manly strife of many descriptions', the English 'regarded assassination as a cowardly and dastardly evasion of those rules of fair conduct to which we were accustomed';

and perhaps we might add that to our abhorrence of the crime we joined a great deal of hearty contempt, because, as a thoroughly practical people, we were naturally apt to despise those who were continually making attempts and never succeeding[57]

– which was a stinging rebuke indeed. It was for both these reasons – his adoption of what Disraeli called 'ensanguined practices',[58] and his continual failures – that Mazzini's stock dipped so low in England in the 1850s.[59] As well as assassination the British also disapproved of those

---

[53] *The Economist*, quoted in *Littell's Living Age* (Boston, Mass.), 2nd Series, vol. 1 (1853) p. 341.   [54] *Morning Chronicle*, 29 March 1851, p. 5; and cf. *ibid*. 15 March 1851, p. 5.
[55] *Weekly Dispatch*, 20 February 1853, p. 113.
[56] 3PD 149, c. 33 (1 March 1858). The same view was expressed in 3PD 148 cc. 1027 (9 February 1858), 1748, 1753, 1764, 1814, 1825 (19 February 1858); and by Sir Arthur Hallam Elton, *The Case Against the Late Ministry Plainly Stated* (1858), p. 5: 'Englishmen despise and abhor assassination, whether in practice or in theory.' In 1864, however, *The Times* was found giving a kind of grudging sanction to tyrannicide in certain circumstances: '. . . to stake life against life, to brave torture and shame and death, to stifle the voice of conscience, and to put the soul in jeopardy for the sake of one supreme vindication of retributive justice, may be sinful, may be pernicious to society, may be, or rather must be, contrary to the laws of God and man, but it can hardly fail to be sublime'. What was *not* sublime was assassination by remote control, which Mazzini was supposed to engage in, at no risk to himself – *The Times*, 14 January 1864, p. 8.   [57] 3PD 148, c. 939 (8 February 1858).
[58] Quoted in Rudman, *op. cit.*, pp. 111–12.
[59] *Ibid.*, ch. 6, 'The Ebbing of the Mazzinian Tide'; and cf. M. B. Urban, *British Opinion and Policy on the Unification of Italy 1856–61* (New York 1938), p. 61.

international secret societies whose 'mysterious agency' was supposed by some of them to 'spread terror and guilt' in Europe,[60] though there were very few people in Britain who shared the continental conservative obsession with these.[61] But possibly what the refugee's enemies distrusted most of all was his revolutionary promiscuity: his willingness to give himself into the arms of any democratic cause anywhere; especially (as we have seen) that of the 'lawless and turbulent Poles' who were 'always found revelling in scenes of violence and anarchy';[62] 'vagabond hirelings, who fought for a country to them utterly indifferent – solely for the paltry pittance of a soldier's pay, and for what plunder might fall within their reach'.[63] 'The large proportion of them', claimed Lord Lyndhurst, were 'men of desperate character and desperate fortunes, hostile to all regular governments, persons accustomed to the use of arms, and ready to embark on any adventure of however bold and daring a kind';[64] unstable bombs whose danger was, perhaps, that they might as well explode in their hosts' faces as anywhere else.

Those who made a particular point of attacking the refugees, however, were a very small band, and for the most part came to tire of it soon after the ferment of 1848 with which the refugees were associated died down. In Parliament the only member who bothered to devote much time to the task was the veteran ex-Lord Chancellor Baron Lyndhurst, who was 80 in 1852. Among the national newspapers of the day *The Times* (which was by far the most widely read and influential of them) appears to have had a special animus against them and their defenders right through the 1850s: especially against Kossuth, whom even before he arrived and for a long time afterwards it pursued and attacked with a rare dedication; and Lord Dudley Stuart, whom it seemed to delight in ridiculing contemptuously and repeatedly.[65] The extreme Tory *John Bull*, though it did not harp on them so much, was also consistently hostile to the refugees.[66]

Yet these do not appear to have represented or determined the general attitude of the British towards the refugees. Few people seem to have positively disliked or feared them. There were even some Englishmen who went along both with the extremer refugees' political objectives, and even with their methods; who were revolutionary socialists themselves, or

[60] *Quarterly Review*, vol. 93 (June 1853), p. 139.
[61] See J. M. Roberts, *The Mythology of the Secret Societies* (1972), p. 206.
[62] 3PD 103, c. 950 (19 March 1849).
[63] Broadsheet of March 1851, in Cowen Papers, TWAD 634/A22.
[64] 3PD 115, c. 626 (27 March 1851).
[65] E.g. *The Times*'s attacks on Kossuth in leading articles throughout October and November 1851 and again on 3 February 1852 and in June 1854; and on Dudley Stuart and his 'Polish Balls' (charity dances in aid of the refugees) on 11 and 19 November 1848, 28 October 1850, and 21 May 1853.
[66] E.g. *John Bull*, 29 March 1851, pp. 201–2, which looked forward to seeing 'our streets flow with the blood of foreign revolutionists' if they tried any kind of demonstration.

who accepted the rectitude, and even the nobility, of tyrannicide. The most notorious example of the latter was Walter Savage Landor, who once offered a prize of £95 to 'the Family of the First Patriot who asserts the dignity, and performs the duty of tyrannicide': although when he appeared to be taken up on it in January 1858 by his old friend Orsini he immediately reserved to himself the right to define a 'tyrant'.[67] By an admirer of Simon Bernard, who was accused of complicity in the same Orsini plot in 1858, it was asserted that 'liberty is . . . dearer than life; and . . . it were not difficult to conceive of alternatives far more to be dreaded than the death of a tyrant'.[68] Orsini himself, the most famous would-be regicide of the day, became the centre of quite a little cult in certain literary circles after his execution.[69] Others who might deprecate violent methods in principle, and in Englishmen, nevertheless excused them in foreigners who were provoked into them, and who did not have the same avenues of peaceful change that Englishmen had. As Simon Bernard's advocate told the jury at his trial:

We, who live under the mild and undisputed sway of a Sovereign who reigns in the hearts of her people, cannot appreciate – perhaps cannot understand, the maddened feelings of those who have long been oppressed – who have been deprived of their liberty by foreign tyranny – and who may deem themselves, therefore, justified in adopting every means to throw off the hated yoke![70]

Most people, however, probably neither sympathised with nor excused the extremists, but agreed with W. J. Fox that among the 'hundreds and thousands of refugees who had found an asylum here' they were 'a very small number indeed',[71] who should not, therefore, be used to blacken the reputations of the rest. Several newspapers were careful to discriminate between sorts of refugees, as *The Times* did between Bomba's victims and the rest.[72] The Tory *Standard,* for example, which was vitriolically anti-catholic, made an exception in favour of 'the gallant and honest men who subverted the tyranny of the Roman Pontiff', who should not, it said, be tarred with the same brush as the other refugees;[73] the *Morning Chronicle* drew 'a line between assassins and honourable exiles';[74] and the *Weekly Dispatch*, which was in general pro-refugee, made an exception *against* the 'cowardly' French.[75] There was no national newspaper apart from *John Bull* which had no good word to say for any of them. More significantly, very few of them ever *initiated* attacks on the refugees. If they ever did

[67] See Rudman, *op. cit.*, pp. 239, 242; and printed copies of Landor to Miss J. Meriton White, n.d., in Cowen Papers, TWAD 634/A485.
[68] 'Lancet', *Life of Dr Bernard. . .* (1858), p. 3. [69] Rudman, *op. cit.*, pp. 242–8.
[70] *State Trials*, n.s., vol. VIII, c. 1007. Cf. *infra*, pp. 102–3.
[71] 3PD 148, c. 948 (8 February 1858). [72] *Supra*, p. 76.
[73] *Standard*, 28 March 1851, p. 2. [74] *Morning Chronicle*, 20 January 1858, p. 4.
[75] *Weekly Dispatch*, 6 April 1851, p. 217; 2 December 1855, p. 9.

criticise them, then it was usually incidentally, in riders to leading articles whose main emphasis was something else: such as – most commonly – a continental demand for their expulsion.

It would appear therefore that if the extremer activities of some of the refugees were known about and disapproved of, they did not, at least until the Orsini affair, make a very significant impression in Britain. The general image or stereotype which attached to the refugees there seems not to have been set by the activities of Orsini and Foschini, or by the highly-coloured characterisations of them which came from the continent, but was more sober, and more favourable towards them. In the popular magazines and novels of the time this was certainly so. Foreign villains appeared in fairly profuse abundance (like Trollope's Lopez); foreign *refugee* villains never.[76] The best fictional portrayal of a refugee was probably Wilkie Collins' 'Professor Pesca', treated entirely sympathetically, if patronisingly, and in a novel (*The Woman in White*) whose main villain (chosen, said Collins, because he 'thought the crime too ingenious for an English villain')[77] was an Italian anti-refugee spy. When refugees were written about at all in the 1850s, it was usually by men and women who had refugee friends (as Collins did), or were especially sympathetic towards their causes,[78] or were even refugees themselves.[79] Consequently their portrayal in the literature of the time did not necessarily accurately reflect public opinion. Nevertheless it is significant that there was no counter-image to theirs in mid-Victorian literature: as there was, for

[76] There is a very minor refugee villain – a Pole called Koratinsky – in Charles Lever's *The Dodd Family Abroad* (1852), but living in Belgium and not England. In the same novel Lever allows his characters one or two little grumbles about refugees generally: 'We hear', writes the hero, 'a great deal of talk about the partition of Poland, and there is an English lord keeps the subject for his own especial holdings forth; but I am convinced that the greatest evil of that nefarious act lies in having thrown all these Polish fellows broadcast over Europe. I wish it was a kingdom to-morrow, if they'd only consent to stay there' (1859 edn., vol. 1 p. 76). A little later his wife expresses a similar view: 'What a fuss they're making all over the world about these "rapparees", or refugees, or whatever they call them. My notion is, Molly, that we who harbour them have the worst of the bargain; and as to our fighting for them, it would be almost as sensible as to take up arms in defence of a flea that got into your bed!' (vol. 1 p. 306). These sentiments, of course, are not necessarily the author's, nor are they necessarily intended by the author to be representative of the opinion of any section of contemporary British society. The 'Dodds' clearly are supposed to have minds of their own, and in any case, as Irish catholic encumbered gentry, are hardly characteristic Victorians.
      Without having wasted a lifetime reading inferior two-volume nineteenth-century novels it is of course impossible to be absolutely certain that no refugee villain appears in any of them; but if there was one I have not heard of him, and his 'image' does not appear to have impressed itself greatly. Henry James' *The Princess Casamassima* (1886) and Joseph Conrad's *The Secret Agent* (1907) were probably the first significant English-language novels to paint political refugees in more sinister colours.
[77] Wilkie Collins, *The Woman in White* (1860; new edn. 1975, p. 591).
[78] See Rudman, *op. cit.*, and Wicks, *op. cit.*
[79] E.g. the novels of G. Ruffini; and articles by Otto von Wenckstern and 'Miss Birkbeck', *cit supra*, p. 67 fn. 3.

example, later in the century. There is very little sign here, or anywhere, that when most Victorians thought of a political refugee, the picture which came to their minds was anything like that which continental reactionaries would like to have placed there.

There is little sign either, however, that the Victorians thought much of political refugees at all. There was really very *little* about them in the literature of the time; in novels, which are otherwise so rich a reflection of English social life, they scarcely featured; in the periodical magazines there was barely a mention of how and where they lived and what they did: which indicates that editors and novelists discerned little public interest in them that they could tap. More common than either approval or disapproval of the refugees appears to have been a broad apathy towards them. Few people had any really strong feeling for or against them, or their views. 'The people of this country,' said the Liberal M.P. Monckton Milnes in 1852, '. . . were not in the habit of taking much interest in the affairs of foreign refugees.'[80] Even those Englishmen who were closest ideologically to the new refugees of the 1850s did not seem as concerned about them as might have been expected. The Chartist and democratic press was full of Harney's and Jones' fraternal celebrations of them, and appeals on behalf of them, but underlying them all was the strong impression that the leaders were almost alone in the interest they took in them, and that the mass of English democrats were bored by them. By the British democratic leaders themselves, and also by many of the refugees, it was often noted, sadly or contemptuously, how lacking the English working classes were in the true democratic spirit of international class-solidarity. The middle classes, who had a different kind of internationalism of their own, were scarcely more interested. In England, said *The Times*, the refugee 'meets with little notice'. 'He finds no enemies, and makes no allies . . . The refugee in England vegetates in safety'.[81] If this was not absolutely true it was very substantially so; and not entirely unwelcome to many of them, who, fearing that any notice which was drawn to them might have hostile effects, worked hard to cultivate a 'low profile' image among their hosts. We have seen[82] that they took little or no part in British politics. They were careful that new arrivals did not for long remain a financial burden on the British, before they dispersed and were looked after by their own communities. They rarely caused any kind of trouble among the English, except a few beggars, and a couple of murderers, and some Italian rioters in Holborn. Those of them who competed for work with Englishmen generally did not do so in large enough numbers to

---

[80] 3PD 119, c. 488 (1 April 1852). Milnes himself however took a prominent interest in them; he was on the Council of the Literary Association of the Friends of Poland, and spoke frequently in Parliament on matters affecting them.
[81] *The Times*, 18 January 1858 p. 6, and 19 September 1850 p. 4.   [82] *Supra*, pp. 39–41.

provoke a distinct prejudice against them. They tried as far as they could to
avoid touching the political and social fabric they were passing through,
and they succeeded in making a very minimal impression on it. The result
was that, except by a handful of Englishmen, and on one or two occasions
for special reasons, they were ignored.

The coolness of the British public's interest in the refugees was illustrated by the poor response it made to monetary appeals on their behalf.
The refugees always needed money, and particularly when they first
arrived: usually because they could not find work to live by, sometimes
because they did not want to. Some of them, like the French and the
Germans, did not appeal in any systematic way to the British for funds, but
instead tried to furnish them from their own and their compatriots'
resources. Those on whose behalf appeals *were* made to the British were
those who it was felt had the likeliest claim on the latter's sympathies: the
oppressed nationalities of Italy, Poland and Hungary. For them efforts
were made on a number of levels to raise funds. The Poles were fortunate
in having, since 1834, a yearly sum from the national exchequer for the
relief of some of them. That grant, however, was never princely – not
more than £15,000 at its maximum in 1839, which was very much less than
the French at that time gave to *their* Polish emigrés; and by the mid-
century it was much lower – only £4,300 in 1852, declining to little more
than £3,000 in 1862, which sum was only very grudgingly given, and then
not to new arrivals.[83] For the rest the supplicants had to rely on private
charity, which was organised mainly by 'Societies of the Friends of' the
various nationalities, and distributed (like most Victorian charity) with a
scrupulous discrimination. That the sums collected by these societies – a
few hundred pounds per annum[84] – were not sufficient for their purposes
was evidenced by the testimony of their organisers, and by the continuing
poverty of many of the refugees.[85] Some of the latter was attributed by
English democrats to malevolence on the part of the relieving societies,
which were mainly middle-class, towards refugees who were too radical,
or who refused to be shunted off to America.[86] Consequently in the early

[83] 3PD 122, c. 119 (7 June 1852); 3PD 168, c. 592 (21 June 1862); and PP (1841) xiii. These
totals include a few Spaniards too.
[84] In 1854–5 the income of the Literary Association of the Friends of Poland (excluding
money entrusted to it by the government for conveying refugees to Turkey) was
£1,306–8s.; of which £905–12s.–6d. was raised by a public dinner, £215–10s. came from
subscriptions, £93–17s. from donations and £91–8s.–6d. from a legacy (*Annual Report*,
1855, p. 75). In 1857–8 the total income had declined to £522–2s., and the next year to
£469–12s.–6d. (*Annual Reports*, 1858 p. 55 and 1859 p. 49).
[85] In 1855, which was not a bad year financially for the Literary Association of the Friends of
Poland, its secretary reported that 'There are unfortunately among the Polish refugees
many in a state of great destitution (though most anxious to obtain employment), whom
the association is unable to relieve' (*Annual Report*, 1855, p. 21).
[86] See *Friend of the People*, 22 March 1851, p. 116. In 1858 the Literary Association of the
Friends of Poland explained that its hostility towards certain sections of the Polish refugees

1850s English democracy launched its own appeals on behalf of its refugee friends, which were hardly more successful. Those who took it upon themselves to help the 262 Hungarians who arrived in Liverpool in March 1851, for example, found it very difficult to make headway, and could only claim to have succeeded if 'adverse circumstances' and 'the many disadvantages under which their friends laboured in raising funds for their support' were taken into account.[87] At least one local organiser found himself personally out of pocket after it all.[88] Then on 9 May 1852 Harney formed a general 'Democratic Refugee Committee' for the refugees' relief; which by August had gathered such an 'insignificant' sum that it was 'ashamed to divide it amongst the committees of the nations',[89] and in May the next year had to be dissolved, after collecting altogether only £69 11s., which 'thoroughly satisfied the members of this committee of the absolute indifference of the great mass of the British people to the claims of the political exiles'.[90]

To Harney there was 'something monstrous and unnatural' in this; in 'the cruel, cold-hearted apathy of our countrymen, to the condition of the refugees'.[91] It may have been so: or it may have been that Englishmen of all classes had a certain prejudice against dispensing charity to able-bodied men, however much they might like them. Like Herzen later, Ugo Foscolo, one of the earliest Italian exiles, noticed in 1823 how in England poverty was regarded not as a misfortune but as a crime: 'The English are a humane people, but will have nothing to do with one who wants bread.'[92] This was the purport too of Herzen's remark about life in Britain being 'bad for the weak, for the frail, for one who seeks a prop outside himself'.[93] Victorian Britain was a cruel enough place for anyone to live in who was unable or unwilling to support himself, and refugees it was believed should make the same efforts to toil and earn as everyone else.[94] And if there was charity to give, many will have agreed with *The Times* that there were others more entitled to it:

We would merely suggest that the English Lazarus has a prior and a better claim. His sores indeed are unpoetical, and his hunger is not embellished by legend or tradition. Job Smith and Abel Brown are out of work and hungry – they, their wives, and their little ones. Their woe is very heavy and very sad, but very stupid

---

was not on account of their opinions, 'but on account of the intolerant spirit in which these opinions are professed' (*Annual Report*, 1858, p. 11).

[87] The *Refugee Circular* (published by the 'Operatives Committee for the Relief of the Polish Hungarian Refugees', Liverpool), no. 9, 16 August 1851, p. 33: in Cowen Papers, TWAD 634/A87.

[88] See copy of a letter from Joseph Cowen to the *Newcastle Chronicle*, 14 February 1852, in Cowen Papers, TWAD 634/A146.

[89] *Reynolds's Newspaper*, 8 August 1852, p. 13.   [90] *Ibid.*, 15 May 1853, p. 9.

[91] *Star of Freedom*, 18 September 1852, p. 88.

[92] Quoted in 'Anglomane' [Anthony Gallenga], 'Foscolo and English hospitality', in *Fraser's Magazine*, vol. 31 (April 1845), p. 401fn.   [93] *Supra*, p. 23.   [94] Cf. *supra*, p. 75.

. . . We have not yet heard of a Typhoidal Hilton Ball, nor of a Fancy Fair in behalf of Bethnal Green.[95]

That the paucity of their direct financial support for the refugees was not necessarily any true guide to Englishmen's sympathies is suggested by the contrast presented by their very much larger contributions to some of the refugees' *causes*: to the Garibaldi fund set up in 1856, for example, which is said to have collected £30,000 in four years.[96] Englishmen may have been keener on supporting revolutionaries in action than revolutionaries in idleness.

Some of the refugees, as we have seen, felt aggrieved at their hosts' lack of concern about them: but in fact it may not have been altogether a bad thing for them. Though it meant that they were not particularly loved, it will have meant also that they were not greatly feared, and not being feared made them more easily tolerated. We have seen already that the refugees did a great deal to assist this, by deliberately refraining from acting fearsomely;[97] but the average Englishman's unconcern about the effect they were having on his society stemmed not only from this, but also from his confidence, which seemed unshakable, in the resilience of that society. This confidence was not altogether intelligible to continental conservatives, by whose understanding of the mechanism of revolution Britain was as vulnerable to it as any other European power: perhaps more so, because of the laxity of her defences against it. Throughout the 1850s they were continually warning her that the refugees in her midst threatened *her* security as well as theirs; that the system which the republicans and democrats among them wished to overthrow embraced Britain (as it did); that socialism was no greater friend to parliamentary than to monarchical capitalism: that, as Princess Lieven wrote to Lord Aberdeen in 1850, 'ils peuvent vous atteindre'.[98] In 1850 came a warning from the Prussian government that some Germans in London were plotting to assassinate Queen Victoria;[99] in 1851 a report from Paris that 'socialist emissaries' were being sent over – Germans being selected rather than French 'from their generally speaking the English language with greater facility and less accent' – to 'pervert the spirit of the manufacturing population'.[100] The

---

[95] *The Times*, 16 November 1848, p. 4; and cf. *ibid.*, 11 November 1848, p. 4. Hilton is a village in Dorset which was afflicted by a typhus epidemic in 1848.

[96] N. J. Gossman, 'British aid to Polish, Italian, and Hungarian exiles 1830–1870', in *South Atlantic Quarterly*, vol. 68 (1969), pp. 236–7. Gossman however presents as a firm fact a figure which his source (Rudman, *op. cit.*, p. 303) makes it clear is only a very rough guess, and may be exaggerated.   [97] *Supra*, pp. 37–9.

[98] 26 September 1850, quoted in E. Jones Parry (ed.), *The Correspondence of Lord Aberdeen and Princess Lieven*, vol. II (1939), p. 515.   [99] *Supra*, p. 57 fn. 35.

[100] Normandy to Palmerston no. 92, 10 April 1851: PRO FO 27/900; and cf. Princess Lieven on 'le travail que Louis Blanc et Mazzini font en Angleterre, et surtout dans les districts manufacturiers': Parry, *op. cit.*, p. 515.

virus these men brought with them, claimed Charles de Bussy in 1858, was already spreading in Britain; the growth of the new monster of trade unionism was a symptom, and to be expected: 'Celui-là appelle le feu sur la maison qui donne asile aux incendiaires.'[101] Yet in the face of it all the British authorities remained, in Princess Lieven's words again, 'orgueilleux, . . . dédaigneux des dangers',[102] revealing a blind folly which was almost beyond the continentals' comprehension. A wild tiger was there amongst them, unrestrained, ready to pounce; from the other side of the Channel Britain's friends were shouting themselves hoarse to warn her of it: and she affected not to hear.

There were times in the middle of the century when some Englishmen, at least, could be persuaded to listen, and when the effect the refugees might have on Britain was feared just a little. One was in 1848, when for a moment, as was recorded in his journal by Lord Campbell (who a decade later was to have much to do with the refugees):

we seem to have arrived at an entirely new era in the annals of the human race. The religious movement at the time of the Reformation was nothing to the political movement which we now behold. The cement which held society together is suddenly dissolved, and it seems about to become a confused mass of ruins.[103]

The British people held firm, acting, in the words of the *Morning Chronicle,* as 'the moral breakwater of Europe';[104] but, asked *The Times*, for how long?

It cannot be denied that the public mind, stunned and confounded by the events of the continent, had become, as the ancients would have expressed it, *meteoric,* unsteady, open to strange impressions, and diffident of its most habitual belief.[105]

While this mood was still on them, London suddenly seemed to fill with foreigners. 'We need only walk from Temple-bar to Charing-cross to satisfy ourselves that London contains an unusual number of good citizens from a powerful military republic within sight of these shores', said *The Times* again. 'Doubtless they mean no harm, but why are they here?'[106] Some observers had no doubt: 'to incite the people to revolt', wrote Henry Greville in his diary, 'and to teach them their Parisian fashions'.[107] It was widely anticipated that they might involve themselves in the great Chartist demonstration on Kennington Common planned for 10th April.[108] In

---

[101] Charles de Bussy, *Les Conspirateurs en Angleterre*. . .(1858), p. 78.   [102] Parry, *loc. cit.*
[103] Mrs. Hardcastle (ed.), *Life of John, Lord Campbell* (1881), vol. II, p. 247.
[104] *Morning Chronicle*, 11 April 1848, p. 4.   [105] *The Times*, 12 April 1848, p. 4.
[106] *Ibid.*, *loc. cit.* On April 11 Lord Beaufort brought to the attention of the House of Lords 'the great number of foreigners that were to be seen at present filling the streets of London,. . . among whom. . . were several who were known to be the worst characters of France': 3PD 98, c. 135.
[107] Viscountess Enfield (ed.), *Leaves from the Diary of Henry Greville*, vol. I (1883), pp. 255–6.
[108] E.g. Hardcastle, *op. cit.*, vol. II p. 236.

the event, as Lord Palmerston wrote to his ambassador in Paris the next day, 'The Foreigners did not shew'; which Palmerston thought was just as well for them, as 'the Constables Regular and Special had sworn to make an example of any whiskered & bearded Rioter whom they might meet with, and I am convinced would have mashed them to jelly'.[109] Nevertheless vigilance was still necessary. In the present state of things in Europe, said Lord Lansdowne, a government minister, in Parliament on April 17th, 'no one knew when compulsion might be necessary to check or prevent the interference of foreigners in the affairs of this country' or, more likely, of Ireland.[110] The Tory Earl of Ellenborough 'believed the danger from aliens was much greater now than at any former time'.[111] The Home Secretary Sir George Grey was less alarmed; but still he held that 'we have a right to protect ourselves against foreigners – to prevent foreigners interfering with us – taking upon themselves to be the apostles of [republican] principles, and coming to us as propagandists'.[112] And so was passed, by large majorities in both Houses, the Alien Act of 1848: 'a measure', said Lord Lansdowne, 'which the Government owed to the people, and particularly to those of middle classes, who would feel greater security under its provisions':[113] as doubtless they did during the two years that it ran.

The only other occasion when Britons feared for themselves from the activities of the refugees was the early part of 1851, when rumours were fairly widespread that they might try something under the cover of the Great Exhibition. These rumours mostly originated from the continent, where it was widely believed that the occasion would be used by the socialists to foment 'an universal revolution' which would begin in England and then fire the continent;[114] and from America, where the *New York Herald* saw the hand of American catholics in it, co-operating (incredibly) with continental socialists to put Bishop Hughes of New York on the papal throne.[115] Another report sent to the Home Office by a well-known English balloonist of the day, who claimed he had elicited his information

---

[109] Palmerston to Normanby (private), 11 April 1848: Palm. P. GC/NO f. 474.
[110] 3PD 98, cc. 398, 265 (17 and 13 April 1848).   [111] *Ibid.*, cc. 266–7.   [112] *Ibid.*, c. 560.
[113] *Ibid.*, c. 1061. The 1848 Alien Act (11 & 12 Vict. c.20) empowered, 'for a Time to be limited', a Secretary of State or the Lord Lieutenant of Ireland to expel any alien who he had 'Reason to believe, from Information given to him. . .in Writing, by any Person subscribing his or her Name and Address thereto' threatened 'the Preservation of the Peace and Tranquillity of any Part of this Realm'. Any alien so expelled was entitled to know the reasons for his expulsion, and to appeal to the Privy Council against it, with facilities for summoning witnesses and examining them on oath. Foreign ambassadors were exempted, as were children under 14 and any foreigner who had lived in Britain for more than three years. The Bill passed its final reading on May 11 by 146 to 29 votes; the 'Noes' included Cobden, Bright, Fox, Stuart and Urquhart. It was never implemented, and lapsed in the summer of 1850.
[114] *The Times*, 26 March 1851, p. 6 (from its Paris correspondent).
[115] *New York Herald*, 29 March 1851: cutting in PRO HO 45/3518A.

from foreign friends, depicted a lurid scenario which was supposed to be directed by Ledru-Rollin, Louis Blanc and others from a public-house in the Haymarket, and involving 90,000 foreign refugees who would simultaneously set fire to the houses they lived in, aided and abetted by 200,000 Irish and by catholic priests cunningly disguised during the day as matchsellers:

I have had described to me some of the missiles intended to be used, one of them termed Crabs, are round Balls with spikes protruding from them in every direction, in order to lame the horses, or men, either Police or troops, that may be engaged against them; also another is a tube in the form of a cane, 3 or 4 are appointed to each Leading thoroughfare; the tube contains a Ball of an inflammatory nature; this is unobserved Blown by the Breath into the various shops towards the evening of the day of the intended outbreak, these Balls explode at a given time and the places will be instantly in a Blaze; at the same time the Lodging houses, in the various parts of the Metropolis will also be in Flames, and any Man, Woman or Boy running out to give notice to the Fire Engines offices will be instantly stab^{d}, at this time of consternation and alarm, it is intended to make an attempt upon the Bank of England, . . . on Buckingham Palace, and other buildings.[116]

These rumours were given their most authoritative backing by the Chartist Feargus O'Connor, who by publicly warning British workingmen in April not to get involved in such plots tacitly implied that such plots did exist.[117] They were taken seriously by many Members of Parliament;[118] by the old Duke of Wellington;[119] and by the Metropolitan Police Commissioner Sir Richard Mayne, for whom the possibility that 'Refugees . . . of extreme democratic Revolutionary Principles' might combine with 'the Political agitators of our own country' to 'create mischief or alarm' was at least a contingency which should be prepared against.[120] But they were denied hotly by the British working-class radicals who were supposed to be involved in these refugee conspiracies, and also by the refugee leaders themselves.[121] And they were by and large not credited by the press, with the exception of *John Bull*, which was sure it was going to happen, and the *Morning Post*, which thought it just possibly might.[122] Other newspapers

---

[116] G. Graham, 'aeronaut', to Sir George Grey, 8 April 1851: PRO MEPO 2/43. The purpose of this letter was to persuade the police to adopt a kind of riot shield ('a street Shield') which he had just invented. Other similar warnings, though accompanied by less impressive details, were received by the Home Office and the Foreign Office during the first months of 1851: e.g. Forbes Campbell to Palmerston, 8 March 1851, in Palm. P. GC/CA/42; J. Smith to Home Office, 24 April 1851, in PRO HO 65/17 p. 459; and anonymous letter of 25 February 1851, in PRO HO 45/3623.

[117] *Northern Star*, 5 April 1851, p. 1.

[118] See 3PD 115, cc. 621–9 and 882–5 (27 March and 1 April 1851).

[119] Wellington to Lord John Russell, 9 April 1851 (copy), in Russell Papers, PRO 30/22/9C f. 31. [120] Mayne to Waddington, 4 November 1850: PRO HO 45/3623.

[121] E.g. *Northern Star*, 12 April 1851, p. 1 and 19 April 1851, p. 4; *Friend of the People*, 12 April 1851, p. 160 and 19 April 1851, p. 166; *The Times*, 8 April 1851, p. 5; *Voix du Proscrit*, vol. I (1850–1), pp. 345–7.

[122] *John Bull*, 29 March 1851, pp. 201–2; *Morning Post*, 29 March 1851, p. 4.

derided it as 'absurd', 'ridiculous', 'ludicrous'; 'the brains must be addled', said the *Weekly Dispatch*, 'that could conceive the notion':[123] even *John Bull* admitted that it was likely to be laughed at.[124] And laughed at it was: by Charles Dickens in *Household Words*, for example, who mocked quite mercilessly those 'nervous old ladies, dyspeptic half-pay officers, suspicious quidnuncs, plot-dreading diplomatists, and grudging rate-payers' who believed that foreigners would take over the country 'while the Metropolitan Police and the Guards . . . (to a man) pretend to be fast asleep';[125] and by *Punch*, which was equally scornful at the expense of the 'bigotted Englishman, belonging to the fine old John Bull school', who expected, from the presence in London of all those foreigners 'with long moustachios, long beard[s], . . . long hair, and dirty habits, . . . nothing less than the Plague in consequence'.[126] This was before the event. When the event came and passed, and nothing happened more untoward than a few pickpocketings – not the slightest whisper of the threatened revolution – the satire was stepped up, and the Cassandras were ridiculed off the stage.[127] After this it became difficult ever to start up such a rumour again. For very many years after May 1851 virtually nothing was heard inside Britain of any threat which the refugees might pose to Britain's institutions and stability. In the lengthy debates about the 'refugee question' which periodically cropped up during the 1850s and sixties, this consideration almost never entered.

For some Englishmen the safeguard they had against subversion by foreigners lay in the endemic xenophobia of their countrymen. In 1851 the Metropolitan Police Commissioner, at the same time as he was worrying about political agitation by foreign refugees, also felt he had to provide against possible clashes between them and 'the lower classes of our own people'.[128] Much earlier in the century, this was what J. W. Ward, a Tory M.P. and future Foreign Secretary, relied on: the upper classes, because

---

[123] *Weekly Dispatch*, 6 April 1851, p. 217; cf. *The Times*, 10 April 1851, p. 5. The most scathing account appeared in the *Manchester Guardian*, 9 April 1851, p. 4.
[124] John Bull, *loc. cit.*   [125] *Household Words*, vol. III no. 57 (26 April 1851), p. 103.
[126] *Punch*, vol. 20 (January–June 1851), p. 104.
[127] E.g. *Punch*, vol. 20 (1851), p. 193 carried a cartoon depicting Victoria and Albert among smiling flag-wavers with the caption 'Her Majesty, as she appeared on the First of May, Surrounded by "Horrible Conspirators and Assassins" '; and a letter (p. 198) signed 'Titus Oates', revealing another 'horrible great plot and conspiracy. . . hatched by American, French and German Socialists, not only against the Constitution and the Church, but also against the British people at large, and particularly against that portion of them vulgarly termed Cockneys.' *Household Words* on 11 October 1851 (vol. IV no. 8, pp. 60–4) carried a similar lampoon by George A. Sala: 'The foreigners! *That* was the *cheval de bataille* of the prophetic brigade. The nasty, dirty, greasy, wicked, plundering, devastating, frog-eating, atheistical foreigners! . . . The foreigners in London! war, ruin, and desolation! Middlesex and the *département de la Tamise*, and three regiments of Cossacks bivouacking at Price's Patent Candle Manufactory. . .' and so on in the same vein.
[128] Mayne to Waddington, 8 April 1851: PRO HO 45/3623.

HER MAJESTY, as She Appeared on the FIRST of MAY, Surrounded by "Horrible Conspirators and Assassins."

3. *Punch*'s comment, after the event, on fears that the opening of the Great Exhibition in May 1851 would be made the occasion for an uprising fomented by foreign revolutionaries in London.

they travelled, he told the Commons in 1820, had 'had their animosities rubbed down', but the middle and lower classes 'retained their national prejudices in all their strength and sharpness. This country was, more than any other nation, separated from its neighbours by those pre- judices'.[129] 'As to looking for sympathy from the Chartists', said *Fraser's Magazine* in 1851, 'that is the most forlorn of all forlorn hopes. In the first place, the Chartists are Englishmen, and have a national distaste for foreign aid . . .'[130] As soon as a foreigner stood up to speak to an English audience, said Lord Auckland in 1816, 'the first word that [he] would have to utter, in which the letters *th* or the letter *w* occurred, would overthrow any attempt he might be disposed to make inimical to the public peace'.[131] If things had changed by 1848 Joseph Hume, for one, had not noticed it: 'Was it possible', he said in May of that year, 'that any sane man could believe that if a Frenchman or a German were to stand up in a meeting of Englishmen, Scotchmen, or Irishmen, and to advocate revolution and the overthrow of the British constitution, he would receive anything else for his trouble but hissings and hootings?'[132] Others thought the same.[133] It may be that they made too much of this. Foreigners did address British audiences, and were received well despite their thick accents. 'Again and again', observed a reporter at Louis Blanc's first address to an English audience, 'bursts of applause, terminating with the English "Hurrah!" repeated over and over, preceded and followed the speech of the People's friend';[134] and Kossuth was always received enthusiastically – to the annoyance of *The Times*, which however took comfort in the belief 'that a popular meeting will cheer anything that is uttered with emphasis, fluency, and confidence'.[135] And of course there were other ways of subverting than by persuading mobs. After the middle of the century English conservatives took rather more comfort from other considera- tions. *The Times*, for example, reposed great confidence in the protective capabilities of the Metropolitan Police: 'Far be it from us', it said in April 1851, 'to disparage the revolutionary daring of Parisians, but they have never yet encountered constables whose daily duty it is to drag frantic Irishmen from a fifth story to the station-house.'[136] Most of all, however, the mid-Victorians felt their institutions were safe because they felt they were good.

---

[129] 2PD 2, c. 297 (7 July 1820). [130] *Fraser's Magazine*, vol. 43, February 1851, p. 136.
[131] 1PD 34, c. 1060 (11 June 1816). [132] 3PD 98, cc. 581–2 (1 May 1848).
[133] E.g. Fox, *ibid.*, c. 576; and Lord Arundel, *ibid.*, c. 852 (11 May).
[134] *Friend of the People*, 23 February 1851, p. 81.
[135] *The Times*, 14 November 1856, p. 8. G. J. Holyoake called Kossuth 'the chief of the few foreigners who took at once a high place as a public speaker in a new tongue' (*op. cit.*, vol. II, p. 258). See also Otto Zarek, *Kossuth* (1937), p. 256, on his 'amazing mastery of English and his magnificent oratory'; and Jánossy, *op. cit.*, pp. 86–7.
[136] *The Times*, 10 April 1851, p. 5.

This was the nub of it, the fundamental reason why the refugees were so little feared. Few people believed that Britain could be subverted by foreigners, chiefly because few people believed she could be subverted at all. 'People must surely be unconscionable alarmists', said *The Times* in 1851, 'to persuade themselves . . . that Englishmen would submit to be driven by foreigners *when they would not even be led of themselves.*'[137] Where their own Milton and Harrington and More had failed, said W. J. Fox in 1848, was it reasonable to suppose that Frenchmen and Germans could succeed?[138] To believe so, added Sir William Molesworth, was to pay 'a very poor compliment to the institutions of the country and to the feelings of the people'.[139] About those feelings, of the British people towards those in authority over them, the mid-Victorian middle and upper classes felt confident, and also proud. It was an object lesson to foreign rulers, how far the British people, even *en masse*, could be trusted to behave *themselves*, with virtually no coercion from above. *The Times* remarked on it when the French emperor visited London in 1855:

Nowhere else can be beheld such masses of population obedient to order and animated by sentiments calculated to command respect for great communities of men. A thin line of police-constables dotted at intervals along the pavement suffices to keep them all in their places. The presence of a single soldier is unnecessary, and there is something inexpressibly sublime in the confident self-reliance in their own right feeling with which they muster.[140]

It was a sign of the 'good sense and loyalty' which for example Joseph Hume believed reposed in the British people[141] that this should be possible, the maintenance of order and social stability so easy and unforced. In England, the democrat Joseph Cowen told a public meeting in Newcastle in 1858,

Our Queen was safe . . . If all our soldiers and all our policemen were abolished, the Queen might walk through among all ranks of the people and not a soul would harm her, *because she ruled righteously and justly.*[142]

[137] *Ibid., loc. cit.* (my italics).   [138] 3PD 98, c. 576 (1 May 1848).   [139] *Ibid.*, c. 567.
[140] *The Times*, 17 April 1855, p. 9. Cf. *Daily News*, 2 May 1851, p. 4, on the opening of the Great Exhibition: 'The military were nowhere to be seen, the police required a close and searching gaze to find them out.' It was, said the *News*, a 'lesson' for foreign absolutists, as well as for foreign republicans.
[141] 4PD 98, c. 582 (1 May 1848).
[142] *Northern Daily Express*, 24 February 1858, in Cowen Papers, TWAD 634/A552 (my italics). Cf. *Daily News*, 17 April 1851, p. 4: 'In any assemblage of the broad public of England the Queen is more safe from insult, and more certain of the most affectionate respect, than in any knot of officials or diplomatists which it may please this or other courts to acredit or bedizen'; and John Waters, *The Refugees, and other Poems* (1862), p. 20:

> Look at Victoria seated on her throne!
> Her subjects' happy welfare is her own;
> All hearts beat for her, and she cares for them,
> The brightest jewels in her diadem.

This last was really the key factor. The British were loyal and obedient because they were governed well. Ultimately the 'good sense' of the people was attributable to the even better sense of their rulers, who were wise enough not to give them serious cause for dissatisfaction and disaffection.

This equation of satisfaction with social stability was, as we have seen already, fundamental to most mid-Victorians' way of looking at the political world. Basically, they were disinclined to believe in the subvertability of any institution which did not deserve to be subverted. The lever of subversion required a fulcrum, and in the 1850s it was felt that Britain was just too well-governed, her habitual path of reasoned and orderly progress too enlightened, to provide one. This was *The Times'* happy conclusion in April 1848, after England's Chartist version of the Continental revolutionary movement had failed so dismally:

> We shall have our revolution the same as we have had year by year for centuries – the same as that which has affected a greater social improvement in this country than either the revolution of 1789 or that of 1830. We shall go on probably extending and purifying the constituency. We shall make more laws than ever for the people, for the emancipation of industry and the protection of the poor. We shall fill the gulf that yawns between poverty and wealth. We shall give to Ireland the benefit of England's resources and her own. Doubtless the vivid march of revolution abroad will quicken our pace at home; and whatever actual benefits are there attained will shortly be naturalised in our soil. But we shall still move naturally, equably, and surely – not by an alternation of frenzy and trance, but by the uniform and simultaneous action of all parties in the State.[143]

It was this procedure which served to protect Britain from the kinds of challenge currently being mounted to the stability of other European polities. Elsewhere revolutionary subversives might justifiably be feared – as in France, where, said Sir William Molesworth, 'the monarch had been self-seeking and hated . . . the upper classes profligate and despised, and the middle classes indifferent to the institutions of the country'; but not in England, where 'these elements of revolution did not exist'.[144] What made the difference, said W. J. Fox, between England's institutions and the continent's was the former's 'elasticity', which by accommodating them peacefully to necessary change ruled out the threat of *violent* change.[145] Richard Cobden pursued the same idea from another tack: if Britain *were* vulnerable to foreign agitators, then it must be because her institutions

> Her strongest guard, a loyal people's love
> Which will in danger's hour sufficient prove;
> There is no murmur, discontent's unknown,
> Conspiracy has perish'd with a groan,
> Never to rise again; here unity is power,
> And liberty, and faith, and hope's bright shower.

[143] *The Times*, 15 April 1848, p. 4. [144] 3PD 98, cc. 567–8 (1 May 1848). [145] *Ibid.*, c. 574.

were in some way defective: and the remedy was to repair them.[146] Whatever might be wrong, 'subversion', whether imported or home-grown, could not be considered the cause of it. Consequently it was not to be feared.

All this made up a neat and tidy parcel of assumptions, at once moralistic and mechanistic. Revolutionary subversion was a kind of automatic retribution for national wrongdoing. A state which behaved well towards its people, as Britain did, had nothing genuinely to fear from it. Revolu-tionary minorities could rant and infiltrate and plot as they liked, but they would be impotent while the mass of the people, the essential material for an effective revolution, felt themselves justly treated, their reasonable aspirations satisfied. In this very simplistic form the idea was not, of course, universally accepted at any time. Some Englishmen could always be found who had contrary, more continental notions about 'subversion'; like the Earl of Arundel, who knew well (he told Parliament in 1848) 'how easily a small number of men might produce great confusion and bloodshed, and damage to life and property, if so disposed'.[147] Disraeli, too, was inclined to a more 'conspiratorial' view of revolution.[148] After the Orsini plot of 1858, which nearly succeeded, many people were forced to modify the model a little, if they were honest, to allow for the occasional potency, at least, of accidental variables. Nevertheless, it is remarkable how general and deep-rooted this happy notion was after the middle of the century, and perhaps until the 1870s. It may have been a natural corollary of that sort of liberalism, associated with free trade, which liked to picture the political and economic world as a kind of self-regulating mechanism which, if it were only left to itself, would right itself: a comforting philosophy and also, of course, a convenient one from many points of view at the time. The natural tendency of things – so went the argument – was for aberrant growths to wither in a free soil; so that socialism and terrorism eventually could be made to disappear, by means short of repression – indeed by means which were the very antithesis of repression. For liberals this made everything so simple, and so hopeful; it precluded the need for agonised choices – how much restraint to tolerate in the interests of a broader freedom, where to strike the balance; and it boded well for a liberal future. The idea seemed to be that freedom, the absence of artificial restraint, encouraged a healthy growth, which enabled the grow-ing organism better to resist or repel threats to it. Thus freedom of trade would encourage the growth of a healthy economy which would be more fit to withstand any damage done to some sectors of it by the foreign competition which was thereby permitted; and similarly, freedom of association and speech would make for a healthy polity better able to

[146] *Ibid.*, cc. 859–60 (11 May 1848).   [147] *Ibid.*, c. 581 (1 May 1848).
[148] See Roberts, *op. cit.*, pp. 3–7; and B. Disraeli, *Endymion* (1881 edn.), pp. 32–3.

withstand the impact of the pernicious doctrines allowed under it. Both courses of action had risks attached to them: risks which continental governments, and also in the early stages many British politicians, regarded as unacceptable and foolhardy. But in the short- and middle-term, at least, both risks turned out to be, apparently, vindicated by events: which will have reconciled to them some of the waverers. Free trade was vindicated by Britain's phenomenal commercial and industrial growth and prosperity in the 1850s and 1860s, which more than compensated for the sectional damage done by the repeal of the Corn Laws. The other freedoms were vindicated by the fact of Britain's resilience against the revolutionary tide in 1848, when less free countries (except Russia, which was the least free) for a time went under. Just as her prosperity was attributed to her policy of free trade, so was Britain's stability naturally attributed to her free politics. It could have been looked at in another way: free trade seen not as a cause but as a result of Britain's prosperity; free speech as a luxury only made possible by the fact that she was stable. But the Victorians preferred to see themselves as reaping the rewards of their own liberal wisdom. It appealed to their national chauvinism, to believe that they were favoured because they were, essentially, *better*, and that the problems the continent was having were its own reactionary fault.

Of course this was a somewhat idealised way of looking at things, which if it were rigorously tested against the reality might be seen to be defective. In the first place the establishment of liberal freedoms in Britain was by no means complete yet. Continentals were not slow to seize on the most blatant flaw in the garment, which was Ireland;[149] and there were others – Jews, for example, could not yet be Members of Parliament, and trade unionists were very much less free to combine than employers. Even those freedoms which were constitutionally and juridicially established could in practice be made less available to some men than to others, by imperfections in the administration of the law and inequalities of access to it. Working-class radical leaders tended to be less impressed than middle-class liberals with the range of effective freedoms they could draw on, and also with the claim that was made, mainly by the middle and upper classes, that the British people were disinclined to revolution because they were satisfied with things as they were. Their own experience of 1848, and the years before, suggested to them that their own poor showing then had had more to do with force and the threat of force by the authorities, than with liberty; and that the people were submissive now not because they were contented, but because they were cowed. (This view was also held by the Metropolitan Police Commissioner, who claimed that at the 1851 Exhibi-

---

[149] De Bussy, *op. cit.*, pp. 39–40.

tion popular trouble had only been averted by the precautions he had taken against it.)[150] Working-class radicals also tended not to accept that the middle and upper classes' new-found tolerance was as hardy a plant as was painted; the tool of repression, they suspected, was always there in the background, kept well sharpened, and ready for use if needed – if the 'consent', the voluntary submission, of the working classes were ever withdrawn; so that the fact that its use was for the time being relaxed said nothing significant about the nature and intentions of the ruling power.[151] But even if it were taken entirely on its own terms, the liberal model had fundamental flaws in it: some of which were revealed by the economic slump of the 1870s, which could be seen as a failure of laissez-faire; and also by the working-class radical revival of the 1880s which, if it was not to invalidate the model, took a deal of explaining to reconcile with it. As yet, however, these clouds were far over the horizon. In the sunnier 1850s and 1860s the complacent liberal assumption was a fair one, or at least a natural one. At a time of burgeoning national prosperity, which for the moment it was not unreasonable to assume would benefit all classes; a time also of relative quiescence on the working-class radical front, with Chartism in discredited disarray, and its socialist successor still as yet gestating; and a time when both these happy circumstances were dramatically highlighted by the starkly contrasting picture abroad: to such a time this complacent, optimistic philosophy was well suited. Nearly everyone seemed to share it to some extent: at any rate nearly every significant organ of opinion, of whatever political colour, liked to think that Britain was impervious to subversion because she was enlightened, and the continental powers par-ticularly vulnerable to it, because they were not. It was a feeling which was peculiar to the 1850s and sixties, and never so ubiquitous before or after; but it was powerful then. And to a great extent, for that time, it was justified. In most ways which were important, Britain was during those years demonstrably and significantly more 'free' than any of the other great European powers; her people more acquiescent and 'moderate'; and her

[150] Mayne to Waddington, n.d. [after 5 June 1851], in PRO MEPO 2/92; and see Viscountess Enfield, *op. cit.*, vol. 1 p. 389.

[151] A modern writer has made the same point. 'The authority of the state rests on the duality of force and consent, but at different historical moments one or other tends to predomi-nate. During the first half of the nineteenth century this authority relied primarily on the use of overt force, but with the emergence of liberal-democracy, it came to rest increas-ingly upon consent. . .

'The nature of this "consent" must be understood. It was gained from the working class by a combination of violence and ideological attrition – against the political movements of the class and against its individual members, both in the factory and outside in daily community life. There is no way, however, in which this consent can ever be assumed to prevail automatically – for no amount of mystification can veil the real nature of the wage-labour relation or the revolutionary potential of their class': T. Bunyan, *The History and Practice of the Political Police in Britain* (1976), p. 301. This is not a claim which can be tested empirically.

ruling classes, for whatever reason, 'safer' from the kinds of perils which threatened, seriously, the ruling classes of the continent.

To the dire warnings which came to them from the continent, therefore, of the subversion which the refugees could set under way in Britain – which continental powers believed should justify Britain, in her own interest, banding together with the emperors in their mutual protection society against the forces of revolution – the British turned a deaf ear. They failed to see that Britain's freedom was as vulnerable as the emperors' despotisms, that the cancer could take hold of her healthy body as easily as their poorly ones; and by and large their self-confidence was justified. They did not think to protect themselves from the foreign virus in their midst because they did not have to; they were *not* part of the continental system; the Channel *was* an ideological frontier; her political system *was* more resilient than theirs, and her revolutionary tinder damper. For most Britons the danger of revolution being fomented by foreigners was the least of their worries, and after the spring of 1851 it was scarcely ever thought of.

But of course when continentals complained to Britain about the activities of the refugees there, they were thinking less of her interest than of theirs. The main purport of their complaints, as we have seen, was that Britain was harbouring men who were doing *them* harm: which it was claimed was inconsistent with international amity. This was a thing which it might have been thought they were the best judges of, but even on this there were those in Britain who thought they knew better. There were of course many who accepted the continentals' version of events – rather more than those who accepted their version of the harm the refugees were doing to Britain. These were usually found amongst those who had a particular hatred of the refugees, or a particular liking for them: men like Lord Lyndhurst who openly sympathised with the continentals' irritation,[152] or men like Harney who needed to believe that the refugees' efforts were effective and wished them well of it.[153] Between these two extremes, however, there was a broad measure of agreement that foreign rulers and foreign refugees both exaggerated the latter's effectiveness: either in the sense of the trouble that could follow from their activities, or in the sense of the attribution to them of real responsibility for that trouble. This in turn had a bearing on the response which 'public opinion' in Britain made to the charges and demands of continental governments on the question of the refugees.

A degree of scepticism about the political potency of the refugees was

---

[152] E.g. 3PD 124, cc. 1046–58 (4 March 1853); Walsh in 3PD 119, c. 518 (1 April 1852); *Quarterly Review*, vol. 93 (June 1853), pp. 138–42.
[153] See Harney's *Democratic Review*, *passim*, and *Red Republican*, *passim*.

natural, and in part clearly justified. Continental governments were very often less than scrupulous in supporting with solid or even convincing circumstantial evidence the charges they showered on the refugees: too willing to see evildoing where none existed: too eager whenever two refugees whispered together immediately to smell cordite, and when they met in threes and fours to see the sinister tendrils of the Secret Societies there; too apt possibly to *provoquer* or even to fabricate crimes, in order to blacken the reputations of their enemies. In Britain there was consequently a widespread distrust of continental motives and methods. This distrust was strengthened by a habit of mind among the upper and middle classes which was genuinely less suspicious and less frightened than the continentals – which refused to believe, for example, that violent talk was necessarily the same as violent action or even violent intent; which was less impressed by the power of the written word to subvert, and by the subvertability of the ignorant masses, than were continentals; and which needed material proof of the worst before it would believe it. If the continental conservative attitude towards the refugees tended to paranoia, there may have been on the other hand something a little naïve about this English attitude: about the attitude of those men who never could see, for example, as Lord Dudley Stuart professed he could not in 1852, any sign of 'conspiracy dangerous to the Governments of Europe'.[154] How could a man pose a threat to a country when he was so far away from it? was a question which was often asked, supposedly rhetorically.[155] *The Times*, which thought that the danger to foreign governments from the refugees had been 'greatly exaggerated', claimed that

A foreign politician in London is almost *hors de combat*. Surrounded by the unsympathetic, the busy, or the incompetent, with few friends except the compassionate or the quixotic, he can compose elaborate treatises, fanciful theories, vapouring exhortations, and harmless philippics. With his tongue, his eye, and the whole man in exile, his pen retains but little of its power.[156]

The *Morning Chronicle* agreed: 'isolated as they are, meeting with more charity than countenance from the English population, we doubt if they could be any where where they could work less harm to the governments that dread them'.[157] Lord Truro believed that, while they *meant* harm to their own governments, they were nevertheless 'in truth, destitute of all means to effect any such evil intentions which they may form'.[158] Of course they might go back, and get up to mischief on the continent. But in

[154] 3PD 119 c. 491 (1 April 1852).
[155] E.g. *Standard*, 25 February 1852, p. 2: 'in what possible way can they affect the security of the Austrian Government while sitting in England. . .?'
[156] *The Times*, 19 September 1850, p. 4.   [157] *Morning Chronicle*, 3 April 1851, p. 5.
[158] 3PD 124, cc. 1056–7 (4 March 1853). Cf. Lord Beaufort in 3PD 119 cc. 660–1, 663–4 (5 April 1852); and *Punch*, vol. 22 p. 2 (January 1852): 'no chickens are produced in England from what may be termed Gallic cocks eggs'.

A DISCUSSION FORUM (!) AS IMAGINED BY OUR
VOLATILE FRIENDS.

4. Continental and British views of the refugee question: from *Punch*,
March 1858.

A DISCUSSION FORUM (!) AS IT IS IN REALITY.

Affectionately Presented to our French Neighbours.

that event, said *The Times* again, the mischief was done there, not in England; the continental powers should blame themselves for letting them in, not Britain for sheltering them; indeed if they were being consistent they would be pressing Britain 'not so much to expel the refugees, as to detain them here'; which was a nice point.[159] The argument had the appearance of being a reasonable one, but to continentals, who felt they *knew* how much harm the refugees could do to them, it will have seemed unreal. The innocence of the Englishman's viewpoint clearly derived from his own limited national experience, which recently had known little of 'conspiracy' and assassination and the like, and could have no idea of their potency. Lord Cowley, who as a British diplomat in Europe for thirty years was familiar with both points of view, saw this. 'The fact is', he wrote to the Foreign Secretary in 1852,

the longer I live abroad, the more I am convinced that insamuch as I never yet met with a Foreigner who really understood England & the English character, so I suppose that we are not more wise in our generation, & that we are apt to measure others by ourselves. You will meet now with few people abroad who are not convinced that we are doomed to be revolutionized by Mazzini & Co. We, on the other hand, cannot understand the alarm with which a few hundred Refugees & half a dozen violent Newspapers inspire half the Govts. of Europe, & yet both may be wrong. We *may* be able to support the exciting language of the foreign democrats, who overrun us, but there may be danger in setting before excitable people like the French & Italians or indeed the Germans, such doctrines as those preached & printed in Switzerland.[160]

It was this mutual incomprehension which, on both sides of the Channel during the 1850s, gave rise, as we shall see, to so much distrust.

Blanket disbelief, however, was not the most common response to tales from abroad of refugee wrongdoing. If most people doubted some of them, others they had to credit, and in most cases to deplore; no one could seriously question, for example, that Mazzini, if he was not guilty of all the charges levelled at him by his enemies, was nevertheless up to something conspiratorial, after the Milan *attentat* of 1853 if not sooner. After 1853, in fact, the British view of these things became a good deal more realistic. Refugee wrongdoing was much more widely acknowledged, and, as we have seen, deplored. It was very generally recognised that there were limits which should be set to the activities of revolutionaries in exile: a line to be drawn between the proper enjoyment of the right of asylum, and its 'abuse'. 'So long as the unfortunate fly to the altar', said *The Times* in March 1853,

---

[159] *The Times*, 5 March 1853, p. 5; and cf. *ibid.*, 28 January 1858 p. 6 and 2 February 1858 p. 8; and the *Globe*, 18 January 1858, p. 2: 'It is not in London that plots against foreign Powers can both be formed and executed. It is with these Powers that must rest primarily the duty of vigilance for their own safety.'

[160] Cowley to Malmesbury (copy), 14 March 1852: Cowl. P. PRO FO 519/209 pp. 13–14. Cf. *supra*, p. 51.

and confine themselves to it, they may hope at least for safety, and may even live to conquer; but, if they forthwith mount the towers of the sacred structure, man its battlements, and turn it into a fortress, they simply draw on it the fire of the enemy, and involve the building and its innocent inmates in their own ruin[161]

– which was the reason for drawing the line. Where exactly it should be drawn was a matter of controversy. Those who were most hostile to the refugees and most sympathetic to the European autocrats drew it very low indeed: Sir John Walsh, for example, held that refugees only really fulfilled the obligations of their asylum when they were 'satisfied to remain quiet, and to sleep under the shade of the British oak'.[162] *The Economist*, whose view of this was similar, acknowledged that it might be frustrating for the refugees.

It is hard, no doubt, that they should be prohibited from the great solace of an exile life; it is painful to feel that their hands are tied, their time wasted, and their faculties idle and rusting; it is irritating to think that they can no longer aid their fellow-countrymen who have remained at home in their struggles for the common cause:– *but these are the tacit conditions on which a place of refuge has been afforded them.*[163]

Others were more permissive. The *Morning Chronicle*, for example, while it deprecated 'downright conspiracy', would allow what it called 'mere agitation': though it recognised that the ground between them was 'debateable'.[164] *The Times* in 1864 was able to be rather more precise. 'With the organisation on our soil of mere schemes of political revolution, however questionable', it said, 'it is difficult for us to interfere . . . But there is a clear and broad distinction between offences which are only political crimes, however grave, and acts which are direct violations of the criminal law of any civilized country.'[165] That was a convenient formula because it merely disallowed activities which were prohibited anyway under British law. It was probably the consensus view.[166] It tolerated a wider range of activities than suited many continental governments. But it acknowledged too that certain refugee activities were wrong, and that asylum was a thing which could be 'abused'.

It still did not follow, however, that for those 'abuses' of the asylum Britain granted to the refugees she herself was in any way responsible. In the first place, it was widely considered to be impertinent to hold Britain

---

[161] *The Times*, 1 March 1853, p. 4. Cf. *Morning Chronicle*, 16 April 1853, p. 6: 'We are entitled to expect that all who avail themselves of our hospitality will be satisfied with the security which they enjoy, and will not make this country the focus of hostile enterprizes against their political antagonists.' [162] 3PD 119, c. 518 (1 April 1852).

[163] *The Economist*, quoted in *Littell's Living Age* (Boston, Mass.), 2nd series, vol. i (1853), pp. 342–3. [164] *Morning Chronicle*, 2 March 1853, p. 5.

[165] *The Times*, 15 January 1864, p. 9.

[166] Every national daily newspaper in the 1850s acknowledged that asylum carried 'duties' and could be 'abused'. Working-class radical weeklies like *Reynolds's* tended to regard as permissible a wider range of activities than did the 'respectable' dailies, on the grounds that they were provoked and excused by the violence of the despots.

accountable for the actions of men the complainants themselves had sent there. 'We don't invite these people', said *The Times*; France had driven them to Britain because she could not manage them, and now demanded that Britain 'keep a better watch on these people than the French did themselves': which was hardly reasonable.[167] 'It is by direct act of the president of the French Republic' – and a president, it was pointed out more than once, who had himself benefited from Britain's asylum, and himself abused it[168] – 'that these refugees are living among us; and we are at a loss to understand how governments which have just banished their political adversaries to a land where all control over their persons and opinions must cease, can address themselves to this country, as if we were to aid them in the work of persecution'.[169] 'Now, just fancy the impudence', commented a Scottish newspaper in 1858, ' . . . of continental Governments shovelling these wretched men upon us, and then flying into a rage because we keep them!'[170] In the second place, asked the sceptics: how could Britain be held to blame for conspiracies which she had not provoked, and did not encourage? 'What lands produced this legion of incendiaries?' asked *The Times* in 1853. 'Who bore them, who nurtured them, who drove them forth into insurrection and crime?'[171] It was their own countries which had made them into assassins, said W. J. Fox of Orsini and his friends, and not England, whose atmosphere discouraged it.[172] If men, said the Liberal M.P. Richard Monckton Milnes, 'were in any degree affected by the opinions of those around them – if there was such a thing as a moral atmosphere – the last place in which conspiracies to assassinate would be formed was in this country'.[173]

When such a man found himself no longer an object of general surprise – when he found that the policemen at the ends of the streets did not know even his name – when he found that, instead of exciting universal fame and admiration, his name hardly ever appeared in a newspaper, or was mentioned at a public meeting – there was a moral exercised in that position of a refugee which ought to moderate and temper his opinion.[174]

If there was any violence still left in the man after a course of such therapy, then it was all the more the fault of those towards whom he harboured the violence, for implanting it so deeply in him.

So was the blame returned firmly on to the head of Britain's accusers. As a pamphleteer wrote in 1858:

The Government of the Emperor has stifled all constitutional opposition to its power, and foreclosed all means of legitimate appeal against its acts. A Govern-

---

[167] *The Times*, 4 February 1858, p. 8.
[168] E.g. 3PD 119 c. 492 (Stuart, 1 April 1852); 3PD 148, cc. 763, 961 (Roebuck, 5 and 8 February, 1858).   [169] *The Times*, 9 February 1852, p. 4.
[170] *North British Daily Mail* (Glasgow), quoted in *Reynolds's Newpaper*, 31 January 1858, p. 13.
[171] *The Times*, 5 March 1853. p. 5.   [172] 3PD 148, cc. 947–8 (8 February 1858).
[173] *Ibid.*, c. 1027 (9 February 1858).   [174] 3PD 119, c. 488 (1 April 1852).

ment, placing itself in such a position, virtually declares that it can only be reached by the secret and dastard hand of the assassin; and thus becomes remotely responsible for the crimes against which it appeals.[175]

'The risk of assassination', said *The Times* in 1864, 'is one peculiar to sovereigns who are beyond constitutional checks, and will always be in inverse proportion to the liberty of speech and legislative action.'[176] The implication of this was that those states which complained about conspiracies against them would have no conspiracies at all if they were run as well as Britain. This was a favourite British riposte to the continentals' charges. It was of course a natural corollary of the theory which attributed Britain's security against subversion to her national virtue: if that were so, then if other countries were vulnerable to subversion it must be because they were bad. In the distant past, explained the *Examiner* in March 1853, 'conspiracy' really had been 'a powerful and efficient mode of operation'. But in modern times,

with populations of millions to appeal to, depend upon, disgust, or conciliate, anything like individual conspiracy must dwindle into insignificance, unless it be identified with that great conspiracy into which a whole people silently enter without consulting each other, and from the mere tacit sympathy of common resentment and disaffection.[177]

This total rejection of a 'conspiracy theory' of revolution was shared by others: for example by the Liberal *Daily News*, which regarded the idea that insurrections could be caused by 'conspiracies' as 'ridiculous': 'The only dangerous conspiracy', it held, 'is that of common right and common sense, revolting by electric unanimity against ignorance, absurdity, and oppression.'[178] It followed that, in the words of the *Examiner* again,

If rulers would but look to this large conspiracy and appease it, without idly inquiring who are its chiefs, for in fact it has no chiefs, they would be doing something towards the consolidation of their thrones.[179]

Consequently, wrote Henry Greville in his diary in 1853,

instead of venting their indignation and ill humour in abuse of us and our institutions, it would be better for [other Powers] if they would set about improving their own systems of government, and endeavour to remove the real grounds there are for discontent and disaffection.[180]

'Let Louis Napoleon', said the *Daily News*, ' . . . rule wisely, fairly, honestly, decorously; and he may defy revolutions, be they red or white'.[181] To *The Times* this somewhat patronising point had a particular

---

[175] 'An Englishman out of Office', *A Voice from England in answer to 'L'Empereur Napoleon III et l'Angleterre'* (1858), p. 22.   [176] *The Times*, 14 January 1864, p. 8.
[177] *Examiner*, 5 March 1853, quoted in *Littell's Living Age*, 2nd ser., vol. I (1853), p. 343.
[178] *Daily News*, 3 April 1851, p. 4.
[179] *Examiner, loc. cit.*   [180] Viscountess Enfield, *op. cit.*, vol. II, p. 41.   [181] *Daily News, loc. cit.*

appeal. Why, it asked, 'are they so afraid of such frothy declamations as Kossuth's, and such visionary schemes as Mazzini's, were it not for the unsoundness and unpopularity of their own position at home?'

It must be a very explosive state of things which can be kindled by so mere a spark as a letter from some unfortunate gentleman in his lodgings at Camden-town . . . Proclamations without men, without money, without arms . . . are only waste paper, and need excite no concern, unless, by the fault of the Governments against which they are aimed, they should tell some bitter truths.

'A really good Government', *The Times* concluded: like Britain's ('we are not at the mercy of any traitor or visionary'), 'can afford not to mind them.'[182] It was a highly seductive argument. It played on the Englishman's national *amour propre*. It liberated him from ultimate responsibility for *anything* done by refugees to harm foreign governments, and consequently from the moral necessity of doing anything about it. It might be thought to be a somewhat fragile position: viable only for so long as the domestic complacency on which it was built remained intact – for as long as the British themselves felt safe from 'subversion'. If ever they began not to, then it would crumble, and the continent might begin to expect more sympathy from Britain, and more help. In these days, however, between effective Chartism and an effective British socialism, when Britons of every class and station appeared so satisfied with their lot, and so many continentals discontented with theirs, it seemed to be amply corroborated by experience, and by recent history.

It also fitted in well with Englishmen's feelings about events abroad. It has often been remarked[183] how much public interest there was in foreign affairs in Britain in the 1850s: more interest in *European* affairs, probably, than at any time afterwards until the 1930s. This was an unusual phenomenon, because generally foreign politics was considered to be a fairly specialist interest, particularly by the specialists themselves, who preferred it this way. One reason why they preferred it was that when the public did take an interest in foreign politics it was usually a different kind of interest from their own. In particular, they tended to view it from a moral perspective which foreign policy-makers generally – not always, as we shall see – believed to be dangerously irrelevant to what in their view should have been the main concern of diplomacy. In the 1850s the particular kind of morality which they applied to foreign policy was a political morality (at other times it might be religious, or humanitarian). In the eyes of the British public continental affairs appeared at that time as a drama whose main theme was the struggle between absolutism on one hand, and constitutional liberty on the other. (Socialism and democracy, which the

[182] *The Times*, 28 February 1853, p. 4.
[183] E.g. Derek Beales, *England and Italy 1859–60* (1961), pp. 9–14.

absolutists saw in the place of constitutional liberty as their main adversary, was regarded in Britain, as we have seen, in a less central rôle: as a kind of affliction which beset absolutists as a result of their intransigence in the face of constitutionalism.) In this conflict, though there were some who took the absolutists' side, the overwhelming weight of British public opinion was against them. This was true not only of liberals and radicals but also of conservatives, who were sometimes shocked by different things, but could generally find something to shock them in the conduct of Austria or Russia (sequestrations of property by Austria in Lombardy, for example – an activity hitherto more usually associated with 'reds' – seem to have appalled some conservatives more than did the taking of lives).[184] For whatever particular reason, it was generally felt that a vast political and ideological gulf yawned between Britain and her neighbours. Britain was a 'free country'; the continent, apart from a few insignificant liberal enclaves, despotic, autocratic and arbitrary. The difference was so great it was supposed to make each side incomprehensible to the other, as if they were different species. 'The mind of Russia and Austria', said the *Morning Chronicle* in 1852, 'does not interpenetrate that of England . . . England and Austria do not live by the same idea.'[185] It went without saying that the 'idea' Russia lived by was far inferior to Britain's: regressive and unenlightened. This broad liberal view of the constitutional arrangements of European states was shared by many conservatives, who by now had mostly been captured by the idea that things naturally *moved*, so that the truly conservative thing was to move with them. Despotism, the stifling of legitimate liberal aspirations, was not only morally wrong: it was also inexpedient.

Some statesmen shared this kind of anti-continental feeling too, or managed to exploit it: as, most notoriously, Palmerston did for a while. Most of them, however, deplored it, either because they had no sympathy for it, or because they felt that such considerations should have no bearing on diplomacy, which was a game between national interests best played, like chess, without emotion. Lord Aberdeen, whose own relative Austrophilia was unpopular in the country, wrote once to his friend Princess Lieven 'how grossly ignorant the people of this country are in relation to foreign matters':[186] which may have been true, and indeed inevitable in a field where, despite the proliferation of 'Blue Books' which was a feature of the

---

[184] E.g. *Morning Chronicle*, 10 March 1853, p. 4 and 15 April 1853, p. 4; *The Times* 8 March 1853, p. 5, 12 March 1853, p. 6 and 25 March 1853, p. 4. The *Daily News* on 9 March 1853 (p. 4) remarked on this sudden revulsion by the Tory press against Austria, as soon as property, as distinct from mere lives, was involved.

[185] *Morning Chronicle*, 2 April 1852, p. 4.

[186] Aberdeen to Princess Lieven, 29 October 1851, in E. Jones Parry, *op. cit.*, vol. II, p. 598.

period,[187] reliable data were so scanty.[188] Queen Victoria in 1851 attributed the popular 'Kossuth-fever' of the time to '*ignorance* of the man in whom they see a second Washington, when the fact is that he is an ambitious and *rapacious* humbug'.[189] As well as ignorance, this popular feeling was also clearly to a large extent based on, or at least drew upon, other strong emotions which were independent of a strict assessment of the politics of the various continental states. Some of these emotions were fairly positive, like the quite strong Italophilia which survived in many quarters from the 1830s and 1840s.[190] Generally, however, popular feelings about foreign affairs were – as they usually are – negative phenomena, more *against* things disapproved of on the continent than *for* anything. They included anti-monarchism, anti-Napoleonism, Russophobia, anti-catholicism, and a general all-weather xenophobia. Such feelings were widespread in the 1850s, strongly-held, and, as we shall see, a force to be reckoned with by governments concerned for their own survival.

They also had a bearing upon the public's attitude towards questions which involved the refugees: much more so than any opinions the public had about the character and politics and activities of the refugees themselves. Those who disapproved of continental régimes, who were in the majority, were likely as a consequence of that disapproval automatically to sympathise with the refugees, or to want to excuse them, or at least to side with them when they were attacked by those continental régimes. The Lombard sequestrations, for example, led the *Morning Chronicle* to view the cause of the Italian refugees in a new light: 'Utterly as we must condemn the course pursued by Mazzini and his coadjutors', it said in 1853 when news of the sequestrations first came to it, 'it must at least be confessed that, if ever there was a cause to justify armed resistance to a tyrannical Government, it is that of the Italian race.'[191] Russophobia and anti-Napoleonism, which were creatures of venerable origins in British life, redounded to the advantage of the Poles, and of the French republican enemies of the third Napoleon. Fears that the new French empire was about to launch an invasion of Britain in retribution for the failure of the first were a constant feature of the 1850s, and, as we shall see, helped considerably to strengthen the resolve of Englishmen to resist the emperor's demands on the subject of the French refugees, who by them-

---

[187] H. W. V. Temperley and L. M. Penson, *A Century of Diplomatic Blue Books, 1814–1914* (1938), p. vii.

[188] The radical *Weekly Dispatch* generally refused to discuss foreign affairs on the grounds that, due to the undemocratic way in which foreign policy was formulated, accurate information on which alone reliable comment could be based was impossible to come by (20 February 1853, p. 113).

[189] Victoria to King Leopold, 31 October 1851: RA Y77/26.

[190] See Miriam B. Urban, *op. cit.*; and *supra*, pp. 69–70.

[191] *Morning Chronicle*, 10 March 1853, p. 4.

selves could manage to engender hardly a spark of sympathy among the British. Anti-catholicism, which in these days of the 'papal aggression' was probably the strongest of all popular phobias in Britain, benefited all refugees who were in opposition to catholic monarchs, which of course most of them were, but particularly the Italians who were struggling against the temporal powers of Pio Nono. (Of all the refugees in England in the 1850s the most popular was undoubtedly the Italian apostate friar Father Gavazzi, who earned his bread by entertaining large audiences with scurrilous anti-papist propaganda.)[192] For whatever reason, more Englishmen probably disapproved of continental régimes than at almost any other time in history; and more disapproved of them, certainly, than would have had any truck with the wilder refugees' opinions, if they knew them. This made it fortunate for the latter that when the former's opinion was called for, it was usually on occasions when this other question obtruded.

Of course at this time, as at nearly any other, it was and is impossible to say how widely these kinds of feelings really were spread amongst the population as a whole. Newspapers, which are one possible guide, were only read by a small minority, and written and owned by far smaller ones: probably the only opinions the press truly reflected were those of the politicians it purported to preach to, but who in fact influenced it more than it influenced them.[193] M.P.s themselves were only elected by minorities; popular meetings could be filled to overflowing while only attracting a minority: and none of these minorities was ever necessarily representative of the remainder. Nevertheless, though they could be only a rough indication of the opinion of that section of the public which was interested and vocal, these signs in the 1850s pointed unambiguously to a considerable fund of popular sympathy in England for the causes the refugees stood for. For anyone who might doubt it, there were dramatic

---

[192] See Basil Hall, 'Alessandro Gavazzi: a Barnabite Friar and the Risorgimento', in *Studies in Church History*, vol. 12 (Oxford, 1975): especially pp. 342–56.

  Religion had another effect: it tended to put the Irish against the refugees, when they might otherwise have been expected to feel an identity of (nationalist) interest with them. Thus the Holborn riots of 1853 between Irish and Italians (*supra*, p. 43), and the 'Garibaldi' riots of 1862, when Irish papists fought English anti-clericalists in Garibaldi's name (see Sheridan Gilley, 'The Garibaldi Riots of 1862', in *Historical Journal*, vol. 16 no. 4). The situation at this time of Irish catholic nationalism, out of step as it was with every other European nationalism, was scarcely more anomalous than the attitude of English liberalism, which professed sympathy with distant nationalisms but appeared curiously blind to the virtues of this home-grown variety.

  At a popular level some of the more demonstrative manifestations of sympathy with refugee causes may have been more anti-catholic and anti-Irish than genuinely pro-liberal: this was almost certainly true over Garibaldi in the 1860s. Religion, however, was not a vital ingredient; it appears to have played almost no part, for example, in the Kossuth demonstrations of 1851.

[193] See Keith A. P. Sandiford, *Great Britain and the Schleswig-Holstein Question 1848–1864* (Toronto, 1975), p. 16.

demonstrations of it early in the decade. In September 1850, for example, Baron Julius von Haynau, the Austrian commander-in-chief who had suppressed the Hungarian rising the previous year, made a private visit to Barclay and Perkins' Brewery in London, and was set upon by a mob of workers: to the joy of radical leaders, who had not expected them to be so internationally politically conscious – 'I confess', wrote Harney, 'I did not anticipate such an outburst of feeling in opposition to that sanguinary monster . . . Least of all did I imagine that the class of brewers' operatives, coal-heavers, &c. &c., would take the initiative in a work so holy.'[194] To Feargus O'Connor this incident proved, what had been doubtful before, 'that the masses do take a deep, earnest, and living interest in the struggles of their oppressed brethren everywhere'.[195] In October the next year the vast and enthusiastic welcome which was given on his arrival at Southampton to Kossuth, and then to his almost imperial progress across England, was further evidence of public sympathy: and of a broader-based sympathy, probably, than was revealed by the Haynau affair.[196] Garibaldi when he visited England in 1864 was fêted in much the same way.[197] To the authorities such demonstrations were puzzling, and diplomatically highly embarrassing. Some tried to dismiss them as the activities of a mere 'rabble', or a minority of trouble-makers:[198] which however it was difficult to do convincingly in the cases of Kossuth or Garibaldi, especially when for a time Lord Palmerston himself itched to join in.[199] The feeling was there: rooted in genuine humanitarianism, or sympathy for oppressed nationalities, or hatred of autocracy, or xenophobia, or whatever. It came out too in the popular literature of the period, which by no means neglected revolutions abroad as it managed to neglect foreign revolutionaries in England, and generally was on the side of the angels of progress.[200] Whatever the reasons for it, it seemed genuine, and spontaneous, and widespread.

For the main body of the refugees it did not necessarily signify any particular warmth of feeling towards *them*. In the first place, this fêting of the more prominent of them was very selective, confined mainly to those

[194] *Red Republican*, 14 September 1850, p. 97.   [195] *Northern Star*, 7 September 1850, p. 5.
[196] It was on the advice of middle-class radical friends like Cobden that, in order to ingratiate himself with the English, Kossuth tempered his utterances to their conservative taste; including in his first speech, for example, some flattering words about Queen Victoria (see Jánossy, *op. cit.*, pp. 85–6); which however did nothing to ingratiate him with the Queen herself, who according to Charles Greville (*Memoirs*, 1896–8 edn., vol. VI p. 423) was most put out by 'seeing him received at Manchester with as much enthusiasm as attended her own visit to that place'. The best modern account of Kossuth's visit is in Jánossy, *op. cit.*, chs. 14–16; the fullest contemporary account (with engravings) in the *Illustrated London News*, 1, 8, 15 and 22 November, 1851.   [197] *Vide infra*, p. 203.
[198] 'This movement', said *The Times* (10 November 1851, p. 4) of the Kossuth demonstrations, 'has only touched the scum of the nation'; and cf. Charles Greville, *op. cit.*, vol. VI p. 423: 'not one individual of station or consideration has gone near him'.
[199] *Supra*, p. 56.   [200] Rudman, *op. cit.*, *passim*.

5. Kossuth's reception at Southampton and at the Guildhall, London, in September 1851, pictured by the *Illustrated London News*.

who seemed best to fit the middle class's favourite pattern of the romantic nationalist – not extended, for example, to Ledru-Rollin when he came or any of his ilk; and was very temporary, insecurely based, perhaps, on mere 'curiosity, and a love of lion-hunting',[201] and quickly dropped when it became unfashionable: sustaining Kossuth only during his first weeks in England, and then soon forgetting him. In the second place, it was not as refugees that they were fêted, but as heroes. On the occasions when it happened, in fact, neither Kossuth nor Garibaldi was coming to Britain strictly as a refugee, but only as a visitor. Likewise when Haynau was attacked, it was not as the enemy of the refugees but as the enemy of the Hungarians and of struggling nationality.[202] Of course there was a connexion; and of course those who most approved of the demonstrations were probably those who were warmest towards the refugees, and those who disapproved most were those who were coolest towards them. But it was by no means certain that all or even many of the people who expressed such enthusiasm for Kossuth, Garibaldi, the Barclay's draymen and the causes they represented felt similarly towards the other foreign represen- tatives of those causes who lived amongst them. In logic perhaps they should have done; but in practice there may have been a wealth of differ- ence between celebrating a popular hero, or howling down a tyrant, and the more mundane cause of the poor, mysterious, motley refugees. 'We have received the glorious chiefs of Democracy with beating hearts, brightening eyes, and eloquent shouts', said Harney in 1852; ' . . . but, amid our enthusiasm for them, let us not forget the lowly soldiers who have fought in the ranks, and who, though nameless, yet plead with the eloquence of wounds and scars.'[203]

Nevertheless, though the public feeling which was indicated by such demonstrations was not extended to the refugees *as* refugees, it could be harnessed in support of the refugees, quite incidentally, in certain circum- stances. For the refugees as such, very few people felt strongly one way or the other, because very few people had any close experience or knowledge of them. When they expressed any significant feeling about them, there- fore, that feeling was very rarely formed by a consideration of the objec- tive merits of their case (or cases), but was generally a corollary of their very much stronger feelings about matters which were related, but dis- tinct. And when they were called upon to express their feelings about the refugees, it was nearly always, for reasons we shall discover, at times when those other related matters came to the forefront.

Feeling as they did about the continent, and about themselves, it is not

---

[201] 'Miss A. M. Birkbeck', *art. cit.*, p. 92.
[202] Although later the *Quarterly Review* (vol. 93, 1853, p. 135) was to claim that the riot had been 'prompted and paid for' by the refugees.   [203] *Star*, 15 May 1852, p. 4.

surprising that Englishmen tended not to brook easily criticism of them-selves emanating from the continent. It was therefore highly significant that when the refugee question came up as an issue in British politics it was invariably as a result of initiatives from the continent which seemed to imply criticism of Britain; which fact may have had more effect on the public reaction to the refugee question than did anything else. The British were not particularly bothered about the refugees; the continent was. It was natural therefore that it should be the continent which brought up the subject, usually in the form of a complaint. What the public was asked to react to, therefore, was not primarily any opinion or activity of any refugee, but a complaint from a foreign power against Britain for tolerat-ing a refugee opinion or activity; a criticism therefore of her own policies and institutions, sometimes backed up with a demand, or even a threat. This made a considerable difference to the British response. The main issue was not the refugees' conduct, about which most people might have concurred with the complainants, but Britain's own. To many people what was at stake were some of the most fundamental of their liberties – not merely asylum, but others too; those liberties which, in their eyes, were what marked Britain off from the great powers of the continent, and gave her her vast superiority over them.

It was this superiority which had given rise to the problem in the first place. As the *Morning Advertiser* proclaimed proudly in 1853: 'It is because there is no other spot in Europe hallowed by the perpetual presence of Freedom, that our soil swarms with refugees.' It was for that reason too, it added, that Britain was so 'hated and abhorred by the Absolutist Govern-ments of Europe' – which fact therefore was not to be regretted too much: 'It would indeed be a sad symptom were they to begin to regard us with friendly feelings.'[204] The *Daily News* thought the same:

it is the country itself – England, and its habits, and its ways of thinking, that are odious and intolerable to the Austrians. We have the misfortune to be a constitu-tional people, and to enjoy the liberties of association and the press. For these qualities Louis Napoleon dreads and Prince Schwarzenberg detests us.[205]

As well as being the source of the problem this made it impossible for Britain to solve it in any of the ways the continent demanded. For Euro-pean countries it might have been an easy matter to do the things they asked of Britain, involving merely minor alterations in their laws and procedures, if any were required at all. For Britain it was a much bigger thing, because her national institutions were so fundamentally different from theirs, so much more 'free'. It is important to understand precisely in what this 'freedom' consisted, insofar as it related to the refugee ques-

[204] *Morning Advertiser*, 1 March 1853, p. 4.   [205] *Daily News*, 27 February 1852, p. 4.

tion.[206] It was not merely a matter of what the *Advertiser* called the 'right of free ingress, sojourn, and egress',[207] though this 'right' was vigorously defended throughout the 1850s, as one of Britain's age-old constitutional freedoms. By some the 'right to exercise hospitality' was regarded, as it was for example by the *Standard*, as 'an inherent natural right – the boundary which the merciful Lord of heaven and earth has imposed upon the cruelty of man'.[208] Panegyrics to the principle of asylum were offered as a matter of course by most Englishmen who discussed the refugee problem in the 1850s.[209] But this was not the only 'freedom' in question. Tied up with it were far older and more fundamental British freedoms: matters which, in the view of the *Morning Chronicle*, 'went to the very root of the primary rights of man'.[210] Two obvious ones were freedom of speech and of association. 'We cannot', said the *Chronicle* in 1853, 'prevent the refugees from assembling in their squalid haunts and indulging in uncomplimentary observations on the men who have proscribed them. Our laws grant them as much license in grumbling as we claim for ourselves.'[211] Nor could they institute separate, discriminatory laws for foreigners – have as the *Daily News* put it 'one law for ourselves and another for the "stranger that is within our gates" ': for it was another essential pillar of the British constitution that 'laws must be of general application'.[212] Another pillar of the constitution was that the executive should be strictly answerable to Parliament and to the law, and the scope of its action rigidly and narrowly circumscribed. Consequently no 'extraordinary and unconstitutional power' over the refugee could ever be granted to a Minister of the Crown: for there was, said the *Morning Chronicle*, 'fortunately, great jealousy of an authority so open to abuse'.[213] These principles, which were designed to safeguard freedom, ruled out certain kinds of laws and arbitrary procedures against refugees. If action was to be taken against any of them, then it had to be under laws which applied to the English too, and by processes which were free, open and universal.

---

[206] It goes without saying that it had nothing to do with 'democracy', which was a matter quite distinct from mid-nineteenth-century notions of 'freedom' or 'liberalism', and more often, in fact, regarded at this time as antagonistic to both.

[207] *Morning Advertiser*, 22 January 1858, p. 4. The Victorians also at this time resisted the idea of 'passports' – impediments to the right of free 'egress'.

[208] *Standard*, 25 February 1852, p. 2.

[209] *Supra*, p. 7. Examples are too numerous to need citing; they are to be found in all the parliamentary debates on the subject, and most press comment.

[210] *Morning Chronicle*, 23 July 1857, p. 4.

[211] *Ibid.*, 2 March 1853, p. 5. Another much-prized 'freedom' was the freedom of a man to invest his capital where he liked: which the *Daily News* saw as a reason to defend the Mazzini Italian bonds: 'capitalists have a right to do what they like with their own money' (3 April 1851, p. 4).   [212] *Daily News*, 28 January 1858, p. 4; 27 July 1857, p. 4.

[213] *Morning Chronicle*, 29 March 1851, p. 5; and cf. *ibid.*, 7 April 1852, p. 4: 'public opinion is clear and unmistakeable as to the inexpediency and danger of strengthening the hand of the Executive against political offenders, of whatever nation'.

It was this last requirement which posed the greatest obstacle to any really effective conciliation of the continental powers. Some of the most cherished liberties of nineteenth-century Englishmen were those which were protected by certain legal processes: *habeas corpus*, the presumption of innocence, the rules of evidence; and also by certain restrictions on the investigative powers of the police designed to safeguard the privacy of innocent men – of all men, that is, who had not been proved guilty. It was these processes and restrictions which, more than anything, prevented more vigorous action being taken even against those refugees whose activities one could be morally certain had contravened British laws. Foreign governments complained chiefly of 'conspiracies' among the refugees in Britain; and by their nature conspiracies were not easily detected without very special means being employed, or easily proved except very circumstantially. In English law the concept of 'conspiracy' had a well-established place; yet it could be a slippery one. 'Conspiracy?' said one commentator interrogatively in 1853: 'Define it . . . Is conspiracy a concerted plan, an understanding, or a conversation, or a mere suspicion? . . . Where does the natural and inevitable intercourse of exiles end? Where does conspiracy begin?'[214] More to the point: how was it to be proven? On the continent, where 'hearsay' and 'notoriety' were acceptable as evidence in courts of law, it was comparatively simple, but English rules of evidence were stricter. For this reason, as *The Times* pointed out in 1857, the evidence which in a French court was found adequate to convict Mazzini in his absence of complicity in the Tibaldi plot 'would not have procured his conviction in England'.[215] Without more substantial proofs refugees could not be convicted; and without having been convicted, nothing could be done against them: 'we cannot swerve', wrote a pamphleteer in 1858, 'from our old English rule of treating men as innocent until they are proved to be guilty'.[216] In some ways this was a pity. In very few minds could there have been much doubt that the rigidity of English law in this matter meant that some criminals, including criminal refugees, went scot free. It was a hindrance to the apprehension and punishment of the guilty. But this deficiency in the English legal system was intentional, designed to safeguard the innocent, and consequently the liberties of Englishmen: and so, as the *Morning Chronicle* affirmed in 1853, 'the mechanism of our criminal law for sifting the truth can never be sacrificed to a political necessity'.[217]

This made it difficult to punish criminal activities by refugees. The nineteenth-century feeling for privacy was supposed to make it scarcely less difficult to detect or to prevent them. This was widely believed to be

[214] 'An Englishman', in *Morning Advertiser*, 4 March 1853, p. 4.
[215] *The Times*, 11 September 1857, p. 6.   [216] Sir Arthur Hallam Elton, *op. cit.*, p. 5.
[217] *Morning Chronicle*, 8 March 1853, p. 4.

no bad thing either. To *The Times* it was a matter of considerable pride that Britain's 'engines of police' were so much less effective than those of continental states, so that she had to 'give up all idea' of preventing refugee conspiracies in Britain, or even of finding out which of the refugees were in the country: 'we neither know nor care who are living in this metropolis'.[218] The difference between her police system and the continent's was supposed to be another sign of that fundamental gulf which existed between her liberty and their despotism. For decades France and other European countries had been willing to use – Britons would say 'stoop to' – almost any means to elicit information about and to incriminate political offenders.[219] Britain was very much more fastidious. For a long time she had been unwilling to tolerate the existence of any official police force at all, partly because of its continental associations; by the 1850s she had had one for only a very short time, and was still supremely jealous over any matter where her 'liberties' might seem to be compromised by it, and very careful to limit strictly both its area and its mode of operation. So, for example, it was not allowed to have any overtly political functions: 'we have no political police', *Household Words* proudly proclaimed in 1850; 'no police over opinion'.[220] When in 1851 the Prussian chief minister complained to the British ambassador in Berlin that the English police seemed only to be interested in 'the apprehension of Robbers and Murderers', and were not at all 'in the habit of pursuing political criminals', Bloomfield replied that he was happy to confirm this, and that 'it was the conviction of the people of England that the police were solely employed in this manner which commanded respect for the Establishment throughout the Country, and which ensured the voluntary and immediate coöperation of the respectable classes of Her Majesty's Subjects whenever circumstances occurred which called for their assistance'.[221] 'It is to catch thieves', confirmed the *Daily News* in 1853, 'not to entrap theorists, that that respectable and efficient body has hitherto been maintained'.[222]

Nor were the police supposed to be allowed to use any techniques which smelt of 'espionage' – a word which had not yet assimilated itself completely into the English language, and was still pronounced in a way which implied distaste. 'Espionage' covered a very wide field of activities, some of which in any other age or place would be considered normal. In 1845, for example, a police constable was severely disciplined by his superiors for disguising himself as a cobbler in order to observe and arrest a counterfeiter;[223] and in 1851 another constable was rebuked for hiding behind a

[218] *The Times*, 26 February 1852, p. 5; 23 July 1857, p. 8; 28 February 1853, p. 4.
[219] See Howard C. Payne, *The Police State of Louis Napoleon Bonaparte* (Seattle, Wash., 1966).
[220] *Household Words*, vol. I no. 26 (21 September 1850), p. 611 (by Henry G. Wreford).
[221] Bloomfield to Palmerston no. 30, 14 August 1851: PRO FO 64/332.
[222] *Daily News*, 2 May 1853, p. 4.   [223] PRO HO 45/1107.

tree to observe an 'indecent offence'.[224] Such methods were considered underhand and dishonourable, and the results that could be obtained by them too dearly bought by the erosion of freedom they involved. Espionage was a system, said the *Standard*, 'such as our whole social system abhors'; 'We are not a sharp people; there is nothing of the spy in the national character.'[225] 'Everybody knows what this means', said the *Daily News* when it was suggested that the French and British police forces co-operate to watch the refugees.

It means a glass lid on every letter-box, and a spy at the corner of every street. It means the annihilation of things which we and our fathers have held for generations most dear, and the permanent establishment of a system repugnant to every feeling, sentiment, and principle of English life.[226]

The *Morning Advertiser* talked of 'espionage, domiciliary visits without legal warrant, preventive arrest, in short, *moucharderie* of the worst character'.[227] 'Political espionage', wrote the novelist Mayne Reid in 1853, 'is cuneiform. Give the vile system but the smallest insertion, and, wedge like, it will help itself, until it has cleft the columns of our glory and sapped the foundations of our dear liberty.'[228] So it was proscribed – 'legally at least', said the *Morning Advertiser,* which had its suspicions;[229] and the refugees were left as a result free from any kind of effective surveillance by the British police. That this was so was not accepted by everybody: not for example by 'the Ministers of arbitrary Governments' themselves, whose 'misfortune' it was, said the *Morning Chronicle*, 'that they are unable to understand the limits of police regulations in a free country';[230] not by some of the refugees, who were not used to such innocence in their own countries and could hardly credit it in England; nor by Chartists who knew that the police had set spies on *them* in the past and did not trust them not to do the same with the refugees. Both Chartists and refugees also remembered, and often recalled, the famous letter-opening affair of 1844, which showed what the authorities were capable of, and might do again.[231] On a couple of occasions during the 1850s there broke through the veil faint indications of some of the improper things which were in fact being done by the police, as we shall see, in secret: which more radically inclined politicians and newspapers made as much of as their tenuous information

---

[224] PRO MEPO 7/15. See also L. Radzinowicz, *A History of English Criminal Law*, vol. IV (1968), pp. 184–9. In Wilkie Collins's *The Woman in White* (1975 edn., p. 445) the hero considers employing a disguise in his pursuit of the villains, but resists the temptation: 'there was something so repellant to me in the idea – something so meanly like the common herd of spies and informers in the mere act of adopting a disguise – that I dismissed the question from consideration, almost as soon as it had risen in my mind'.
[225] *Standard*, 25 February 1852, p. 2; 27 January 1858, p. 4.
[226] *Daily News*, 3 February 1858, p. 4.   [227] *Morning Advertiser*, 19 February 1858, p. 4.
[228] *Daily News*, 25 April 1853, p. 5.   [229] *Morning Advertiser*, 22 January 1858, p. 4.
[230] *Morning Chronicle*, 25 February 1852, pp. 4–5.   [231] *Supra*, p. 54.

allowed.[232] Nevertheless these seem not to have been generally credited: not by *The Times*, for example, which regarded accusations made by Kossuth in 1853 that he was being spied on (which in fact were true) as 'wild and improbable';[233] nor by most commentators, who believed, or perhaps merely wanted to believe, that the British people never would (as the *Daily News* put it) 'subject themselves to a preventive political police, such as prevails on the Continent, with its *espionage*, violation of the confidences reposed in the Post-office, and other enormities'.[234] This being so, concluded the *Standard*, 'they who stand in need of such dirty work' would have to 'find dirty fellows of their own to execute it'.[235]

In view of all this, it is remarkable that English commentators and politicians in the 1850s persisted in maintaining that the system was quite adequate to control the refugees. 'With each and all these things', said the *Morning Herald* in 1855 – with conspiracy, libel, sedition and the rest – 'the law of England is perfectly competent to deal'.[236] To continental rulers statements like this appeared demonstrably untrue, inconsistent with the facts. The truth is, of course, that they were not wholly intended as assessments of fact. They were value judgments. What was meant by them was that the law of England was adequate to deal with conspiracies and the like which *deserved* to be dealt with; and that if some conspiracies and libels complained of by the continentals had not been legally proscribed or punished, it was because they did not merit it: because they never existed, or were not what they were made out to be, or because inadequate cases had been made out against them to satisfy English law officers, or because they were not in English eyes, and therefore were not *at all*, activities which should be regarded as criminal. In this sense the English law was an adequate protection against reasonable complaints. In any other sense, of course, it was not. It was not adequate to detect crimes which could only be detected by low and unworthy means, or to convict men who could only be convicted on perjured or hearsay evidence. It was not adequate to prevent men from exercising what was merely their natural right to free speech. It was a liberal law, and consequently was a poor blunt tool for illiberal ends. To convert it into anything else would involve a price no free-born Englishman was willing to pay.

This whole area, therefore, was a highly sensitive one: more sensitive probably than continentals ever understood. There were ways of prevent-

---

[232] For example in 1851 *Reynolds's Newspaper* believed it had discovered a 'foreign branch' of the police force recently set up (6 September 1851, p. 7); in 1853 *Reynolds's* (1 May, p. 4) and the *People's Paper* (26 March, p. 4) reported irregular police activities in connexion with the Rotherhithe rocket-factory affair (*infra*, p. 145); and in 1858 *Reynolds's* reported in detail Sanders's illegal entry into Orsini's lodgings: *infra*, p. 189.

[233] *The Times*, 26 April 1853, p. 6.   [234] *Daily News*, 28 January 1858, p. 4.

[235] *Standard*, 25 February 1852, p. 2.   [236] *Morning Herald*, 29 October 1855, p. 4.

ing refugee conspiracies, said the *Manchester Guardian* in 1858: police surveillance, letter-opening, espionage and the rest. But –

It is sufficient to say that to subject them to this system would involve a total change in our views of the province of executive authority . . . Among the things which seem to us as natural and indefeasible as the air we breathe are the right of perfect freedom of communication, of passing from place to place without inquiry, of enjoying absolute privacy in our own homes, and, generally speaking, of being left, not only in appearance but in truth, to our own devices until we fall under the censure of the law. By long habit we have grown to consider these things not in the light of privileges, but as the primary conditions of existence, and they appertain to foreigners as a necessary consequence of their residence in the country.

Some of the refugees abused quite deplorably the asylum Britain granted to them; but it just could not effectively be stopped, without imperilling the whole national fabric. 'The abuse is an excrescence on the fair growth of a plant which we cherish among the most valued of our possessions.' Kill the excrescence, and the plant would die too.[237] *The Times* agreed: 'in the deliberate judgment of the people of England', it said in 1852, 'these evils' – the harm that was done by the refugees – 'are more than compensated by the great principle of freedom under which they occur'.[238] 'Any attempt', said the *Morning Advertiser*, 'to change the character of this broad English law is calculated to imperil our own civic liberty'.[239] This was what was at stake. These demands that the continentals were making on Britain were in fact, though they themselves might not have realised or intended it, direct attacks on Britain's constitutional freedoms: and so were treated and resisted as such. It is fair to say also that many Englishmen were only too willing to see the matter in this light if they could: very eager to take offence, in a way which puzzled and irritated, for example, the *Morning Chronicle* in 1858: what had come over 'John Bull', it asked, – 'that respectable and, generally speaking, self-satisfied personage, that he should manifest all at once such extreme sensibility to the censures and even the innuendoes of foreigners?'[240] The reason was that their sense of national superiority made them resent all the more criticisms from inferior polities, especially when those criticisms were tinged with menace, and when the British ruling class's willingness to resist them could not altogether be counted on. We shall see that this last fear was by no means groundless. Consequently, the resistance of 'the country' had to be made quite plain. On this issue it was impossible to be too vigilant, or too sensitive.

The demands and criticisms of the continent, therefore, were seen as a kind of aggression: just as, on their side, the continentals saw Britain's

[237] *Manchester Guardian*, 28 January 1858, p. 3.   [238] *The Times*, 9 February 1852, p. 4.
[239] *The Morning Advertiser*, 22 January 1858, p. 4.
[240] *Morning Chronicle*, 4 March 1858, p. 4.

harbouring of refugees as a kind of aggression. Words like 'appeasement', 'submission,' 'subserviency', 'prostitution', and phrases like 'pandering to despotism' and 'truckling to absolutism', were widely applied to any suggestion that the British government might agree to any part of what the continentals asked.[241] It was a theme most forcefully taken up, of course, by newspapers like *Reynolds's*: 'Englishmen', it declared in 1857: 'you are asked, and *expected*, to become the jackals and the bloodhounds of continental absolutism. You are asked, and expected, to make of England a penal settlement, and a trap for the chased Republicans of Europe . . . '[242] But milder journals pursued it too: like the *Daily News*, which declared it to be no part of a British minister's business 'to prostitute the power and authority which belong to the executive of a free nation in political prosecutions, to appease the baffled fury of despotic Governments abroad';[243] or the *Globe*: 'no country will allow laws to be dictated to it founded not on domestic but on foreign ideas and interests';[244] or the *Morning Post*, which saw it as 'an act of base subserviency' to attempt to convert English law 'into an engine of foreign police and a political man-trap';[245] or the *Weekly Dispatch*, which professed unwillingness 'to lay the fruits of the battle of so many years at the feet of the French ambassador';[246] or the *Morning Advertiser*, which regarded as 'craven and impolitic' any 'proposal to alter our laws and conform them to the absolutist *codes of Continental nations*'.[247] This theme, of a free country 'submitting' to despotism, was the one most enthusiastically exploited by those who opposed any changes at all in the laws affecting refugees, and the one, it seems, which was least easily resisted by the less committed. And when foreign demands were accompanied by direct and explicit threats, as they seemed to be in 1853 and 1858, the final decisive ingredient was added to this line of reasoning, which thus became almost irresistible. If Englishmen were not to be told what to do by foreigners, they were less likely to be frightened into it. 'We have yet to learn', said the *Daily News* proudly and defiantly in 1858, 'that a free nation can be suddenly bullied into the fabrication of new laws by having the naked sword of a despotic ally brandished in its face.'[248] In February 1858, when feeling in the country over the refugee question reached its pugnacious climax, this was the element in it which gave it its force. Of every argument that was put

---

[241] 'Appeasement': *Daily News*, 16 April 1853 p. 5 and *Reynolds's Newspaper*, 12 June 1853 p. 7; 'submission': *Daily News*, 8 February 1858 p. 4; 'subserviency': *ibid.*, 3 February 1858 p. 4 and *Morning Post*, 5 March 1853 p. 5; 'prostitution': *Daily News*, 16 April 1853 p. 5 and *Weekly Dispatch*, 21 February 1858 p. 9; 'pandering to despotism': *ibid.*, 30 March 1851 p. 201; 'truckling to absolutism': *Daily News*, 16 February 1852 p. 4.

[242] *Reynolds's Newspaper*, 2 August 1857, p. 8.

[243] *Daily News*, 16 April 1853, p. 5.   [244] *Globe*, 2 March 1853, p. 2.

[245] *Morning Post*, 5 March 1853, p. 5.   [246] *Weekly Dispatch*, 31 January 1858, p. 9.

[247] *Morning Advertiser*, 10 February 1858, p. 4 (italics in the original).

[248] *Daily News*, 3 February 1858, p. 4.

forward against the Conspiracy Bill of that month (which was supposed to be the Government's concession to the French), although the rationale may have been different, this was its emotional heart. 'If England wishes to hold her place among the nations,' said Roebuck in the House of Commons, 'if she wishes still to maintain her own independent position, no solicitation of an ally, no threatenings on the part of anybody, ought to lead us to alter our laws . . . if our ancestors treated with contempt and defiance the menaces of *Napoleon le Grand*, should we, their descendants, quail before the threats of *Napoleon le Petit*?'[249] It was a seductive cry: seductive enough, as we shall see, to bring over to the side of those who were anyway opposed to being 'dishonoured'[250] by submitting to foreign advances, many others who were less concerned for their constitutional virginity, and might otherwise have given in – but not in the face of threats. Seduction was one thing: rape was quite another.

This aspect of the refugee question was probably the most important of all in determining the nature of the public reaction to it. People disliked being told to alter their superior laws at the request or dictation of foreign governments. This did not render the asylum Britain gave to refugees absolutely secure. But it made it more secure – better protected by public opinion – at those times when it appeared to be most under attack: which was when people felt most strongly about rallying to it. Early in 1852, for example, and then again in the spring of 1853 and the first months of 1858, it was defended manfully in the press, in parliament and at public meetings. These various manifestations of opinion appeared to indicate quite clearly, as Monckton Milnes warned Palmerston in 1852, that any move in the direction of appeasement on this issue 'would bring destruction on the heads of any government, and produce a general feeling of indignation throughout the whole realm'.[251] Scarcely anyone in Parliament in those years, and scarcely any national newspaper, doubted for example that any overt Alien Act was entirely outside the realm of political possibility. Even 'the most powerful administration', if it even contemplated it, said the *Morning Advertiser* in 1853, would be swiftly 'extinguished'. An Alien Bill would be

one of the most unpopular, and, to themselves, the most perilous acts which Ministers could contemplate. The country would be up in arms against any Government that could make such a proposal. The Tories would be no less indignant than the Liberals: nor would they be one whit less strenuous in their opposition to it.[252]

[249] 3PD 148, cc. 766 and 771 (5 February 1858). The same argument is repeated again and again in the debates of February 8, 9 and 19: 3PD 148 cc. 933–64, 979–1081, 1741–1847.
[250] *Daily News*, 31 October 1855, p. 4.   [251] 3PD 119, c. 487 (1 April 1852).
[252] *Morning Advertiser*, 1 March 1853, p. 4, and 23 February 1853, p. 4. Cf. *Morning Chronicle*, 25 February 1852, pp. 4–5, 7 April 1852, p. 4 and 2 March 1853, p. 5; *Morning Post*, 2 March 1853, p. 5; *Daily News*, 31 October 1855, p. 4 and 25 January 1858, p. 4; *Morning Herald*, 30 October 1855, p. 4; and *Weekly Dispatch*, 6 March 1853, p. 153.

Anything less than an Alien Bill was not quite so unthinkable, but was widely resisted nevertheless, insofar as it seemed to be proposed in response to foreign pressure. In 1851, 1852 and 1853 not one national newspaper was in favour of amending the law in any way to take account of refugee conspiracies, except *John Bull*, whose demands were as draconian as they were idiosyncratic:[253] though the *Morning Chronicle* thought 'the time may come' when, regrettably, such an amendment might be necessary.[254] In 1858, when an amendment was actually proposed to Parliament, there was far less unanimity: but still the balance of metropolitan press opinion was against it.[255] In 1853 there were public meetings called to protest against reports of police 'spying' on Kossuth and other refugees.[256] In 1858 there were popular demonstrations in many major cities to protest against the Conspiracy Bill: one in Newcastle 'crowded to suffocation' even after that Bill had been withdrawn.[257] The scale of popular protest over the refugee question was not as great as that over other leading issues of the day, like Parliamentary reform or the Eastern question or the papal aggression, but it was significant. Perhaps more significant was the fact that there were never any protest meetings held on the other side, against the refugees.[258] All this demonstrated that there was a reservoir of public feeling to tap, among the middle and working classes, on the refugee question, and on the side of the refugees. But it had to be on occasions when 'foreign dictation', or some other matter about which Englishmen felt more strongly than they did about the refugees *per se*, dominated. The merits of the case – of the continental complaints against Britain – hardly mattered. The simple principle was that no law should ever be passed in England – and certainly no acts outside the law instituted – at the behest or suggestion of a foreign country. This applied to Alien Bills as well as any other: 'Every act of that description which has been passed', said Milnes, 'related solely to our own security, and our own internal defence, and never in any one case had we admitted the principle

[253] *John Bull*, 29 March 1851, pp. 201–2 and 28 February 1853 pp. 137–8.

[254] *Morning Chronicle*, 29 March 1851, p. 5.

[255] In favour of the Conspiracy Bill were *The Times, Morning Chronicle, Morning Post* and *Globe. John Bull* opposed it, but only because it was too tepid. Against the Bill were the *Daily News, Standard, Morning Advertiser, Weekly Dispatch, Reynolds's Newspaper* and the *People's Paper*. The *Morning Herald* and the *Press* took up no strong position either way.

[256] See *People's Paper*, 14 May 1853, p. 2, reporting a meeting in the Horns Tavern, Kennington on May 11; and *ibid.*, 21 May 1853, p. 7, reporting another meeting at Southwark on the 18th: both to protest against the 'spy system' used against Kossuth.

[257] *Northern Daily Express*, 24 February 1858, in Cowen Papers, TWAD 634/A552. The biggest one was planned to be held in Hyde Park the day after the Bill was in the event defeated. Some of the others were noticed in *The Times*, 16 February p. 12 (London), 26 February p. 6 (Bury, Manchester) and 19 March p. 12 (Birmingham).

[258] Except for a meeting of the loyal inhabitants of Jersey in 1855 to protest against Pyat's 'letter' to the Queen: which was probably not spontaneous, but arranged by the Governor of the island to give force to his decision to expel some of the refugees: *vide infra*, p. 165.

6. Broadsheets announcing demonstrations in London and Newcastle against the Conspiracy Bill, 1858.

that we were the guardians of the peace of foreign countries.'[259] This was not strictly accurate,[260] but it was a compelling myth in the chauvinistic fifties. Consequently, when the criticism from abroad was most outspoken, and the demands most overt – which was usually when they were most justified, and when therefore it would have been reasonable to give a little – the stiffer resistance to them became.

It followed from this, however, that when the 'foreign dictation' element was less in evidence, resistance was likely to be less stiff. This was what the *Daily News*, for example, feared: that an Alien Bill might slip through when popular vigilance was relaxed. It believed that such a situation might have arisen in the summer of 1857: 'At no period of our history', it warned, ' . . . has there been less likelihood of a resolute and general opposition being offered, should a Bill be introduced into Parliament to impose limitations or restrictions upon that right of asylum which from time immemorial has been enjoyed by political exiles in England.'[261] Another similar occasion was the autumn of 1855, when 39 refugees were actually expelled from Jersey after the publication there of a libel on the French emperor.[262] The action was arbitrary, and even possibly illegal. Yet the reaction in England was conspicuously more muted than to any 'refugee question' at any other time in the 1850s. There were some petitions in protest, and some meetings held against the expulsions, but by most accounts the latter were hard to fill.[263] There was no mention of the affair in Parliament when it met in January. And the national press was unusually acquiescent: only the most radical papers objecting to the expulsions, and not even all of *them* – the *Weekly Dispatch* and the *Morning Advertiser* joining, on this one occasion, the ranks of the refugees'

[259] 3PD 119, c. 486 (1 April 1852).
[260] The early Acts clearly had a European as well as a British purpose. In 1816, for example, the government of the day refused to accept an Amendment which would have prefaced to the Alien Act a declaration that it was designed to conserve 'the peace and safety of the realm' only, and Lord Sidmouth admitted 'that the peace of Europe, with which the welfare of this country was so closely connected, was also one of the objects of the Bill': 1PD 33, c. 1083 (12 June 1816). On the same occasion Castlereagh nevertheless persisted in maintaining that in enforcing the act he had always 'acted entirely upon a British policy': *ibid.*, c. 171 (1 May 1816); but as Romilly pointed out, 'It might be thought to be an object of British policy to oblige a foreign minister': *ibid.*, c. 172.
[261] *Daily News*, 27 July 1857, p. 4.
[262] *Infra*, p. 165.
[263] A meeting held in Newcastle on 11 November was reported by the *Newcastle Messenger* as being 'not more than three parts filled' (16 November 1855, in Cowen Papers, TWAD 634/A407), but by the *Daily News* as being 'crowded to the doors' (15 November, *loc. cit.*, A405). Other meetings were held on 12 November in St Martin's Hall, London; on 19 November in Finsbury Square; on 26 November in Friar Street; on 26 November in Paisley ('numerously attended' according to one observer, 'very thinly attended' according to another: Cowen Papers, TWAD 634/A438 and A435); and on 27 November in Glasgow. See K. W. Hooker, *The Fortunes of Victor Hugo in England* (New York, 1938), pp. 124–32.

enemies.[264] For the first time there was considerable press support for the idea of their expulsion altogether from British soil. The *Morning Post* called on the government to 'sweep this foul factory out of the Queen's dominions'.[265] This was echoed by the *Morning Advertiser*, the *Standard* and (more predictably) *John Bull*.[266] Never before had resistance to the idea of an Alien Act been so low.

But in 1855, unlike 1852, 1853 and 1858, what had been done was not done in response to any foreign demand that was known about: and therein lay the difference. Of course it was suspected by radicals that the occasion for the expulsion was such a demand, made secretly;[267] but this could not be explicitly demonstrated. The *Northern Daily Express* believed that it was significant that it was 'neither at the request of Louis Napoleon, or Francis Joseph', or even of the English government that 'the first proceedings were taken', but 'in accordance with the popular voice, rising in detestation of the infamous principles promulgated in the republican ukase'.[268] There were other differences too. Britain was at war – and a popular war – in alliance with France, and it was an alliance which was known to be both vital and fragile. Then again, the 'libel' which had been the reason – or the pretext – for the expulsions had embraced the English Queen as well as the French emperor, which soured nearly everybody's attitudes to the expellees. 'This free nation', declared *Lloyd's Newspaper*, 'must still be the home of the unfortunate; but being so, it must not be perverted into an asylum for the cowardly preachers of assassination, and worse still[!], the slanderers of women.'[269] Even the *Daily News*, which was the only daily newspaper which remained consistently faithful to them at this time, was affected: 'We should', it said, 'have expressed ourselves more strongly did we not feel that the Jersey *proscrits* have to

---

[264] The *People's Paper*, *Reynolds's* and the *Daily News* campaigned fiercely against the expulsions. The *Morning Herald*, while implying mild disapproval of them, did not spell it out. The *Morning Advertiser* began by supporting the expulsions, but then (October 25) suddenly turned around and began following the *Daily News* line. The *Morning Chronicle* and the *Press* ignored the affair editorially. Consistently in favour of the expulsions were *The Times*, *Morning Post*, *John Bull*, *Weekly Dispatch*, *Standard*, and *Globe*.

[265] *Morning Post*, 18 October 1855, p. 4. The *Morning Post* was largely inspired by Palmerston, who was Home Secretary at the time.

[266] *Morning Advertiser*, 18 October 1855, p. 4: 'We apprehend that such a case has arisen as would justify the passing of an Alien Act'; *Standard*, 17 October 1855, p. 2: 'If they cannot be deported to Western Australia or New Caledonia, let a law for that purpose be passed in the very first week of the session'; *John Bull*, 27 October 1855, pp. 680–1: 'The sooner the summary power of expulsion from the British soil against aliens who misconduct themselves is revived, the better.'

[267] E.g. Cowen at the Newcastle meeting on November 11 claimed it was done 'at the dictation of the Emperor of the French' (*Northern Daily Express*, 13 November 1855, in Cowen Papers, TWAD 634/A402); and the *Daily News* claimed it was 'obviously provoked by alien interference' (22 October 1855, p. 4). See also *Reynolds's Newspaper*, 21 October 1855, pp. 7 and 9; and *Morning Advertiser*, 2 November 1855, p. 4.

[268] *Northern Daily Express*, 14 November 1855: Cowen Papers, TWAD 634/A403.

[269] *Lloyd's Newspaper*, 17 November 1855: *ibid.*, A411.

thank their own indiscretion for the treatment they complain of.'[270] 'It is plain', commented the *Edinburgh Daily Express*,

that an agitation cannot be got up for their benefit. There was a considerable agitation; but this was when the country was indignant at their offence and loudly called upon the Government to notice it; and as soon as the expulsion took place, all agitation subsided.[271]

Many Liberals were disappointed, and even ashamed. The *Daily News* predicted that 'The future historian of the nineteenth century will point to the Jersey outrages, and to the apathy with which they seem likely to be endured by the English public, as the darkest blot on the Liberals of this age.'[272] (Had it survived to hear that future historian, it would have been disappointed at his reaction too.) This Jersey episode and its reception in the country demonstrated just how precarious was the status of the refugees when those other extraneous considerations, which at other times redounded so to their benefit, were absent. Insofar as their security was founded on public feeling in England, it was not so much a feeling for them, as against their enemies. So long as the Englishman's (not unreasonable) xenophobia was distracted by the larger light of the despots abroad, foreigners at home were safe. But if that light receded or grew dim, then the refugees might have brought home to them sharply, what many of them knew already: that the upper and middle classes of England, and probably most of the lower classes too, approved of them scarcely more than they approved of their erstwhile masters.

The refugees in England, therefore, were in a curious situation. Most of them were unloved by most Englishmen, who made them feel very little welcome, but tolerated their presence in deference to what purported to be a great and selfless humanitarian principle: the doctrine of asylum. To this doctrine of asylum a great deal of obeisance was paid, and a moderately wide and deep attachment probably felt; but the attachment was deeper and wider to certain other principles of the British constitution which affected Englishmen themselves more intimately, and which it was thought would be endangered by any effective action taken against the refugees. All these principles were supposed to demonstrate, and were very largely valued for the way they demonstrated, Britain's moral and political superiority over her continental neighbours, at this time in history when they were probably further separated ideologically than at any other. They were also supposed to explain why Britain was safe from viruses, carried by the refugees, which the continent was highly vulnerable to. When these inferior polities, not fully aware of the implications of what

[270] *Daily News*, 22 October 1855, p. 4.
[271] *Edinburgh Daily Express*, 30 November 1855: Cowen Papers, TWAD 634/A435.
[272] *Daily News*, 31 October 1855, p. 4.

they were doing, made demands upon Britain that she amend her freer and better institutions to suit them, it was, naturally, widely resented: and it was this resentment which, more than anything else, determined the response of 'public opinion' in Britain not only to the demands, but also to the 'refugee question' itself which was the occasion of them. Herein lay the refugees' main security against the designs of governments which, as we shall see, did not altogether share these popular feelings, and to whom the presence and activities of the refugees appeared as less mitigated an evil. They were also assisted by a peculiar domestic political situation of the time which rendered governments particularly susceptible to what was taken to be 'public opinion'; and by all kinds of accidentals, which on one or two occasions, for reasons quite unconnected with the merits of any of these cases, helped to turn that 'public opinion' in their favour.

5

The Government

In those years after 1848 when things were so bright and promising for the English middle and upper classes by contrast with their fellows on the continent – when the wisdom of relaxing the restraints on trade was demonstrated by their prosperity, and that of relaxing the restraints on the free expression of opinion vindicated by the total absence of any convincing extra-constitutional challenge to the *status quo* – it was one of the fondest and proudest beliefs of those middle and upper classes that this *status quo* was maintained in Britain, not by the forceful exercise of authority, but by the willing consent of all her people. This consent, it was further claimed, was forthcoming not merely because of the rulers' readiness to concede and adapt to the feelings and wishes of those they ruled, but also because in very large measure they themselves shared those feelings and wishes: especially, as the *Morning Chronicle* put it in 1858, 'all those sentiments of liberty and attachment to the laws which are a special characteristic of the English people'. In this respect Britain was happily distinguished from the class-riven polities of the continent. 'There is not, here', continued the *Chronicle*, 'that bane of some continental countries, a line of demarcation between the aristocracy, from among whom Statesmen for the most part spring, and the other classes of the community. A general fusion of feelings and interests permits the formation of a homogeneous public opinion.'[1] There was no conflict, no essential friction between leaders and led, ministers and people. Both shared the same ideals and values. When the government acted, it was for the people; when the people spoke, it was in the same sense as their leaders. On fundamental issues at least, their hearts beat as one.

If this had been totally true, it would have been very remarkable. Of course all governments of the time had to take account of and show sympathy for public feeling, if they were not to run the risk of political defeat and exclusion from power. This was probably more true during the 1850s and early 1860s than at almost any other time, because of the unusual weakness of party loyalties and discipline then, which caused allegiances in

---

[1] *Morning Chronicle*, 8 March 1858, p. 4.

the House of Commons to bend and break to the slightest popular wind: so that Palmerston, for example, if he decided on a policy which was unpopular had nothing like the chance Disraeli with more docile and tractable forces had twenty years later, of carrying it through regardless. This may have rendered government policies then more accountable to the 'general will' than they ever were in later and more 'democratic' times, and so created perforce a kind of identity between the two. Yet it is inherently unlikely that there was a perfect unanimity, an entire absence of tension between what 'the nation' and what government wanted. On this refugee issue there were several ways in which governments of all political colours were likely to feel differently from the public, merely – if for no other reason – by virtue of being governments. As governments, for example, they might be said to have a special interest in maintaining law, order and social stability, and in that case would tend to regard more seriously than most any direct threats to these *desiderata* which the refugees might be supposed to offer. Governments also had access to information which was unavailable to the public, which might lead them to different conclusions about the reality of such threats. Most important of all: governments had to bear in mind a much wider range of priorities and pressures than the public customarily considered; how these priorities interacted, and the repercussions which actions taken to further one priority might have on the achievement of other possibly more desirable ones. Any of these considerations might have influenced governments in the 1850s and 1860s away from the general public attitude, and against the refugees: if for example they feared them, had intelligence which seemed to give substance to their fears, or had a special and vital national interest in view, like a French alliance, which was likely to be jeopardised by too unyielding a stand on this other, less material issue. All this was quite apart from any antipathetical feelings of their own towards the refugees, which might derive from the fact that government ministers were generally recruited from those sections of society which tolerated the refugees and their causes least, and towards which the refugees themselves, for their part, were most hostile.

That there were tensions and conflicts became fairly clear during the early months of 1858, when a ministry was turned out for (ostensibly) running counter to the popular will on the refugee issue. The 'dualism' between government and people then, wrote Gladstone very soon after this event, 'is beyond all doubt. Nothing could be more contradictory in their letter and in their spirit than the proceedings of the Ministry and of the nation; the dogs were coupled, but they could not hunt together.'[2] This hardly squared with the *Morning Chronicle*'s rosier picture of the relation-

---

[2] [W. E. Gladstone], 'France and the late Ministry', in *Quarterly Review*, vol. 103 (April 1858), pp. 527–8. The Ms. of this article is in the Gladstone Papers, BL. Add. Ms. 44689.

ship, which was published at the same time and in the same context: but of the two it did seem to fit that context better. There were, as we shall see, tensions over this issue at other times too, though often they were hidden by official secrecy, or else by the government's not pressing its view in order to avoid an open conflict. When foreigners, as a way of being charitable to British governments, assumed that they were sometimes forced to act against their better inclinations by a 'democracy' which it 'dislikes and condemns, but. . . cannot resist', British ministers, resenting strongly the notion that they would bow to any pressure, but especially to a 'democratic' one, hotly denied it:[3] but there was something in it. Governments did feel hampered and restricted in their dealings over the refugee issue during most of the 1850s, by a public feeling they did not altogether share, but whose force and effectiveness they sometimes declined to contest.

Nevertheless the *Morning Chronicle* was not entirely in the wrong. There were quite large areas of consensus between government and people on this question, which were at least as significant as the areas of difference. On many points their views coincided. They coincided, for example, in the view they took of the danger to be apprehended from the refugees to British society. Governments feared them scarcely more than did anyone else, and were given very little cause to by their special sources of information. Of course they were careful not to take chances, and dutifully checked out, for example, the rumours of foreign plots which surrounded the opening of the Great Exhibition in May 1851;[4] but they very rarely gave much credence to them, or did anything to suggest that they considered the refugees to be other than harmless to their hosts. When the question was raised in the House of Lords in 1849 Lord Lansdowne for the government assured his fellow-peers that 'it was not the case' that refugees 'habitually misbehaved themselves in this country': indeed, he went on, 'insofar as the authorities went, the argument went the other way; for it had been proved that they were not inclined to take part in disturbances'.[5] No one, wrote the Queen to King Leopold in the same year, believed that they were engaged 'in doing harm *here*'.[6] During the preparations for the Great Exhibition in 1851 the Home Secretary was able to give it as his considered opinion that the likelihood of 'the internal peace and tranquillity of this country . . . being menaced by the conduct of foreign refugees resident in this country' was 'a very distant one, and a very improbable one'.[7] To the Russian government, which on this matter appeared far

---

[3] Clarendon to Westmorland no. 18, 2 March 1853: PRO FO 7/412.
[4] E.g. Palmerston to Grey, 10 January 1851: Palm. P. GC/GR/2588; police inquiries recorded in PRO HO 45/3720.   [5] 3PD 103, c. 951 (19 March 1849).
[6] Victoria to Leopold, 18 December 1849: RA Y94/55.
[7] 3PD 115, c. 884 (1 April 1851).

more worried on Britain's account than she herself was, Lord Palmerston gave the same assurance, that 'Her Majesty's Government have no fear that the internal tranquillity of this Country will be disturbed' by foreign visitors to the Exhibition, chiefly because the cost of coming would deter 'any great number of persons below a certain class in society', and for those who were not deterred, and had hostile designs, there would be waiting in London 'Two million of people, the great mass of whom are deeply interested in the maintenance of order', and who would rally round to defend it if required.[8] At the other end of the decade a Conservative Home Secretary, when it was suggested to him that French refugees might be planning to sabotage telegraph wires and railway track simultaneously with a French invasion, poured scorn on the notion that they would be likely to want to carry out the schemes of the government which had proscribed them.[9] On the periphery of government there were some men who felt differently. Permanent under-secretaries may have done so; and also British ambassadors abroad, who tended sometimes to take on some of the colour of their surroundings and to express very continental opinions on the matter, whether or not they were asked for them.[10] (George Hamilton Seymour, for example, who was British ambassador in St Petersburg from 1851 to 1854 and then in Vienna, was strongly of the opinion that between Britain and the continent there was 'a great community of interests' over the question of the refugees, who he believed 'would avail themselves with equal alacrity of an opportunity of promoting insurrection in London or Manchester' as they would in Paris or Berlin.)[11] At the centre, however, cabinet ministers of whatever party showed very little sign at all of concern over it, either in public or, so far as it is possible to discover, in private.[12] By and large they appear to have shared the general incredulity at the very idea that Britain could be subverted by foreigners.

Nor was this mere bravado. The government's confidence was well founded: firstly on what *The Times* called 'the experience of ages',[13] which had thrown up very few examples in the past of refugees actively engaging themselves in British affairs; and secondly, in the fairly good intelligence which, from about 1850, they had of the refugees' activities from the Metropolitan Police, and from which scarcely a suspicion of danger

[8] Palmerston to Bloomfield no. 56, 7 March 1851: PRO FO 65/387.
[9] 3PD 160, c. 287 (27 July 1860).   [10] *Vide infra*, pp. 142–3.
[11] Seymour to Granville no. 40, 31 January 1852: PRO FO 65/407.
[12] The private papers of prime ministers and home and foreign secretaries which are available for this period reveal not the slightest hint of any concern for the effect of the presence of the refugees on British domestic politics. In a letter to the Home Secretary, Sir George Grey, on 10 January 1851, Palmerston wrote that he was far more uneasy about the state of Britain's military defences than he was about any of the rumours then current that foreigners were conspiring against the life of the Queen: Palm. P., GC/GR/2588.
[13] *The Times*, 19 September 1850, p. 4.

appeared. The extent of police surveillance of the refugees will be discussed later. It may not have been completely thorough or reliable. But it was fairly extensive and, so far as can be gathered, generally reassuring on this issue. Only one of the police reports which still survive contains any suggestion that refugees might be involved in domestic British politics.[14] At other times they ignored the possibility, or dismissed it: 'I have not heard them once say the least thing', reported one police spy of their meetings in 1850, 'to lead anyone to fear of their meddling with this country.'[15] Of course this, as we have seen, was what the refugees themselves very much wanted the authorities to believe, but it was probably true too. Such assurances will have neutralised any feelings which ministers might have had, that the country might be just a little less fireproof, a little more receptive to revolutionary agitation, than was widely assumed. If there was no sign that the refugees were making fire, then it was unlikely that the country could be fired by them.

If governments therefore differed a little from the public in their opinions of the refugee question, as we shall see they sometimes did, it was not because they regarded the refugees as more of a threat to themselves. If they had it would undoubtedly have been worse for the refugees. Nor was it, initially at any rate, because they accepted any more fully than public opinion did the continentals' assessment of the threat the refugees posed to *them*. Among the dominant political élite of the day the same liberal theory of revolution prevailed as among the mouthpieces of opinion: that civil rebellion and disaffection had broad and not narrow causes, and were not to be as easily provoked as the continental conservatives assumed, if the people were justly and liberally treated, by secret societies and red agitators, but were generally the result of bad government; and *could not*, therefore, in the nature of things, possibly be blamed on the actions of any individual or group of individuals at all. Palmerston in the House of Commons in 1852 found a vivid metaphor for it.

A single spark will explode a powder magazine, and a blazing torch will burn out harmless on a turnpike road. If a country be in a state of suppressed internal discontent, a very slight indication may augment that discontent, and produce an

[14] On 20 November 1855 a policeman in Jersey retailed – without comment or corroboration – information he had received that 'Mazzini, Ledru Rollin, Kossuth, and many other Refugees are not strangers to the disturbances in London, and that their object is to keep up the excitement. . . to push the people to violence': PRO HO 45/6188. The 'disturbances' here referred to were probably the serious 'bread riots' which affected London and other cities in February, June and October 1855: see *Annual Register* 1855, Chronicle pp. 32–3, 106–7, 157.

[15] Anonymous report of 19 May 1850 (by J. H. Sanders), in PRO FO 27/887. Cf. Police report by Field, [20] October 1849, in PRO FO 27/859: 'My informant positively states that the French Refugees have nothing whatever to do with any party in England'; also Mayne to Waddington 12 August 1851, in PRO FO 27/921; and police report (Sanders) of 5 March 1853, in PRO HO 45/4816.

explosion; but if the country be well governed, and the people be contented, then letters and proclamations from unhappy refugees will be as harmless as the torch upon the turnpike road.[16]

To Seymour in St Petersburg in 1851 he expressed the same idea, that 'men with the most dangerous intentions who are living . . . in exile can have little means of creating disturbances in their own Country, unless there exists in that country a great mass of political discontent'; and also its corollary: that it was 'generally within the Power of all Govt⁵ so to order the internal affairs of the Countries which they rule, as to remove any just causes of general dissatisfaction', and hence the real roots of revolution.[17] This line of argument was a particular favourite at this time of Palmerston's, who used it especially to berate Austria for the illiberalism which, in his view, undermined her long-term security and consequently her credibility as a pillar of the European balance. But the same idea was shared too by the Liberal foreign secretaries who came after him, and especially by Lord Clarendon, who was at the Foreign Office for the bulk of the decade, and who believed strongly that it was to Austria's own advantage to be more liberal, in order to give her people 'a *personal* interest in checking revolution' which would render all the machinations of Kossuth and Mazzini impotent.[18] If he had been an anarchist, he once told the Austrian ambassador Colloredo, he would

prefer one proclamation of Marshal Radetskys [sic] to any number of Mazzini's or Kossuths [sic], as far more likely to promote the objects I had in view: . . . the latter excited universal disgust and contempt, but . . . the indiscriminate sequestration of property in Lombardy and the wholesale expulsion of thousands of poor harmless peasants in retaliation for four Capucin monks having been sent out of Tessin, were deeds almost without parallel in modern history, which must create a spirit of resistance and revolution, even if it did not exist before, and alienate from Austria the wealthy, the intelligent, and the moderate persons of all classes, whom a really conservative Govᵗ would desire to rally round the throne.[19]

Sometimes it appeared to him that the emperors were merely using the refugees as a kind of diversionary scapegoat, to avoid having to deal with their problems at their roots: 'It is far easier to attribute to them the risings and revolutionary spirit that prevail than to look into the causes of popular discontent at home.'[20] All this was the pure milk of mid-century liberalism, as smug and arrogant as anything that appeared in the pages of the *Daily News*: in perfect unison with the mood of the time.

Palmerston and Clarendon also shared the popular view that the conti-

[16] 3PD 119, cc. 511–12 (1 April 1852).
[17] Palmerston to Seymour no. 53, 28 October 1851: PRO FO 65/390.
[18] Clarendon to Westmorland (private), 29 March 1853: Clar. P. c. 125 pp. 175–89.
[19] Clarendon to Westmorland no. 25, 10 March 1853: PRO FO 7/412.
[20] Clarendon to Lord Howard de Walden (private), 1 March 1853: Clar. P. c. 125 pp. 23–5.

nentals in any case greatly exaggerated the harm the refugees could do to them if they wanted. If this, wrote Clarendon to Westmorland in Vienna after making some inquiries about them, was

the 'Central Committee of London' about wh. so much has been said and written, I can only congratulate the Austrian Govt. upon the numbers and character of its enemies in the Country and assure them that the *English* Govt. has many more such committees and of a far more formidable description, constantly but harmlessly at work for its destruction.[21]

There is, he wrote to Westmorland on another occasion, 'exaggeration about these Refugees and . . . many things are attributed to them of wh. they are not guilty'.[22] His own opinion was

that though the Refugees desire the destruction of their respective Govts. they do little or nothing to promote their detestable objects. In fact they *cannot*. They have no money and they find no countenance in England. They may write a few letters and suggest risings but such things always depend on the circumstances of time and place and can never be effectually directed from a distance.[23]

Consequently Clarendon told Colloredo in March 1853 'that the more I reflected on this subject the more convinced I had become that Austria had comparatively little to fear from the Refugees, so long as they remained in England'.[24] Palmerston's view was identical. To the French ambassador Marescalchi in 1851 he was reported to have said

that he believed the number of Italians in London to be small, and . . . that the distance between England and Italy is great and that the means of communication between them are difficult, and that it seems doubtful how far the Italian Refugees in London can exert any sensible action upon the conduct and proceedings of their Partisans in Italy.[25]

'How are they to do it?' he asked the House of Commons in April 1852 – by sending money?

Why, good Heavens! the money that those unhappy refugees, who were living in lodgings in back places, some of them of the lowest kind, and who could hardly pay for their daily subsistence – what kind of danger could there possibly arise to any foreign Government from the money which such persons could send?[26]

That the refugees themselves professed violent intentions was of course beside the point. Palmerston never had been in the habit of taking threats at their face value. In another (Irish) context he told Normanby in 1848 how in his opinion 'there is some distance between saying and doing; and

[21] Clarendon to Westmorland (private), 29 March 1853: Clar. P. c. 125 pp. 175–89.
[22] Clarendon to Westmorland (private), 1 March 1853: *ibid.* c. 125 pp. 12–17.
[23] Clarendon to Westmorland (private), 8 March 1853: *ibid.* c. 125 pp. 63–9.
[24] Clarendon to Westmorland no. 25, 10 March 1853: PRO FO 7/412.
[25] Addington to Waddington, 1 February 1851: PRO HO 45/3720.
[26] 3PD 119, cc. 511, 512 (1 April 1852).

Bragging and swaggering are not always the forerunners of action'.[27] This notably unhysterical and sceptical approach of both of them was, again, fully in tune with the times.

It will probably therefore mainly have *derived* from the times, and from those assumptions and prejudices and modes of reasoning which determined the popular attitude too. It was a naïve view of things, out of touch with continental realities, and based very largely upon peculiarly English conditions from which no general deductions should properly have been made. Ministers appear for example to have had a very simple and fixed idea of the kind of man who was likely to be conspiratorial and violent: generally the 'lower classes' of refugee, and not the 'respectable' classes who, supposedly, had less need to be.[28] This was convenient and reassuring, because it was also assumed that to foment revolution from a distance required money, which the 'lower classes' were usually conspicuously short of. But government ministers also had better reasons for playing down the harm that the refugees were supposed to do. In the first place they had very good cause to distrust the continentals' version of things. They knew better than anyone, for example, how dubious were some of the methods by which foreign police forces elicited their intelligence: through spies and *agents-provocateurs* who were less intent on finding out the truth about the refugees than on incriminating them, and whose efforts were occasionally, as we have seen,[29] revealed to the British police by the refugees themselves. 'I receive all these histories with some amount of distrust', wrote Lord Cowley from Paris to Clarendon after another of the many conspiracies against the French emperor's life had been uncovered in July 1853, 'because it is known now that while Maupas was Minister of Police, plots were got up in order that the necessity of a Minister of Police might be shewn';[30] 'the French Government', wrote Clarendon to Cowley four years later, 'Employ such a number of spies & pay them so absurdly high that they must furnish something for their wages & I am sure that all manner of absurdities are sent to Paris'.[31] When pressed, even the French government could occasionally be got to acknowledge that their secret

---

[27] Palmerston to Normanby (private), 18 July 1848: Palm. P., GC/NO f. 482. Palmerston might have been pleased to know that this was (or was to become) Karl Marx's opinion too: 'Shouting and doing are irreconcilable opposites' – letter to Jenny Marx, 11 April 1881, in Karl Marx and F. Engels, *Correspondence 1846–1895* (1934) p. 390.

[28] In 1854 the intelligence that a Pole who was suspected of being a Russian spy was lodging with a 'respectable' Englishman was enough to persuade Palmerston that he was not one: see PRO HO 45/5684; and police inquiries into refugees were often allowed to stop when it had been ascertained that the men under surveillance, and their acquaintances, were 'respectable'. E.g. Grey to Foreign Office, 10 July 1849: PRO FO 27/858; Police report by Field, 12 February 1851: PRO HO 45/3720; and by Sanders, 30 December 1851: PRO MEPO 2/43. [29] *Supra*, p. 38.

[30] Cowley to Clarendon (private), 6 July 1853: Cowl. P., PRO FO 519/211, pp. 8–9.

[31] Clarendon to Cowley (private), 23 June 1857: *ibid.*, PRO FO 519/175, ff. 963–9.

agents were not totally dependable: 'Fould admits', wrote Cowley again, 'that these fellows accusations are liable to suspicion.'[32] Invariably, therefore, police reports from France or from any other foreign country were handled warily.

The distrust which the British authorities felt towards them was confirmed by information they had from their own sources, which frequently showed them up to be exaggerated, or even sometimes fabricated. Although the refugees were not widely known to be under the surveillance of the British police we have seen that they were, so that British governments were not forced to rely on foreign governments for knowledge of them. The British police, however, when they looked saw very different things from the foreign spies, or, more often, saw the same things but interpreted them differently: saw merely smoke where the spies saw fire, for example, or hopeless dreams where the spies detected material conspiracies. Consequently this pattern of events was common: that a British ambassador in, for example, Berlin would be shown a report from the Prussian secret police in London, which was full of fire and fury and talk of revolutions and assassinations being hatched around Leicester Square; which he passed on to the Foreign Office, which in turn sent it to the Home Office, which gave it to the Metropolitan Police Commissioner to look in to, who put one of his detectives on to it: who reported back that, yes, there was some wild talk, but nothing dangerous, and that in reality the refugees' activities were mild and harmless and even a little pathetic. Again and again alarmist reports from foreign governments were doused in this way, shown up to be (as the Commissioner commented to the Foreign Secretary about one of them in June 1852) 'either wholly untrue, or so exaggerated as to amount to misrepresentation . . . the production of an agent wishing to make information out of very slender materials'.[33] It became the normal official response to reports of this kind to disregard them – sometimes mistakenly: the authorities' first reaction to news of Mazzini's Italian loan, for example, was to disbelieve it.[34] Foreign police authorities for their part, when they were confronted by the British police versions of these matters, were similarly incredulous: a British report sent to him on some French refugees in 1857, commented the French Minister of the Interior, was 'en complet desaccord' with the information he had received from every other source, whose veracity he regarded as 'incontestable'.[35] Usually it was not the evidence which conflicted, so much as the interpretation of that evidence,

[32] Cowley to Clarendon (private), 28 June 1857: *ibid.*, PRO FO 519/221, pp. 283–5.
[33] Mayne to Malmesbury, 5 June 1852: PRO MEPO 1/46.
[34] See Waddington to Foreign Office, 14 November 1850: PRO HO 45/3234; and Addington to Koller, 18 November 1850: PRO FO 7/384.
[35] Billault to Walewski, 26 July 1857, enclosed in Cowley to Clarendon (private), 7 August 1857: Clar. P., c. 75 ff. 74–9.

which depended on the very different assumptions the two sides brought to it. Between the two channels of intelligence there was no common ground; no common premise or conclusion. To the English police the French seemed sensationalist; to the French the English appeared naïve.

Whatever were the rights or wrongs of this, however, the consequence of it was that the British authorities' earliest reaction to continental complaints about the refugees was to underrate them. Sometimes they appeared to believe that they were not intended seriously. The refugee issue was merely a pretext, for launching a diplomatic offensive on Britain whose fundamental cause was something else. To the Austrian ambassador Count Colloredo in February 1853 Clarendon expressed his 'apprehension' that it was 'less on account of the protection we gave to Refugees' that they were so disliked on the continent, 'than of the example afforded by our institutions', combined, he said, with the Church of Rome's 'ill will' towards their religion.[36] To Hamilton Seymour he attributed Austria's bad feeling to simple jealousy: 'Our institutions and our perfect tranquillity with perfect liberty are offences she can't pardon.'[37] By itself therefore the refugee question was not intrinsically important: or if it was, then because it was based upon unreasonable fears of the harm the refugees were capable of, when these fears were proved groundless it would *cease* to be important. This devaluing of the force of the continental complaints, though it appeared dangerous to some of Britain's ambassadors who were closer to and consequently more aware of the real depth of feeling on this question at foreign courts, was nevertheless a genuine enough conviction on the part of Liberal foreign secretaries in the early 1850s; who on the basis of it made a show, at any rate, of trying to persuade the continentals of the baselessness of their fears. After all, Clarendon asked Colloredo in 1853, 'what can their possible machinations amount to?' – and he went on to rehearse to him all the familiar arguments for disbelieving their capacity for evil: their cowardice, their poverty, and at the bottom of it all the fundamental liberal tenet, that not conspiracy but repression was the cause of revolutions.

Her Majesty's Government have no wish, and claim no right, to interfere in the internal affairs of other Countries, but as our own system of Government is now seriously criticised I may be permitted to observe that so long as arbitrary Government is carried on to its utmost limits on the Continent, and so long as measures of desperate and undiscriminating rigour such as those now applied to Milan are

---

[36] Clarendon to Westmorland no. 18, 2 March 1853: PRO FO 7/412; and cf. Clarendon to Victoria, 25 February 1853 February 1853, in *Letters of Queen Victoria 1837–61*, vol. II, p. 535. To Bloomfield in Berlin Baron Manteuffel confirmed this analysis in February: see Bloomfield to Russell no. 76, 22 February 1853: PRO FO 64/353.

[37] Clarendon to Seymour (private), 23 March 1853: Clar. P. c. 125 pp. 142–3.

resorted to, so long will popular discontent exist and its manifestations by revolutionary outbreak must be expected.[38]

'Nobody likes to be told of their faults', wrote Palmerston in 1851;[39] and Austria predictably accepted none of this. It was no use, Westmorland reported back from Vienna, 'telling them that their own mode of governing is in fault, for they turn round at once & say it is the constant conspiracy agst. us which you nourish in your bosom which forces upon us the measures you find fault with'.[40] Again the ideological chasm yawned between them, as between different worlds, with so little common ground between them as to make understanding impossible, let alone agreement.

Government ministers always managed to sound, and in all probability were, genuinely aggrieved by the virulence of the continental attack on them over this issue. It was considered unjust for all kinds of reasons: not only because the continent's troubles were considered to be fundamentally its own fault much more than that of the refugees, but also because many of the refugees themselves had been deliberately shipped by continental governments to Britain, which had not asked to have them and whose inability to police them had always been made absolutely clear. Britain felt she had as much a grievance for being forced to put up with them as had the continent for having to bear the impact of their conspiracies. In the 1830s we saw that she frequently made protests to continental governments against their practice of making England a 'penal colony' for their political malcontents,[41] and these protests were resumed in the 1850s.[42] That after sending them there they should then complain of their being there was almost unendurable: Palmerston likened it to a thief slipping stolen goods into the pocket of a 'respectable gentleman' and then putting the police on him.[43] 'It really is too bad of the French Police', wrote Clarendon in 1857, 'to drive over here all the Italian Refugees & every other vagabond whom they want to get rid of & then complain that we harbour them.'[44] The French initially made the rather lame response that if Britain was so certain the refugees were harmless she should not mind their being sent to her, but they were eventually made to see the point, and

[38] Clarendon to Westmorland no. 18, 2 March 1853: PRO FO 7/412; and cf. Clarendon to Westmorland no. 25, 10 March 1853: *ibid.*, *loc. cit.*
[39] Palmerston to Westmorland (private), 21 November 1851: Palm. P. GC/WE f. 202.
[40] Westmorland to Clarendon (private), 23 March 1853: Clar. P. c. 1 ff. 64–6.
[41] *Supra*, pp. 52–3.
[42] E.g. Palmerston to Normanby no. 346, 24 July 1849: PRO FO 27/837; Palmerston to Normanby no. 84, 11 March 1851: PRO FO 27/893 and HO 45/3518; Cowley to Malmesbury no. 407, 12 July 1852: PRO FO 27/935; Anglo-Belgian correspondence, July–August 1854, in PRO HO 45/5635; Cowley to Clarendon no. 1158, 16 August 1857: PRO FO 27/1202; and Malmesbury to Malakoff, 4 December 1858: PRO FO 27/1275.
[43] Palmerston to Clarendon, 28 February 1853: Clar. P., c. 3 ff. 1–2.
[44] Clarendon to Cowley (private), 25 July 1857: Cowl. P., FO 519/176 ff. 25–9.

stopped the practice.[45] British governments felt they had other reasons to complain too. It was not ever said to his face, but it was considered to be impertinent of Napoleon III to protest against conspiracies hatched in exile in England when his own return to France in 1848 had been the result of a conspiracy hatched in exile in England by him.[46] And it was considered equally unjust to complain of Britain's ineffective policing of the refugees when the continent's own record in this respect was so imperfect. Continental police forces were always railing against Mazzini's being allowed so often to slip into Europe from England: yet they were never themselves smart enough to spot him as he came in, even though by all accounts his features were not the easiest to disguise; and in the case of the Orsini plot, for example, did nothing to stop it even though they were told of it in advance.[47] British ministers and diplomats were hardly ever found to have a good word to say for foreign police forces, who were supposed to be as inept at detecting political crimes when they occurred as they were ingenious at fabricating them when they did not. ('When I hear of a Continent[l] State in difficulty', wrote Seymour privately to Clarendon in 1857, in this context, 'my first idea is why don't they get rid of their Police.')[48] Very often it was felt that when foreign police authorities complained against Britain it was merely to cover up their own failings.[49] After all, as Scotland Yard pointed out in 1853, Mazzini was out of England for weeks before the Milan *émeute* in February, and was likely therefore to have incriminated himself more deeply abroad than in England – why blame England for not suspecting him when he was acting innocently, when the Austrian police had failed to detect him when he was acting guiltily?[50]

Which was all very fair so far as it went, except that it did not really touch the core of the continentals' sense of grievance: which was against the sight of sanguinary deeds being plotted by men in a refuge near them yet out of their reach, and with nothing being done about it by those who *had* authority over them; which did not make things *easier* for the continental

[45] See Normanby to Palmerston no. 100, 14 April 1851: PRO FO 27/900; and Foreign Office to Home Office 5 June 1851: PRO FO 27/920, which reports that the practice has been stopped. There is a file on this, containing some of the Anglo–French correspondence, in the Home Office papers: PRO HO 45/3518.
[46] E.g. Seymour to Clarendon no. 100, 3 February 1858: PRO FO 7/539.
[47] See Howard de Walden to Clarendon (private), 15 January 1858: Clar. P., c 83 ff. 17–18; Clarendon to Cowley (private), 20 January 1858: Cowl. P., PRO FO 519/177 ff. 65–73.
[48] Seymour to Clarendon (private), 4 August 1857: Clar. P., c. 87 ff. 367–9.
[49] E.g. Charles Wood to Clarendon, 9 March 1853: Clar. P., c. 4 ff. 278–82.
[50] See Addington to Clarendon, 24 February 1853: Clar. P., c. 1 f. 3; and enclosure in Clarendon to Westmorland (private), 1 March 1853: *ibid.*, c. 125 ff. 12–17. Count Buol's reply to this was that 'although as your Lordship stated Mazzini left England to direct the immediate outbreak in Italy, yet he [Buol] considered it was to reap the fruit of a conspiracy which had previously been organised': Westmorland to Clarendon no. 161, 13 April 1853: PRO FO 7/418.

police authorities, however inept they might have been. And with this general grievance British government ministers did feel some considerable sympathy. *They* did not like the sight of such things being done in England either. 'Exhortations and Incentives to assassination', wrote Palmerston to Sir George Grey in 1855, 'do not belong to the range of that Political discussion, the freedom of which is entitled to respect.'[51] To the House of Commons he offered the opinion in 1858 that

> it can never be the wish of the English people that, under the pretence of enjoying security against oppression, men should be allowed to be here plotting offences of the deepest dye, and instigating others to commit crimes involving other countries in scenes of anarchy and bloodshed by the assassination of those who may be at the head of the Government.[52]

To foreign complainants ministers made strenuous efforts to emphasise this disapproval.[53] Sometimes those foreign complainants appeared to doubt it: but it was genuine.

The reasons why foreign governments sometimes doubted the genuineness of Britain's professions of hostility to revolution on the continent have been touched on already.[54] In their eyes, and with their explanatory 'model' of revolution before them, too many of Britain's diplomatic and political actions in the recent past appeared to be feeding the flames of revolution to make them confident that this was not deliberate. In fact it was certainly not. None of the leading statesmen in office in the 1850s, be he a Liberal or a Whig or a Protectionist or a Peelite, could be said to be a natural sympathiser with revolution, unless perhaps it were revolution of the most gradual kind for which really the word was a misnomer. To all of them it went without saying that social revolution of the sort dreamt of by the socialists and democrats of the time was anathema, antipathetic to their own material interests as well as to their principles and ideals. Not wanting these things for themselves, it is of course feasible that they might have welcomed them for the continent, for malevolent reasons – in order to destroy it. It is also feasible that the 'liberals' among them might have been more sympathetic towards revolutions of another kind: revolutions which aimed to liberate 'nationalities' from alien control and establish them as autonomous states. Nationalism after all was a close relation of nineteenth-century European liberalism; for many people the one automatically predicated the other. Nevertheless this was not so for most British ministers in the 1850s, least of all for those

[51] Palmerston to Grey, 12 October 1855: Palm. P., BL. Add. Ms. 48579, f. 80.
[52] 3PD 148 c. 1073 (9 February 1858).
[53] E.g. in Clarendon to Westmorland no. 18, 2 March 1853: PRO FO 7/412; and see Clarendon to Reeve 4 March 1853: Clar. P., c. 535 box 3, asking him in an article he is about to write to 'take care to condemn strongly the abuse of hospitality by the Refugees', in order to make the Liberals' position clear to the continent.　　　[54] *Supra*, pp. 55–7.

most concerned with the conduct of foreign policy. Neither was it true that any British minister wished to encourage any other sort of revolution on the continent in order to destroy it. If for no other reason, neither of these courses of action could possibly have been entertained, because both of them were entirely incompatible with the main principles of British foreign policy, based firmly upon Britain's own national interests, as they were officially conceived then.

No British government wished to see the continent of Europe destroyed, or revolutionised, or broken up into nationalities. Their main concern was to see her settled and at peace, which they believed would best be guaranteed by a 'balance of power' between the major states of Europe. What was chiefly feared was an upsetting of that balance in favour of one state or another, which might impel Britain to involve herself expensively and damagingly in the affairs of the continent, in order to correct the balance to resist the domination of Europe by one power, or because she was directly threatened herself. That was the prevailing orthodoxy of the time. It followed from it that a country destroyed would endanger the balance, by tempting other states to aggrandize themselves at her expense; as would a country successfully revolutionised, which if historical experience was anything to go by would be likely to turn into an aggrandising power herself. For the same kind of reason it was not considered to be in Britain's interest for putative nationalities to become nation states, if it was done in a way which would weaken another power. A little later in the century, under the tutelage of Gladstone, British liberalism became largely won over to the cause of European nationalism, even for Britain's own constituent nationalities. In the 1850s among the political establishment, however, this had not yet happened. This was not wholly understood even at the time. Lord Clarendon in 1854 regretted the 'popular clamour' that was being got up among the 'rabble' by 'Revolutionaries' in England 'for the purpose of getting it believed abroad that England is in favour of distinct nationalities'.[55] The misunderstanding may have arisen from a widespread confusion between the concepts of liberalism and nationalism, which for both Clarendon and Palmerston (and even at this time for Gladstone)[56] were perfectly distinct. What they wished upon Europe was her liberalisation: which we have seen was regarded by continental conservatives as only one short step away from a direr fate, but which Englishmen saw as a means to avoid such a fate. It was the sympathy he felt towards their liberal aspirations which engendered the support Palmerston gave to the Hungarian dissidents between 1848 and 1851, and not any sympathy for their national aims, which he did nothing at all to promote. Hungarian nationalism was a natural product of illiberal repres-

[55] Clarendon to Westmorland (private), 7 June 1854: Clar. P. c. 129 p. 34.
[56] See J. Morley, *The Life of William Ewart Gladstone* (1903), vol. II pp. 12–13.

sion: but it was nonetheless undesirable in itself, and indeed he believed it would be unnecessary, and seen to be such by the Magyars themselves, were Hungary to be governed, still by Austria, but liberally. Besides this, a separate Hungarian nationality would weaken Austria, which would unsettle the European balance of power, and thus in the end hinder the advance of moderate liberalism in Europe which needed the kind of stability guaranteed by the balance to provide the best conditions for it. There were other places where such amputations might not have this effect, and where therefore Palmerston might be prepared to give his sanction to them. Austria's Italian provinces, for example, he believed to be only a source of weakness to her; which if they were separated from her could only assist her to perform better her 'balancing' rôle in Europe, and which in addition might also, in independent confederation with other northern Italian states, serve as a much-needed buffer state between Austria and France. But with nationalism for its own sake – the national-ism of the Italian and Hungarian and Polish and Wallachian refugees in England – Palmerston had no truck at all.

This was a difficult distinction for continental statesmen to grasp, and it may not have been a distinction which was commonly made by Palmerston's countrymen. But Palmerston was quite clear about it. To Lord Westmorland in Vienna in November 1851 he spelt out the strength of his support for the Austrian empire, and the particular nature of that support. What, he asked, were 'the general Feelings of this country about Austria among men who understand the subject . . . ?' (He meant primar-ily himself.)

Not hostility to Austria as a Power but dislike & disapproval of the Policy of the men who direct & have directed the affairs of Austria. No man who comprehends the Interests of Europe & the Interests of England as connected with those of Europe can doubt for a moment that there should be in the middle of Europe a great Power like Austria to hold the balance between Russia & France . . . Men here do not think indeed that for this purpose it can be necessary that Austria should hold northern Italy in chains, nor do men believe that the occupation of Milan & Venice is a source of strength to Austria[;] they think on the contrary that it is an Element of weakness. But no impartial & rational man could wish to see Hungary, Bohemia, Gallicia & Austria separated from each other. A wise & enlightened Policy on the part of the Austrian Govt. might have cemented these several parts into a coherent whole instead of leaving the Austrian Empire to be that which Metternich represented Italy as being[,] only a Nom Geographique. Now all this must be to reasoning & enlightened men a matter of deep regret, but only of Regret.[57]

Lord Clarendon's attitude towards Austria diverged not at all from this:

we shall probably be told to mind our own business . . . but believe me we are animated by feelings of sincere good will towards Austria, we desire to see her

[57] Palmerston to Westmorland (private), 21 November 1851: Palm. P. GC/WE f. 202.

strong and respected for her own sake as well as for ours, we are sure that the antagonism of the two Govts. would be a European calamity because it wd. remove a guarantee of peace and we cannot therefore as honest friends or honest men refrain from giving our opinion upon matters wh. we think discreditable and dangerous.[58]

Although their recipe for ensuring it might seem a curious and unacceptable one to Austria's own rulers, a powerful Austria – and also a powerful (but not too powerful) France, Russia and Prussia – were considered to be fundamental British interests. Another fundamental British interest was to avoid direct armed conflict with any of these states over a trivial issue (like the question of the refugees), from which she would have nothing to gain if she won, and which if she were alone in it she might very possibly lose. This was almost self-evident.

These general but nonetheless imperative considerations of national policy meant that British governments took no pleasure at all in the sight of Austria or any other of the European great powers being discomfited by the activities of nationalist or democratic refugees in England. (It was a different matter in the case of lesser powers, like Naples, whose discomfiture Liberal ministers did greatly relish and indeed positively and materially abetted.)[59] As well as these broad considerations there were narrower ones which worked to the same effect. The two European great powers which suffered most from the activities of the refugees, and which therefore complained most about them, were Austria and France. As well as general reasons for wishing these two countries to be strong, there also came to be in the 1850s particular reasons for wishing them to be friendly to Britain. In the tortuous diplomatic conflict over the Eastern question which culminated in 1854 in the Crimean War, when Britain's antagonist was a supposedly overweening Russia, it was important for Britain that Austria should at least be held back from an alliance with Russia to which many common affinities and some common interests between them seemed to point; and absolutely vital that the alliance with France be held firm. Successive foreign ministers in the 1850s placed emphasis on the French entente; none more so, however, than Palmerston, whose attitude towards the new French empire was notably warmer than his public's. His speedy recognition of Louis Napoleon's *coup d'état* had been a factor contributing to his fall in December 1851; and it is significant that when he returned as Prime Minister Palmerston revealed himself, in 1855 and in 1858, to be far more sympathetically responsive to foreign complaints

[58] Clarendon to Westmorland (private), 29 March 1853: Clar. P., c. 125 pp. 175–89.
[59] E.g. Gladstone's campaign against King 'Bomba'; and Panizzi's plot, assisted by Palmerston and some others, to free some of his prisoners: H. Rudman, *Italian Nationalism and English Letters* (1940), pp. 206–7, 251–7, 263–5. That Palmerston and also Clarendon were implicated in the Panizzi plot is corroborated by letters from Palmerston to Clarendon, 29 July and 2 August 1855, in Clar. P., c. 31 ff. 360–1, 374. See also *supra*, p. 33 fn. 84.

about the refugees when they came from France, than when they came from any other continental country. During the course of the Crimean War, when France and Britain for a period seemed to be pulling in different directions – Britain wanting to fight on, France to settle – the good will of France was particularly essential. All this put a kind of personal premium too on the life of the French emperor, on which it was widely supposed the Anglo-French alliance entirely depended, so that, as Henry Greville observed in September 1855, 'were anything to happen to him, the whole edifice would crumble at once'.[60] The worst nightmare of all was that something might happen to him at the hands of the refugees in England, which he visited in April that year: 'what a calamity for Europe in general & Engd *in particular*', wrote Clarendon to Cowley, 'if an attentat were to be successful here ! ! !'[61]

There can be no doubt at all that for the refugees, their causes and their activities, British government ministers in the 1850s had no sympathy at all, but rather the reverse. They had good reason to dislike them, and even – for the effect they were liable to have on Britain's foreign relations – to fear them. Of all ministers foreign secretaries disliked them most, partly perhaps because they were constitutionally less sympathetic to their ideas, but mainly because they were closest to the diplomatic nerves which the refugees could touch. More hostile even than secretaries of state were the professional diplomats and permanent officials, who lived their whole lives in foreign fields, and far apart from those moods and prejudices of their own people towards which even the most aristocratic foreign secretary – even though he might resent it – was supposed to have some direct responsibility. (This tendency of the diplomatic cadre was admitted by some diplomats themselves, like for example Henry Bulwer, who in 1855 gave as one of his reasons for approving Lord John Russell's cabinet mission that 'in transacting any business of great importance with another state one of the most essential qualities is to have a thorough acquaintance with the spirit and interest of our own: a point on which a mere diplomatist generally fails'.)[62] Consequently the men of affairs who most regretted the absence of Alien Acts at this time were ambassadors, like the first Lord Cowley who in 1845 called their repeal 'absurd';[63] and permanent under-secretaries like Henry Waddington, who in 1850 was strongly in favour of renewing the Act of 1848.[64] For this kind of reason too ambassadors sometimes appeared to support foreign demands over the refugees to a point which put in doubt whether they saw it as their main function to

[60] Viscountess Enfield (ed.), *Leaves from the Diary of Henry Greville*, 2nd. series (1884), p. 243.

[61] Clarendon to Cowley (private), 19 March 1855: Cowl. P., PRO FO 519/171 ff. 225–8.

[62] Bulwer to Russell, 28 March 1855: Russell Papers, PRO 30/22/12D f. 56.

[63] F. A. Wellesley (ed.), *The Diary and Correspondence of. . .First Lord Cowley* (n.d.), p. 302.

[64] Note in Waddington's hand, n.d., in PRO HO 45/3272.

represent British views abroad, or foreign views to Britain. But this could not be true to the same extent of ministers of state: who, whatever their own personal inclinations might have been, had perforce to be more aware of what could, in a British context, be done. Lord Malmesbury, for example, when he was probed on the question of the refugees by Louis Napoleon in March 1853 admitted willingly that 'as we knew that half of them were rascals we should be very glad to get rid of them'; but the fact was that they could not. 'Every country', he went on, 'had its subject on which no cession could be made. The Holy places in the East was that of Russia, the Refugees was ours.'[65] Lord Clarendon also called them 'rascals', from whose presence he said Britain suffered greatly: 'but we cant help this consequence of our free institutions, & we must take the good & the bad of them together'.[66] It was regrettable, but it was so: and for all kinds of ultimately good reasons. This was what they told the continent.

The main reasons were that the British government had absolutely no power to banish or exclude refugees or any aliens at all; and that although it did have powers to discipline refugees in certain circumstances, those powers were very much narrower than any the continental complainants would consider sufficient. The fact that the government could not deport aliens was a main pillar by which Britain's policy of asylum – 'one of her dearest liberties'[67] – was supported. It was also a way of relieving her from the necessity of rejecting applications from foreign governments for the expulsion of certain refugees, or having to make invidious distinctions between them:

for supposing that a law for the expulsion of political refugees were passed, the Government would immediately be overwhelmed with applications to send away individuals said to be dangerous or conspiring against their respective Governments. To indiscriminate demands founded on rumour & the reports of foreign police, it would be impossible for the British Govt to yield without an utter abandonment of its dignity & independence, to investigate each particular case would always be difficult and often impossible: many demands would unavoidably be rejected and more irritation would be caused by constantly recurring refusals, than under the present system when our inability to comply with any such application is notorious.[68]

The only exceptions to this general rule were extradition treaties: which however at this time were very few indeed, specifically excluded political offences, and which anyway – certainly in the case of the treaty with France which dated back to 1843 – were in practice, for technical reasons,

---

[65] Lord Malmesbury, *Memoirs of an ex-Minister* (1885 edn.), pp. 299–301.
[66] Clarendon to Loftus (private), 21 July 1857: Clar. P. c. 139 p. 306.
[67] Bloomfield to Clarendon (private), 25 March 1853, retailing his own words to his Russian colleague in Berlin: Bloomfield Papers, PRO FO 356/30.
[68] Clarendon to Westmorland no. 18, 2 March 1853: PRO FO 7/412; cf. Granville's circular despatch of 13 January 1852: PP (1852) liv, pp. 72–4.

dead letters.[69] All that could be done to curb the refugees, therefore, had to be done in England. Even then it could not be done, as we have seen, in a discriminatory way – refugees forced to observe different codes of conduct from other subjects of the British Crown; and it had to be done according to the strict principles and procedures of English law, which ruled for example that nothing could be done before a crime was actually committed, and that the burden of proof of any offence lay with the prosecution. These restrictions meant that some refugee offenders, against whom there might be little 'moral doubt' of their guilt, would go undetected and unpunished. This, however, for reasons we have discussed, was accepted in England, and could not be altered.[70]

Yet until April 1858, when Simon Bernard was acquitted of complicity in Orsini's plot against the life of the French emperor, the claim was usually made by British governments as we have seen it was by the press, that despite all these limitations English law was 'amply sufficient' if not to prevent what should be prevented at least to punish what should be punished: or as the Home Secretary Sir George Grey somewhat tautologically put it in 1851, 'to punish by penalties the violation of the law by foreigners after we have been satisfied that these foreigners have really committed themselves in any case in which legal proceedings can be instituted'.[71] They held to this despite the fact that it was never once during the 1850s proved or even properly tested: scarcely any refugee charged with any serious offence in England, and not one convicted. When foreign governments pointed this out the British reply was always the same: that the men the continentals wanted charged (like Ledru-Rollin for complicity in the Tibaldi plot, for which a French court had found no difficulty at all in convicting him in his absence) were in fact innocent; or that there was simply no proof. When Britain asked foreign governments to provide proof they seldom gave satisfaction: 'It is now nearly two months', wrote Clarendon to Palmerston in May 1853, 'since we asked Buol for some of the facts "notorious to all the world" respecting the "London Central Committee" wch originated & executed every Continental Crime & the

---

[69] Between 1843 and 1852, of 14 applications made by the French government to Britain for the extradition of offenders, only one succeeded: 3PD 122, c. 193 (8 June 1852). The difficulties of working the old convention with France were described during the debate of 1852 over the ratification of a new one: *ibid.*, cc. 192–214, 498–508, 561–2, 1278–84. In the end that convention was not ratified. 'The reason that the passing of Extradition Acts is so difficult', wrote the Permanent Under-Secretary for Home Affairs in December 1857, 'is the extreme jealousy felt by the people of this country upon the subject of any interference by our Police or Magistrates with foreigners coming to this Country, upon the mere allegation of their own government that they have been guilty of some crime': Waddington memo. enclosed in Grey to Clarendon, 19 December 1857: Clar. P. c. 70 ff. 70–1.
[70] *Vide supra*, pp. 112–16.
[71] 3PD 115, c. 885 (1 April 1851). Cf. Lord Malmesbury the next year: 'the same law which inexorably protects will as inexorably punish them if they bring their conspiracies into a practical shape which clearly breaks it': 3PD 119, c. 675 (5 April 1852).

enclosed is the only result . . .'[72] In 1857 Clarendon was pressing the same point with the French government: that the whole British legal system was still willing and waiting and ready to go into action against refugees, the moment it was given some evidence:

if the French Government have any proofs . . . we will go to the utmost limits of English law to prevent such iniquity on the English soil but the Emperor must be aware that we cannot act upon the unsupported evidence of spies . . . He must also remember that during 3 years exactly the same things have been said about our harbouring the wd be assassins of the Empr but not one particle of proof has ever been furnished that any such plot was hatching beyond the wild & revengeful language in wch refugees always indulge. However let us be furnished with anything real and tangible and the Emperor may be sure that nothing which we can do for his protection shall be wanting.[73]

Of course it was not really up to foreign governments to furnish proof of crimes committed in England, and the British authorities themselves were by no means backward with their own efforts to bring refugee offenders to book. These only emphasised however the difficulties of the task. In 1853 in response to pressure from Austria[74] they went to considerable lengths to try to implicate Kossuth in a rocket-making enterprise in Rotherhithe which had contravened the explosives laws, but at the end of it all were unable to bring him to court because their only prosecution witness was a man with a known grudge against him which, as the police officers in charge of the investigation themselves admitted, 'might in a legal view prejudice his credibility'.[75] Other similar efforts foundered on the same rocks: the Law Officers of the Crown recommending against

---

[72] Clarendon to Palmerston, 6 May 1853: Palm. P., GC/CL/506.
[73] Clarendon to Cowley (private), 23 June 1857: Cowl. P., PRO FO 519/175 ff. 963–9.
[74] The investigations into this affair were begun at a time when Austrian government demands on Britain to institute proceedings against one or other of the refugees were most vociferous: see, for example, Aberdeen to the Queen, 27 February 1853: RA A23/14; Westmorland to Clarendon (private), 27 February 1853: Clar. P. c. 1 ff. 9–10.
[75] Police report of 26 March 1853: PRO HO 45/4816. At the beginning of the year the police were given information by a German refugee that war-rockets were being made for Kossuth at an arms factory run by a Mr Hale in Rotherhithe. A watch was put on the building then but nothing incriminating noticed. Surveillance was resumed again in March, but to no better effect, chiefly because it was found that the factory had for the time being stopped operating (*ibid., loc. cit.*, and see Palmerston to Clarendon 3 April 1853: Clar. P. c. 3 f.12). When it began manufacturing again Palmerston on 13 April ordered 'a Grand Razzia' on it, which revealed a quantity of explosive weapons there, 'nicely packed for Exportation' (Palmerston to Clarendon, 14 April 1853: Clar. P. c. 3 ff. 13–14), on the basis of which the government hoped to be able to charge Kossuth under the Foreign Enlistment Act (Palmerston to Prince Albert, 14 April 1853: RA J12/22). In the event, however, the connexion between the rockets and Kossuth could not be proved (Palmerston to Prince Albert, 15 April 1853: RA J12/25), and the best that could be done was to convict Hale for exceeding, marginally, the amount of gunpowder the law permitted him to keep on his premises – what Clarendon called 'a mere *pyrotechnicality*' (Clarendon to Palmerston, 14 April 1853: Palm. P. GC/CL/505). Some of the incidental implications and repercussions of this affair are mentioned *infra*, p. 162.

prosecuting Mazzini for his Italian bonds, for example, on the ground that material proof against him 'appears to be wanting';[76] or Kossuth for proclamations inciting Hungarian troops to mutiny on the ground that, although they bore his name; it could not be positively proved that he authorised its use.[77] In public government ministers always tried to uphold the adequacy of existing laws in these matters, but in private they were forced to admit, as Lord Aberdeen did to the Queen in 1853, that 'It cannot be denied that the state of the Law is very defective in this respect.'[78]

In the background to all this there was however another reason too for the government's inability to bring refugees to justice, and for the Law Officers' reluctance to recommend that they be brought to justice: which was that justice in criminal cases involved juries, and as the permanent under-secretary at the Home Office pointed out to Clarendon in 1855, 'you can never be *quite* sure of a Jury'.[79] In cases like these, involving foreign governments, juries were widely suspected to be undependable. In the atmosphere of the 1850s English courts proved to require a great deal of convincing to convict a refugee whom they believed to be the victim of persecution by a foreign despot in league with the English aristocracy. The trial of Simon Bernard in 1858, for complicity in the Orsini plot, was the most famous example of a jury seizing on the minutest gap in an otherwise convincing chain of evidence to acquit a man they believed to be the object of a political prosecution.[80] There had been a similar case, though not such an outrageous one, five years before when the Home Secretary instituted proceedings against a Frenchman called Eduard Raynaud who had been caught trying to conspire with the Prince de Joinville to assassinate Louis Napoleon, but was acquitted because the jury did not believe he was serious about it.[81] On other occasions the government, aware of the hazards, did not in the end attempt to prosecute. Asked for his opinion on the possibility of instituting proceedings against Mazzini in 1853 the Attorney-General Sir Alexander Cockburn replied that, although 'in point of law' he believed that 'such a prosecution could be sustained', yet he thought that 'the chance of obtaining a conviction would be very slight, as popular feeling would run very strong against the prosecution'.[82] Clarendon was quite open about this to the Austrian government: they could institute proceedings, he wrote, but it would be 'a course of such doubtful policy, – the evidence of the witnesses brought forward by the accused, and the inflammatory speeches of his Counsel, might so operate on the minds of the Jury, that the prospect of obtaining a verdict would be very

[76] L.O.O. of 11 March 1851, in PRO HO 45/3720 and 3234.   [77] *Ibid., loc. cit.*
[78] Aberdeen to Queen Victoria, 27 February 1853: RA A23/14.
[79] Waddington to Clarendon, 15 October 1855: Clar. P. c. 34 ff. 548–9.
[80] *Vide infra*, pp. 190–3.   [81] *The Times*, 18 August 1853, p. 9.
[82] Cockburn to Clarendon, 28 February 1853: Clar. P. c. 1 ff. 13–14.

problematical'; and if they failed things would be left worse than they had been before.[83] They were most reluctant to bring charges in cases of libel by refugees against foreign monarchs; which as Clarendon pointed out to the French government in 1855 even if a prosecution (in this case against *Reynolds's Newspaper* for carrying a libel by Félix Pyat) were successful, would do more harm than good by providing an opportunity for all the libels to be repeated in court, and more widely reported.[84] Where crimes with political motives or overtones were involved, an English jury was a highly deficient instrument for pacifying irate European allies. As the Law Officers tried to explain to the Austrian government over another such case in 1861, 'in matters of this description, whatever the English Law may be, the application of it depends entirely on the pleasure of the Jury, who are uncontrollable Judges both of Law and facts'.[85] That was the root of the problem.

This being so, it appeared to the *Quarterly Review* in June 1853 'absurd' that foreign governments should be expected to be content with such a situation, and with for example ' a system of trial which, as to political charges in times of popular excitement, has been found utterly ineffectual'. The *Quarterly Review* wanted a change in the laws.[86] But to almost everyone else in England it was clearly apparent that, for exactly the same reasons that convictions were difficult to come by under the existing laws, so would any alteration of the laws to the detriment of the refugees be difficult too; especially if it was felt, or could be represented, to be done in response to foreign pressure. Continental governments found it difficult to credit this – to see why, if a ministry had a parliamentary majority, it could not pass any measure it liked; or at least how it was able to tell that it could not, when it had not even tried. In 1853 Count Buol was totally bewildered by it; where, he asked Westmorland in February, was the difficulty, when as well as the coalition's own supporters 'the late Conservative Govt. wd. certainly join the present Govt. in carrying such a law if it was proposed'?[87] Prince Esterhazy, whose knowledge of English proverbs was somewhat better than his command of English spelling, voiced what seemed to be a general continental opinion when he told Clarendon that 'where there is *a will* their[*sic*] is *a way*';[88] and throughout the 1850s (or at

[83] Clarendon to Westmorland no. 18, 2 March 1853: PRO FO 7/412.
[84] Clarendon to Cowley (private), 31 October 1855: Cowl. P., PRO FO 519/172 ff. 405–10. France took Britain's advice and refrained from insisting on a prosecution; see Cowley to Clarendon (private), 14 November 1855: Cowl. P. PRO FO 519/217, p. 186.
[85] L.O.O. of 15 February 1861, in PRO HO 45/7233; and Russell to Apponyi, 22 February 1861: PRO FO 7/617.   [86] *Quarterly Review*, vol. 93 (June 1853), p. 141.
[87] Westmorland to Clarendon (private), 1 March 1853: Clar. P. c. 1 ff. 21–8.
[88] Esterhazy to Clarendon, 1 March 1853: Clar. P. c. 1 ff. 29–30; cf. Westmorland to Russell (private), 21 February 1853: Clar. P. c. 1 ff. 4–6; Clarendon to Queen Victoria, 25 February 1853, in *QVL 1837–61* vol. II p. 535; Clarendon to Westmorland no. 18, 2 March 1853: PRO FO 7/412; and Westmorland to Clarendon no. 107, 8 March 1853: PRO FO 7/417.

least until February 1858) most European governments held to the notion that Britain's failure to legislate in their interests was due not to lack of competence but to lack of 'will'.[89] In England, however, it looked otherwise. We have seen how newspapers and backbench politicians sought to persuade governments that if they tampered with the laws affecting asylum it would be to their own ruin.[90] Governments of all political complexions generally believed them. Palmerston on at least one occasion toyed with the idea of trying an Alien Bill and had to be argued out of it by his colleagues,[91] but all the other most prominent prime ministers and foreign secretaries of the day accepted that, as Malmesbury put it to Lord Westmorland in 1852 'no Government which complied with such demands could exist a month'.[92] Derby and Aberdeen both said the same thing;[93] as did Clarendon, repeatedly: 'I need not tell you', he wrote to Lord Howard de Walden in 1853, 'that any attempt to pass an alien Bill could have but one result namely to turn out the Govt. that proposed it';[94] and to Cowley in 1857: 'we might as well try to bring the moon by act of Pt. as to get the H. of Cs. to consent to such a thing'.[95] This was what they believed. With popular feeling as it was in the country, and the weakness of party structures at the time, there can be little doubt that they were right. It was not very long before they were proved to be so.

Whether they ever privately hankered after an alien law, or some other means by which 'this detestable question of the Refugees'[96] might be summarily disposed of, ministers very rarely said. As it was out of the question anyway there was little point – and certainly no electoral mileage – in crying for one. By 1852 at the latest nearly all government ministers were aware that as it was the situation was not entirely satisfactory: that foreign governments did have 'some cause for complaint'[97] against Britain, that English laws and procedures were not adequate to meet even their reasonable demands, and that those demands were meant seriously,

[89] E.g. *supra*, p. 50; and *infra*, p. 170 fn. 1.   [90] *Supra*, p. 119.   [91] *Infra*, p. 175.

[92] Malmesbury to Westmorland (private), 8 March 1852: Malm. P. 9M73/1/4, and printed in Malmesbury, *Memoirs. . .*, p. 235. Cf. 3PD 119 c. 675 (5 April 1852); Malmesbury to Walewski, 8 March 1858: Malm. P. 9M73/1/5 pp. 27–8; and his Diary for 20 March 1853, in *Memoirs* pp. 299–301.

[93] E.g. Aberdeen to Queen Victoria, 27 February 1853: RA A23/14; Derby to Clarendon, 19 January 1858: Clar. P. c. 103 ff. 724–5.

[94] Clarendon to Howard (private), 1 March 1853: Clar. P. c. 125 pp. 23–5.

[95] Clarendon to Cowley (private), 5 August 1857: Cowl. P. PRO FO 519/176 f. 57. Cf. Clarendon to Westmorland (private), 24 Febuary 1853: Clar. P. c. 125 pp. 5–7; Clarendon to Cowley (private), 1 March 1853: Cowl. P. PRO FO 519/169 ff. 12–17; Clarendon to Westmorland no. 18, 2 March 1853: PRO FO 7/412; Clarendon to Seymour (private), 8 March 1853: Clar. P. c. 125 pp. 51–2; Clarendon to Seymour (private), 11 August 1857: Clar. P. c. 139 p. 410; Clarendon to Cowley (private), 19 January 1858: Cowl. P. PRO FO 519/177 ff. 53–63.

[96] Clarendon to Westmorland (private), 12 April 1853: Clar. P. c. 125 p. 256.

[97] Clarendon to Cowley (private), 1 March 1853: Cowl. P. PRO FO 519/169 ff. 12–17.

and might have damaging repercussions. Closely entrapped however within the restrictions placed around it by 'public opinion' in England no government could publicly reveal any dissatisfaction it might feel, or any substantial sympathy for the grievances of its allies, least of all when those grievances were expressed most forcefully.[98] When the continental onslaughts came, therefore, the official British responses were always correct and unyielding. Despatches on the refugee issue stood firm on principle, and were parsimonious with concessions, because despatches were, or could become, public property. To the simultaneous remonstrances sent by the Northern Courts in December 1851, for example, the Russell government's very carefully considered reply, sent on January 13th and soon after published in a Blue Book, was that aliens could not legally be expelled from Britain, that the British people would be unlikely ever to allow them to be, but that the government disapproved of refugees 'exciting insurrection' and would 'endeavour by every legal means to prevent them from abusing the hospitality, so liberally accorded to them by the British laws, to the prejudice of countries and Governments in amity and alliance with Great Britain'.[99] Two months later, a new Conservative government's reply to a still unappeased Austria followed very closely the same lines.[100] In March 1853 the Aberdeen coalition took a rather stronger line with Austria (Aberdeen himself worried that it might seem 'rather too pugnacious')[101] – assuring her that it was as indignant as she was at 'the base and unworthy manner in which a few individuals have abused the protection they enjoy in this Country', and that the Government would prosecute any they could, but insisting forcefully – even angrily[102] – that legislation was out of the question, and that it was foolish, wrong and possibly malicious for other countries to demand it of Britain.[103] In 1858 Palmerston's Liberal government was turned out because it did not make any formal reply at all to France's remonstrances then; but its informal response, insofar as it was revealed for public consumption at home, was in the words of the British ambassador in Paris 'clear and

---

[98] Because of this the British government sometimes tried to persuade foreign governments not to make demands on the grounds that such demands would make concessions more difficult – which may have cut some ice for a time, until it became clear that no concessions were going to be made anyway. E.g. Seymour to Clarendon no. 124, 13 March 1853: PRO FO 65/425.

[99] Granville's Circular Despatch of 13 January 1852, in PP (1852) liv, pp. 72–4. This despatch appears to have been drafted by Russell: see Granville to Labouchere, 5 January 1852, in Granville Papers, PRO 30/29/20/2 f. 113.

[100] Malmesbury to Buol, 15 March 1852, in PP (1852) liv, pp. 96–7.

[101] Aberdeen to Clarendon, 7 March 1853: Clar. P. c. 4 f.7.

[102] 'The discussion became rather warm. . .': Clarendon to Queen Victoria, 25 February 1853, in *QVL 1837–61*, vol. II, p. 535.

[103] Clarendon to Westmorland no. 18, 2 March 1853, recounting a conversation with Colloredo: PRO FO 7/412; and Clarendon to Westmorland no. 58, 5 April 1853: PRO FO 7/413.

straightforward', and to the same effect: that the right of asylum was a 'great principle of our Constitution' which could not, in any circumstances, be infringed upon.[104] So far as appearances were concerned, that was the end of it.

On the surface of things, therefore, British governments of every political colour stood firm against the demands which assailed them on the refugee question in the 1850s, at least until 1858, when Palmerston's government gave an inch and was thrown out for it: dramatically seeming to confirm what British statesmen had been telling the continent for the previous six or eight years, that it could not be done. Yet there were some things that could be done by the government for the continental powers, and were. These were things which did not involve legislation or litigation, and which therefore did not require the sanction or even the knowledge of 'the public', either as M.P.s or jurymen. Of course they were not as effective as legislation would have been. Nevertheless they had, as we shall see, some effect on the refugees' activities, and enough anyway to mollify some of the less intransigent of Britain's continental critics.

The most important of the British government's positive actions with respect to the refugees was the systematic watch which it began to keep on the refugee community from 1851, with the purpose of helping and advising foreign governments: though the advice given was, as we have seen, not always found acceptable by them. Proper surveillance of the refugees appears to have been a new departure in the 1850s. Before 1848 if it existed at all it was probably ineffective: by all accounts in 1844 the police were unable to find Mazzini even when he was making no attempt to hide.[105] In April 1851 Palmerston was suggesting that, if the French government were so afraid of refugee plots in London, then they should send over 'Some sharp Detectors' of their own, as 'our police are good for ~~nothing~~ [*sic*] little for such purposes, and besides they are not *linguists*'.[106] We have seen already that there was a considerable prejudice in England at the time against methods which would have made an efficient surveillance possible.[107] During the 1848 revolutions and just afterwards the authorities relied for information about the refugees on four kinds of source. The first was *ad hoc* inquiries by Metropolitan Police detectives diverted from their

[104] Cowley to Clarendon, 20 February 1858: PP (1857–8) lx p. 131; and *vide infra*, p. 182.
[105] Police Report of 12 January 1844, in PRO FO 7/320: 'I beg to report that I have made every possible enquiry at the different Foreign Hotels, Lodging Houses, the Passport Office and the Steam Navigation Companies Office, respecting two Foreigners named Mazzini and Fabrizzi, but cannot find any person who knows either of them.' At the time Mazzini was – and had been for 3½ years – living openly at no. 4, York Buildings, King's Road, Chelsea; as the police could easily have found out if they had tried, from Mazzini's many English Liberal friends or from the Carlyles. See also F. A. Wellesley, *op. cit.*, p. 303.
[106] Palmerston to Normanby (private), 3 April 1851: Palm. P. GC/NO f. 592.
[107] *Supra*, pp. 113–16.

normal domestic duties for the purpose, whose reports (or those of them that survive) were notably unrevealing.[108] Then there were rumours retailed unsolicited by ordinary members of the public, which were generally sensationalist and unfounded.[109] The third source was reports from foreign police spies which came through the Foreign Office, and whose veracity, as we have seen already, was invariably mistrusted.[110] Lastly there were the revelations of the British authorities' own informers and spies, not themselves members of the police, who as far as it is possible to tell acted as such voluntarily (probably for the money), and may have furnished the most reliable information.[111]

In 1849 one of the most reliable of these informers was a young man of about 24 called John Hitchens Sanders, who despite his English name was sometimes taken for a Frenchman,[112] and could pass himself off easily as a radical refugee. Sanders attended refugee meetings and passed very detailed information about their activities to the Metropolitan Police and the Foreign Office in 1849 and 1850.[113] In August 1850 he joined the Police himself, left shortly afterwards, and then re-joined in January 1851,[114] as a detective-constable attached to the 'A' (Whitehall) division. Whether or not he was recruited for this specific task, very soon he was Scotland Yard's specialist in refugee matters, reporting directly to the Commissioner, Sir Richard Mayne. Until his death from 'apoplexy' in August 1859 at the age of 35[115] he remained, as he was described in 1858, 'Mayne's right-hand detective in matters connected with the refugees'.[116]

During the course of 1851 this surveillance of the refugees, which until then had been *ad hoc* and irregular, appears to have been made more

---

[108] E.g. reports by Insp. Haynes, Supt. Evans and Insp. [?]Shuckell, 1848, in MEPO 2/43; report by Sgt John Gray, 10 July 1849, and by Insp. Charles Field, 13 July 1849, in PRO FO 27/858; reports by Field, 4 and 20 October 1849, in PRO FO 27/859; report by Insp. John [?] Lund, 30 September 1850, in PRO FO 27/890; and report by Field, 12 November 1850, in PRO HO 45/3272. [109] E.g. *supra*, pp. 86–7. [110] E.g. *supra*, p. 134.

[111] PRO MEPO 2/43 contains records of the recruitment of some of them, in 1851. One of them, Joseph Blareau, agreed to 'discover all the private arrangements of the members of the divers clubs held by the strangers now in London', for a salary of 30 shillings per week, 'which said salary might be augmented in proportion to the importance of my information' (10 May 1851). There is no indication here of whether the authorities on their side agreed to this arrangement.

[112] Sanders' Marriage Certificate (3 May 1845) gives his residence then as 'Boulogne sur Mer, France'. To Cowley Clarendon on 18 January 1858 offered to send to France 'a Frenchman here employed in the Metropolitan Police' who is likely to have been Sanders – he went to Paris soon afterwards: see despatch no. 92 (in cypher), PRO FO 27/1233. See also *infra*, p. 189.

[113] See 'J. H. S.' to Field, 19 October 1849: PRO FO 27/859; 'S' to Foreign Office, 15 May 1850: PRO FO 27/887; 'J. S.' to Foreign Office, 19 May 1850: *ibid.*, *loc. cit.*

[114] Information supplied by the Metropolitan Police Office, New Scotland Yard.

[115] From Sanders' death certificate.

[116] Hammond to Cowley, 17 February 1858: Cowl. P. PRO FO 519/187, ff. 61–2. He also undertook some counter-espionage work in England and in Jersey, and may have had other duties too.

systematic. The Chartist *Northern Star* in September of that year reported rumours of a 'recently established foreign branch of the English police force' set up for that purpose,[117] which cannot be confirmed for certain but is substantially possible.[118] If such a branch was set up it will probably have grown out of the preparations which were made for the Great Exhibition of that year, which included a fairly wholesale recruitment of informers on refugee meetings in April and May,[119] and more co-operation than had been usual before with foreign policemen sent over, as they understood it, with a view to watching their own exiles' political activities.[120] By November 1851 Sanders' reports were coming in regularly, and full of convincing detail. In August 1852 he made the first of a number of trips to Jersey to inquire into the activities both of French spies and of French refugees there.[121] Police surveillance of the refugees was now regular and professional: probably for the first time ever.

It may also have been pushed beyond the boundaries of what was considered to be proper police practice at the time. What methods Sanders used are uncertain, and appear to have been a mystery even to the Home Office: 'he has some means of obtaining information about these persons',

[117] *Northern Star*, 6 September 1851 p. 7, and 13 September 1851 pp. 4–5.
[118] Metropolitan Police records were quite considerably culled before being deposited in the Public Record Office, and little trace of this side of the police's activities survives. Apart from the bare facts of his recruitment, the only record of Sanders' service with the force at all is a note of his death in Police Orders for 1859. However, more than a hundred of his reports survive, in various locations. The Metropolitan Police papers are the least helpful, although MEPO 2/43 contains a few reports from 1851–3; MEPO 3/22–34 (especially 22) contain his reports on the Bernard investigation in 1858; and MEPO 1/46 has a report by him on a rumoured conspiracy in Liverpool later that year. Most of his surviving reports are among the Home Office papers: especially HO45/3518 (from 1851), 4302 (from 1852), 4547A (from Jersey, 1852), 4816 (from 1853), 5180, 5635 and 5680 (from 1854), and 6188 (from Jersey, 1855). There are a few others in other Home Office files, but none for 1856 and 1857. For these later years, however, one or two copies of his reports are preserved in the Clarendon papers, c. 2, c. 32 and c. 75, and more in the Cowley papers, PRO FO 519/171–4, 176, 185–6.   [119] See PRO MEPO 2/43.
[120] Thirty-five foreign policemen came over altogether. Information about them is in PRO HO 45/3623 and in PRO MEPO 2/92. A letter from Palmerston to Bloomfield, no. 111 of 13 May 1851 (PRO FO 65/388), makes it clear that by Britain their purpose was supposed to be 'to point out to the English Police those persons of bad character belonging to their respective Countries who may come to London. . . and whose proceedings while in London may, for British interests, require to be watched'. Consequently their salaries were paid by the British authorities. The governments which sent them, however, saw them as a means of 'discovering conspiracies which had for their object the spread of socialism' on the continent, for which the avowed purpose of 'rendering assistance to our own [English] police' was a mere 'cloak' – Bloomfield to Palmerston no. 30, 14 August 1851: PRO FO 64/332; and cf. Seymour to Palmerston no. 98, 29 April 1851: PRO FO 65/392. Duty reports made out by them are in PRO MEPO 2/91–104. They include information about dangerous republicans, as well as about thieves, confidence tricksters and the like. Occasional notes scribbled on them by Mayne suggest that he was more interested in the criminals than the politicos.
[121] See PRO HO 45/4547A. The local Jersey police were ineffective and untrustworthy, because they were amateur, and elected by the community.

Sir George Grey's Permanent Under-Secretary once minuted to him obscurely, 'which are peculiar to himself'.[122] There is little indication that he or anyone else in authority ever resorted to the bad old practice of 1844 and opened private letters,[123] apart from one occasion in 1858, when it was done without the agency of the police.[124] Probably he relied heavily on informants, whose use was a well-established and accepted police practice at the time.[125] But he may also have directly spied on the refugees, by disguising himself as one of them: which was not. His early reports (before he joined the police) were made from direct observation: 'in haste', he finished one report back in 1849, 'for I am writing this in the same room (*with them*)'.[126] It is by no means impossible that he was able to maintain his 'cover' for some time after that, and most of his reports right through the 1850s read as if they were first-hand accounts. In 1853, although Palmerston refused to admit it in Parliament, the police were known (and privately acknowledged) to have disguised one of their constables as a removal man in order to examine Kossuth's belongings, which was highly improper;[127] and in 1858 Sanders himself was found resorting to lies and subterfuge in order to gain entrance illegally to Orsini's lodgings in London, which embarrassed his superiors greatly: 'the less is said about it', wrote the Permanent Under-Secretary at the Home Office, 'the better'.[128] How often this kind of thing went on is impossible to establish. In the vigilant and innocent 1850s, the rules of the game, if they were adhered to strictly, were very disadvantageous to the police in dealing with men so secretive and subtle as some of the more conspiratorial refugees undoubtedly were, and it is likely that they were bent occasionally.

All this was done, partly in order to find out what harm the refugees were planning to do to England; but much more in order to discover what schemes they were hatching for the continent: in the direct interests therefore of the continent, to be able to forewarn it, and so put Britain in

[122] Note by Waddington attached to Wodehouse to Waddington, 14 March 1855: PRO HO 45/6188.

[123] Palmerston expressly disallowed this in 1853 – see Palmerston to Clarendon, 9 May 1853: Clar. P. c. 1 ff. 21–2; and when Sanders tried to make arrangements for letters to be opened in Jersey he seems to have been stopped – see Fitzroy to Love, 24 October 1853: PRO HO 99/10 f. 154. [124] *Infra*, p. 189.

[125] PRO HO 45/6126 contains accounts of 'money expended in treating Refugees & other persons from whom it was supposed that information could be obtained' in 1855.

[126] Report of 19 October 1849, in PRO FO 27/859; and cf. his report of 19 May 1850 (PRO FO 27/887): 'I have attended several of their private meetings and in fact I have been in their company every day this month.'

[127] See police report (by Supt Samuel Hughes) of 24 March 1853: PRO HO 45/4816. Questioned on this in the House of Commons on 5 May 1853, Palmerston avoided giving a direct answer: 3PD 125 cc. 1142–67. To Mayne in private on 12 May, however, he asked for the police to be cautioned 'against similar proceedings in future': PRO HO 45/4816.

[128] Note by Waddington on Stephens to Grey, 22 January 1858: PRO HO 45/6512; and *vide infra*, pp. 189–90.

better diplomatic odour there. By those radical critics of the police who suspected that this kind of thing was going on, it was naturally assumed that it worked to the disadvantage of the refugees and their causes, and to the advantage of what the *Northern Star* in 1851 called the 'detestable and blood-thirsty purposes' of the despots.[129] It is likely, however, that on balance it did not. It has already been indicated how gentle and moderate the British authorities' picture of the refugees' activities was, by contrast with the continentals'. Most of this picture was compiled out of materials provided by Sanders. The distinctive features of Sanders' reports were that they were discriminating, and that in cases of doubt he gave the benefit to the refugees. Occasionally his inquiries confirmed continental suspicions about the refugees. The vehemence of the refugees in Jersey by comparison with those in London always shocked him: 'their excitement and violence has been beyond description', he wrote back once in 1852; '. . . They utter daily threats . . . that they would not be satisfied until they had torn the flesh of Louis Napoleon and his *Valets* with their teeth . . .';[130] and it was from the *proscrits* there that he believed the greatest material danger to the continent lay. In 1855 he warned from Jersey that 'unless measures are taken I fear that it may become serious'[131] (we shall see that measures were taken very soon afterwards); and back in London for a time in 1856 and 1857 he appears to have been concerned that some of the French, and more of the Italians, were becoming 'really dangerous' and actively preparing for an attempt on Napoleon's life.[132] He did not always therefore deal in anodynes. More often, however, this was the effect of his diagnoses. They generally confirmed, not the picture of the refugees which emerged from the reports of continental spies, but the image the more responsible refugees wished to give of themselves: harmless, impoverished, strictly law-abiding. The dull, low-key, policemanly style of his reports itself contrasted markedly with the histrionics of his foreign counterparts.

In answer I beg most respectfully to state that in some back rooms at the rear of the house No. 10 Little Compton Street, Soho, a dozen poor Refugees, Frenchmen, have formed a Society, they have made the rooms a sort of 'cafe' where, every day

---

[129] *Northern Star*, 13 September 1851, pp. 4–5.
[130] Sanders' report of 10 October 1852: PRO HO 45/4547A. Cf. reports of 10 and 14 August 1852, *ibid.*, *loc. cit.*; and report of 5 October 1855: 'they use in their speeches foul language, taking the most dreadful of oaths, using threats against all the Kings and Queens, down with the Aristocracy and all persons in opposition to them, threaten, should they ever gain power, to guillotine all persons who have adhered to the Government of the assassin and perjurer Napoleon': PRO HO 45/6188.
[131] Sanders' report of 7 August 1855: Cowl. P. PRO FO 519/172 ff. 151–2.
[132] Sanders' report of 8 September 1857: Cowl. P. PRO FO 519/176 ff. 175–6. Cf. reports of 18 and 25 August 1856, in Cowl. P. PRO FO 519/174 ff. 59, 69–70; 7 July 1857, in Cowl. P. PRO FO 519/176 ff. 15–19; and 6 November 1857, in Clar. P. c. 75 f. 864, which implicated Ledru-Rollin in a plot with Mazzini and other Italians to assassinate Napoleon III.

they meet to drink and smoke their pipe . . . Every evening between 20 and 30 frenchmen meet, during the evening they talk Politics, and sometimes one of them will deliver a rambling speech, concerning the Doctrines of Democracy and Socialism, and also respecting the state of affairs in their Country . . . [133]

Always he leant over backwards to emphasise the peaceableness of the main body of refugees, their innocence of any nefarious designs. His most adverse reports generally contained caveats designed to preserve the reputations of the bulk of them: 'I beg to say', he wrote of the unruly Jersey community in 1852, 'that they are not *all* violent';[134] and when Kossuth was suspected of illegally manufacturing war rockets in 1853 he reported that 'the foreigners generally' were on the side of the government against him.[135] What was perhaps most important from the refugees' point of view were the distinctions he was always careful to make between, in the first place, wild talk and wild intentions, and in the second place wild intentions and the capacity to carry them out. Of the Jersey refugees of 1852 again he claimed that although they 'talk much' they were 'not to be feared';[136] and when the London refugees seemed to him to be most menacing of all, in 1856–7, he was reluctant except in the extremest circumstances to believe that they could actually do harm. Either lack of funds would prevent them, or lack of nerve:

Mazzini and his Committee . . . appear sanguine of success, but, from good information, I believe they will not succeed in raising sufficient money to carry their plans into execution . . . The assassination of the Empr. Napoleon appears to be their aim, but they cannot find any of their party brave enough to do it.[137]

If anything at all suspicious came to his notice, he always tried to find an innocent explanation before he would accept a guilty one. He was very quick, for example, to smell out *agents provocateurs*: 'it is evident', he reported back after a particularly stormy refugee meeting in Jersey in September 1852, ' . . . that many men who are here as political Refugees, are nothing else but spies, who excite the better class of Refugees to commit themselves'.[138] When later he heard of secret meetings of prominent *proscrits* taking place on horseback on the Jersey beaches, he suggested that it might not be as sinister as it appeared, but intended merely to enable the leaders to get away from the 'lower class of the Refugees', who were the ones egging them on to foolish actions.[139] His assertions tended to be

---

[133] Sanders' report of 1 November 1851: PRO HO 45/3518.
[134] Sanders' report of 10 October 1852: PRO HO 45/4547A.
[135] Sanders' report of 1 July 1853: PRO HO 45/4816.
[136] Sanders' report of 28 September 1852: PRO HO 45/4547A.
[137] Sanders' report of 25 August 1856: Cowl. P. PRO FO 519/174 ff. 69–70.
[138] Sanders' report of 19 September 1852: PRO HO 45/4547A. The same thing happened, he believed, in 1855: see his report of 9 August 1855 in PRO HO 45/6188.
[139] Sanders' reports of 5 March and 15 October 1853: PRO HO 45/4816.

positive and confident: 'I am quite sure he is not drilling any one . . . '; 'I am certain that the Refugees are not plotting secretly . . . '[140] Nearly always his reports gave the impression that his information was complete, his knowledge even of private meetings omniscient: 'The Refugees and other suspected persons are observed, and cannot attempt a movement unless known to me . . . '[141] They were therefore, except on a mere handful of occasions, highly reassuring. They were so reassuring, in fact, that they raise the possibility – though surely a very faint one – that he was in some way in league with the refugees. Whether or not that was so, however, there can be little doubt that John Sanders, a policeman, even possibly a 'police spy', was in effect in the 1850s the refugees' truest and most valuable friend.

His value to them – and his importance for us – lay in the fact that he was virtually the only source of information about the refugees that his superiors trusted, and that they did trust him absolutely. From 1851 through to 1858, all but a handful of the police reports about refugees which reached the Home Office and the Foreign Office (and have survived) were either his, or Mayne's paraphrasing him. His uniqueness could be inconvenient when he was wanted in two places at once: 'It is quite absurd', complained Palmerston in 1855, 'that they [the Police] should have only one man capable of performing duties of this kind.'[142] When for some reason Sanders was not available and another detective had to be put on to the refugees, and his report sent to the Home Office, it was usually with reservations about its reliability added to it by Mayne.[143] Sanders' reports never had any such reservations attached to them. His abilities were rated highly by Mayne, who in 1857 described him as 'a very deserving officer performing his duties with great zeal and intelligence and ready for [duty] at all times night as well as day',[144] and for this rewarded him generously with money, as was customary in the nineteenth century with deserving officers, and with meteoric promotion.[145] The Lieutenant-Governor of Jersey was forever conducting a kind of epistolary tug of war between 1852 and 1855 with Scotland Yard to get him to or keep him in the Channel Islands, and without him professed himself to be

---

[140] Sanders' reports of 11 June 1852: PRO HO 45/4302; and 16 September 1852: PRO HO 45/4547A.   [141] Sanders' report of 26 September 1852: PRO HO 45/4547A.

[142] Palmerston note of 14 January 1855, in PRO 45/6188.

[143] E.g. report by Brinley of 9 September 1852, with a note by Mayne: 'I am not satisfied that this is to be depended on': PRO HO 45/4547A; and see the comments on the efforts of P. C. Larendon in Jersey in 1854 in PRO HO 45/5180; PRO MEPO 1/46 (Mayne to Fitzroy 26 March 1854); and Clar. P. c. 16 f. 679 (Fitzroy to Clarendon 31 March 1854). From November 1857 Sanders was assisted by Sergeant John Rogers, who was (like him) bilingual: see *State Trials*, n.s., vol. VIII, cc. 934–6.

[144] Mayne to Hammond, 3 July 1857: PRO MEPO 1/46. To Addington on 1 November 1852 he wrote of his 'skill and great discretion': *ibid., loc. cit.*

[145] He was promoted to Sergeant at the age of 26 in November 1851, and to Inspector at the age of 31 in January 1856 (information supplied by Metropolitan Police Office).

totally in the dark about the doings of *his* refugees.[146] Lord Clarendon, though in 1853 he seems to have been not altogether satisfied with the information he provided,[147] by 1857 had come to rate him 'worth all the French police agents & spies put together'.[148] His reports found their way from Scotland Yard to Whitehall ministries, to British embassies abroad, to foreign embassies in London, and to the Court.[149] No one in authority ever appears to have questioned his findings, to have found them too trusting or naïve. Sanders was relied upon absolutely for almost all the government's intelligence about the refugees, and the intelligence he provided in general corroborated what they were probably already disposed to believe, or wanted to believe: that the refugees were harmless. Consequently his contribution will have been vital, in confirming – if it did not determine – the stand they took.

So there was police surveillance of the refugees; and the results of this surveillance were sometimes communicated to continental police forces, in ways which, again, if they had been widely known about, would have been disapproved of. For it was another commonly held belief at the time that the British police did not help foreign police forces, even to investigate crimes which were clearly against English law. This was what much of the fuss over the Mazzini letter-opening affair in 1844 had been about: that not only had the letters been opened but that information from them had been communicated to a foreign government, apparently with fatal consequences. In 1849, when the Sicilian government asked the British authorities to investigate a frigate in the London docks supposed to be equipping for war for use by Italian insurgents (and contrary to the Foreign Enlistment Act), Palmerston made the proper response: that

to allow the Government Police to be employed by the Agents of a foreign Government to make enquiries connected with the interests of such Government, would be a precedent which might lead to very inconvenient consequences . . . and . . . be very repugnant to the public feeling in this country.[150]

On another occasion, when the request (from the Saxon government) was for information only, Palmerston replied that it could not legally be complied with, and that Saxony would have to 'employ some agents of

---

[146] Love to Home Office, 6 December 1853: PRO HO 45/4816 – 'when he leaves I shall have no means whatever of knowing the mischief these people are contemplating'. See also the correspondence between Love and the Home Office from January, March, September and November 1855, in PRO HO 45/6188.

[147] 'I must say our Police give us very little assistance. I knew everything that passed in Dublin in 1848' (when he was Irish Viceroy) – Clarendon to Aberdeen, 7 March 1853: Aberdeen Papers, BM. Add. Ms. 43188 f. 24.

[148] Clarendon to Cowley (private), 12 July 1857: Cowl. P. PRO FO 519/176 ff. 11–12.

[149] A few have noted on them that they were sent to the Queen: e.g. reports of 26 April and 25 May 1854: PRO HO 45/5180.

[150] Addington to Waddington, 1 February 1849: PRO HO 45/2736.

their own to seek it'.[151] The collaboration which was carried on with foreign police forces during the 1851 Exhibition was intended to be for British purposes only.[152] The rule therefore was supposed to be a simple and unambiguous one: that any inquiries the British police made, and information they elicited, about the refugees in Britain, were for British purposes and British eyes only: yet it is evident that this rule was frequently broken later in the 1850s. Foreign secretaries very often sent police reports on refugees in England to British ambassadors abroad, either with instructions to pass them on, or else without instructions *not* to pass them on, which may have amounted to the same thing.[153] There also appear to have been more direct contacts between Scotland Yard and the French police authorities, which was also strictly improper: in 1855 Cowley wrote that he had 'no doubt that the French police are in communication with ours' about the Pianori plot;[154] in July 1857 Clarendon confirmed that it would be 'quite right' for Mayne to treat directly with the French Préfet de Police;[155] and it can be established that Sanders paid several visits to Paris[156] and was also by 1857 'well known to Walewski & Persigny'.[157] Insofar as there was such collaboration British ministers tended to be nervous about it, because of the possible effect in England if it became widely known there: 'of course this will put all the Refugees here on the qui vive', wrote Clarendon to Cowley in February 1858 about a report in *The Times* of papers connected with the Orsini affair being sent to Paris; '& we shall be denounced as spies & police agents of France' – as indeed they were.[158] Consequently it was, at other times, kept very secret indeed.

Sometimes the information which was passed on was warning of some conspiracy or other. We have seen that promises to pass on such informa-

[151] Addington to Waddington, [15?] January 1850: PRO HO 45/3263.
[152] *Supra*, p. 152 fn. 120.
[153] Many of Sanders' reports are among the papers of Lord Cowley, who was ambassador in Paris from 1852 to 1867. Usually Cowley was not told what to do with them. Occasionally he was expressly forbidden to reveal them to the French government; on other occasions he was instructed to do so. E.g. Clarendon to Cowley (private), 2 May 1855: '. . .pray let the Empr see them': Cowl. P. PRO FO 519/171 f. 382.
[154] Cowley to Clarendon (private), 29 April 1855: Cowl. P. PRO FO 519/216 p. 54.
[155] Clarendon to Cowley (private), 12 July 1857: Cowl. P. PRO FO 519/176 ff. 11–14.
[156] Sanders report, 18 November 1856: Cowl. P. PRO FO 519/185 f. 292.
[157] Clarendon to Cowley (private), 12 July 1857: Cowl. P. PRO FO 519/176 ff. 11–14; and Clarendon to Cowley (private), 17 February 1858: Cowl. P. PRO FO 519/177 f. 195. He is likely to have met them in London, where both had served as French ambassadors. On 9 July 1857 Cowley wrote to Clarendon about 'a certain M. Roy in the department of the Police here, who is very useful to us' – in what connexion is not specified: Cowl. P. PRO FO 519/222 p. 13.
   Further information about Anglo-French police collaboration is very likely contained in a file in the Archive Nationale in Paris (BB30 419 P1540 dossier 3), on 'Transactions with Foreign Police', cited by H. C. Payne, *The Police State of Louis Napoleon Bonaparte* (1966), p. 276n.; which however I have not seen.
[158] Clarendon to Cowley (private), 2 February 1858: Cowl. P. PRO FO 519/177 ff. 111–19; and see *Reynolds's Newspaper*, 21 February 1858 pp. 1 and 6, and 18 April 1858 p. 1.

tion were made in the 1830s,[159] and they were repeated later, for example in 1850 by Palmerston, who then assured the French ambassador that 'if H.M. Govt should discover that any Plots are being carried on by Frenchmen residing in London against the Internal tranquillity of France, information thereof . . . will be forthwith communicated to the French Govt'.[160] To Count Thun in Frankfort Cowley in 1852 transmitted a similar promise:

that if Her Majesty's Government shd ever become cognisant of any designs hatching in England against the repose and tranquillity of the Austrian Empire, they wd act as Sir Robert Peel's Govt had done, and put the Austrian Authorities on their guard.[161]

British governments kept to those promises thereafter, though possibly only sporadically – in 1853 Napoleon III complained to Malmesbury that his Liberal successor had been less forthcoming in this respect than *he* had been.[162] In January 1851, for example, Palmerston 'privately' told the French Chargé d'Affaires in London of a shipment of arms bound for Italy *via* England;[163] in September 1852 Malmesbury used his private secretary to communicate confidentially to Napoleon information Sanders had elicited about a plot to invade Bayonne from Jersey;[164] and rumours of imminent assassination plots were occasionally flashed across the Channel by telegraph.[165] In 1858 the British police went out of their way to furnish their French counterparts with prosecution evidence for Orsini's trial.[166] On these occasions the assistance accorded by the British government to the continental authorities (however justified) could be looked upon as inimical to the interests and the causes of the refugees. More often, however, it was not, but the reverse: a mere retailing of Sanders' customary assurances about the refugees, to support the official British diplomatic line that the continentals' fears of them were exaggerated. From the continent's point of view all this was something, but it was not very much. Lord Westmorland in Vienna believed that it did a little to mollify the Austrians, by showing that the British at least meant well.[167] But overall

---

[159] *Supra*, p. 53.
[160] Palmerston to Drouhn de Lhuys, 8 February 1850: PRO FO 27/884.
[161] Cowley to Granville (private), 15 February 1852: RA I27/60. The reference to Peel's government must be to the 1844 Mazzini letter-opening affair.
[162] Lord Malmesbury's diary for 20 March 1853, in his *Memoirs* (*op. cit.*), pp. 299–301.
[163] Note by Addington on Grey to Palmerston, 20 January 1851: PRO FO 27/918.
[164] G. Harris to Malmesbury, 2 September 1852, in Malmesbury, *op. cit.*, p. 263.
[165] E.g. Clarendon to Cowley, telegram, 25 June 1855: PRO FO 27/1054; Clarendon to Cowley (private), 30 July 1855: Cowl. P. PRO FO 519/172 f. 105; Clarendon to Cowley (private), 15 August 1855: Cowl. P. PRO FO 519/172 ff. 163–7; Malmesbury to Cowley no. 228, 15 April 1858: PRO FO 27/1235.
[166] Mostly *via* the Foreign Office, whose private correspondence with Cowley in Paris between mid-January and mid-March 1858 is full of references to this: in Cowl. P. PRO FO 519/177, 187, 196 and 223; and Clar. P. cc. 84 and 141.
[167] Westmorland to Clarendon (private), 8 March 1853: Clar. P. c. 1 ff. 38–41.

European governments could not have been greatly satisfied or impressed with the intelligence they got from the British police in the 1850s, which was not very often forthcoming, and when it was, was not often the kind of information they wanted. They did better to rely on their own sources, which were more numerous, more skilled at this kind of work, more able to recognise a conspirator when they saw him, and more willing to provide the kinds of answers the continental governments wanted, than were Detective-Sergeant Sanders and his foreign department at Scotland Yard.

There was however something else that the British government could do for the continent, and did, which was to send some of the refugees away. From north America it was agreed by nearly everybody that they could do less harm to the continent than from England,[168] and many of them, especially after a few months of semi-starvation, proved not at all unwilling to go there, if they could only find the money to. The first occasion when the government provided funds for this purpose appears to have been in 1850, for a group of Poles who arrived at Southampton from Malta.[169] It was done again in 1851 for the Polish and Hungarian refugees who were released from Turkey in that year and arrived in large numbers at Liverpool and Southampton, after an attempt had been made to get Lord Dudley Stuart to raise the money privately, which he claimed was impossible.[170] In 1852 it became established as a general principle that any *bona fide* refugee could be given his fare to America and a little spending money besides (about £10 in all): so long as it was done 'without any public notice being taken of the means by which they are sent'.[171] The money came from the Foreign Office's 'Secret Service Fund', which did not have to be accounted for to Parliament; later it was supplemented by money secretly provided by the French Government.[172] Secrecy was thought necessary to avoid protests not only from British taxpayers but also from

---

[168] Clarendon did *not* agree; in the U.S.A., he wrote to Cowley on 20 January 1858, 'they wd. be there under democratic influence &. . . wd. meet with far more encouragement & pecuniary aid than in Engd': Cowl. P. PRO FO 519/177 ff. 65–73.

[169] Referred to in Lord Dudley Stuart to Russell, 11 February 1851: Russell Papers, PRO 30/22/9B ff. 71–4. It was also normal practice before 1851 to commute the pensions granted by Parliament to Poles who desired it, to a lump sum to enable them to emigrate. See paylists in PRO T [Treasury] 50/95–6.

[170] Stuart to Russell, 11 February 1851, *loc. cit.*, and see PRO HO 45/3720 and 3725.

[171] Memorandum by (?) Granville, n.d. (January 1852?): PRO HO 45/4302. The fact that they were offered passages to America, however, was not a very successfully kept secret: see *Daily News*, 3 April 1851, p. 4.

[172] The Treasury was always highly reluctant to bear this expense, and in 1857 cut the grant: see Hammond memo. of 23 April 1858 in Malm. P., 9M73/1858–9/3. That memorandum also confirms that the government expected eventually to be reimbursed from France, whose government agreed to this at about that time; see also Hammond to Cowley 12 April 1858: Cowl. P. PRO FO 519/187 f. 154; and Hammond to Mayne, 24 April 1858: PRO MEPO 2/43.

the United States: 'the moment it was known that we were making them our penal settlement', wrote Clarendon in 1858, 'there wd. be an uproar & protest from one end of the Union to the other & not a man wd. be permitted to disembark'.[173] The task of establishing the refugees' *bona fides*, and also of getting them on to the boats before all their fare-money was spent on drink, was entrusted to Sanders.[174] Of course this expatriation could only be voluntary, although there were some doubts about the early Hungarians, who it was claimed in some quarters had their arms twisted a little to go.[175] Nevertheless it did rid Britain of more than 1,500 refugees between 1850 and 1858,[176] which was a very large proportion of the whole, and it was claimed by the British government to be politically effective. In 1854 Clarendon tried to make out that 'all the worst and most dangerous refugees' had been sent away, which was patently untrue.[177] In December 1857 Sanders gave it as his opinion that 'the Emigration of Political Refugees to the U.S. of America' had 'completely ruined the Democratic influence here for nearly all the Refugees who have left were men of education and energy, and they had great weight'. Where there used to be thirty meeting together in clubs, he said, 'there are now nine, and very few of those remaining of any importance'.[178] Of course it was in Sanders', and Clarendon's, interest to believe so. Foreign governments in general thought less of it. To Sir Richard Mayne in December 1857 Pietri, the French police chief, was reported as saying that 'as long as the Chiefs were harboured here it did not much signify what became of the Diminués of revolution',[179] which was considered less than grateful, considering the fact that, as Clarendon put it to Cowley, 'the operation is rather a costly one & a pure act of goodwill towds. France as the residence of such men here does us no harm'.[180] It was intended as 'a proof of our desire to meet

[173] Clarendon to Seymour (private), 3 February 1858: Clar. P. c. 141 pp. 65–9.
[174] PRO MEPO 2/43 contains some of Sanders' reports on these assignments, including one of 13 June 1853 explaining how he kept back the free clothing allowed to the refugees until just before they embarked, because when he had used to issue it earlier, he had 'found that they had pawned them to drink with their friends previous to departure'. To furnish the refugees with free clothing as well as a free passage appears generous beyond the call of necessity. It may be that the authorities found that it was a necessary inducement for them to leave; or that they wished to avoid putting the American authorities on their guard, by fitting the refugees out respectably.
[175] *Red Republican*, 13 July 1850 p. 25 and 20 July 1850 p. 37; *Northern Star*, 21 September 1850 p. 1. They were also subject to pressure from other refugees to stay: see Sanders' report of 25 August 1856: Cowl. P., PRO FO 519/174 ff. 69–70.
[176] Clarendon told Cowley on 21 January 1858 (no. 117: PRO FO 27/1233) that to that date 1498 had been granted passages – 960 men, 305 women and 233 children; which tallies roughly with detailed but incomplete accounts covering the years 1852–8 in PRO MEPO 2/43.   [177] Clarendon to Cowley (private), 15 August 1854: Clar. P. c. 129 pp. 216–17.
[178] Sanders' report of 8 December 1857: Cowl. P., PRO FO 519/176 ff. 374–5.
[179] Clarendon to Cowley (private), 10 December 1857: Cowl. P., PRO FO 519/176 ff. 368–72.
[180] Clarendon to Cowley (private), 2 June 1856: Cowl. P., PRO FO 519/173 f. 323.

the wishes of our allies'.[181] Whether it was taken as an adequate proof, or the sacrifice involved really appreciated by less cost-conscious peoples than the British, was doubtful.

Continental governments wanted much more than this. What they wanted most of all was for strong and decisive action to be taken, not against the small fry, but against the leaders of the refugee community, the central conspiratorial ganglion. It was remarkable what even an unsuccessful effort in this direction could do to calm them. In 1853, for example, the news that Palmerston was going to prosecute Kossuth for his alleged bomb-making activities in Rotherhithe[182] was reported to put the Austrian ambassador, recently so full of (real or simulated) anger towards Britain, 'in a state of enchantment over it', and to put Baron Manteuffel in Prussia in a state of 'joy'.[183] When the Rotherhithe bubble burst, and Kossuth was in fact not touched, it seemed to make no difference. From Berlin Lord Bloomfield reported that 'Notwithstanding the probable failure' of the case against Kossuth the Prussian government was 'much gratified with the readiness shewn by H.M. Govt. in making this seizure', which had produced 'the best effect' there; and from Vienna Lord Westmorland described the Austrian government as 'excessively pleased that our Govt. shd. have taken the step agt. the machinations of the refugees & that Palmerston shd. have had the direction of it'.[184] (Palmerston was Home Secretary at the time.) The point was that they had made an effort, which might possibly have a deterrent effect. (They had also, as was pointed out by Clarendon, who was not above this sort of thing, more effectively smeared Kossuth's reputation than if they had brought the case to court, and failed.)[185] Three months after the event Clarendon was still highly delighted at the good which had come out of it: 'the case conducted & concluded as it has been has benefitted our foreign relations far more than the *worth of the rockets*', he wrote to Palmerston in July; 'Since Hale's arrest' – Hale was the owner of the bomb factory, convicted eventually of a minor technical offence – 'there has not been a murmer [*sic*] even from Austria about Refugees.'[186]

If this could be the effect of an honest effort which failed, there was

[181] Clarendon to Westmorland (private), 24 February 1853: Clar. P., c. 125 pp. 5–7.
[182] *Supra*, p. 145.
[183] Clarendon to Cowley (private), 15 April 1853: Clar. P. c. 125 p. 269; Bloomfield to Clarendon (private), 15 April 1853: Clar. P. c. 1 ff. 496–7.
[184] Bloomfield to Clarendon (private), 22 April 1853: Clar. P., c. 1 f. 502; Westmorland to Clarendon (private), 26 April 1853: Clar. P., c. 1 f. 112.
[185] 'The consequence has been that instead of sympathy with the victim as Kossuth would have been considered if the case had failed, there is now a general though vague conviction in the public mind that he was concerned in this manufacture of arms' – Clarendon to Westmorland (private), 3 May 1853: Clar. P., c. 125 pp. 395–7.
[186] Clarendon to Palmerston, 21 July 1853: Palm. P., GC/CL/516.

no saying how much good could be done by one which succeeded. In England we have seen that the main obstacle to success was nearly always the fact that the executive was unable to act effectively except through the courts, which put certain difficulties in the way of conviction: which obstacle however did not exist in the island of Jersey, where consequently the government's best chance of success always lay. Jersey in the 1850s possessed a distinctive and archaic form of government, presided over by a Lieutenant-Governor (under the Home Office) who for his little domain had far wider executive powers than did any minister in Whitehall for the mainland. He could, for example, expel people. Jersey also housed a community of mainly French refugees who were, by Sanders' testimony, more 'violent' than most; were more feared than most by the French government because they were so much nearer to them; and were also considered by the island's governor to be a standing threat to public order there.[187] The danger to France was acknowledged in 1852 by Derby's Conservative government, which ordered a steamer patrol of the island with the dual purpose of preventing a refugee landing on the French coast and a possible French *coup de main* against the Channel Islands.[188] It also led Palmerston as Home Secretary to place a special ban on the exportation of arms from the Channel Islands in June 1854.[189] The possibility of expelling some of the Jersey refugees was mooted as early as 1852,[190] but was never taken up because the prevailing view continued to be that they were less harmful to France than the French themselves supposed. This was for example the opinion of the Liberals' natural Home Secretary, Sir George Grey, in the summer and autumn of 1855: that the refugees' antics were best countered by ignoring them, and that they were safer in Jersey, where they could be 'more easily watched', than in London where they would be able to hide and plot more secretly.[191]

---

[187] *Supra*, p. 40.
[188] See Derby to Malmesbury, 3 September 1852: Cowl. P., PRO FO 519/196 ff. 161–2; Cowley to Horace Hamond, 4 September 1852: Cowl. P., PRO FO 519/202 p. 126; Sanders to Love, 7 September 1852: PRO HO 45/4547A.
[189] Waddington to Love, 12 June 1854: PRO HO 99/10 f. 197.
[190] 'I do not know whether the laws of Jersey would allow of our removing the Refugees from a position the proximity of which to France affords some justification for the Espionage practiced by the French Government. If we can do it, we certainly ought' – Derby to Malmesbury, 3 September 1852: Cowl. P., PRO FO 519/196 ff. 161–2. In December the Lieutenant -Governor of Jersey wrote to the Home Office assuring it that he was empowered to remove 'at pleasure any foreigner whom he may consider from his conduct to be dangerous to the morals or peace of the Island. . .' – Love to Jolliffe, 10 December 1852: PRO HO 45/4547A.
[191] See Jolliffe to Love, 9 August 1855: PRO HO 99/10 f. 243; Grey to Clarendon, 10 August 1855: Clar. P., c. 29 ff. 63–4; and memorandum by Grey, 4 October 1855, attached to Love to Grey, 29 September 1855: PRO HO 45/6188. The Parliamentary Under-Secretary for Foreign Affairs in Derby's government, his son Lord Stanley, also believed the refugees in Jersey were harmless: see memo. by Stanley to Jolliffe, undated (early December 1852?): PRO HO 45/4547A.

Palmerston however disagreed. Soon after he became Prime Minister for the first time in 1855 his government was plagued informally with irritated complaints from the French government about the Jersey refugees,[192] which were renewed again in August when the brother of the putative regicide Pianori was traced to Jersey, and rumoured to be about to try to complete his brother's unfinished work.[193] Sanders was sent to find him, and failed, but while he was looking sent back some alarming reports of the activities of the other refugees there.[194] Palmerston was convinced in August that

these French exiles ought to be sent away from the Channel Islands where they are doing far more mischief to France & to England than they could accomplish in London. The best way would be to send them off gradually, the most violent first, the rest by instalments afterwards. The identity of language & similarity of Race give them Powers of mischief in those Islands, together with the nearness of the Islands to the French Coast which they could not possess in England.[195]

Consequently, after it was first established that it could be done without bothering with law courts and juries and the like,[196] the Lieutenant-Governor of Jersey was given leave on the 15th of August to expel as many as he thought fit; with a rider added however by Sir George Grey (who in all these refugee affairs appears as a dove among hawks) impressing on him 'that the power should not be exercised in any case without proof of its necessity'.[197] This, or a concern for the reaction of the public if it were done too hastily, delayed the event for a couple of months yet. Palmerston, irked by the harm the refugees – 'pushed on by Russian agency' – were doing to his precious Crimean alliance at a uniquely delicate point, held that his government was

not doing justice by our faithful and zealous ally the Emperor of the French, by allowing a knot of his mortal enemies to be plotting within an hour's sail or row of his shore, when we have the power of sending them away from thence.[198]

This was in October. In the middle of that month the deed could be done. On September 22 Félix Pyat had delivered a speech to a meeting of refugees in Jersey, which Victor Hugo considered to be 'éloquent, ironi-

[192] See Wodehouse to Waddington, 14 March 1855: PRO FO 27/1091.
[193] See Clarendon to Cowley (private), 25 June 1855: Cowl. P., PRO FO 519/171 ff. 716–17; Clarendon to Cowley (private), 30 July 1855: Cowl. P., PRO FO 519/172 f. 105; Correspondence between Police and Home Office, July–August 1855, in PRO HO 45/6188.
[194] See Sanders' reports of 7 and 16 August 1855, in Cowl. P., PRO FO 519/172 ff. 151–2 and 183; and 9 and 12 August 1855, in PRO HO 45/6188.
[195] Palmerston memo. to Home Office, 14 August 1855: PRO HO 45/6188.
[196] See note by H. W[addington] on Sanders' report of 9 August 1855 in PRO HO 45/6188; and two letters from Grey to Clarendon of 10 August 1855, with a note by Waddington enclosed: Clar. P., c. 29 ff. 60–6.
[197] Waddington to Love, 15 August 1855: PRO HO 79/5, pp. 14–18.
[198] Palmerston to Grey, 12 October 1855: Palm. P., BM. Add. Ms. 48579, f. 80.

que et spirituel',[199] but which by the British authorities, less familiar perhaps with the customary excesses of the French declamatory style, was regarded as particularly offensive, combining as it did incitement to assassinate the French emperor with an attack on the British Queen couched, somewhat insensitively, in sexual imagery.[200] While the slander was only spoken, however, it was difficult to proceed in law against it.[201] But then in October the Jersey refugee paper *L'Homme* took it up and published it: which was the pretext the authorities wanted.[202] The Lieutenant-Governor called a public indignation meeting of the loyal islanders on the 13th, which was suitably indignant,[203] and armed with this expression of popular feeling put into operation his instructions of August, by expelling the proprietor, editor and vendor of the journal which had contained the libel. This will have been moderately satisfying, but it did not completely satisfy Lord Clarendon, who on the 16th wrote to the Home Office that he only wished the 'people of Jersey' would 'take the law *into their own hands* and settle the Refugee question in the Island';[204] nor did it appear to satisfy the French government, which addressed another complaint to Clarendon about the refugees on the 20th.[205] It may have been in response to this that the Cabinet on the 22nd of October decided to expel thirty-six further refugees who had signed a declaration of support for the original three: 'The question now', wrote Palmerston to Grey, 'is whether these Islands belong to us or to Victor Hugo & Co.'[206] Victor Hugo was among those expelled a few days later, to the accompaniment of shouts of 'down with the bloody Reds' from some bystanders at the docks.[207]

It was all done very expeditiously and without hitches. It was enabled to be done because both the courts and Parliament (which was, fortuitously, in recess at the time) could be short-circuited. Some popular protest was expected on the mainland, and prepared for.[208] There were a few petitions

---

[199] H. Dechène, 'Les Proscrits du Deux-Décembre à Jersey (1852–1855)', part III, in *Etudes Religieuses*, vol. CLII (1917), p. 53.

[200] 'You have had your knee kissed by thirty Arabian chiefs UNDER your garter. . . You have put General Canrobert in a BATH. . . and kissed Jerome. . . *Yes, you have sacrificed ALL:–the Queen's dignity!–the woman's delicacy!. . .–* ALL – EVEN CHASTITY! – for the love of that Ally! . . .' English translation in PRO HO 45/6188.

[201] See Waddington to Clarendon, 6 October 1855: Clar. P., c. 34 ff. 487–8 – 'there is no witness who can speak to the exact words used. . .with sufficient certainty to lay the foundation of any proceedings'.

[202] Pyat's 'Letter' appeared in *L'Homme* of 10 October.

[203] See Sanders' report, 14 October 1855: PRO HO 45/6188. According to Sanders, 'The inhabitants are very much excited, and it is with great difficulty that the police prevent the destruction of property.'

[204] Clarendon to Waddington, 16 October 1855: PRO HO 45/6188.

[205] Persigny to Clarendon, 20 October 1855: PRO FO 27/1094.

[206] Palmerston to Grey, 23 October 1855: PRO HO 45/6188. The Cabinet decision is mentioned in Grey to Palmerston, 23 October 1855: Palm. P., GC/GR/2451.

[207] Love to Waddington, 3 November 1855: PRO HO 45/6188.

[208] The Governor of Jersey, hearing in January that the expulsions were to be brought up in

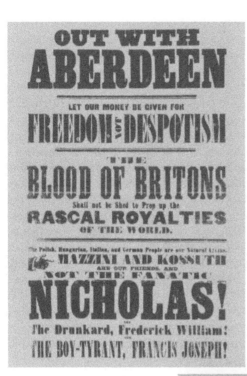

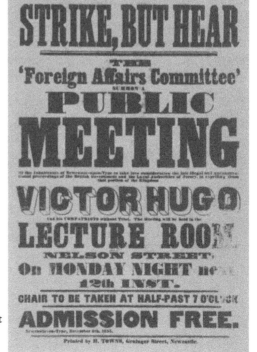

7. Broadsheets of 1854 and 1855, the latter directed against the Jersey expulsions.

and protest-meetings, and some press opposition.[209] Victor Hugo claimed that it was enough to dissuade the government from going further and bringing in an Alien Act: 'Ce bon et fier peuple montra les dents; Palmerston et Bonaparte durent se contenter de l'expulsion.'[210] But Hugo (as he often did) exaggerated; there is no sign of a projected Alien Bill at this time, and if there had been the scale of the protest against the expulsion would have been no deterrent. There was, for example, no mention of the affair made in Parliament when it met in January, and we have seen already how muted the protest was otherwise. What was contemplated by the government for a while, and then dropped, was a charge against *Reynolds's Newspaper* for publishing the Pyat letter in its own columns: but the decisive factor in this case was the old one, that a trial would allow the libel to be repeated and embellished.[211] The government's offensive against the refugees in Jersey had succeeded so well because it had deliberately avoided this kind of thing: chosen a place and a weapon which circumvented immediate and direct public accountability, and an issue on which the public to whom its actions were ultimately accountable were less likely, because of the way their own Queen had been involved, to feel sympathetic to the refugees than on most issues.

It showed what could, in these unusually favourable circumstances, be done to appease the continent. It therefore showed willing, which may have had a mollifying effect on the continent. It was also in itself quite a concession to the continent, in the sense that, by taking punitive actions against men who were not tried or even charged, it contravened what were supposed to be some very fundamental principles of English freedom: and all for the good of another. Governments which were more arbitrary themselves, however, may not have realised the generosity of it. To the refugees themselves, who as we have seen were liable to exaggerate both the desire and the capacity of the British government to limit their activities, it might have had a greater deterrent effect than it really merited. As it always did when it was able to do some little thing to meet the continent's wishes, the government made as much of this as it could. Clarendon told Cowley, to pass on to the French government, that its action had got rid of 'the whole of the *bad* Refugees', whose fury therefore 'knows no bounds'.[212] In fact, however, what had been done was really rather little. The expelled refugees did not go very far: some only to

Parliament 'for the purpose of embarrassing the Government', sent the Home Secretary legal ammunition for his use, and also offered to take full responsibility for the expulsions if the Government looked like getting into trouble – Love to Grey, 29 January 1856: PRO HO 45/6333.
[209] *Supra*, p. 122; and petitions in PRO HO 45/6188.
[210] K. W. Hooker, *The Fortunes of Victor Hugo in England* (1938, reprinted 1966), p. 133.
[211] *Supra*, p. 146.
[212] Clarendon to Cowley (private), 12 November 1855: Cowl. P., PRO FO 519/172, f. 488.

Guernsey, others to London; there was no question of extraditing them altogether from Britain. None of them was ever indicted, although their offence was technically indictable. They were still free to threaten the security of the French empire and the life of its emperor; from a little further away now than they had been before, but still too close for Napoleon's comfort. The Jersey expulsions of 1855 were the government's most dramatic victory against the refugees: but it was a victory which was more symbolic than effective.

If it was not effective, however, it might be seen as revealing. Government ministers in the 1850s generally tried to give the impression that they shared the attitude they found they had to take about continental demands over the refugee question on other occasions: that when they said they could not act arbitrarily against the refugees, it was not with any real regret, but with a total acceptance of the moral necessity for not so doing. Yet when they were allowed to act arbitrarily we find them doing so, and not apparently with any great reluctance. Released from the constraints put upon them by the law and the constitution, they showed their true mettle, the hungry despotic wolves under the liberal sheepskins. Some ministers were more wolflike than others – Palmerston and Clarendon more willing or eager to put aside their liberal qualms, for example, than Grey: but in the end all of them succumbed. Perhaps if they had been allowed a similar freedom of executive action on the mainland, the same would have happened there: the principle of asylum been the more precarious, if it had had only governments to defend it.

In fact there can be little doubt of this. On this particular occasion in 1855, there were exceptional factors explaining and perhaps excusing, if it required to be excused, the government's infringement of strict liberal principle. In the first place the infringement was a small one, not affecting any of its victims' liberty in a really material way. In the second place it might not have been called for at all if the dice had not been so inconveniently and unfairly loaded against the proper course of action in such a matter, which was to take it to court. Pyat's letter was clearly libellous, yet it could not be prosecuted because if it were the renewed publicity it would receive would negate the effect even of a guilty verdict. This is what the British authorities persuaded the French, who could if they had wanted have proceeded on their own behalf.[213] It could be argued that this justified the rather rougher justice of the expulsions. Thirdly: the circumstances which surrounded the expulsions were supposed to be very special. The action was taken in response to a very great necessity of the time, which was to keep a fragile Anglo-French alliance going and fighting in the

[213] Clarendon to Cowley (private), 31 October and 12 November 1855: Cowl. P., PRO FO 519/172 ff. 405–10, 488; Cowley to Clarendon (private), 14 November 1855: Cowl. P., PRO FO 519/217 p. 186.

Crimea. Not even the most principled Liberal who has ever lived has believed in putting every small detail of his principles before any necessity. The ministers who were most willing to offend against principle in this case (and also, as we shall see, in 1858) were those who were closest to the necessity: Palmerston and Clarendon, the men directly involved in conducting Britain's foreign affairs. From this it did not at all follow that this government, or any other one, would be so ready either to take such measures as these under any lesser pressures, or to take more illiberal measures at all. But it did follow that no government could be positively guaranteed not to do one of these things. Insofar as governments in the 1850s were liberal and permissive in their policies towards the refugees, it was very likely less because of the strength of their principles than because in the first place they could afford to be so, and secondly they had to be. They could afford to be because the refugees posed no direct threat at all to them, and not yet a critical indirect threat. They had to be liberal towards the refugees because their constituents (not always for very liberal reasons) demanded it of them and could give force to their demands. The licence the refugees enjoyed in England in the 1850s depended upon these two factors. If both of them had been reversed their position would have been (self-evidently, perhaps) less secure. We shall see what happened in 1858, when one of these factors was reversed, but not the other: when it seemed for a time that the government could no longer afford to persist in its old policy towards the refugees, but were still forced to by a 'public opinion' whose priorities differed from theirs.

6

The Orsini Affair

Overall what British governments had found themselves able to do to
appease the continental courts before 1858 had amounted to very little,
especially when put into the scales together with their generally intransigent official statements on the refugee question; and the continental courts
were not appeased, nor were their suspicions entirely allayed, that Britain
could have done more if she had tried, but had not wanted to, for nefarious
motives of her own.[1] When therefore on the evening of January 14th, 1858,
the ex-refugee Orsini's Birmingham-made bombs exploded near the
Place de l'Opéra in Paris, it was predictable that Britain would come in for
most of the blame: and she did. The Foreign Secretary Lord Clarendon
always complained bitterly thereafter that the greater part of that blame
was not deserved: for if every measure which had ever been pressed by the
continent on Britain had been adopted in its entirety, even an Alien bill,
how would that have stopped Orsini and Rudio: whom nobody – French
or English – had suspected of any guilty intent beforehand, and whom
therefore it would have occurred to no one to charge or to expel?[2] What
difference could it have made if Mazzini and Ledru-Rollin, whom the
French government *had* suspected quite obsessively, had been expelled,
when in this case neither of them appeared to be implicated at all?[3] How
could the British police have been expected to detect and prevent the
conspiracy in England when the French police so abjectly failed to detect it
when it reached France, even though apparently they were amply fore-
warned?[4] And who after all had sent these men – one of them, at least – to

---

[1] 'There is not a Government in Europe that is not convinced that England cd. prevent much
that is inimical to them to take place within her territories, if she would' – Cowl. P., PRO
FO 519/223, ff. 59–61.

[2] See for example Clarendon to Cowley (private), 19 and 20 January 1858: Cowl. P., PRO FO
519/177 ff. 53–73.

[3] *Ibid.*, *loc. cit.* Mazzini's innocence was confirmed by British police inquiries (Sanders'
reports of 21 and 25 January 1858: PRO MEPO 3/22), and is accepted by e.g. M. St J. Packe,
The Bombs of Orsini (1957). France at the time did not accept it: Walewski told Cowley in
January that 'if the chiefs, as he called L-R[ollin], Hugo & Mazzini, were not allowed to
reside in England, their subordinates wd. soon disappear' – Cowley to Clarendon (private),
17 January 1858: Cowl. P., PRO FO 519/223, ff. 38–44.

[4] See Howard de Walden to Clarendon (private), 15 January 1858: Clar. P. c. 83 ff. 17–18;
Palmerston to Clarendon 21 January 1858: Clar. P. c. 82 ff. 53–4.

8. Orsini preparing the bombs used in the *attentat* of 14 January 1858 (below); and his accomplice Simon Bernard (left).

England in the first place?[5] Clarendon's indignation was not wholly unreasonable, but of course it did not really touch the heart of the continent's grievance against Britain. That grievance was related less to the actual circumstances of the Orsini plot, than to the reservoir of resentment which had been building up against Britain over the past seven or eight years; which, if Britain had done more to appease it before, though it might not have forestalled the Orsini plot, would have made it very much less likely that Britain would have been abused so virulently on account of it. The continentals had always claimed that by harbouring Mazzini and the rest Britain's policy of asylum was bound to lead, some time or other, to an eventuality such as this. Britain had always claimed in reply that the continent's fears were exaggerated. The Orsini plot seemed to prove that they were not; and though this conclusion did not necessarily follow, in the heat of the moment to maintain otherwise appeared a sort of choplogic. Morally Britain was suddenly pushed on to the defensive.

Most British ministers *felt* themselves to be on the defensive, and felt that the continental onslaught against them, if neither reasonable nor justified, was at least understandable. All of them appeared genuinely shocked by the *attentat* and its bloody effects, and by the thought of 'the universally dreadful consequences' which would have entailed if it had succeeded.[6] Clarendon expressed himself 'ashamed of the protection wh. assassins enjoy here', and admitted to a considerable sympathy with France: 'The more I think of the whole matter', he wrote to Cowley, 'the more allowance I make for the feelings of the French & the less I am inclined to complain of the language of men who believe themselves to be in imminent danger and that England if she chose might put them in safety.'[7] '*We are a nuisance to Europe,*' he wrote on another occasion; 'we have our systems and our policy . . . and their external result is terror and danger to others and people are therefore justified in voting us a pest.'[8] Palmerston agreed that the feelings of the French were 'perfectly natural, and would have been ours in as great a Degree if attempts and outrages of the same kind had been repeatedly committed in London by criminals issuing from Paris'.[9] Others in the cabinet expressed similar views.[10]

[5] Cowley discovered that one of the conspirators, Pierri, 'was actually sent to England by the French authorities themselves' – Cowley to Clarendon (private), 18 January 1858: Cowl. P., PRO FO 519 pp. 44–8.

[6] Clarendon to Cowley (private), reporting the feeling of the Cabinet, 15 January 1858: Cowl. P., PRO FO 519/177 ff. 45–6.

[7] Clarendon to Howden (private), 22 January 1858: Clar. P., c. 140 pp. 651–2; Clarendon to Cowley (private), 21 January 1858: Cowl. P. PRO FO 519/177 ff. 77–83.

[8] Clarendon to Cowley (private), 16 January 1858: Cowl. P., PRO FO 519/177 ff. 49–52.

[9] Cabinet memorandum by Palmerston, 21 January 1858: Palm. P., CAB/A/89.

[10] E.g. Granville believed that France had a good case in international law against Britain (memo., n.d.: Clar. P. c. 82 f. 213); George Cornewall Lewis that she had 'a reasonable case against us' (Lewis to Clarendon, 19 January 1858: Clar. P. c. 82 ff. 199–202). Lord Argyll called the French reaction 'natural but illogical' (memo. in Palm. P., CAB/A/98).

Sympathy with the French was compounded by a degree of apprehension too, lest the issue be put to dangerous use, not only by France to damage an alliance which the British government still placed much weight on, but also by other hostile powers against Britain. The French emperor was supposed to be as loyal as ever to the entente, but finding it increasingly difficult to hold out for it against pressure inside and outside France.[11] Clarendon was very nervous for its survival, and became more so as time went on; by the beginning of February he was holding out almost no hope 'of maintaining friendly relations',[12] and reported to be 'haunted' by the fear of a French invasion.[13] And that was not the worst of it. Russia too was rumoured to be ganging up with France against Britain.[14] If it went on the movement could encompass the whole of Europe. Two days after the *attentat* Clarendon wrote to Palmerston that 'we must be prepared for a Continental League agst. us of one kind or another'.[15] It was a possibility he returned to frequently,[16] and a particularly ominous one at a time when, with much of the army tied up in India putting down the Mutiny there, 'we have no troops & no ships for home defence'.[17] Possibly – as was suggested to him in February by his ambassador in St Petersburg – they might soon have to give India up, in order to save themselves.[18] That was the scale of the problem.

Although Clarendon had some grounds for his fears – notably the behaviour of Persigny, the French ambassador in London, whose talk at times appeared wild and warlike, and the utterances of some leading politicians in France[19] – it is likely that his judgment was at fault on this occasion, and that things were not so black as he believed. Lord Cowley in Paris for example never shared his pessimism, and the eventual resolution of the crisis in March, more easily and amicably than Clarendon in February could have thought possible, suggests that the breach was not so wide as he assumed. There were some more auspicious signs too even in February: such as the reluctance of Prussia to join in the hue and cry against Britain, and, much more significantly, the moderation of Austria, who on previous occasions had led the hunt but now appeared to want to use it to

---

[11] See Cowley to Clarendon (private), 22 January 1858: Cowl. P., PRO FO 519/223 pp. 53–8.
[12] Clarendon to Palmerston, 8 February 1858: Palm. P., GC/CL/1149; Clarendon to Cowley (private), 8 February 1858: Cowl. P., PRO FO 519/177 ff. 137–41; and Clarendon to Lewis, 15 February 1858: Clar. P., c. 533 folder 1 – 'I wish we were better prepared for its rupture.'
[13] *Greville Memoirs* (1898 edn.), vol. VIII, p. 161.
[14] Wodehouse to Clarendon (private), 30 January 1858: Clar. P., c. 86 f. 141.
[15] Clarendon to Palmerston, 16 January 1858: Palm. P., GC/CL/1140.
[16] E.g. Clarendon to Lord Howden (private), 22 January 1858: Clar. P., c. 140 pp. 651–2; Clarendon to Forbes (private), 27 January 1858: Clar. P., c. 141 p. 35; Clarendon to Wodehouse (private), 10 February 1858: Clar. P., c. 141 pp. 111, 114.
[17] Clarendon to Palmerston, 21 January 1858: Palm. P., GC/CL/1144.
[18] Wodehouse to Clarendon (private), 13 February 1858: Clar. P., c. 86 ff. 146–7.
[19] *Vide supra*, p. 62.

ingratiate herself with Britain at France's expense.[20] Clarendon may have been wrong in his assessment of the situation: nevertheless it was Clarendon who at the time had his finger on the continental diplomatic pulse, and consequently it was presumably his assessment which, together with Palmerston's, carried most weight with the cabinet. Clarendon was certain that something had to be done. If it were not, he emphasised to his cabinet colleagues in January, then 'the excitement agst us in France will increase daily & will be stimulated by every Govt of Europe until the whole Continent is leagued agst us when demands inconsistent with our national honour will infallibly be addressed to us'. It was therefore 'a question of the gravest political importance to Engd'.[21] Together with Palmerston he set to to work out some measure which would appease the French, and so prevent the nemesis he so much dreaded.

Of course nothing could be done by Britain which really would effectively preclude the repetition of outrages like Orsini's; this, as we have seen, Clarendon was aware of. But this was not really necessary anyway. 'What we want', he told the cabinet, 'is not so much a law to prevent foreign conspiracies in Engd as a measure to satisfy public opinion abroad':[22] which was a different matter. It was not what was done which was important so much as the doing of it; what was needed was a gesture, a response not to the specific grievances of France, which were unjust and not very seriously meant, but to the general grievance, which was just and also quite real; nothing necessarily effective, but something which would demonstrate merely 'that we are not unmoved at the dangers to wch. France & the Empr. are exposed & that we are doing something *ad hoc*'.[23] Yet it had to be something substantial. The most substantial thing, of course – the power to expel foreigners from England whenever a foreign government demanded it – was 'utterly out of the question' so far as opinion in Britain was concerned: 'We might just as well ask Parliament to annex England to France, & yet I suppose that nothing short of that wd. satisfy the demands wch. Frenchmen moved by spite & fear are prepared to make.'[24] Between doing that, which was impossible, and doing nothing, which was also impossible, there were other courses of action the government might consider, so long as France left them some room for manoeuvre by not making overt demands on them. These were explored during the weekend following the *attentat*. From Paris Lord Cowley, who like Clarendon believed that it did not much matter '*what* is done provided *something* is done to conciliate public opinion in this country', suggested

---

[20] See Bloomfield to Clarendon (private), 30 January 1858: Clar. P., c. 86 ff. 43–4; Seymour to Clarendon (private), 24 February 1858: Clar. P., c. 85 ff. 408–9.
[21] Cabinet memorandum by Clarendon, 21 January 1858: Palm. P., CAB/A/92.
[22] *Ibid., loc. cit.*
[23] Clarendon to Cowley (private), 23 January 1858: Cowl. P., PRO FO 519/177 ff. 89–95.
[24] *Ibid., loc. cit.*

finding some way of getting rid of Mazzini, which he thought would do the trick.[25] The objection to this of course was that the government could not do it with the law as it was, and that to ask for 'an act of Parlt ad hominem wd be absurd'.[26] The Attorney-General had the idea of trying to extend the Treason Laws to cover treason against foreign sovereigns, which the cabinet received favourably at first, but then dropped.[27] A new extradition treaty was discussed but also dropped.[28] Palmerston and Clarendon favoured a forthright Alien Bill. Palmerston went to the length of framing one:

> The Government to have for five years to come the Power to send away by order of a Secy of State any Foreigner who might on good grounds be suspected of plotting either to disturb the internal tranquillity of any friendly Power or to use violence agst the Person or Life of any Foreign Sovereign.

Such power was to be protected from abuse by making it accountable to a special secret Parliamentary Committee (Clarendon preferred the three Lord Justices) each time it was proposed to be implemented. France was to reciprocate by promising never again to send refugees to Britain. Palmerston believed that if the leaders of the opposition could be got to promise support for it beforehand such a bill would be 'tolerably certain' to pass.[29] When it was put to the cabinet on January 22nd, however, scarcely any of his colleagues agreed with him. Some of them rejected it out of principle; others because of its likely unpopularity, or because of practical difficulties in the way of implementing it which the Lord Chancellor pointed out to them. Apart from Clarendon and Palmerston only the lightweights Panmure and Clanricarde came out in favour of the Bill.[30] Consequently it was dropped: but not before 'whispers' of what had been in the wind had got out, and into the House of Commons.[31]

What the government eventually came up with was something a good deal milder. It was decided by the cabinet of January 22nd that, instead of bringing in a new law, some way should be found to make the existing

[25] Cowley to Clarendon (private), 20 and 24 January 1858: Cowl. P., PRO FO 519/223 ff. 49–52, 59–61.
[26] Clarendon to Palmerston, 21 January 1858: Palm. P., GC/CL/1144; Clarendon to Cowley, 21 January 1858: Cowl. P., PRO FO 519/177 ff. 77–83; and see note by Grey, n.d., in Clar. P., c. 82 ff. 191–2.
[27] Bethell to Clarendon, 23 January 1858: Clar. P., c. 82 ff. 239–42; Clarendon to Cowley, 23 January 1858: Cowl. P., PRO FO 519/177 ff. 89–95.
[28] See Grey to Clarendon, 30 January 1858: Clar. P., c. 82 ff. 196–7.
[29] Cabinet memorandum by Palmerston, 21 January 1858: Palm. P., CAB/A/89. Clarendon's amendments are in *ibid.*, CAB/A/92.
[30] The pre-cabinet opinions of 12 out of the 15 cabinet ministers are recorded in Palm. P., CAB/A/89–101, together with Argyll's after the cabinet.
[31] 3PD 148 c. 765 (Roebuck, 5 February 1858).

laws more effective, by increasing the penalties and also the chances of conviction for conspirators in England.[32] This was the purpose of the Conspiracy to Murder Bill, which was drawn up hurriedly on January 29th,[33] promised the support of his party privately by Lord Derby the next day,[34] amended and completed by a further cabinet on February 2nd,[35] and introduced into Parliament on February 8th by Palmerston himself.[36] The Conspiracy Bill amended the existing conspiracy laws in two material ways: firstly by making conspiracy to murder a felony rather than a misdemeanour, so enabling the maximum penalty to be increased from two years to life imprisonment; and secondly by establishing what until then had been doubtful, that the law covered conspiracies to commit offences abroad as well as in England.[37] In this form the measure had several advantages from a House of Commons point of view. It was not, in the first place, an Alien Bill, as Palmerston pointed out when he presented it to Parliament, as if the possibility of bringing in one had never crossed his mind: 'Sir, it is needless for me to say that it is not the intention of Her Majesty's Government to propose any measure of that kind . . .'[38] It did not even refer specifically to refugees or foreigners – although in an earlier draft it appears to have done so.[39] Consequently it was not what the continent had asked for, and not something against which popular and parliamentary resistance had already stiffened. On its merits it was very difficult to object to: the laws relating to conspiracy to murder undoubtedly were, as Grey pointed out to Lord John Russell to secure his support for the bill, 'in an uncertain & unsatisfactory state', and badly needed improving.[40] From a diplomatic point of view the advantage of the Bill was that it was a *measure* of response to continental demands, which, though it did not appear adequate, continental rulers could pretend to accept as adequate, if they were as anxious as Britain's were – and as Louis Napoleon was known to be – to cool things down. Herein undoubtedly

---

[32] See Argyll's memorandum, n.d., in Palm. P., CAB/A/98. The first recorded suggestion of such a measure is the memorandum by M. T. Baines, Chancellor of the Duchy of Lancaster, in *ibid.*, CAB/A/100; subsequently however it was credited to Waddington, Permanent Under-Secretary at the Home Office – see Grey to Clarendon, 1 February 1858: Clar. P., c. 82 ff. 154–5.

[33] Bethell to Clarendon, 29 January 1858: Clar. P., c. 82 f. 244.

[34] Clarendon to Palmerston, 30 January 1858: Palm. P., GC/CL/1146.

[35] Palmerston to Queen Victoria, 2 February 1858: RA J77/92.

[36] 3PD 148, c. 933.

[37] *Ibid.*, cc. 937–8. About the latter, however, there was some controversy: Lord Chief Justice Campbell claimed that the applicability of the old laws to overseas offences was not really in doubt, and that the Attorney-General only maintained it *was* in order to make his bill appear more necessary. See *ibid.*, cc. 1848–51 (22 February 1858) and 2069–70 (1 March 1858); and Mrs Hardcastle (ed.), *Life of John, Lord Campbell*, vol. II (1881), p. 357.

[38] 3PD 148, c. 934 (8 February 1858).

[39] See Clarendon to Palmerston, 30 January 1858: Palm. P. GC/CL/1146; Grey to Clarendon, 31 January 1858: Clar. P., c. 82 ff. 194–5.

[40] Grey to Russell, 2 February 1858: Russell Papers, PRO 30/33/13E ff. 212–15.

lay the appeal of the Bill for the government. Russell described it well when he spoke of it in Parliament as being 'an exceedingly skilful, an exceedingly cunning artifice, if I may use the expression, by which neither the people of England nor the Emperor of the French will be offended'.[41]

It left the government, however, an exquisitely delicate task. The success of the Bill on the continent depended upon its being thought more than it was; its success in England depended upon its being thought less than it was. Public pronouncements to one side were bound to be overheard by the other side. If the government emphasised to the House of Commons too strongly the Bill's harmless aspects, in order to secure its passage, that would be taken amiss by the continent and consequently render its passage valueless. If on the other hand in order to secure its acceptance by the continentals they made it appear to them too strong, that would arouse the alarm and resentment of the Commons who would probably then not pass it. 'The fear may be', wrote Clarendon to Palmerston on the day of the first reading, 'that in recommending the Bill we shall explain too clearly to the French that in fact we do nothing for them.'[42] He tried to counteract this effect by insisting privately to the French government how magnificent in fact the concession was: how it was 'a great & almost unprecedented act of friendship on our part directly or indirectly to meddle with our laws with reference to other Countries';[43] and how effective it would be – not in its actual provisions, but in its power to terrify and deter the refugees who had only 'the vaguest notions & the extremest fears about what the English law will call conspiracy & the means that may be used for implicating them'.[44] The Bill, he wrote to France after its first reading, 'fell among them like a bomb'; they were 'all frightened out of their wits':

& indeed I cd. not have expected that the Bill wd. be so completely successful or seem to be so evidently just the measure that was required. The vagueness of the term conspiracy & the extreme severity of the punishment are enough to frighten people the majority of whom are rank cowards.[45]

To Seymour in Vienna Clarendon wrote that in fact the Bill, together with 'the Police regulns. wh. can be put in force without act of Parlt.', would be far *more* effective than an Alien Act because penal servitude for life would be more of a deterrent than mere deportation to America.[46] This is what he

[41] 3PD 148, c. 1046 (9 February 1858).
[42] Clarendon to Palmerston, 8 February 1858: Palm. P., GC/CL/1148.
[43] Clarendon to Cowley (private), 10 February 1858: Cowl. P., PRO FO 519/177 ff. 149–53.
[44] Clarendon to Cowley (private), 11 February 1858: Cowl. P., PRO FO 519/177 ff. 155–9.
[45] *Ibid.*, *loc. cit.*, and Clarendon to Cowley (private), 13 February 1858: Cowl. P., PRO FO 519/177 ff. 169–74.
[46] Clarendon to Seymour (private), 3 February 1858: Clar. P., c. 141 pp. 65–9. What he meant by 'the Police regulations' is unclear. To Normanby on 11 February he referred to them as 'the vigorous measures of Police *observation*' (underlining in original): Clar. P., c. 141 pp. 135–7.

tried, privately and almost desperately, to convince the continent of; but not of course his own countrymen, who had the thing presented to *them* as if it were a mere trifle, a minor repair to England's general laws, and hardly a concession to foreigners at all.[47]

With France Clarendon seems to have succeeded quite well: which however posed its own danger. If they were too well persuaded of the magnitude of the Bill then the French might start crowing openly. 'I am delighted at the Division', wrote Cowley to Clarendon after the first (successful) reading; 'All I fear now is some insulting paragraph in some of the French Papers to the tune that France has only to hold up her finger and England must obey.'[48] This kind of danger was always very near. However much the leaders of the two countries might like to see this question settled, they were not entirely the masters of what they did. An intemperate or undiplomatic or even misunderstood speech or newspaper article might undo weeks of painstaking diplomacy. Both countries had their 'mobs', as Clarendon called them,[49] and their press; Palmerston had his House of Commons besides, and Napoleon his army. Feelings ran high and offence was easily taken. A characteristic attack on the French emperor by Roebuck in the House of Commons on the first reading of the Conspiracy Bill set Cowley scurrying to smooth down the feathers it had ruffled in Paris.[50] An indiscretion by a French minister to the Paris correspondent of *The Times* about police co-operation between the two countries had him rushing again to warn him of the fuss such sensitive revelations might cause in England.[51] An unfortunately-timed rumour, of the emperor's having granted a pension to a man his uncle had hired to assassinate the Duke of Wellington, had the diplomatic fire-service out working again: not with any great success, for the story turned out to be true.[52] A speech by Persigny in London on January 23rd, and others in France, some of which were almost wilfully misinterpreted in England, had the diplomats

[47] See especially the first reading debate, 8 and 9 February 1858: 3PD 148 cc. 933–64, 979–1081.

[48] Cowley to Clarendon (private), 10 February 1858: Cowl. P., PRO FO 519/223 pp. 93–8.

[49] Clarendon to Cowley (private), 20 February 1858: Cowl. P., PRO FO 519/177 ff. 211–16.

[50] 3PD 148 cc. 957–64 (8 February 1858); Cowley to Clarendon (private), 10 February 1858: Cowl. P., PRO FO 519/223 pp. 99–100. The emperor complained at Roebuck's not having been called to order or replied to by Palmerston; through Clarendon, Palmerston explained the Parliamentary procedures which prevented both of these reactions – Palmerston to Clarendon, 11 February 1858: Clar. P., c. 82 ff. 87–8; and Clarendon to Cowley (private), 11 February 1858: Cowl. P., PRO FO 519/177 ff. 155–9. On February 16th, at Clarendon's insistence, Palmerston addressed a general appeal to M.Ps to stop abusing the emperor – 3PD 148 cc. 1470–1; Clarendon to Cowley (private), 16 February 1858: Cowl. P., PRO FO 519/177 ff. 187–93.

[51] Clarendon to Cowley (private), 2 February 1858: Cowl. P., PRO FO 519/177 ff. 111–19; Cowley to Clarendon (private), 3 February 1858: Cowl. P., PRO FO 519/223 pp. 81–5.

[52] Clarendon to Cowley (private), 8 and 10 February 1858: Cowl. P., PRO FO 519/177 ff. 137–41, 149–53; Cowley to Clarendon (private), 15 and 16 February 1858: Cowl. P., PRO FO 519/223 pp. 109–11, 113–18. Clarendon decided to keep quiet about it.

almost in despair. And then came some openly provocative addresses from French army regiments to the emperor, printed in the official *Moniteur*,[53] whose effect in England proved incapable of being doused; and which consequently sent the whole brittle structure collapsing to the ground.

Clarendon from the very beginning of this affair had repeatedly warned the French government that if it wanted something to be done by Britain it would have to be careful to avoid menace, or the appearance of menace. 'Let it once be said or thought', he wrote to Cowley two days after the *attentat*, 'that we are *threatened* by a foreign Power and there will be an end to any hope of a vote even if we could propose any measure'.[54] Now, he wrote again on the 4th of February, 'what I foresaw has occurred'; Englishmen would put up with abuse: 'but that which no man here can or will stand is a threat, and there is no risk or danger to which Englishmen would not expose themselves rather than submit to menace'.[55] Many Liberal M.P.s, including most notably Lord John Russell, regarded the *Moniteur* articles as reason enough to refuse to give countenance to any measure, however reasonable it might be in itself, out of 'regard for national dignity'.[56] Palmerston regarded Russell's attitude as 'childish' and unlikely to gain much support in the Commons:[57] and sure enough when the Conspiracy Bill passed its first reading on the 9th it was by a comfortable majority of 200, the *Moniteur* notwithstanding. ('This House of Commons', commented Sir James Graham, who was plotting at the time with Russell and Gladstone and Aberdeen to bring the government down on the Bill, 'is abject, afraid of France, and bold only in the massacre of Chinese.')[58] The 200 majority, however, was misleading. Lord Aberdeen on the 10th felt that the Bill stood 'no great chance of success' despite it.[59] Many M.P.s who fully intended to vote against it ultimately, on this occasion desisted from doing so for tactical reasons and because they believed the intrinsic merits of the bill deserved an airing.[60] Others were genuinely perplexed by the dilemma the bill put them in: like Gladstone:

if the Government succeed in showing a *fault* in our law then we shall have to choose between refusing to amend what is bad, on account of circumstances other

---

[53] To Cowley Napoleon explained that he could not have refused to publish the regiments' addresses without offending them: and Cowley was aware how much he depended upon the loyalty of his army – Cowley to Clarendon no. 174: PRO FO 27/1243.

[54] Clarendon to Cowley (private), 16 January 1858: Cowl. P., PRO FO 519/177 ff. 49–52.

[55] Clarendon to Cowley (private), 4 February 1858: Cowl. P., PRO FO 519/177 ff. 121–8.

[56] Russell to Grey, 2 February 1858: Russell Papers, PRO 30/22/13E ff. 216–17.

[57] Palmerston to Clarendon, 4 February 1858: Clar. P., c. 82 f. 76.

[58] Graham to Russell. 11 February 1858: Russell Papers, PRO 30/20/13E ff. 224–5.

[59] Aberdeen to Graham, 10 February 1858: Aberdeen Papers, BL. Add. Ms. 43330 ff. 31–2.

[60] Aberdeen, Graham, Sidney Herbert and Cardwell, for example, believed that this was the right course to take, and criticised Russell for coming out against it too early, which they believed damaged their cause. See Aberdeen to Graham, 10 February 1858, *loc. cit.*; and S. Herbert to Gladstone, 10 February 1858: Gladstone Papers, BL. Add. Ms. 44211 ff. 1–2.

9. The Orsini *attentat,* 14 January 1858: from the *Illustrated Times.*

than the merits, and the disadvantage of doing what is good under apparent dictation and under circumstances which as far as I understand them amount to insult.

Gladstone abstained to mull it over, but it was clear even then which way his vote eventually would go: 'My prepossessions are strongly adverse to altering English Laws for other than English occasions.'[61] If therefore it had come to a straightforward vote on a second reading, the issue would remain in doubt in spite of the massive majority on the first. It is clear also that there were many Members of Parliament in February 1858 who wanted an opportunity to bring Palmerston down, for all kinds of reasons unconnected with this affair, but who because of the way in which the bill was framed found it difficult to, without for example seeming to be voting for murder. They needed another pretext. That pretext was quickly to grow out of a seed planted in the Commons by the independent M.P. J. A. Roebuck on February 5th, when he asked the government, in connexion with the *Moniteur* addresses, to lay on the table of the House the corres-

---

[61] Gladstone to Graham, 9 February 1858: Aberdeen Papers, BL. Add. Ms. 43071 ff. 376–7. Gladstone was also a little worried that his action might do violence to his 'pacific principles': but on the other hand, he wrote, 'My indisposition to meddle with others is in some ways balanced with a proportionate dislike of being meddled with.'

pondence which had passed between France and Britain in the past few weeks on the refugee question.[62]

This was inconvenient for the government, because the only correspondence which could be published appeared somewhat one-sided: a strong despatch from the French Foreign Minister Walewski communicated to Clarendon on January 21st, very accusatory in its tone towards England (and to those who wished to find fault, easy to present as more insulting than it was), and making clear though unspecific demands on the British government, to which as yet – a fortnight later – no official British reply had been sent.[63] Walewski's despatch was published on February 6th. It took a little time, however, for people to realise what its implications were – or what could be made of it.[64] By the time of the second reading of the Conspiracy Bill on the 19th they knew. 'Public opinion' too was lumbering into activity. There was a sharp controversy in the daily and weekly press, and indignation meetings were being called all over the country, including a 'monster' one in Hyde Park for the 21st. 'John Bull', wrote Lord Malmesbury in his diary, 'has got his back up.'[65] To 'John Bull' the chain of events now appeared clear: Walewski's accusations and demands, backed by threats from the French army given official sanction by being printed in the *Moniteur*, instead of being stoutly resisted by the government had forced from it this Conspiracy Bill as a cowardly response. If they passed it in circumstances such as these, said Sir Robert Peel (son), it would 'entail shame and degradation on this House and on the country'.[66] Consequently it must be resisted.

This version was not entirely fair. The Conspiracy Bill was certainly a response to the French government's demands,[67] but not to the French army's menaces, which were published after the Bill was drafted. Neither was it quite true that Clarendon had made no reply to Walewski's despatch. The trouble was that the replies he did make, contained in his private letters to Cowley, were not the kinds of replies his critics would

[62] 3PD 148, cc. 762–71.
[63] Walewski to Persigny, 20 January 1858: PRO FO 27/1273, and printed in PP lx (1857–8) pp. 113–17.
[64] On February 8th, for example, it had still not sunk in that the government had made no rebuttal or reply of any kind to it: see Kinglake's amendment, 3PD 148 c. 939.
[65] Diary for 9 February, in Lord Malmesbury, *Memoirs of an ex-Minister*, p. 415.
[66] 3PD 148, c. 1792 (19 February 1858). See also *Daily News*, 3 February 1858, p. 4; *Morning Advertiser*, 10 February 1858, p. 4; and the Commons debates of 9 and 19 February: 3PD 148 cc. 979–1078 and 1741–1844.
[67] Clarendon constantly maintained that this was not so: for example in a private letter to Wodehouse in St Petersburg, 3 February 1858, where he claimed it was 'a spontaneous act of the Govt &. . . brought forward without the instigation or indeed the slightest approach to pressure on the part of the French Govt.' – Clar. P., c. 141 pp. 59–62. This can only be accepted as true in a very pedantic sense: even the first intimations that the government might legislate were prompted by Cowley's reports that the French would demand it, and their first serious discussions of what to do were a direct result of Walewski's despatch.

have found reassuring, chiefly because their object was, as we have seen, to convince the French that the nature and purposes of the government's actions were precisely what those critics objected to. To have replied more firmly in the sense they demanded would, he wrote on February 19th, 'have done no earthly good'; it had already been said to them '50 times over in the course of the last few years' and if repeated again to men 'so frightened & excited as the French were at that moment' would only have exacerbated the quarrel.[68] Instead Clarendon's replies were intended to temper the wind. About the despatch of Walewski's which his critics demanded he repudiate, Clarendon instead told Persigny that he 'thought it a proper dispatch & that I need not renew to him the assurance that any thing wch it was in our power to do shd. be done for the satisfactn. of public opinion in France . . .'[69] To Cowley he wrote on February 2nd to tell Walewski that 'we shall have a Bill to be introduced on the 1st night of the Session . . . & you may rely upon it that with the more active Police regulations wch we can establish without the intervention of Parlt. this will be amply sufficient to keep the Refugees in order . . .'[70] None of this (especially the new 'Police regulations') could have been revealed to the House of Commons without seeming to confirm its worst suspicions; and indeed when much later Lord Clarendon, to clear himself, did reveal to the House of Lords some of his private communications with Cowley – including both of the letters from which these passages are taken – it was only in versions so censored and distorted as to be dishonest.[71] Walewski's dispatch, therefore, had to go before the Commons naked, its impact unsoftened by any sign or hint of a rebuttal by the British government, or an explanation by the French.

By the time the second reading came along, it had been nearly a month since the despatch had been received and still it had not been replied to. It was this which tripped the government. To some M.P.s it appeared that if no other reply was sent then the Conspiracy Bill itself must be intended as the government's reply, which was in effect to admit to the justice of Walewski's accusations.[72] For other M.P.s it provided the pretext they were seeking to combine with those of Palmerston's erstwhile supporters who were genuinely in agreement with his 'Conspiracy' policy at this time to bring him down. The Conspiracy Bill had been cleverly designed to make it difficult for a majority to vote against it; now its opponents came up with some of the same kind of cunning, and put together an amendment 'ingeniously framed', said the Conservative Bentinck, 'to catch birds

---

[68] Clarendon to Cowley (private), 19 February 1858: Cowl. P., PRO FO 519/177 ff. 207–10.
[69] Clarendon to Cowley (private), 21 January 1858: *ibid*. ff. 77–83.
[70] Clarendon to Cowley (private), 2 February 1858: *ibid*. ff. 111–19.
[71] 3PD 149, cc. 65–6 (1 March 1858). 'Doctoring' correspondence for publication was not unknown at this time, but in this case the scale of the deception is unusual.
[72] E.g. 3PD 148, c. 1764 (19 February 1858).

of every kind'.[73] Milner Gibson's Amendment, proposed on the 19th and seconded by Bright, while expressing abhorrence of the Orsini *attentat* and a general readiness to remedy defects in the law of England if they could be 'proved to exist', nevertheless regretted that the government, before putting this measure to a second reading, had not 'felt it to be their duty to make some reply' to Walewski's despatch.[74] The point of this formula, of course, was to bring over to the side of those who opposed the bill as many as possible of those who did not: and it worked. To the 99 M.P.s, mainly Liberals, who had voted against the first reading there joined another 135, mainly Conservatives, who had not; and the amendment was carried by 19 votes. ('Disraeli's face', wrote Lord Malmesbury, 'was worth anything – a mixture of triumph and sarcasm that he could not repress.'[75]) Palmerston's ministry resigned the next day, in an atmosphere of anger and recrimination.

Undoubtedly the most put out of all the government ministers by this débâcle was Lord Clarendon, who had not shown the coolest judgment throughout this affair, and whose direct responsibility, of course, the defeat was: for it had been his job to reply to despatches. 'I can not understand', wrote Lord Derby to him, '. . . why no answer was sent'; but Clarendon knew why, and was unrepentant.[76] What irritated him most was the fact that Parliament should have presumed to interfere at all in this kind of thing; 'The more one thinks about it', he wrote to Cowley, 'the more patent appear the inconvenience & danger of a H. of Cs. deciding how & when & what dispatches shall be written in utter ignorance of all the circumstances necessary for coming to a decision.' This kind of interference was bad enough, he said, in home affairs; in foreign affairs it was 'immeasurably worse'.[77] It offended against all the canons of diplomacy: that into its secret, delicate, aristocratically-ordered world should come blundering the *hoi polloi*, with their total ignorance of its finer points, the nuances, the significance of things left unsaid, the subtlety of it; ruining everything by their stupidity. It was an invasion of what was still, in a political world becoming increasingly vulgarised, very much an aristocra-

---

[73] *Ibid.*, c. 1788 (19 February 1858).   [74] *Ibid.*, c. 1758.

[75] Diary for 20 February 1858, in Malmesbury, *op. cit.*, p. 417.

[76] Derby to Clarendon, 20 February 1858: Clar. P., c. 103, ff. 731–6.

    Clarendon will not, of course, have made the decision on his own. Lord Granville's recollection of the event twenty-three years later, however, suggests that it might have slipped through a rather tired and off-guard Cabinet. 'I remember hours being spent in discussing the [Conspiracy] Bill and the prudence of presenting it to Parliament at that time. As we were about to separate, the despatch of Count Walewski was referred to, and Lord Clarendon said – "How am I to act with regard to the despatch? I think I had better not answer it at all." Lord Palmerston said – "I think that would be the best way." And in that the whole of the Cabinet acquiesced without saying a word.' – 3PD 261 cc. 787–8 (House of Lords, 19 May 1881).

[77] Clarendon to Cowley (private), 22 February 1858: Cowl. P., PRO FO 519/177 ff. 217–23.

tic corner; and by the aristocrats who had charge of that corner it was greatly resented.

Yet the vote of February 19th was a curious affair. In a way it was fortuitous: Clarendon described it as 'one of those accidents or rather dishonest combinations to which every Govt. in this country is exposed', especially 'at the present time when parties are so much subdivided & allegiance sits upon them all so lightly'.[78] Palmerston explained to the Queen how his government had been taken by surprise: many of his supporters, 'not anticipating any danger' after a spanking victory on the India Bill the previous day, having 'gone out of town for a few days'.[79] Apparently the government whips hardly exerted themselves.[80] There can be no doubt that the thing was greatly bungled. 'The truth is', wrote one of the defeated ministers, 'that Pam. mismanaged the House grossly.'[81] His speech at the close of the debate was widely deplored for its intemperate vindictiveness. The delighted *Daily News* likened it to 'the last convulsive struggles of a sperm-whale in "the flurries", when the lance has been driven deep into its vitals, amid the exultant acclamations of the assailing boats' crews'.[82] Lord Derby, who was the main beneficiary of it all, claimed that he himself was as surprised as anybody by the result.[83] By defeated ministers, on the other hand, he was blamed for having engineered or at least exploited it for partisan advantage.[84] Among the majority votes there were clearly some which were not given solely on the merit of the question, but for extraneous reasons: by Tories for party political reasons, by disaffected Liberals, it was suggested, because of Palmerston's recent appointment as Privy Seal of Lord Clanricarde, who (wrote Prince Albert) 'is looked upon as a reprobate', and during the debate was present, provocatively, in the Peers' gallery.[85] Much specula-

[78] Clarendon to Lord Howard de Walden (private), 26 February 1858, and Clarendon to Lord Howden (private), 23 February 1858: Clar. P., c. 141 pp. 237–8, 204–5.

[79] Palmerston to Queen Victoria, 19 February 1858: *Letters of Queen Victoria 1837–61*, vol. III, p. 336.   [80] *Greville Memoirs*, vol. VIII, p. 167.

[81] Argyll to Aberdeen, 2 March 1858: Aberdeen Papers, BL. Add. Ms. 43199 ff. 124–6. Charles Greville agreed: see his *Memoirs*, vol. VIII, pp. 169–71. Some contemporaries, puzzled by the government's ineptness in falling into a trap it could (in their opinion) so easily have avoided, wondered whether it might not have been done on purpose, to avoid having to face a much more disagreeable question, which was a debate coming up soon on Clanricarde's appointment: see *ibid.*, p. 170; Countess of Strafford (ed.), *Leaves from the Diary of Henry Greville*, vol. III, p. 107; and Argyll to Aberdeen, 2 March 1858: 'I prefer a fall on this – where I think we were clearly right – to a fall on such things as the P[rivy] Seal': Aberdeen Papers, BL. Add. Ms. 43199, f. 126. Derby was also suspicious that it might be a tactical withdrawal on the government's part, 'for the purpose of going through a crisis in order to come back again with new strength' – memorandum by Prince Albert, 21 February 1858: *QVL 1837–61*, vol. III, p. 339.   [82] *Daily News*, 22 February 1858, p. 4.

[83] Derby to Clarendon, 20 February 1858: Clar. P., c. 103, ff. 731–2.

[84] E.g. Palmerston to Queen Victoria, 19 February 1858: *QVL 1837–61*, vol. III, p. 336.

[85] Memorandum by Prince Albert, 21 February 1858: *ibid*, p. 336; *Greville Memoirs*, vol. VIII, pp. 164–6.

tion was aroused also by the collaboration against the government of Sir James Graham (who ironically enough while Home Secretary back in 1844 had been the philorefugees' main villain in the Mazzini letter-opening affair) with Gladstone and Lord John Russell: to what purpose no one quite knew, except that it was in all likelihood a devious one. Russell's motive may have been to get the Liberal party back in power in his own hands, and reconstituted on a new kind of basis with the Peelite Gladstone there too;[86] towards which aim the February 19th vote was a small step. (A second step would be to defeat Derby while Palmerston was still discredited.) It was a time of considerable flux and instability in British party politics; of cross-currents which were likely, quite unpredictably, to upset any legislative vessel. Palmerston may on this occasion have been merely unlucky.

Or he may have brought it on himself. It is clear that to a great extent the target of the Parliamentary attack on the 19th was Palmerston personally, who had only himself to blame for provoking it. When Parliament had first met at the beginning of February, although not many people had thought the government would fall on this issue it was widely predicted that it would fall on something: probably the India Bill or reform.[87] For this vulnerability Palmerston was supposed to be responsible. Charles Greville at the time took note of 'the diminution of Palmerston's energy and power'. ('He is', he wrote, 'always asleep, both in the Cabinet and in the House of Commons, where he endeavours to conceal it by wearing his hat over his eyes.')[88] Others were said to resent what the *Morning Chronicle* described as his 'dictatorial' manner, 'the dull despotism with which he has weighed down his contemporaries'.[89] Distrust and dislike of Palmerston in the Commons may have gone deeper than the majorities he was regularly able to command suggested: what preserved him, of course, was his popularity in the country, and the Liberals' awareness of this. 'I have no faith in Palmerston', wrote Graham to Gladstone in January; 'I think him a very dangerous Minister; but the Liberal Party is bought and sold to him; and the delusion in his favour in the Country has not yet passed away.'[90] That 'delusion' may have dissuaded some M.P.s who otherwise would

---

[86] On 26 January Graham had written to Gladstone that Russell wished 'to get the Government into his own hands, but does not see his way': Gladstone Papers, BL. Add. Ms. 44164, ff. 145–51. The obstacle, of course, was Palmerston. The *Moniteur* addresses gave him the clue: 'It is clear', wrote Graham to Aberdeen on February 4, 'that Ld. John thinks he had Palmerston on his Hip': Aberdeen Papers, BL. Add. Ms. 43192 ff. 199–200. Russell and Gladstone worked closely together over the Conspiracy Bill, and their victory on the 19th prompted Russell to comment, in reference to their co-operation, that 'In six months we may have a union of the liberal party which may be a foundation for the future' – Russell to (?) Dean, 23 February 1858: Russell Papers, PRO 30/22/13E ff. 234–5.

[87] *Greville Memoirs*, vol. VIII, pp. 159, 165.　　　[88] *Ibid.*, p. 162.

[89] *Morning Chronicle*, 22 February 1858, p. 4.

[90] Graham to Gladstone, 26 January 1858: Gladstone Papers, BL. Add. Ms. 44164, ff. 145–51.

have liked to from voting him down, at least until they got a chance to on an issue where he might not secure popular support: where he might be parted from his public. The Conspiracy Bill seemed to be that issue. It was a measure on which Palmerston could be attacked with Palmerstonian weapons. 'Throughout the second half of his long public life', said the *Morning Chronicle*, 'Lord Palmerston has led the vulgar captive by his arrogant and offensive policy. He was regarded as the Champion of England against all encroachments by Foreign Powers, and yet now his enemies are able to taunt him with having "betrayed the honour of his country".'[91] Surely enough, they did. A case against the Conspiracy Bill *per se* was, as we have seen, not an easy one to sustain, and on the second reading only one member seriously tried to do it.[92] But this was a much more promising line: that by failing to rebut Walewski's despatch the government had compromised Britain's good name. Milner Gibson's Motion, as the *Morning Chronicle* again put it, hit Palmerston 'in the tenderest point of his reputation'.[93] The irony of it delighted his enemies; the more so as it was almost universally assumed that his downfall on this issue was final.

In a way, therefore, the refugees 'escaped' in February 1858 only because peculiar political circumstances at the time allowed them to: weak parties, shifting allegiances, clever manoeuvres, plots, resentments, blunders and accidents; all quite apart from the issue which was supposed to be in question. On the other hand there was a feeling in the country for the refugees – or rather, against the French colonels – without which none of these things could possibly have helped them. What those peculiar circumstances did was simply to make the House of Commons more amenable than it otherwise might have been to this feeling: so that by another way of looking at it it was not quite so fortuitous. The refugees' escape was not a mere incidental side-effect of a political wrangle which had nothing to do with them: the Conspiracy Bill a kind of innocent casualty of the party war. If it had been merely this, it would in all likelihood have been re-introduced soon afterwards, and passed. The Tory government which displaced Palmerston wanted it as much as he did. There was no technical reason why it should not have been brought in again. Indeed, it was even questionable whether it needed to be brought in again, or could not be simply taken up as the Commons had left it and carried on with, because strictly speaking it had not been defeated yet. The Amendment which had toppled the government had not attacked the Bill, but merely required that something else be done before it was passed. If that thing was done, it left

[91] *Morning Chronicle, loc. cit.*
[92] McMahon, who argued that conversion of a misdemeanour into a felony would give the government stronger powers of espionage and harassment over the refugees (which was true): 3PD 148, cc. 1775–80.　　　[93] *Morning Chronicle, loc. cit.*

the way clear for the second reading to be resumed. Yet it was not resumed;[94] and it was not resumed because it *could* not be. This suggests that if the victory of the refugee cause in February was lucky, it was not accidental.

The implications for the Conspiracy Bill itself of the vote of the 19th were not immediately clear to everybody. The French saw no reason why under a change of government it should not be persevered with, and indeed warned that if it were not there could be no hope of healing the breach between the two countries.[95] Clarendon too held that the Bill was vital and wrote to Derby telling him so.[96] Palmerston, though he hoped it would be persevered with, understood nevertheless how difficult the task might be – 'for the fact certainly is', as he wrote to Clarendon on the 25th, 'that the Bill is very unpopular all over the Country, mainly indeed from the misrepresentations which have been spread about regarding it'.[97] This last comment was not altogether an unfair one. The Bill was popularly misrepresented, especially in being widely dubbed an 'Alien Bill' (or worse),[98] despite strenuous government efforts to avoid this impression.[99] Although this had not happened at all on the 19th, the idea sprang up and became a powerful mythology that Palmerston, in response to foreign threats, had introduced into Parliament an Alien Bill which the Commons had thrown out; and this made it more difficult to contemplate bringing it in again. Although the Bill had neither been an Alien Bill, nor defeated, the impression that it had, enormously encouraged its opponents in the country and consolidated opposition to any successor to it in the Commons. Derby very soon found this out. Counting likely votes, he found that the 200 majority on the first reading had quite miraculously melted away. It was not only his own minority government which would be put at risk, but something far more important. To Cowley on March 2nd Malmesbury, the new Foreign Secretary, wrote to explain.

We find it utterly impossible to proceed with Palmerston's Bill. Ld. J. Russell has thrown himself into the arms of the Radicals by whom he has been gladly taken & he & Gladstone have pledged themselves with 140 men to interrupt *any* Bill in *any*

---

[94] Natalie Isser, *The Second Empire and the Press* (The Hague, 1974), is wrong to say (pp. 41, 48) that the Bill was passed in March.

[95] Cowley to Malmesbury (private), 1 and 3 March 1858: Cowl. P., PRO FO 519/223 pp. 132–43; Malmesbury to Cowley no. 26, 3 March 1858: PRO FO 27/1234.

[96] Clarendon to Derby, 23 February 1858: Clar. P., c. 525, folder 6.

[97] Palmerston to Clarendon, 25 February 1858: Clar. P., c. 82 ff. 104–5.

[98] The *Morning Advertiser* (e.g. 20 February 1858, p. 4), *Reynolds's Newspaper* (21 February, p. 1) and the *People's Paper* (13 February, p. 4) regularly referred to it as the Alien Bill. In addition it was called 'the French Bill' by the *Weekly Dispatch* (21 February, p. 9); 'the French police act' by the *Morning Advertiser* (10 February, p. 4); 'Louis Napoleon's Bill' by the *Standard* (8 February, p. 4); and 'the French Colonels' Bill' by *Reynolds's* (14 February, p. 9).

[99] E.g. Palmerston's opening remarks on the second reading, 19 February: 3PD 148, cc. 1741–3.

way & for *any* time. If *we* are beaten *now* Ld. John must be the next man. Clarendon agrees with me that all moderate men must deprecate such an advent accompanied by a Reform Bill wh. wd. make the H. of Commons a revolutionary & unmanageable body.[100]

The first stage of Russell's little plot, therefore, had helped to stun the Bill in the first place: now in order to prevent the second instalment of that plot the Bill had to be left to die. The French would find it hard to understand how a measure which had the support of both governments could not be expected to pass in an identical parliament to that which had given it a two to one majority before. Malmesbury wrote personally and privately and in French to Walewski to explain: but a month later the emperor was reported to be 'still *sore* at the *dropped bill*'.[101] Some other means would have to be found to pacify him.

One small propaganda benefit might be said to have come out of this affair: which was that continental governments now surely were persuaded of the difficulty, which British governments had impressed on them all along, of legislating on their behalf. 'Our foreign friends will poco a poco believe', wrote Clarendon even before the vote, 'that a change of law is not the easy matter they have hitherto thought'; and his successor wrote to the Queen that 'at least for some time it will show Foreign Courts how dangerous it is *even to criticize* our *domestic Institutions*'.[102] This may have penetrated later, and prevented demands in the future; but for the moment the failure of the Conspiracy Bill only seemed to make Anglo-French relations worse: this at any rate was the general opinion of Britain's ambassadors on the continent, some of whom seriously expected war to result.[103] With legislation ruled out, but with a serious diplomatic crisis still to defuse, the British government was left now with the laws she had, to appease France and those other continental countries who were suspected of trying to push her to war. Cowley for one thought that if they applied those, the situation might be saved yet.[104] We have seen that these laws, and the agencies that existed to enforce them, were neither of them considered to be totally dependable or effective weapons. But both Palmerston's and Derby's governments worked them on this occasion for all they *were* worth. Every juridical avenue was explored for punishing or assisting the French authorities to punish the perpetrators of and acces-

---

[100] Malmesbury to Cowley (private), 2 March 1858: Cowl. P., PRO FO 519/196 ff. 237–8; and in Malmesbury, *op. cit.*, p. 420.

[101] Malmesbury to Walewski, 8 March 1858: Malm. P., 9M73/1/5 pp. 27–8; Cowley to Malmesbury (private), 2 April 1858: Cowl. P., PRO FO 519/223 pp. 207–12.

[102] Clarendon to Cowley (private), 19 February 1858: Cowl. P., PRO FO 519/177 ff. 207–10; Malmesbury to Queen Victoria, 7 March 1858: Malm. P., 9M73/1/6 p. 11.

[103] E.g. Howard de Walden to Clarendon (private), 22 February 1858: Clar. P., c. 83 ff. 100–3; and Cowley to Malmesbury (private), 1 and 3 March 1858: Cowl. P., PRO FO 519/223 pp. 132–43.   [104] Cowley to Malmesbury (private), 1 March 1858: *ibid.*, *loc. cit.*

sories to the Orsini plot, and anyone else who came within their purview. Lord Clarendon, though it was not his department's responsibility, indefatigably immersed himself in all the tiniest details of the inquiries about Orsini, Pierri, and the other conspirators, as did Cowley in Paris, who found the day 'not long enough to meet the demands upon one' when 'the duties of a Police officer are added to those of an Ambassador'.[105] 'The French Govt. will therefore see', wrote Clarendon proudly, 'that we are doing our utmost – indeed I am sure that if the attentat had been agst. the Q. instead of agst. the Empr. more activity & bonâ fide zeal cd. not have been displayed here.'[106] Zeal was the word. To help furnish the French authorities with evidence against the conspirators they had arrested, the British police were not discouraged from breaking rules – from entering and searching houses, for example, 'without any of the previous preliminaries required by law'.[107] A letter from 'An Exile' in *Reynolds's Newspaper* described one such incident:

On the night of Friday, the 22nd, at half-past twelve, a tremendous noise was heard at the door of the house lately inhabited by Signor F. Orsini, in London. The servant and the other inmates, awakened by the noise, came to the window with the natural question, 'What do you want?' 'We have a letter from Count Orsini for you,' was the answer. 'Put it under the door, and I will take it.' 'No, you must come and receive it.' The servant then went down stairs and opened the parlour window, asking for the letter. 'We cannot give it to you; come to the door. We must have a receipt.' The servant went to the door and opened it. The men rushed in; but lo! there was the chain. The servant again asked them for the letter; but the men, seeing they could not obtain admission, dared to assume the authority of English police officers, and one of them said, 'I am Mr Sanders, Superintendant of the Detective Police (he spoke very good English), and must search the house.' The servant, terrified, let them in. There were four of them. They took some waste papers and a bottle of wood naphtha, and, after half-an-hour or more, left the house. The worthy who had assumed the name and quality of an officer of English police, had the effrontery to hand a card bearing the name of 'Sanders' to the servant girl. They then left with the plunder they had obtained, telling her to call the next day at Scotland-yard. Surely these men were French police; as English police would not enter a house at midnight under false pretences, and without exhibiting a search warrant.[108]

In April the Home Secretary did what may not have been done since 1844, and instructed the Post Office to intercept letters to the wife of one of the conspirators.[109] 'A great deal', admitted Clarendon, 'has (most properly)

---

[105] Cowley to Clarendon (private), 14 February 1858: Cowl. P., PRO FO 519/223 pp. 105–8.

[106] Clarendon to Cowley (private), 9 February 1858: Cowl. P., PRO FO 519/177 ff. 143–7.

[107] Clarendon to Cowley (private), 30 January 1858: *ibid*., ff. 103–10.

[108] *Reynolds's Newspaper*, 31 January 1858, p. 1.

[109] On 7 April Walpole instructed the G.P.O. to intercept letters to a 'Mrs. Bugden' in Camden Town – *alias* Mrs Thomas Allsop – from the U.S.A. The G.P.O's reply, 12 April, stated that nothing had yet arrived for her from the U.S.A. besides a newspaper with a paragraph marked, which it dutifully forwarded to the Home Office: PRO HO 45/6512.

been done by our Police wch. is not legal',[110] but which it was hoped would be of immeasurable value in establishing to France the genuineness of the British government's desire to help. (To one Radical, in fact, it demonstrated 'how successfully the English police authorities had conformed to the Napoleonic pattern'.)[111] Unfortunately it was not felt that the French police reciprocated quite so generously – Clarendon suggested it was because if they did it would show them up for the incompetents they were[112] – when the British authorities sought on their side to take action against those of the conspirators who it was believed still remained in England; and especially against Simon Bernard, whose capital indictment on a charge of complicity in the murder of a guard who was killed by one of Orsini's bombs was to be, especially after the failure of the Conspiracy Bill, the British government's prime peace-offering to the French.

Almost from the beginning it was known that the Orsini conspiracy had involved others in England besides the four who had been arrested in Paris, including two Englishmen, who were pursued but managed to get away;[113] and a Frenchman, Simon Bernard, who was arrested in the middle of February.[114] In Bernard the authorities for a time thought they had the leader of the whole conspiracy;[115] and although he was probably not that, by dint of great effort and expense[116] the police had assembled, by the end of March, what the government regarded as the most damning case they had ever had against a refugee.[117] Originally they had intended to try him for conspiracy, which was the charge he was arrested on. On March 13th, however – which was the day Orsini and Pierri were guillotined in Paris – Derby's government decided to go for the more serious

---

[110] Clarendon to Cowley (private), 2 February 1858: Cowl. P., PRO FO 519/177 ff. 111–19.

[111] 'Lancet', *Life of Dr. Bernard*, n.d. [1858], p. 10.

[112] Clarendon to Cowley (private), 28 January 1858: Cowl. P. PRO FO 519/177 f. 103. See also Cowley's complaints about the way Pietri, the French police chief, treated Scotland Yard officers sent to consult with him, in his letters to Clarendon of 30 January and 1 February 1858: Cowl. P., PRO FO 519/223 pp. 71–80.

[113] Thomas Allsop and J. D. P. Hodge, who were both deeply implicated in the plot, but managed to get away to the U.S.A. and Piedmont respectively. Much of the correspondence which passed at the time between the Foreign Office and the French government is about their whereabouts and possible extradition. The implication of a third Englishman, G. J. Holyoake, was not suspected at the time.

[114] First of all his brother Martin was suspected – Clarendon to Palmerston, 23 January 1858: Clar. P. c. 82 ff. 57–8; 'but it turned out to be the other' – Clarendon to Cowley (private), 28 January 1858: Cowl. P., PRO FO 519/177 f. 97. Simon Bernard was arrested on February 14th.

[115] Clarendon to Lord Howard de Walden (private), 15 February 1858: Clar. P., c. 141 pp. 153–4.

[116] The cost of procuring witnesses alone came to more than £5,000. The Treasury was still grumbling about the expense in the autumn: see PRO HO 45/6512; MEPO 3/31; and MEPO 1/46.

[117] Clarendon to Cowley (private), 16 February 1858: Cowl. P., PRO FO 519/177 ff. 187–93.

10. Simon Bernard before the magistrate: from the *Illustrated Times*.

charge of accessory to murder, for which the penalty was death.[118] At
around the same time some other lesser fry were also indicted: a publisher
called Edward Truelove for bringing out a pamphlet advocating tyrannicide; and a bookseller, Stanislaus Tchorzewski, for selling a manifesto by
Pyat justifying the Orsini *attentat*. The conviction of these three was
believed by the government to be desirable in itself, but also essential in
order to establish to continental governments the effectiveness of Britain's
existing laws: in a very real sense, wrote Lord Malmesbury, not only
Bernard and Truelove and Tchorzewski were on their trial, but also the
English law itself.[119] If these actions succeeded, then all well and good. If
they failed on points of law, then it might be damaging: but it might also
do some good, by strengthening the government's hands to reform the
law: which would be 'an unexpected boon' for France.[120] When the trial of
Simon Bernard opened, therefore, on April 12th, much was felt to rest on
it. And when, six days later, the verdict was announced, and Bernard was
acquitted, much harm was supposed to have been done by it.

There was never very much doubt or disagreement over the reason for

[118] Malmesbury to Cowley no. 80 (telegram), 13 March 1858: PRO FO 27/1234; and *State
Trials*, n.s., vol. VIII, cc. 891–2.
[119] Malmesbury to Cowley no. 26, 3 March 1858: PRO FO 27/1234; Malmesbury to Cowley
(private), 4 and 6 March 1858: Cowl. P., PRO FO 519/196 ff. 252–63, 269–76.
[120] Malmesbury to Walpole, 4 March 1858, in Spencer Walpole Papers (communicated to me
by Mr David Holland); and Malmesbury to Queen Victoria, 7 March 1858: Malm. P.,
9M73/1/6 p. 11.

Bernard's acquittal. The judge, Lord Campbell, in his own words 'summed up strongly for a conviction';[121] and not without good cause. The
chain of evidence linking Bernard with the Orsini plot seemed complete:
'as unbroken', said the *Morning Post*, 'as any we have seen submitted to a
jury';[122] and the only reasonable doubt which remained in it was whether,
in supplying Orsini with the grenades which did the deed, Bernard could
be proved to have been aware that they were intended for that particular
task. The jury no doubt seized on this as a pretext to acquit him:[123] but the
real motive for his acquittal was political. All along this had been regarded
as a political trial. By Bernard's advocate, Edwin James, who turned out
later to be a rogue but was at this time also a successful barrister with a way
with juries,[124] this was made the main pillar of his defence: that the
prosecution of Bernard had been 'directed by foreign dictation, to bring
about a state of political subserviency to foreign governments which the
Executive of this country has not the courage to submit to the sanction of
the English House of Commons . . . to gratify a foreign potentate'.[125] On
the jury's verdict, he claimed at the outset, hung not only Bernard's life but
also 'consequences most serious both to public and private liberty in this
country, and to the cause of freedom and civilisation throughout
Europe'.[126] Throughout the trial he skated perfunctorily over the material
evidence but lingered over, for example, the 'foreign police spy' angle.[127]
At the end of the trial G. J. Holyoake, who was there, 'heard with
amazement his ornate appeal so materially destitute of facts'.[128] His peroration was a calculated but passionate plea to the patriotic and xenophobic
instincts of the jury:

Be not intimidated into giving a verdict which you may hereafter regret, and with
which your children hereafter may upbraid you. He, at whose instigation this

---

[121] Mrs Hardcastle, *op. cit.*, vol. II, p. 358.   [122] *Morning Post*, 19 April 1858, p. 4.
[123] They may also have been flattered by Bernard's reply at the beginning of the trial, when he
was asked whether he wished to exercise his privilege of having six aliens on the jury: 'I
trust with confidence to a jury of Englishmen': *State Trials*, n.s., vol. VIII, c. 900.
[124] Edwin James (1812–82) began his working life as an actor, but left the stage because he
looked too much like a prize-fighter. He was called to the bar (where this was apparently
no disadvantage) in 1830, and assisted the defence in the famous Palmer poisoning trial of
1856. In 1859 he became M.P. for Marylebone and supported Palmerston. In 1861 he went
bankrupt, and was also disbarred for fraud and corruption. He emigrated to the U.S.A.,
and became a member of the New York bar until he was disbarred there too. He returned
to acting in 1865, then to England in 1872, where he started up again in law, this time as a
solicitor, and then got into debt again. He had visited Garibaldi's camp in Italy in 1860.
Dictionary of National Biography, vol. 10, pp. 643–4.
[125] *State Trials*, n.s., vol. VIII, c. 1005.   [126] *Ibid., loc. cit.*
[127] E.g. his cross-examination of Rogers, *ibid.*, cc. 934–6.
[128] G. J. Holyoake, *Sixty Years of an Agitator's Life*, vol. II, p. 32; and see 'Lancet', *op. cit.*, p. 12:
'Mr. James did not examine minutely all the evidence adduced by the Crown, but simply
fixed upon a few of its most obvious defects; and pressed the strength of his argument and
appeal into what every clear-sighted observer felt to be the real *animus* of the case – its
political origin and aims.'

prosecution was undertaken, little knows the firmness, the attachment to the law, the regard for mercy, and the unconquerable love of liberty which animates the breasts of the English people. Tell him that no threats of mighty armaments – no insane dread of foreign invasion – will for one instant intimidate you. Tell him that the jury box is the sanctuary of English liberty. Tell him that that glorious institution will survive the wreck of a thousand empires. Tell him that on this very spot your predecessors have not quailed before the arbitrary power of the Crown, backed by the influence of Crown-serving and time-serving judges. Tell him that, under every difficulty and danger, your predecessors have maintained inviolate the liberties of the people . . . Tell him that you will acquit the prisoner – and that though 600,000 French bayonets glittered in your sight; though the roar of French cannon thundered in your ears, your verdict will be firmly and courageously given – careless whether that verdict pleases or displeases a French despot, or secures or shatters for ever the throne which a tyrant has built upon the ruins of the liberty of a once free and still mighty people[129]

which must have moved the jury, as it certainly moved the public gallery, who applauded it wildly;[130] as they did the verdict when it was given, in 'a scene unexampled perhaps in an English tribunal':[131]

The moment these words [Not Guilty] were uttered the excited audience raised a loud and continued cheer, such as had seldom been heard in a court of justice, and this they repeated again and again, and in which even some members of the bar joined. Men, in their frantic joy, raised their hats, and ladies in their wild enthusiasm stood on their seats and waved their handkerchiefs, and cheered and cheered again.[132]

'The Judges', reported one observer 'were evidently quite disconcerted, and they made a hasty retreat from the Court, the Lord Chief Justice not even addressing one word to the Jury or paying them any compliment for their long and patient attendance.'[133]

English radicals and the refugees themselves regarded the verdict as a victory of 'the people' of England over the forces of continental reaction abetted by a subservient aristocracy: and rejoiced in it. 'Twelve English-men *from the people*', wrote Herzen, 'would not agree (as the aristocrats and wealthy middle class would have liked them to agree) to purchase Napoleon's favour . . . with the life of Bernard.'[134] The political establishment did not rejoice. Lord Campbell was reported to be 'very much put out' by it all, as well he might be.[135] 'This acquittal of Bernard', wrote

---

[129] *State Trials*, n.s., vol. VIII, c. 1024.   [130] *Ibid., loc. cit.*   [131] *Ibid.*, c. 1062.
[132] *People's Paper*, 24 April 1858, p. 3. Other contemporary press reports corroborate this picture: e.g. *The Times*, 19 April, p. 11. See also 'Lancet', *op. cit.*, pp. 13–14, which goes into more detail.   [133] 'Lancet', *op. cit.*, p. 14.
[134] Herzen in *Kolokol*, 1 May 1858, quoted in A. Kimball, 'The Harassment of Russian Revolutionaries Abroad', *Oxford Slavonic Papers*, vol. VI (1973) p. 60n.
[135] Diary of Lord Broughton (John Cam Hobhouse) for 17 April 1858: BL. Add. Ms. 43761 ff. 65–6.

Malmesbury to Cowley, 'is a very painful affair – there was cheering and every sort of rascally demonstration disgraceful to our country';[136] and the Queen regarded 'the acquittal, the conduct of the Jury, the speech of Mr. James, and the manner in which the acquittal was received, *most* disgraceful and discreditable to this Country and to its Institutions.'[137] Nearly everybody was surprised by the verdict, though some professed not to be.[138] A few commentators tried to make the best of it by convincing themselves that it really had been based on reasonable doubt of Bernard's guilt, and that the demonstrations inside and outside the courtroom were the work only of foreigners and democrats, and not of right-thinking Englishmen:[139] but with no great conviction. In general it was agreed to have been, on the evidence, a perverse verdict, which owed everything to the political circumstances which surrounded the case. Lord Broughton thought that 'the Jury believed the man did intend to assist in destroying the despot, as James called him, and approved of his intention'.[140] The radical author of a pseudonymous *Life of Dr. Bernard* wrote of the 'healthy substratum of genuine sympathy with the struggles of the enemies of continental despotism' which existed 'in the deep heart of the English people' and inspired the jury's judgment.[141] A more charitable view was that the jury was not necessarily moved by sympathy either with Bernard's specific aim or with his general cause, but by a resentment at the way the case was handled. The weekly *Press* shortly after the trial pointed out that 'A State prosecution, conducted by the great law officers of the Crown, and originating in political circumstances, has ever been looked upon with disfavour by that class of persons from whom common juries are chosen.'[142] *The Times* agreed. 'Every one who remembers', it said on the 19th, 'the strong democratic bias of the class from which the London petty juries are taken will be prepared to learn that they feel a strong sympathy with any one whom they conceive to be prosecuted at the instigation of a despotic court.'

. . . Indeed, whatever may be the recommendations of Judges . . . Juries will not restrain themselves from looking at State prosecutions in a political light . . . When this Act of Parliament was evoked for the prosecution of a refugee for a plot against the life of a despotic Sovereign, and when, moreover, it was plain that the prosecution was the result of a diplomatic tempest and a Ministerial change, we

[136] Malmesbury to Cowley (private), 17 April 1858: Cowl. P., PRO FO 519/196 f. 373.
[137] Queen Victoria to Derby, 22 April 1858: RA J78/66.
[138] See Lord Broughton's Diary for 19 April 1858: Delane told Broughton on the 17th that 'a conviction was certain', yet *The Times* of the 19th 'says that *they* always thought Bernard would be acquitted': BL.Add.Ms. 43761 f. 66.
[139] See *Manchester Guardian*, 19 April 1858, p. 2; *Globe*, 19 April 1858, p. 2; and Lord Howard de Walden to Malmesbury (private), 23 April 1858: Malm. P., 9M73/1858/5.
[140] Diary of Lord Broughton for 17 April 1858: BL.Add.Ms. 43761 ff. 65–6.
[141] 'Lancet', *op. cit.*, p. 16.
[142] *Press*, 24 April 1858, p. 388.

may well conceive that a Jury would consider that the law was being strained to effect a political purpose, and that their duty was to defeat the attempt.[143]

For *The Times*, consequently, the fault for the whole fiasco was the Attorney-General's, who had brought the prosecution, and who should have known better.[144]

The failure of the Bernard prosecution was particularly galling for the government because it was not even the second-best outcome it had hoped for: which was that the case would be thrown out on a legal technicality, and so strengthen its hands in trying again for new legislation. If Bernard had been found guilty he would have appealed to the 'fifteen judges', who might well have quashed the conviction on the ground that the act under which he was convicted did not cover crimes committed abroad. (Even before the case ended Lord Campbell had reserved this point to them.)[145] This might have been embarrassing for the government, some members of which consequently expressed relief that it had not come to this.[146] Nevertheless it would also have given it a cast-iron excuse, which no M.P. this time could have disputed, for amending the law in this respect. This is what Malmesbury had meant when he had said that in this case the law itself was on its trial as well as the defendant. A not-guilty verdict, however, meant no appeal, and therefore that this point of law was *not* tested: and so Derby's government was left in exactly the same position as Palmerston's had been in before. If anything had been found wanting by the Bernard verdict, it was not the law, but the strictness of English rules of evidence and the judgment of juries: neither of which (as Malmesbury pointed out to Walewski)[147] stood the slightest chance of being altered to suit the convenience of the continent, or of anybody.

Again it seemed that the government's effort to appease the continent over the refugee question had foundered on the principles and prejudices of those English middle classes from which juries and parliamentary constituencies were both recruited. For ten years until 1858 the refugee question had never been put for a direct verdict either to the House of Commons or to a jury, partly for fear of what they would do to it: a fear which appeared very sharply vindicated now that it had been put to both, and had been decided by both resoundingly against the government. The government consequently was prevented from pursuing the course it wished to pursue by 'the people', who on this question scored quite a notable victory over their rulers. This was not the only way of looking at

---

[143] *The Times*, 19 April 1858, p. 8.
[144] *Ibid.*, 20 April 1858, p. 9, and 23 April 1858, p. 9.
[145] *State Trials*, n.s. vol. VIII, cc. 896, 1001–2.
[146] See Hammond to Cowley, 17 April 1858: Cowl. P., PRO FO 519/187 f. 162.
[147] Malmesbury to Walewski, 24 April 1858: Malm. P., 9M73/1/5 pp. 115–17.

it, but it was a valid way. Of course there had been a great deal of luck in it. The outcome of this confrontation was always in doubt, and in fact at the beginning the odds were if anything on the government, who in a way threw away their advantage by their blunders. The first victory especially, on February 19th, owed much to factors which had nothing to do with the refugee question; and the second victory, on April 17th, owed much to the impetus which was given to public feeling on the refugee question by the first. Both victories may have owed more to the French colonels than to anything else, for without James's '600,000 French bayonets glittering in your sight' it is difficult to envisage popular feeling ever coming down as strongly as it did on the side of a group of foreign socialists and conspirators scarcely anybody really approved of; even in defence of 'English liberty'. Nevertheless in a still very largely oligarchic age it was remarkable that 'public opinion' should have proved as powerful as it did: especially when it is borne in mind that these measures which were wrecked by it were hardly draconian, even by the far more liberal standards of their own time: the Conspiracy Bill doing nothing at all to limit the traditional British policy of unrestricted political asylum, and the Bernard prosecution light-years away from being simply, in the strict sense of the term, a 'political trial'. What says more for the power of 'public opinion' at this time may be the fact that governments were deterred by it from proposing anything stronger, like for example the Alien Bill Palmerston hankered after; but were reduced instead to such pallid alternatives as the Conspiracy Bill, because they believed that they were the very most that the 'people' would allow.

When these failed, the government immediately gave up the struggle. When Bernard was acquitted of the main charge against him they decided to drop a second, minor (conspiracy) charge too, on the ground that it would only produce the same fiasco all over again;[148] and also the prosecutions which had been planned against Truelove and Tchorzewski, to the disgust of Lord Campbell, who regarded the decision as 'pusillanimous'.[149] For the same reason they also turned down an offer from the radical G. J. Holyoake to turn in his friend Allsop for the reward which had been offered of £200.[150] Juries were not to be trusted; and so litigation, like legislation, was ruled out as a means of disciplining the refugees.

In the end, therefore, the British government had nothing to show

---

[148] Derby to Queen Victoria, 21 April 1858: RA J78/65; and *State Trials*, n.s. vol. VIII, c. 1064.
[149] Mrs Hardcastle, *op. cit.*, vol. II, p. 359.
[150] See Holyoake and Langley to Home Office, 9 June 1858, and the Home Office's reply, 13 July 1858: PRO HO 45/6512; and Joseph McCabe, *Life and Letters of George Jacob Holyoake* (1908), vol. I, p. 253. According to the latter Allsop, who was in the United States, wished to stand trial in England, if money could be found for his defence. The £200 was to be used for this. In the event the government's decision not to proceed allowed him to return from exile.

France for all the efforts it had made, apart from some bruises sustained on her behalf. The French authorities were less than satisfied. Napoleon was reported to be 'very much put out'[151] by the Bernard verdict, as were his empress and his Foreign Minister, who both wrote to complain.[152] Malmesbury replied personally and directly to the latter to try to persuade him that in fact the British government had if anything tried to do too much for France, which is why it had failed, and that the best thing now would be to let the whole thing drop, 'in the *interests of the alliance*' as well as for any other reason.[153] The French were still not entirely reconciled, and at the end of the month the emperor was reported to be hardly more hopeful than before about 'the possibility of maintaining friendly relations between the two countries, if similar unpropitious circumstances continued to occur'.[154] For a few months afterwards consequently the government nervously chased up any slightest hints of new conspiracies in Britain[155] in case one of them turned out to be the final straw on the already much-strained back of the entente: and found nothing. Nevertheless, though the Bernard verdict and its repercussions did nothing to improve Anglo-French relations, neither did they provoke the horrors which might have been expected from them two months before. For whatever were the feelings of others on both sides of the Channel in the early spring of 1858, neither the French nor the British governments had ever wanted the Orsini affair to destroy their alliance; and between them they had already in March managed to patch up a kind of agreement, which saved some face on both sides, and enabled them to survive the Bernard episode. It was a very artificial kind of settlement, the product of some clever diplomacy by Malmesbury, Walewski and Cowley rather than a real material exchange: but it did the trick. In effect the basis of the settlement was that Britain gave nothing, and France 'explained' how Walewski's notorious despatch had really *demanded* nothing, which made the whole quarrel out to have been a misunderstanding.[156] Of course it had not been a misunderstanding, and the settlement was in fact a climb-down on France's part. 'We must not forget', wrote Cowley to Malmesbury while he was negotiating it, 'that we are asking them to eat their disp. as well as to put up with the abandonment of *the Bill* – that in fact, therefore, they will have made a stir

[151] Cowley to Malmesbury (private), 18 April 1858: Cowl. P., PRO FO 519/223 p. 239.
[152] Empress to Cowley, 18 April 1858: RA J78/64; and see Malmesbury to Walewski, 24 April 1858: Malm. P., 9M73/1/5 pp. 115–17.
[153] Malmesbury to Walewski, 24 April 1858: *ibid.*, *loc. cit.*
[154] Cowley to Malmesbury no. 351, 30 April 1858: PRO FO 27/1248.
[155] For example: rumours of a conspiracy in Cardiff in mid April (see correspondence between the Home and Foreign Offices in PRO FO 27/1276B); a report of 'infernal machines' being made by an Italian in Liverpool in May (see Malaret to Malmesbury, 18 May 1858, in PRO FO 27/1273, and Sanders' reports in MEPO 1/46); and a plot suspected in Dublin in July: PRO HO 45/6512.
[156] The correspondence is printed in PP lx (1857–8) pp. 119–25.

for nothing, and that you can offer nothing even in prospective. We ought therefore to make the retreat as easy for them as we can.'[157] So the impact was cushioned by some soft words, and the settlement was not treated as a diplomatic victory by the British. Nevertheless it was a defeat for France. She had had to give in, because Britain had proved utterly incapable of doing so voluntarily. The vote of February 19th, once it was explained by the government, had demonstrated that; the verdict of April 17th confirmed it. If France had still insisted on getting what she wanted, it could only have been got by means of war. For France the issue was not worth that.

France however was unable to shed thereafter a small sense of grievance and humiliation, as Cowley's dispatch to Malmesbury at the end of April makes clear;[158] and there can be little doubt that, despite Malmesbury's healing touch, the whole affair left Anglo-French relations in a worse position than it had found them. It was the opinion of the Foreign Under-Secretary Edmund Hammond at the end of February – though this may have been too much influenced by his chief's pessimism at that time – that what had happened up to that point had 'exposed the alliance to the severest shock which it has yet been called upon to encounter'.[159] The bad feeling the crisis created was felt on both sides, for little had happened during it to temper the distrust of Napoleon which was already a widespread feeling in England, even among some of those who preferred to see him at the head of affairs in France than Bourbons or Blanquists. On the other hand these mutual feelings of distrust had long been there between Britain and France before Orsini or any other refugee had stepped in to exacerbate them, and scarcely needed an excuse to show themselves, so deep-seated did they appear; and very shortly after the Orsini affair's immediate repercussions had died down other much bigger questions, like Italy, came along to cast much longer shadows: by the side of which this crisis came very soon to appear a very little one indeed, and its long-term diplomatic effect hardly more than mildly irritating. In the broader picture of the history of Anglo-French relations in the mid nineteenth century, therefore, the Orsini affair was not of very great lasting significance: except perhaps as a symptom of the vast gulf in fundamental political attitudes which separated the two nations at this time, and which may help to explain what lay beneath some of the other more important rifts between them. For the refugees, however, and for the history of refugee policy in Britain, the significance of this affair was decisive. Whoever

---

[157] Cowley to Malmesbury (private), 5 March 1858: Cowl. P., PRO FO 519/223 pp. 150–2.
[158] Cowley to Malmesbury no. 351, 30 April 1858: PRO FO 27/1248.
[159] 'Memorandum on the State of Foreign Relations at the close of Lord Palmerston's Administration', prepared by Hammond at Clarendon's request, 25 February 1858: Aberdeen Papers, BL. Add. Ms. 43355, f. 235.

exactly had been the 'victors' of February 19th and April 17th, their victory was a considerable and long-lasting one, whose effects were still to be felt, strongly, twenty years afterwards. However precarious the issue had been before the vote in February, however marginal and fortunate that first success had been, it turned out to be a solid one: certain, unambiguous, irrevocable; as permanent as any political achievement can be. From April 1858 until the end of our period, the events of 1858 stood as an example and a warning to all governments, British and foreign, who came after: that to try to change or even to enforce English laws against refugees at the request of continental governments was just not worth the candle. 'Of this we may be assured', wrote one commentator in 1858: 'Louis Napoleon will never play that game again.'[160] Neither, as it happened, would any of his continental peers or successors; or Palmerston when he came back to power in England, or any of *his* successors: until very far in the future, when the memory of 1858 had faded, and new necessities beckoned.

[160] 'Lancet', *op. cit.*, p. 14.

7

Aftermath: Conclusion

1858 marked the end of the refugee question as a serious diplomatic issue between Britain and the continent: the last brilliant flash of the meteor as it sped across the Victorians' sky. It did not however finally remove it: nothing could have done so, short of Britain's absolute capitulation to the continent's demands, or the continent's absolute conversion to English liberalism. While refugees from Europe remained in England and continued to conspire (even if they had not conspired, for they would have been suspected of it anyway) there were bound to be tensions between the governments they had fled from and the government whose protection they had fled to, which the resolution of the 1858 crisis could not hope to relieve and indeed might exacerbate. The meteor was dark now, but not destroyed; it was there in the diplomatic firmament still, and no less able to exert some pull on the bodies around it for not burning so brightly as it once had. Nevertheless it was very dull, and the refugee question never again so urgent and significant as it had seemed in the 1850s: for which the events of that decade itself were partly responsible. Those events cast a long shadow. In a way everything that occurred in the 1860s and 1870s was a kind of unravelling of their implications; a postscript to the drama of the Orsini affair and the Conspiracy Bill debate and the Bernard trial. To a great extent that episode set a pattern for the future, and determined for example that what had happened then would not be allowed to happen again.

The outcome of the crisis of 1858, however, was not the only reason for the waning of the refugee question afterwards. Many continental countries had begun to lose interest in it long before then anyway. The high point of European agitation against Britain over the refugees had really been earlier, in the months between the autumn of 1851 and the spring of 1853, when it had involved several continental powers together. After 1853 the general clamour had by and large died down, leaving just one shrill voice, that of France, to be heard again at intervals. The Orsini crisis, serious as it may have been, was a quarrel almost exclusively between Britain and France. Except for Russia no other power made even a show of solidarity with France over it: not even the Austrians, whose interest in frustrating Orsini's designs was surely almost as great as Louis Napoleon's, and who had not been backward in the past, but made no move now. British statesmen and diplomats could never quite credit this, and still in the first couple of months of 1858 daily expected the issue to become a general European one. The disparity of practice, and consequently the conflict of interest, between Britain and nearly all the continental states on this issue were, they believed, fundamental; so much so that eventually Britain must be forced by a combination of European states into line, if she did not step there voluntarily.[1] But that combination never came about, and in fact showed few signs of coming about after 1853. The issue was, after all, not so important as it had once appeared.

There were good reasons for the continent's loss of interest in the refugee question, quite apart from the events of 1858. Throughout the nineteenth century refugees tended to create most stir when they were on the move, as for example in the 1830s; and by 1853 they had stopped moving in large numbers into Britain. Until 1871 there were no more of those dramatic exoduses out of Europe and Turkey which had marked the early 1850s, and consequently the refugees were noticed rather less. There were also, as we have seen, some exoduses of them out of England; and those who remained were undoubtedly less active. More important was the fact that the continent's original agitation over the refugees had been related closely to the very recent events of 1848–9: which as they receded into the past seemed to diminish also the menace the refugees in England were felt to hold for the continent. As the reactions which initially appeared so precarious survived longer, they became more confident, and consequently less frightened of their enemies. France's particular spell of anti-red paranoia, for example, was already well past its peak in 1858, and with the amnesty of 1859 could be said to be over.[2] That amnesty was impressive proof of conservatism's victory over the exiled revolutionaries, whose own hopes evaporated as the reactionaries' rose, making them appear less ferocious still. As every year passed, so did the almost obsessive (if understandable) anxiety of continental rulers about the internal stability of their régimes; which anxiety had been the main factor fuelling their resentment against Britain over the question of the refugees. The issue was never unimportant; but as time went on it became less central and urgent and vital.

It came to seem less vital too as other issues appeared more so. It was abnormal in the nineteenth century for domestic preoccupations to figure quite so overtly in international relations as they had done, with this issue, in the very early 1850s; and it did not last long, before the states of the

[1] See Seymour to Malmesbury no. 199, 3 March 1858: PRO FO 7/540.
[2] See H. C. Payne and H. Grosshans, 'The Exiled Revolutionaries and the French Political Police in the 1850s', in *American Historical Review*, vol. 68 (1963) pp. 970–2.

continent began again to look outside themselves, at the kinds of inter-state issues which were the more customary concerns of European diplo-macy: of which there were at this time a number, of rising urgency and importance. The years from the beginning of the Crimean War to the end of the Franco-Prussian war were a time of abnormal activity and move-ment on the continent: when states whose boundaries had been fixed and steady for forty years – even through the trauma of 1848 – disintegrated and regrouped in the space of just fifteen years; when the map of Europe at a dozen points was transformed, and when all the major continental wars of Queen Victoria's reign were fought. Since 1815 there had been no such elemental shifts in Europe as there were in these years, and were not to be again until 1914. In all this there was much more to concern any European power, than the hypothetical dangers arising from the presence of a few thousand mainly penniless refugees on English soil. The difference be-tween Britain and the continent on the question of asylum and its 'abuse' remained as wide as ever through the late 1850s and the 1860s, but not so prominent as before, because with all these other more vital matters to concern continental governments it could not be; neither could they allow it to be, for in such times to quarrel over so minor a matter with a nation whose support in the future might be needed over a much greater matter would have been foolish. Quite naturally, therefore, the refugees receded from view.

They did not, however, disappear altogether; and if they had wanted to continental statesmen could easily have found pretexts – even good reasonable causes – to raise the issue again. In the 1860s, and despite the amnesties, there were several thousand political refugees in England still, including some of the most feared. In the early 1870s they were joined by more, from Paris. They behaved in much the same way as they had in the 1850s, if perhaps without quite the same enthusiasm or effectiveness as before. They gave out threats which seemed as bloodthirsty as before, and with nothing being done to stop them by the authorities. In 1861, for example, Carlo di Rudio, one of Orsini's accomplices who had been sentenced to death with him, then imprisoned at Cayenne instead, and then escaped, came to Britain and began stumping the country boasting of and justifying his part in the plot: which cannot have pleased his intended victim.[3] Others did more than talk. Kossuth for example in 1861 resur-rected an old refugee device when he started printing his own revolu-tionary banknotes, which were intended this time not only to raise funds on the security of the revolution, but also to bring on the revolution directly by undermining the official currency of the Habsburg empire.[4] A little later refugees were found enlisting themselves, and also recruiting Englishmen, to fight for revolutionary causes in Poland and Italy, against

[3] See PRO HO 45/6994.   [4] *Infra*, p. 212.

the very explicit provisions of the Foreign Enlistment Act.[5] In January 1864 a plot was uncovered by the Paris police against the life of the French emperor, by some Italians who had been refugees in England, recruited it was claimed by Mazzini who was a refugee in England still, using English-made weapons, and involving even a junior member of the British government, James Stansfeld, whose address was found on papers in the possession of one of the conspirators.[6] There was talk too of other assassination plots, some of it surrounding Marx's International Association which was founded in London in 1864.[7] That same year Garibaldi came to England, and met – to what purpose no one knew – some of the most notoriously conspiratorial of the refugees, including Mazzini and Ledru-Rollin.[8] What was worse, from the continentals' point of view, was the way he was received by the English, including some very eminent ones. The rapturous welcome Garibaldi received in 1864 was highly reminiscent of Kossuth's in 1851,[9] and was resented as much on the continent, where it was taken to indicate that the toleration which Britain afforded to her allies' enemies was not wholly involuntary: not quite the matter for regret her government had always made it out to be. It was small wonder therefore that in the 1860s the continent still did not feel entirely safe from the machinations of the refugees in England, and that resentment and a sense of grievance and suspicion remained against the part played in it all by the British government.

It was small wonder too that for the British government itself the refugees remained a source of anxiety, for the same reasons as before. Although the outcome of the crisis of 1858 had seemed to settle the matter for the time being, ministers were not to know that it had settled it for good. Lord Malmesbury, for example, who had been chiefly instrumental in effecting that settlement, had never believed it was permanent, and had predicted that if anything like the Orsini affair ever happened again then France this time might well press the matter to its end: which would mean war.[10] When the Greco plot – which did bear striking resemblances to the

---

[5] A brigade of emigrés was recruited and fitted out in England and France to help in the Polish insurrection of 1863, but never reached there: see E. H. Carr, *The Romantic Exiles* (1968 edn.), pp. 208–10. The efforts of the British Legion in the Italian wars of unification are described in G. M. Trevelyan, *Garibaldi and the Making of Italy* (1911), pp. 259–60.

[6] *The Times*, 9 January 1864 p. 10, 12 January p. 6, *et passim*. Mazzini denied any complicity in the Greco plot, in a letter to *The Times*, 15 January, p. 9. Stansfeld had allowed his address to be used as a *poste restante* for letters from Italian revolutionaries to Mazzini, in order to circumvent the Austrian postal censors: see 3PD 174 cc. 259–63 (17 March 1864).

[7] *Infra*, p. 215 fn. 54.

[8] See H. W. Rudman, *Italian Nationalism and English Letters* (1940), p. 325; and Noël Blakiston, 'Garibaldi's visit to England in 1864', in *Il Risorgimento*, vol. XVI no. 3 (Milan, October 1964), pp. 133–43.

[9] Queen Victoria was as much put out by this as she had been on the previous occasion: see her letter to Russell, 13 April, in *QVL 1862–78*, vol. I, p. 169.

[10] Lord Malmesbury, *Memoirs of an Ex-Minister*, p. 424 (Diary for 13 March 1858).

Orsini plot – was discovered in 1864 it looked as if that moment might have come. Strong feelings were expressed in France, especially against the supposed involvement in the plot of James Stansfeld, and on the English side were greatly resented, not least by Russell who waxed very indignant about it in private correspondence with Cowley.[11] Similar strong feelings were aroused by the Garibaldi visit;[12] and an only slightly lesser degree of irritation by some of the other activities of the refugees in England.[13] For the occasional fleeting moment, the ingredients appeared to be there for a repeat of the crisis of 1858. The likelihood was real enough, as we shall see, to cause the British authorities to try to do something to allay it, within the very restricted parameters the events of the 1850s had left them. But in fact the menace always receded: and the main reason for that was that continental governments had themselves learnt from the events of the 1850s that there was no point, but only danger, in pressing the issue with Britain too far.

There were other reasons too. Sometimes the activity or incident which was resented on the continent was just too trifling to merit any serious complaint. On other occasions the continent may have been soothed by British efforts to prevent or punish the abuse. If less was made of contraventions of the Foreign Enlistment Act than they sometimes seemed to merit, then it may have been because enlistment in England on the revolutionary side – for Garibaldi's army – was so nicely balanced on the other side by the recruitment of Irish to fight for the pope.[14] But generally the reason for the continentals' self-restraint, when they did feel they had a grievance, was the knowledge that protest was useless and might even react against them, if it were made too peremptory and official. Consequently during the row over the Greco affair the French government was very careful, whatever feelings it might express in private, to hold back from making any formal accusations or demands. When in March 1864 the French empress angrily took Cowley to task for the harm which she believed was being done to her husband by 'the state of the law in England with regard to strangers', she took care to add that 'she knew the law could

---

[11] See Cowley to Russell (private), 8 March 1864: Cowl. P., PRO FO 519/231 pp. 118–19; and Russell to Cowley (private), 26 March 1864: *ibid.* /200, ff. 279–80.

[12] E.g. Bloomfield (Vienna) to Russell no. 215, 31 March 1864: PRO FO 7/668; Odo Russell (Rome) to Russell, 27 April 1864, quoted in N. Blakiston (ed), *The Roman Question* (1962), p. 285; Elliot (Turin) to Russell, 16 April 1864, quoted in N. Blakiston, 'Garibaldi's visit to England in 1864', *loc. cit.*, pp. 139–40.

[13] See for example Bernstorff to Stanley, 9 July 1866, about a libel in *Der Deutsche Eidgenosse*: copy in PRO HO 45/7914; Musurus Pasha to Clarendon, 19 January 1870, about an article in the *Hurriyete*: copy in PRO HO 45/9472/A38025; Apponyi to Russell, 5 February 1861, about the Kossuth banknotes, in PRO FO 7/617. Foreign states also occasionally requested information about political refugees: see for example HO 45/7783 (a French request for information about a M. Ansas, in December 1865).

[14] There are papers about enlistment on both sides in 1860, in PRO HO 45/7019.

not be altered', and consequently 'did not presume to expect it'.[15] This probably was the emperor's reason for restraint too. France had come to accept the inevitable: although as Cowley pointed out it was not without a great deal of frustrated resentment, which lingered.[16] No official communications at all were exchanged over the Greco plot or the complicity in it of Mazzini and Stansfeld – and so the peace was preserved. (Over Garibaldi's visit too only the very mildest kind of protest was allowed to be made *officially*.) On all sides among diplomatists it was well understood how extremely sensitive the whole refugee issue was, and so there was a tacit agreement to avoid it. It was a kind of taboo. When on one occasion Lord Lyons, who was Cowley's successor in Paris, wrote home suggesting that his government might like to look into the activities of some refugees who were supposed to be plotting Louis Napoleon's murder, he was very careful to make it clear that the whole idea was wholly his own, and that not the slightest allusion to it had been made to him 'either by the Marquis de Moustier or by any other French authority'.[17] It is significant that he felt that this was important to say. Neither side was eager for the refugees to become a diplomatic issue again. The lessons of 1858 had struck home.

Britain and the continent were no closer on this issue in the 1860s, therefore, than they had been before; but now the difference had become accepted. On the continent Britain's perversity and stubbornness was deplored, but deplored much like a fact of geography might be: regarded like a range of mountains, obstructive but unalterable, which could not be levelled and so had to be somehow circumvented instead. Like the democracy of the United States, there could be no thought of making it the pretext for a crusade. The continentals may have been encouraged in this tolerant attitude by the realisation eventually, after some years of doubting it, that the British government was in fact anxious to do something about the refugees, and had proved it on more than one occasion, but was genuinely prevented from doing more by factors which it really could not control: though this belief will have been undermined a little by Garibaldi's welcome and the Stansfeld affair. More important, the events of the 1850s, and of 1858 especially, will have strengthened for them the realisation that this whole issue for Britain was – however incomprehensible that might seem – a fundamental one, on which she would not bow to any diplomatic pressure however forceful, short of war. So if a continental power wished to make anything of it again, that was what she would have to be prepared for: either war, or else the sort of undignified climb-down which France had been forced into in March 1858. When this fact had got

[15] Cowley to Russell (private), 8 March 1864: Cowl. P., PRO FO 519/231 pp. 118–19.
[16] Cowley to Russell (private), 29 March 1864: Cowl. P., PRO FO 519/231 p. 124.
[17] Lyons to Stanley no. 625, 11 July 1868: PRO FO 27/1707.

home, as it had not generally before 1853 – later in France's case – it put an entirely new complexion on the matter. It quite suddenly turned the refugee question into one of those issues, like cows for Hindus, which was of far greater importance and significance for one of the parties in dispute over it than it could possibly be for any of the others. Consequently it was best left alone.

For Britain the lessons of the 1850s were similar, but not quite the same. Those years for her had been salutary in more ways than one; if they had taught British governments what could not be done against the refugees, they had also impressed on them the dangers of not trying to do something against them, and so risking the ill favour of their allies. They were anxious to avoid another popular defeat like that of 1858, but they were also anxious to prevent the kind of diplomatic crisis which had provoked that defeat in the first place; and these two desiderata were not – as they never had been – easily compatible. Even more than in the 1850s, the impression is persistent in the following decade, of a ruling class restrained and shackled in its desire to curb the refugees (though not necessarily in ways which were particularly repressive) by powerful and uncontrollable popular (but not necessarily proletarian) forces beneath it; and resorting therefore, in its efforts to meet the continent's desires, more and more to measures which avoided the issue being raised in any of the central and effective arenas of public discussion and legislation. Which of course (from its own point of view) was an unsatisfactory way of proceeding, and was ultimately unsuccessful. During the 1860s and 1870s almost no inroads were made into Britain's policy of political asylum at all, nothing to appease the continent fully and prevent another 1858 crisis; which therefore was only prevented really by the fact that the continent was as anxious to avoid it as Britain.

The deterrent effect of 1858, and of the proud myth which the events of that year had fashioned, was very apparent in the 1860s and seventies. The only year in which public opinion was ever really tested on the refugee question was 1858, and the results of that test were taken for years afterwards to be immutable. It ruled the ultimate sanction of an Alien Bill absolutely out of the question: this scarcely needed to be said, though the possibility was raised occasionally.[18] The broad principle of asylum had to

---

[18] E.g. in the House of Commons on 27 July 1860: 3PD 160 cc. 282–7; and in the House of Lords by the Marquess of Westmeath on 29th February 1864: 3PD 173 c. 1242. Technically there was still an Alien Act in force in the 1860s, whose only requirement was that foreign arrivals in Britain should show their passports if they had them – not if they did not. In fact it was never enforced. In 1861 there was some correspondence between the Foreign and Home Offices over whether it might not, in that case, be repealed. In the end it was decided that repeal was not worth the bother, and that the law might as well be left alone but not acted upon: PRO HO 45/7063.

be sacrosanct, untouchable even in the slightest degree or the most defensible way. Towards the end of the 1860s, when the improvement of Britain's untidy and ineffective system of extradition treaties came up for discussion, a Select Committee recommended modifying it to allow political assassination, alone among political offences, to be taken out of the category of exempted crimes and made extraditable: but when it came to it Gladstone's government could not do it, and the Act which resulted from it all in 1870 went to considerable lengths to safeguard the traditional immunity afforded to the refugee.[19] Governments also held back from applying existing laws of conspiracy or libel against the refugees, where they required juries to arbitrate on them. When the possibility was raised in 1861 of charging Rudio, for example, it was turned down: 'He forgets', minuted the head of the Home Office against one such suggestion, 'that the prime mover in this affair was triumphantly acquitted by an English jury.' There were in this case technical impediments to a successful prosecution too: but the memory of 1858 will have deterred the government from risking failure.[20] It may also have dissuaded them from implementing the laws of libel or conspiracy in other similar cases. One solitary exception was the Turkish refugee paper *Hurriyete*, whose publisher at the request of the Turkish ambassador was charged in 1870 for printing an article calling for the assassination of the Sultan.[21] When on the other hand the Prussian ambassador in 1866 asked for the German refugee newspaper *Der Deutsche Eidgenosse* to be prosecuted for a libel on his king the government decided not to, on the familiar ground that it would only give greater currency to the libel.[22] In 1873 no action was taken against a French revolutionary manifesto whose libellous character no one disputed, possibly for the same reason.[23] For similar reasons the Foreign Enlistment Act, though it was repeatedly contravened by Poles and 'Garibaldinos' in

[19] *Report from the Select Committee on Extradition*, PP (1867–8) vii, recommendation no. 5, p. 131; House of Commons debates of 16th June and 4th July: 3PD 202 cc. 300–5, 1425–6; Extradition Act, 1870: 33 & 34 Vict. c. 52, para. 3. Austin Stevens, *The Dispossessed* (1975), p. 46, claims that 'the given target' of the 1870 Act was 'the anarchist', and that despite the fact that it was 'hedged around with exceptions which were supposed to keep the right of political asylum alive', it in fact 'marks the beginning of the end of free immigration into Britain'. I can find no evidence to support such an interpretation of this measure, whose safeguards in favour of political refugees were in fact extraordinarily tight.

[20] PRO HO 45/6994. The legal difficulty arose out of the fact that Rudio's 'seditious libels' were only spoken, not printed; in which case it would have to be shown that they were intended to incite his *audience* to commit some specific offence; and a jury, as Waddington pointed out, would be unwilling to accept that Rudio 'intended to excite the Birmingham men to assassinate L.N.'

In 1863 Rudio wrote to the Home Office asking for assistance to emigrate, which Sir George Grey was inclined to grant him, but not the Foreign Secretary, Russell ('This Rudio', minuted somebody in Russell's department, 'is as great a rogue as exists'): so he was refused it, probably in retribution for the trouble he had caused Palmerston's first government: PRO HO 45/6994.   [21] PRO HO 45/9472/A38025.

[22] See L.O.O. of 31 July 1866, in PRO HO 45/7914.   [23] PRO HO 45/9355/29553.

the early 1860s, was very conspicuously neglected by the government in those years. 'It is all illegal no doubt,' wrote an official against one report in September 1860 of men being recruited for revolutionary service in Italy; 'but this is a law which may be enforced or not according to circumstances'.[24] Circumstances at that time made its enforcement impolitic, at the very least: 'No one in his senses', minuted Waddington at the Home Office against a Neapolitan request for action against these men, 'would embark on a prosecution of this description in the present state of public feeling.'[25] And in the case too of Kossuth's revolutionary banknotes, which was quite a little *cause célèbre* at the time, the government's law officers, though they were in no doubt that 'the fabrication of those notes was contrary to the laws of the country', decided against pressing charges on the grounds that 'any such prosecution would be odious, and the defence most popular'.[26] We shall see that this was not the government's last word; but it was its last word so far as juries were concerned. Their untrustworthiness may have been exaggerated. When at last in 1881 the authorities for the first time since 1858 decided to chance their arm in a 'conspiracy to murder' action against a German refugee, Johann Most, they found that it was in fact not at all difficult to get a conviction out of a common jury, after only twenty minutes' deliberation: and despite the trundling out again by the defence of Edwin James's old 'foreign dictation' ploy.[27] Possibly they could have done the same, if they had tried, in 1871, if not in 1861. The result of the Most trial suggested that maybe governments had been a little over-cautious before, and that juries, if they were still vigilant for the rights of refugees, might not have been so unreasonably so as to prevent any recourse to them at all. The refugee question's reputation of intractability, which the events of the 1850s had given it, may have outlived the reality of it. But the myth survived, and was effective.

[24] Note by Waddington, on W. S. Paulet to Home Office, 5 September 1860: PRO HO 45/7019.
[25] Note by Waddington on Hammond to Waddington, 21 August 1860: PRO HO 45/7019. In September 1863 Captain Alfred Styles, who was busily engaged at this time in recruiting for both the Garibaldian and the Polish revolutionary armies, was brought to trial under the Foreign Enlistment Act: but by the Russian government, not the British: see PRO HO 45/7514.
[26] L.O.O. of 15 February 1861: PRO HO 45/7233.
[27] Johann Most, a German socialist refugee, was tried for incitement to murder in May 1881 after an article had appeared in his German-language newspaper *Freiheit*, published in London, approving of the recent assassination of the Czar. *The Times* of the day expressed strong reservations as to the wisdom of the prosecution, and doubts as to its outcome in view of what had happened before in the case of Bernard (1 April 1881, p. 10). The government was aware of the danger, and did what it could to avoid any hint of collusion with foreign powers, which it thought might prejudice the verdict as it had in 1858 (see Gladstone to Granville, 12 April 1881, in Agatha Ramm [ed.], *The Political Correspondence of Mr Gladstone and Lord Granville 1876–1886* (1962), vol. I p. 256). Nevertheless it is probable that the prosecution of Most was undertaken on the initiative of Count Münster, communicated through the Queen (see PRO HO 144/A3385, which has some early items

The myth of 1858 survived powerfully too in the minds of the police, who if anything lived in even greater awe of it, and for longer. At some time after 1858 their activities against the refugees in England appear to have lapsed almost to their pre-1850 state, and to have remained in that state throughout the 1860s and 1870s. The early death of the unique Sanders may have had something to do with this; together with the fact that with the continent becoming less importunate there was less need for it, and with the bad press the police had got in 1858 it may have seemed less worthwhile. It is never possible to be absolutely certain about police activities in this sensitive area at this time, because the records which have been allowed to survive are so scanty; but it may be significant that they are much scantier for this later period than for the 1850s. Those which do survive suggest very strongly that police surveillance over the refugees at this time was far less systematic than earlier, and less efficient. A police report of 1868, for example, on the refugee meeting in London which Lord Lyons had put the government on to, reads as if it was compiled from a second-hand account: possibly from a newspaper.[28] Another report from 1872 reveals some of the difficulties which the police faced then in gathering the kind of information which had come so easily to Sanders in the 1850s: a police superintendent who tried to infiltrate a meeting of communist refugees in Islington told how

a person (whom I can identify) caught hold of me and assisted by others carried me forcibly out of the room and intimated that if I returned they would break my head. I did not return in order that no breach of the peace should take place.[29]

In the end the Home Office came to the conclusion that if they wanted to find out about the communists it would be best to ask Karl Marx himself:

missing but contains a reference [item 6] to a letter from Münster; and Gladstone to Ponsonby, 21 March 1881, in Gladstone papers, BL. Add. Ms. 44544 f. 146). In the event Most was convicted and sentenced to 16 months' hard labour. Shortly after his release in October 1882, he went to America where he became a leading anarchist, resumed the publication of *Freiheit*, and was imprisoned more than once for offences similar to his English one. There are reports of his trial (and appeal) in *The Times*, 1 April 1881 p. 4; 8 April p. 8; 5 May p. 12; 6 May p. 12; 26 May p. 13; 30 June p. 12; and in *Law Reports, Queen's Bench Division*, vol. VII, pp. 244–69. A more detailed examination of this affair and its implications will be published soon in the *Historical Journal*.

Despite Most's conviction, the doubt about juries remained. When the case of Vladimir Burtsev came up in 1898, the Public Prosecutor warned the government that a jury might not convict because of the 'general feeling that strong language on the subject of Russian institutions is excusable': see Alan Kimball, 'The Harassment of Russian Revolutionaries Abroad: The London Trial of Vladimir Burtsev in 1898', in *Oxford Slavonic Papers*, vol. VI (1973) p. 57. (The Home Office file of Burtsev's case, PRO HO 144/A59222, which Kimball – p. 56 – states was destroyed, is in fact extant.)

[28] Police Report (Williamson) of 23 July 1868: copy in PRO FO 27/1736. Pyat, who was one of the half-dozen most prominent refugees in London, is referred to as 'a M. Felix Pyat, a French refugee' – as if he was an unknown.

[29] Police Report (Williams) of 24 May 1872: PRO HO 45/9303/11335.

who turned out to be very obliging.[30] By 1878 it appears that police surveillance of refugees had subsided almost to nothing, and indeed that all memory of the days when their every move was known to the Metropolitan Police Commissioner had been erased. In October of that year the Russian ambassador asked the Foreign Office whether he might have the help of the London police to find out about the activities of Russian refugees in England; to which the response of the British authorities was illuminating. The Commissioner of the time, Sir Edmund Henderson, claimed that before then this had never been done, 'except when some overt act had been committed and materials were required in a prosecution in this country' – which was not true of the 1850s. He also pointed out how 'The Police action even in the Orsini case visited[?] great animosity against the Government of the day among a large class of the people': which shows how the memory of that event still flickered, pointing the lesson that 'any interference with the right of asylum in this country for political refugees is sure to arouse much feeling'. He claimed too that police espionage would be 'worse than useless', which further confirms the impression that it was not done then.[31] A rider to this was added by the Assistant Under-Secretary at the Home Office. If it were done, he said, and if it became known,

no one can say how far the present feeling against Russia, & the long-established feeling on the subject of absolute government, right of asylum, & secret police would not carry the public, when inflamed by political and social agitators. All sorts of falsehoods, incapable of refutation, would be invented. It would be impossible to make clear to the public exactly what had been done, and what had not been done, they would always say there were secret orders besides given to the secret police. In this respect I think the step would be more resented as an open provocation like that of Bernard.

It would also, he said, be difficult to know where to stop.

Suppose for instance you agreed at first only to watch the refugees here: well, one of them you learnt was just starting for Russia on a Nihilistic campaign – if you announced that to the Russian embassy, the result wd be that the moment the man set foot in Russia, he wd be arrested & either shot or sent to Siberia. Imagine the consequence in England if such a man was a Kossuth or a Garibaldi.[32]

So still the authorities were deterred from acting against the refugees by their fear of the public reaction; and still for evidence of that reaction they looked back, twenty years later, to the events and the men of the 1850s.[33]

[30] Robert Payne, *Marx*, pp. 426–8.
[31] Henderson Memorandum, 15 October 1878: PRO HO 45/9473/A60556.
[32] Lushington to Cross, 15 October 1878: *ibid.*, *loc. cit.*
[33] Things may have changed very soon after this. In the early 1880s Scotland Yard maintained a strict and regular watch on the publications, at least, of foreign revolutionaries in London, partly through the efforts of two Germans in the Metropolitan Police, Inspectors Hagen

Once or twice they were bolder, and succeeded a little way in circumventing those barricades which they believed had been erected in the 1850s. They could not after all absolutely depend upon the self-restraint of the continent, if they were not seen to be doing anything at all for it. So, for example, they brought their action against the *Hurriyete*; and when they were asked to by the Russian ambassador they put customs men on the *Ward Jackson* at Gravesend to see if it really was being fitted out by refugees to help the Polish insurgents; and they may have done what they could to persuade Garibaldi to leave. None of these measures was particularly vigorous, or effective: the *Hurriyete* defendant jumped bail and fled abroad before his case could be heard;[34] the *Ward Jackson* slipped anchor and set sail with the customs men still on board (they were disembarked a little lower down the Thames);[35] and by the time Garibaldi left his visit had already done its harm.[36] But they showed willing.

A more substantial move against the refugees was made in 1861. In that year Palmerston's second government made a more direct attempt to undo the harm that had been done in 1858, by slipping the essential features of the ill-fated Conspiracy Bill into a massive new Law Consolidation Bill which was lumbering its way through Parliament. The trick was spotted, and the clause was amended: the offence of conspiracy to murder reduced back again from a felony to a misdemeanour. Nevertheless the exercise achieved something, which was to dispel the uncertainty which had existed before about whether conspiracies to murder abroad were covered by the law.[37] In the same year a way was also found to stop

and von Turnow. This surveillance may have arisen out of the Johann Most case (*supra*, p. 208); at Most's trial Hagen denied having 'looked after' German political refugees before then; but it certainly continued thereafter. Reports by Hagen and von Turnow are in the (closed) Home Office file of the Most case, PRO HO 144/A3385; which also contains a significant letter from the Home Secretary of the day, Harcourt, to Liddell, 26 March 1881: 'H. Ponsonby has written to me on the subject of a Communistic Meeting reported in the Telegraph where most atrocious doctrines were preached. I have said we can do nothing as we have no authentic record but these meetings should be looked after for the future. Tell the Police to look after them.' Perhaps this pinpoints precisely when the change occurred.

[34] See PRO HO 45/9472/A38025.

[35] See Carr, *op. cit.*, pp. 208–10; and PRO HO 45/7514. Though it had not managed to prevent the crime, the government might still have charged the captain of the *Ward Jackson* with it on his return: and thought of doing so. On June 15 1863, however, the Law Officers advised against it, on the grounds that it could not be proved that he was aware that Poles were to be taken aboard his ship (at Southend) to fight abroad.

[36] In radical and refugee circles it was suspected that the government had something to do with Garibaldi's departure, earlier than was expected. There is no Home Office file on the Garibaldi visit, and very little mention of it in official Foreign Office papers. To Cowley Lord Clarendon wrote privately on April 20 that Garibaldi had decided to leave 'on the advice of physicians and true friends': PRO FO 519/179, quoted in Blakiston, 'Garibaldi's visit to England', *loc. cit.* Gladstone, Shaftesbury and Sutherland were probably among those friends, and may or may not have been prompted by Palmerston. I am grateful to Dr Derek Beales for allowing me to see the results (inconclusive as yet) of his research into this affair.

[37] See Commons debate on clause 4 of the Offences against the Person Bill, 15 July 1861: 3PD

Kossuth printing his private banknotes, without involving a jury: which was for the emperor of Austria to apply privately for a civil injunction. The injunction was granted, but on grounds which were almost universally felt to be dubious and bound to be overthrown on appeal: until Lord Campbell in the Court of Chancery (again therefore unhampered by a jury) found a clever way of upholding it, on the quite different ground that Kossuth's actions interfered with the Austrian emperor's proprietary rights.[38] The judgment, and indeed the whole affair, raised a minor storm in the press and in Parliament:[39] but it was a storm the government was protected from because it had not instituted the action; and the judges too, because by this way of doing it they had reserved the last word to themselves. Consequently it stood: a victory at last, after ten years of trying, by the authorities against Kossuth, who with Mazzini had always been the refugee who had caused the most annoyance. It was followed just three years later by a kind of victory over Mazzini too: not directly but through his English friend Stansfeld, who was forced to resign his junior government post in April 1864 because of his involvement with him. Stansfeld's resignation had nothing to do with foreign governments, who had not requested it; nor was it wanted by the British government, who on the first occasion it was offered turned it down. It was made necessary by a Tory offensive against the government on his account, which his resignation was intended to deflect.[40] Nevertheless it will have caused some satisfaction in France, where the presence in the government of this man who was believed to be a conspirator with the refugees against the emperor had been resented. These three various events could be said to be government successes against the refugees; but (except perhaps for the Kossuth judgment) they were very tiny ones, of scarcely any consequence at all against the background of massive inactivity which characterised these two decades after 1860.

During the 1860s and 1870s, in fact, things returned almost uncannily to the way they had been during the 1830s and 1840s: as if the 1850s had never

163 ff. 924–32. Twenty years later *The Times* (26 May 1881, p. 11) claimed that 'what had seemed so bad in 1858 was slurred over as harmless in 1861', which was an exaggeration.

[38] The original injunction was granted on 27 February and 4 May 1861: see *The Times* 28 February p. 11, 16 April p. 12, 17 April p. 11, 18 April p. 10, 19 April p. 10, 22 April p. 11, 6 May p. 11. The appeal was heard in the Court of Chancery in May and judgment issued on 12 June: see *All England Law Reports (1861–73)* (1971 edn.), pp. 1597–1615. See also Mrs Hardcastle (ed.), *Life of John, Lord Campbell*, vol. II, pp. 408–9.

[39] There were short debates in the Commons (arising out of questions) on 14 and 22 March: 3PD 161 cc. 1975–81, and 162 cc. 214–20. Critics were mainly concerned about how the banknotes came to the notice of the government in the first place: they suspected it was through the agency of an English spy employed in the service of the Austrians. The critics' case is also well elaborated in *The Economist*, 4 March and 13 May 1861.

[40] See 3PD 173, cc. 1256–60, 1931–9 (29 February and 14 March); 174 cc. 189–90, 250–86, 322–43, 396–402 (17 and 18 March, 4 April 1864).

really happened, or had been slept through by those who governed Britain afterwards. It was not as if there was no movement of refugees into Britain at all during this period. In fact after the fall of the Paris commune in May 1871 there was a large new influx comparable with that of the early 1850s: but provoking a reaction by the authorities much more like that of the 1830s, when the main diplomatic issue it had raised was the right of the continent to send its exiles to Britain, than that of the 1850s, when the issue had been the right of Britain to harbour them. Some concern was expressed in the country about the effect these communist refugees were having or might have on the working classes of England, but not enough to provoke more than one very perfunctory debate in Parliament, or any kind of sympathetic response from the government of the day;[41] which shows how far the national self-confidence of the 1850s was from being toppled yet. Privately the government may have been less sanguine, and feared the communists a little more;[42] and this may have been one reason for the diplomatic attack they launched in the spring of 1872 on France for shipping them to England: though they would not admit this. In fact although they were repeatedly asked for them they conspicuously neglected to give their precise objections to the practise, beyond labelling it, rather vaguely, 'a serious breach of international comity'.[43] The impression they tried to give was that they objected to having to support the refugees, who were mostly destitute, when they landed; but when the French government offered tentatively to send them over with money to support themselves it did not abate the British government's objection to them one whit.[44] Whatever the reason for it, they felt they had a grievance. France did not deny it: but she did point out that Britain's difficulties were partly of her own making. France's other neighbours did not allow the communists in, which left only England for them to go to. Of course Britain could not exclude them, though she contrived to give some of the *proscrits*, who came to British embassies and consulates to ask for permission to come, the impression she could by refusing it.[45] This would have made no difference had they decided to come all the same: but the confidence trick may have deterred some. It was, however, a very unfirm kind of ground on which to build an immigration policy. At one point the Foreign Secretary, Granville, on the suggestion of the government's Law Officers,[46] thought of issuing a threat to the French government that if

[41] 3PD 210, cc. 1183–1210 (12 April 1872).
[42] In 1871–2 it asked its ambassadors abroad to find out about the communists' impact there; their conclusions are summarised in a memorandum of 24 February 1872: PRO FO 64/760.
[43] Granville to Lyons no. 206, 16 May 1872: printed in PRO FO 881/2044 p. 10.
[44] Lyons to Granville no. 671, 27 May 1872: printed in *ibid.*, p. 24; and Granville to Lyons no. 240, 1 June 1872: *ibid.* p. 29.
[45] E.g. Delcambre to Lyons, 9 March 1872: *ibid.*, p. 4; Granville to Lyons no. 109, 22 March 1872: *ibid.*, pp. 6–7.   [46] L.O.O. of 4 April 1872: PRO HO 45/9303/11335.

they did not stop shipping them to England Britain would be forced 'to
enact such laws as would prevent its right of asylum being abused'.[47] It was
Lord Lyons in Paris who pointed out to him that this was really no threat at
all, because a law to prevent its asylum being abused was exactly what the
French wanted: and so it was held back (and all reference to it carefully
excised from the public version of this correspondence when it was later
published as a Blue Book).[48] Britain had hardly a foot to stand on. In
cabinet at the end of July, as Gladstone reported to the Queen,

It was argued that this conduct was highly unsatisfactory, and that permanent
submission to it could hardly be contemplated, but that we could only remonstrate
for the present, the law as it stands not supplying us with means of prevention, and
the difficulties of a change being as yet such as cannot be [?]circumvented.[49]

Consequently the communists continued to drain out of France into
England, until most of them were there, and the French government may
at last have made a genuine effort to close the door, after them.[50]

If the government felt some twinges of concern about them and the
subversive effects they might have on the English working class, it does
not appear to have lost them much sleep. When for example the Home
Office was asked (at the suggestion of the German ambassador) for its
thoughts on the subject in July 1871, its reply was quite imperturbable.
Although socialist ideas were 'disseminated and sometimes discussed in
England' it claimed that they had 'no root here'. It was 'notorious that the
leading and most active spirits among the various extreme political
associations in London' were foreigners. Their notions did not appear to
be catching on.

Ideas of revolution effected by force of arms, of destruction of public buildings, of
'popular revenge on detested individuals', have taken no hold on the English
working classes. Vague notions of some enlarged cooperative system under which
property and capital shall be peaceably absorbed for the benefit of all classes of
society, so that the very rich and the very poor shall disappear from the land,
undoubtedly are to be found among the more intelligent leaders of the Trades
Unions, and are generally becoming popularised. But up to this time these notions
are purely speculative, and no considerable section of Englishmen indulge in the
desire of propagating them otherwise than by peaceable discussion and the force of
reason.[51]

[47] Granville to Lyons no. 206, 16 May 1872: Printed in PRO FO 881/2044 p. 10.
[48] Lyons to Granville no. 618, 17 May 1872: *ibid.* p. 15. The expurgated Blue Book is PP
(1872) lxx, pp. 447–78.
[49] Gladstone to Queen Victoria, 31 July 1872: RA A44/43 (*Cabinet Reports from Prime Ministers
to the Crown 1868–1916*, Harvester Press Microfilms, reel 2).
[50] France promised to do what she could to stop it in June 1872 (PRO FO 881/2044 p. 31), but
reports came in of more landings through to November: see letters from Knight, 19 June;
Secretary of Local Government Board, 20 June; Young, 30 June; and Dodson, 10 July 1872,
in PRO FO 27/1968; despatches from Granville 20 June, 11, 20 and 27 July (nos. 272, 326,
350, 374) in PRO FO 27/1913; Enfield to Home Office 6 November 1872, in PRO HO
45/9303/11335.   [51] Liddell to Hammond, 12 July 1871: PRO FO 64/735.

Still therefore the government's view was that no danger was posed to liberal England by this socialist virus in its midst; towards which consequently its attitude was as unhysterical, unparanoid, complacent, even naïve, as it had been in the 1850s. Like then too it stood in marked contrast to the continental view of it, which saw the whole social fabric, as the Spanish government put it in a dispatch it circulated to all its allies in February 1872, 'menaced in its deepest foundations' by the activities of the First International: 'which flies in the face of all the traditions of mankind, which effaces God from the mind; family and inheritance from life; nations from the civilized world', and which therefore in Spain's view could not be tolerated 'even under the most liberal political institutions'.[52] Spain had already resolved to crush it out of existence in her own domains, but was concerned about the ability of the socialists to strike even from outside national frontiers, and so floated the idea of some concerted action between all the states of Europe and the Americas to wipe them out internationally, which will have been aimed above all at Britain, because Britain was by this time the refuge of most of them, and had from its beginning housed the International's headquarters. Bismarck made similar noises.[53] But Britain remained unmoved. In their country, explained Granville to the Spanish government in March 1872, the International 'confines its operations . . . chiefly to advice in questions of strikes', and had got nowhere at all with its more revolutionary designs among 'British workmen, whose attention is turned chiefly to questions affecting wages'. As to its effects abroad, the British government would 'highly condemn any attempts on the part of foreign refugees in England to excite insurrection' against régimes there; and to the German government in 1871 they had already promised to send on, confidentially, any information which might come to their hands concerning such attempts: and did.[54] But they were legally incapable of preventing them, or of taking any kind of

[52] De Blas to Rances y Villanueva, 9 February 1872, communicated to Granville 24 February 1872; translation printed in PP (1872) lxx pp. 718–20.

[53] A. F. Pribram, *England and the International Policy of the European Great Powers* (1931), p. 8, states that in the middle of June 1871 Bismarck corresponded with Granville 'regarding an understanding as to "common defence against the common enemy" and as to the "moral responsibility of England as the native land of the 'International' " '. I have found no trace of such correspondence at the British end (F.O. papers, Gladstone papers, Granville papers) beyond a letter from Bernstorff (the German ambassador) to the Foreign Office, 1 July 1871 (PRO FO 64/731) which may imply but does not openly request such an understanding. Bismarck was at this time co-operating with other European powers, notably Austria and Russia, along these lines – see Russell to Granville no. 250, 11 October 1872: PRO FO 64/747.

[54] Granville to Bernstorff, 17 July 1871: PRO FO 64/731. In September 1871 they passed on to Germany the information that Marx had returned to England – Granville to Petre, unnumbered, 19 September 1871: PRO FO 64/715; and at the beginning of 1872 a report from a man called Lachowa who claimed that he had been deputed by the International to murder Bismarck – Home Office to Foreign Office, 8 January 1872; Enfield to Russell 20 April and 12 June 1872: PRO FO 64/760; FO 244/259–60.

exceptional action against them, and did not consider that 'any ground exists which would justify them, on the present occasion, in applying to the Legislature for any extraordinary or further powers' against them:[55] and there the matter had to rest. The British government, feeling secure in itself, refused to co-operate with the continent, as it had also refused (by and large) in the 1850s.

The Government claimed that their view of this matter was 'shared both by Parliament and the public of this country',[56] and there can be little doubt that they were right. There were a few Cassandras, mostly Englishmen who knew the International best from its continental side; like the writer and Conservative politician Alexander Baillie Cochrane, who regarded it as a menace to civilisation and so led the movement in Parliament to have it outlawed: but he was very poorly supported there.[57] On the whole people thought and knew very little of it. Even some of those who knew more, however, were not as alarmed by it as in continental eyes they should have been; like for example *The Times*, which made quite a thorough study of it during the course of 1871[58] and still found nothing in it to be especially frightened of. Of course its doctrines were ludicrous – although *The Times* did not find them quite as ludicrous as might have been expected: 'an extraordinary medley of sense and folly', it described them in October,[59] which at least gave the socialists credit for some sense. The folly was of no great consequence. 'English working men are no fools, nor do we think they are likely to become fanatics.'[60]

The prevailing idea of English workpeople, if they think themselves ill-used, is a combination for a little more wages and a little less work. If they can achieve that, they are not disposed to attempt more. It is taking them out of their depth.[61]

If they sometimes used more violent language than was comfortable, this was mere rhetoric. *The Times* could not answer for foreigners, who for all it knew 'may be sincere and very practical'.

But we feel sure that when Mr Applegarth and the other Englishmen propose the *abolition of classes*, and inveigh against the maintenance of the domination of the rich by brute force, they know quite well they are using hyperbolical verbiage which has no reference to the state of their own country, or to the opinions of their own class.[62]

The Times even found it in itself to welcome the new trend, which it saw as but the natural result of 'the improvement in the conditions of life' which under Britain's enlightened system of government had been 'gradually

---

[55] Granville to Layard, 8 March 1872: printed in PP (1872) lxx p. 720.
[56] *Ibid., loc. cit.*
[57] 3PD 210 cc. 1183–94 (12 April 1872); and see his letter to *The Times*, 31 October 1871 p. 6.
[58] For example, its issue of 27 April 1871 carried a long and detailed article on the I.W.M.A.
[59] *The Times*, 27 October 1871, p. 9.   [60] *Ibid.*, 15 April 1872, p. 11.
[61] *Ibid.*, 23 September 1872, p. 7.   [62] *Ibid.*, 24 September 1871, p. 9.

spreading downwards for centuries', until it had 'now in no slight degree reached the working class', and so inevitably brought political ambitions in its train: which was laudable and responsible. If the expression of those ambitions at this stage appeared crude it was because they were as yet in their infancy (or a kind of difficult adolescence):

like children grasping at a light, these new politicians stretch beyond it into darkness, and grope amid distant confusion for objects close at their feet.

A few more years would bring maturity and moderation.

We listen, therefore, to all this declamation with a satisfied confidence that in the sober light of day, and corrected by the reflections of a multitude of minds, it will resolve itself into a recognition of our old-fashioned, just, and patient method of redressing grievances and satisfying the reasonable claims of all classes.

This, concluded *The Times*, was 'the way we have got on from the beginning'.[63] So there was no cause at all for concern. The system could take it.

Other countries, which were less fortunate or less wise, could not understand this, or the vital difference it made. In 1871 the London correspondent of a Parisian journal painted this picture of a Britain totally undermined by socialist subversion, and about to topple, but in its blinkered concern only for money-making unable to see it.

The whole of this vast empire is permeated by secret societies. The Internationale here holds its meetings almost publicly. It is said that the greater number of the dispossessed Princes of India, a good number of officers belonging to the Army and Navy, as well as Members of Parliament and even Ministers, are affiliated to it. The Government is aware of the infernal plan by which, at a given moment, the public buildings of London are to be exposed to the fate which befell so many in Paris. Boats are already waiting on the Thames to receive the treasures of the Bank of England – an easy prey, say the conspirators – as soon as the main artery of the Strand shall have been burnt, and the public buildings – the barracks especially – shall have been blown up . . . Careless by nature, and too much engaged with business to think of the morrow, spoiled by a long established liberty and a fabulous prosperity, having for many generations forgotten the scourge of war, foreign or civil, we allow ourselves to drift on without taking heed of the signs of the times.[64]

Of course this was all nonsense: but foreigners would not be persuaded. 'It is in vain to tell them', commented *The Times*, 'that they judge us by themselves; they will answer that we are like them, though we think we are not.'[65] It was the very same difference as before: the same incompatibility of outlook between the continent and Britain, conflicting assumptions, fundamentally opposed views as to the nature and causes of revolution,

[63] *Ibid.*, 27 October 1871, p. 9.
[64] *Ibid.*, 12 October 1871 (from the *Courier Diplomatique*).
[65] *Ibid.*, 24 November 1871, p. 9.

and the means therefore by which social and political stability were best preserved. The continent's warnings to Britain were the same in 1871 as they had been in 1851; the attitude of *The Times*, and of British middle-class opinion in general, identical on both occasions. Nothing had changed; nothing at least to cause Britons to doubt that one great political principle to which nearly all of them held in the middle of Victoria's reign: that subversives could only subvert the subvertible, and that therefore from all these afflictions which beset the continent repeatedly during the nineteenth century they were secure, because their system of government, and their political, social and economic institutions generally, were better.

The end of the Victorian policy of asylum, whose battles had been won in the 1850s, came in 1905 when, to control the flow of Jewish immigrants from Russia and eastern Europe into Britain, a new Alien Act came into being.[66] It was supposed to safeguard still the right of entry into Britain of those who could prove themselves to be genuine victims of political or religious persecution – and so to preserve the principle, which Britons still took at least an abstract pride in, of asylum. But of course it did not preserve the right of asylum in the sense in which the Victorians had understood it. In Victorian times it had been automatic: now it was a matter of discretion. The difference was crucial. In one important area of political activity, a liberal age had come to an end: and there was no possibility that it could return. The old practice anyway had outlived the conditions which had suited it best. Habits of mind were already before 1905 very different from what they had been in the 1850s and 1860s. Attitudes of which the Victorians would have been ashamed had become common parlance, and what the Victorians had accepted as axiomatic was coming to be seen as unrealistic idealism. The existence of a bright new Alien Act on the statute book completed the shift in the climate of opinion. What had once been impossible now became normal. What had been a right became a privilege. A new bureaucracy was spawned whose purpose was to administer the Act, and whose interest was to perpetuate it. War and the insistent demands of national security further entrenched and streng-thened it. After the war other 'controls' were dismantled, but not this one.[67] A generation was now grown to adulthood which had scarcely known a time when there had been no immigration controls. Successive layers were added to the thicket of barbed-wire which now surrounded the British Isles. In it a way through was kept open for political refugees to enter: but not without difficulty. Political asylum now had to be applied for. It was not always granted. Occasionally political refugees were extra-

---

[66] See Bernard Gainer, *The Alien Invasion* (1972); John A. Garrard, *The English and Immigration 1880–1910* (1971).

[67] See T. W. E. Roche, *The Key in the Lock* (1969).

dited back to the countries they had come from. More often they were expelled to somewhere else – a more generous nation than Britain had by now become – on the grounds that they threatened national security, or were subversive. At other times foreigners were refused entry into Britain for neither of these reasons, but because their opinions were merely offensive. None of these things was thinkable in Victorian times. A happy age of innocence had been lost, for ever.

The reasons for this are the reasons for the differences between the nineteenth century and our own. To those who (like the present author) incline towards material explanations of political attitudes and policies, it will be significant that the years when the refugees and their opinions were tolerated most were also years of exceptional economic growth and prosperity for Britain, and when free enterprise capitalism was at the height of its vigour and success. Confidence comes with success, and particularly with the early stages of success; and the confidence which for example *The Times* exuded throughout all these mid-Victorian years, in the resilience of Britain's institutions and their resistance to foreign political infections even when the carriers of them all congregated in their midst, is likely to have been related to the dominant economic euphoria of the time, which nothing but an economic failure could have punctured. Capitalism held the initiative, was winning, and appeared likely to continue to win, because it was its distinctive feature that it was a dynamic rather than a static system, expanding, constantly spreading its benefits wider and deeper, and able always therefore to adapt to or subsume new circumstances and situations. Mid-Victorian liberalism, which in Britain was akin to it, also shared this dynamic quality, this view of itself not as a state but as a process, a constant enlargement of liberty: 'progress'. Herein lay its strength: a strength which was commonly believed at the time to be self-generated and invincible, so that liberalism, and capitalism too, scarcely required protecting, did not need any special vigilance in defence of them even against those who had sworn to destroy them. The system worked on its own; and while it was working so wonderfully well there was no cause to question it or any of the principles which were derived from it. In particular there was no reason, while the long mid-Victorian boom went on, to doubt that Britain really could not be touched by these wild-talking foreigners who fled there, whose ideas had been nurtured in a stonier soil and could not take root in hers. It was this assumption which to a great extent made it possible for Britain to persist in her asylum policy – for surely the latter could not have survived the 1850s or the early 1870s if the refugees had ever been looked upon as a danger; and it was an assumption born of a particular stage of economic development, and its success.

But the boom did not last for ever; and so neither did that almost monolithic confidence in the efficacy of liberal-capitalism which had accompanied it. In the 1870s the system ran into difficulties. Profits fell, the rate of expansion faltered, and there set in what contemporaries called a depression (though they had been comfortable so long it is clear they did not know what a real depression was). The 1880s saw a spate of riots and strikes and 'outrages' in Britain and also in Ireland. The very basis of nineteenth-century society came under ideological challenge from a newly vigorous native socialism, which had connexions with a new breed of refugees, who were wilder than the old ones: anarchists and nihilists who mostly hailed from Russia, and after the assassination of the Tsar in 1881 came flushed with an ominous success. No longer could the material basis of society be said to be congenial to a policy of undiscriminating political asylum. It was not yet absolutely hostile to it. Between the time when the material foundation of the policy began to crumble, and the time when that crumbling seeped through into attitudes and policies, there was a delay while people slowly came to recognise what was happening and to adjust their assumptions accordingly. There was no absolute economic decline: nothing to jolt them violently out of those assumptions. The light of liberalism shone a little less brightly, perhaps, but still enough to give warmth and vigorous life for a few more years yet to the party which professed to be its special worshippers, and to their favourite shibboleth, the principle of free trade. In this frostier but not yet lethal climate the idea of open asylum was able to live on, sustained partly by the impetus given to it by the power of its own myth. In 1881, for example, when Britain was herself under threat from violent men living abroad – American Fenians – and so could understand the problem, still she continued to turn down invitations from continental powers even to join in discussing concerted measures against it, on the grounds, as the Foreign Secretary of the day put it to Gladstone, that acceptance was 'Impossible in the face of all the traditions'. [68] Those traditions therefore still had some force: but it was seeping slowly away. Small signs appeared that the idea was no longer so impregnable as it had been. Gladstone's government, for example, though it would not risk open collusion with the continent over refugees, was able in 1881 to launch a prosecution against one of them for a 'political' offence in a court of law, probably at the prompting of a foreign government, and to win. [69] The idea was no longer powerful enough to prevent that. Neither was it powerful enough to prevent what appears to have been the stealthy and noiseless but nonetheless significant re-erection in the early 1880s, under a Liberal administration, of that whole structure of police surveillance over the refugees' activities which 'public opinion' seemed to have put an end to in the later 1850s and which had lain in ruins, no one

---

[68] Granville to Gladstone, telegram, 11 April 1881: Gladstone papers BL. Add. Ms. 44173, f. 38.   [69] *Vide supra*, p. 208 fn. 27.

daring to lift a stone of it, since then: the resurrection of what might be termed a secret political police in British society, after two decades uniquely free of any such agency.[70] (It cannot be entirely coincidental – though there may be other than directly causal connexions to account for it – that those two decades followed so closely upon what is conventionally regarded as the beginning and end of the mid-Victorian boom.) And then, when the final challenge came in 1905, the idea – eroded as it had been by another twenty years of depression and doubt – proved too weak to withstand it: and it fell, capitulated to the logic of the times and of a stage in the development of capitalism which could afford it less, or thought so.

But this is far too glib. Material factors do not by themselves furnish a sufficient explanation for Britain's almost extravagantly permissive policy towards the refugees in the nineteenth century, or for its erosion afterwards. If the stage of development of capitalism in the mid nineteenth century can be said to have favoured the policy that was adopted at that time towards the refugees, it cannot be said in any rigid sense to have 'determined' it. The most that can be said is that that policy was a response to the material circumstances of the time: which however might have been responded to in other ways. In Britain in the mid nineteenth century those circumstances drew this particular response, because Britain was Britain and different, and different not only in the material basis of her life. We have seen that she very strongly felt herself to be different: freer, more favoured, *better* than her continental neighbours. This feeling of 'difference' may have been fundamentally a middle-class attitude: founded primarily upon the economic imbalance between Britain and Europe, based largely upon ideas of 'liberty' which were especially favourable to middle-class interests, and widely shared both by the working classes, and by the aristocratic classes of society which still to a great extent ran the country, only because the former were so gullible and blind to their real class interests, and the latter so devious in the defence of theirs. Underneath it all it may be possible to discern the dead weight of bourgeois self-interest, controlling and manipulating for its own ends. But the material it had to control and manipulate had a life of its own. Bourgeois self-interest did not absolutely *need* to give the latitude it did give to its political enemies in the 1850s and 1860s: except insofar as it was required to by 'tradition'. Britain in the mid nineteenth century had all kinds of 'traditions' of political life and conduct which were quite independent of capitalism. Freedom of speech; equality before the law; the independence of the judiciary; the ascendancy of Parliament; public accountability in government; a certain flexibility of political attitude on the part of the dominant classes in society, and a penchant for what was called 'moderation': some of these principles even in the recent past had been honoured

[70] *Vide supra*, p. 210 fn. 33.

more in theory than in practice, and none of them was quite so 'traditional' as it was widely thought to be: but all of them together made up a combination of qualities which gave a special character to mid nineteenth-century Britain, marked her off from her continental contemporaries, and also marked her off from other societies which at other times went through a similar stage of capitalist development to the one she was going through then. They helped, as we saw, to guide her response to the material conditions of the time into this particular channel of policy: together with a good measure of xenophobia – for the biggest difference between Britain and the continent at this time was undoubtedly her *sense* of difference; and some luck, which allowed these 'traditions' to assert themselves successfully against obstacles put up against them by (aristocratic) foreign policy makers for foreign policy reasons. Though the material circumstances of the time made Britain's policy towards the refugees possible, it was factors such as these, deriving in the main from distinctively British national attributes, which made it a fact.

And when this policy eventually met its end, it is significant that it was not primarily in response to any change of public attitude on the political question. Rather it was because of social pressures which overrode the political question: the effect upon the lives and the livelihood of native Englishmen of this quite substantially larger immigration of continental refugees amongst them. The suspected anarchist leanings of some of them was a factor, but not a leading one. If the absence of an alien act after 1850 had been sustained by a certain set of dominant political attitudes then – in particular, by a confidence in the non-subvertability of British society – the enactment of an Alien Act in 1905 does not necessarily indicate that those attitudes were now dead. Indeed they were not, but survived long into an age which provided far fewer material grounds for confidence than did the 1850s, which suggests that maybe material circumstances had not all that much to do with it. For example, in the 1850s there had been two ways of diagnosing and treating the phenomenon of 'revolution', counterposed against each other. One saw it as fomented by communist conspirators, held that concession would only encourage the conspirators to demand more, and for the treatment of the disease prescribed repression. This had been the dominant theory on the continent. The other diagnosed it as an effect of widespread and genuine unrest, believed that it was likely to be aggravated by repression, and prescribed concession. This had been the British view. It was still by and large the British view more than a century later. When in 1977 the government of the Republic of South Africa launched one of its periodical campaigns of newspaper closures and detention orders with the object of putting down black unrest there, the London *Evening Standard* adjudged that it had now lent credence to the dangerous political logic of terrorism and subversion. If the machinery of the state acts through brutality, repression of free speech and the use of the law in the service of the crudest racial discrimination, then there is nothing left for the oppressed minority but sabotage, lawlessness and mob violence.[71]

Those words could have been uttered by the *Morning Chronicle* against some act of Austria's in 1853. Repression bred extremism. The corollary of this, that moderation and liberalism inoculated a society against extremism was, in the 1970s, a little less easy to swallow unreservedly than it had been in the 1850s. Baader-Meinhoff, the I.R.A. and a handful of other such organisations seemed to give the lie to it: to show societies which appeared to be moderate and liberal and good still breeding dangerous fanatics, and vulnerable to them. The alternative 'conspiracy theories' of revolutionary politics found a fertile soil to grow in, far more fertile than in 1850. Tiny groups of dedicated 'communist' subversives were infiltrating trade unions, Labour party branches, even schools and universities, with the object of manipulating the whole inert mass of society towards the end set for it by this small, sinister minority. Such a way of thinking would have been (and in fact was) laughed out of court in the confident 1850s. In the 1970s it did not appear so risible. Terrorism (which in the strict sense of the word had hardly been known in the 1850s) appeared to pose a real threat to every European society, including Britain's. To counter it the British authorities could no longer afford to be too scrupulous in the methods they used. They could no longer, as they generally had in the 1850s and 1860s, allow a mere respect for privacy to come between them and a knowledge of what their enemies were secretly up to. They could no longer spurn so haughtily as they had in the 1850s the use of a political police (though for years they denied its existence). They could no longer turn down, as Granville had done so loftily in 1872, suggestions that they work together with their continental neighbours to put the menace down. They had at last become thoroughly Europeanised, as Buol and Schwarzenberg and the rest had always wanted. The ideological gulf had closed up. And yet some traces of the old ways of thinking remained. If it was universally acknowledged that terrorist bombs could injure even liberal societies, and that terrorists could not be appeased out of existence without destroying the fabric of society, yet it was not yet so widely accepted that liberal societies could be *revolutionised* in the same fashion. A revolution required far more than a 'conspiracy' to succeed. A minority could not overthrow a government on its own. It required majority support. If it got majority support it would be because the majority had been wronged. In a liberal society the majority was less liable to be wronged than in a repressive society. A minority could possibly provoke the society into being repressive, which might in the end do the trick; this

[71] *Evening Standard*, 20 October 1977.

in the 1970s was sometimes claimed to be the purpose of activities of
certain sections of the political left wing which otherwise appeared to be
merely counter-productive. But even this, it was said, was less likely to
happen in a society which was 'traditionally' as moderate, reasonable, and
liberal as Britain's was. This was by no means a unanimous feeling in
Britain in the 1970s, but it was a tenacious one, and it still showed through
in the realm of policy. Dissent was still widely tolerated. Even the most
'extreme' political tendencies were allowed to organise and propagandise.
With one exception, and that affecting only a portion of the kingdom, no
political party was banned. Political refugees were still permitted to live
and work for their causes in England, without any great fear that they
might subvert the English. Britain still liked fondly to regard herself as the
home of moderation, mid-way between and in all essentials quite apart
from the left-wing extremism of a Russia and the right-wing extremism of
a Chile: and more secure in her liberty for that reason. Some of the
complacency of the mid-Victorians still survived into this very different,
and for liberals far less hopeful, age.

Nevertheless there was a chasm between the two periods. In the 1970s
the state was fully armed with contingency powers to act against its
enemies if necessary: the weapons were often hidden, but they were there.
In the 1850s Britain's steadfast refusal to arm herself with any but the most
ineffective instruments against internal subversion staggered her continental allies, to whom it appeared as foolhardly as to swim naked among
sharks. The British government not only did not expel or turn away aliens:
it did not allow itself the power to expel them or turn them away; nor was
it even prepared to implement against them the very ordinary and mild
laws it did possess to prevent or punish criminal actions by them. This was
a different order of toleration entirely from the toleration afforded by any
British government to refugees afterwards, or by any continental government at any time at all.

We saw that this very negative policy was partly forced on the government in the 1850s, by a middle-class public whose opinions on this issue it
shared in part but not completely. It was the result of what was widely seen
at the time as a conflict between government and 'people', which the
'people' won. That there was a conflict was perhaps natural. Governments
in the 1850s differed very widely in social composition from the classes of
people they represented. Over large areas of policy this difference was
softened by the considerable 'bourgeoisification' of that section of the
aristocracy which was still so influential in government – its permeation
by the liberal ideas and ideals of the middle classes. But that bourgeoisification was not complete. Patches of unenlightenment still showed through:
especially in the realm of foreign affairs, which was a particular little
corner of government where aristocrats still reigned supreme, and which

they quite strongly believed should be conducted by means – if not necessarily towards ends – which were old-fashioned and aristocratic. Hence Clarendon's irritation at the 'democratic' implications of Milner Gibson's motion in February 1858. More important however was the fact that governments were nearer and consequently more sensitive to repres-entations from foreign powers, from whom – and not from domestic sources – all the pressure to change their policies towards the refugees came. From where the 'people' stood, feeling as they did less passionately than the foreign policy-making élite about such dispassionate concepts as the 'balance of power' and the like, with stronger feelings for what made an Englishman superior to a foreigner, and more shortsighted perhaps than their leaders, those pressures appeared like insults, which had to be resisted. Hence the conflict between government and people. What was less natural was that the 'people' should win it. It was by no means inevitable. British governments never have at other times been absolute slaves to their constituents, but on the contrary have been able and some-times notably prone to contravene the popular will. It is often called leadership, or firm government. It depends however upon a strong control by a government over its supporters in Parliament, formally exercised through the machinery of the Parliamentary party. That control Palmers-ton in 1858 proved not to have. His dominance in Parliament at that time rested not upon this but on his appeal to – his 'touch' with – the people outside Parliament. Consequently when that failed (because on this issue the policy he sought their support for appeared to fly in the face of the principles they had customarily given him their support for) his Par-liamentary base crumbled. That it was so friable, that party discipline and party allegiances were so weak, and that there was on hand in the House of Commons a combination of resentments sufficient to take advantage of this moment of folly to sink him, at this time when the crucial battle over the refugees was fought, was fortuitous. It could have happened the other way, the 'people' have lost; and after a month or two, probably, their strong feelings about it would have been forgotten. The principle of asylum would not have been affected. What would have been gravely damaged, however, were the extreme lengths to which it was taken, and the myth of popular invincibility in defence of it, which may have helped sustain it thereafter. Popular opinion, luck and an easing of the pressures for change after the 1850s together ensured that for another forty-five years British governments would be armed only with the very lightest of weapons, against any threat which might arise from the presence in England of refugees and subversives from abroad.

Of course the fact that they had no effective weapons then to use against the refugees did not mean that those weapons were not to hand, if a domestic need for them arose. The popular opinion which forbade it in the

1850s was not exactly a flawless pillar of liberal strength. It is arguable that, just as none of the small European nationalities which strove for independence in the nineteenth century ever achieved it by its own unaided efforts, but only with the self-interested help of other greater powers, so did other liberal ideas too require the help of more powerful hands before they could win through: from self interest or from prejudice, harnessed to them and furnishing the motive power. In this case the refugees may only have been tolerated because of the assistance which was given to their cause by a massive popular *in*tolerance: the xenophobia which to a large extent powered the movement in their favour. We have seen that it was not quite so simple as that. One element in the xenophobia of the 1850s was the belief that Britain was more liberal than foreign countries. Xenophobia, in other words, was itself founded in liberalism, as well as in those other murkier qualities of the collective mind to which it is generally (and probably correctly) attributed. Usually in the 1850s the foreigners who were most disliked were the least liberal ones, and those states which made efforts to be liberal, as Englishmen understood the term, were exempted from the prevalent odium. So Russia in the 1850s was the worst-liked power, and Piedmont the best. It may be too that a significant thread in the rabid anti-catholicism of the day was disapproval of the Roman church's authoritarianism. The policy of asylum was supposed to be a particularly vivid reflexion, in many various ways, of the difference between Britain and the continent in this regard, and this went far to explain the tenacity with which Britons held to it. Liberalism in mid nineteenth-century Britain was a pervasive creed, and also a fiery and aggressive one. Nevertheless it is giving far too much credit to its practitioners to suppose that it was inviolable. The refugees were never greatly liked in Britain. If they had ever come to seem to present a threat to domestic tranquillity, for example by interfering too boldly in English radical politics, or because their activities elsewhere seemed likely to threaten serious diplomatic repercussions, then it was not at all outside the range of possibility that the government might repair the deficiency in their weaponry, and arm themselves with the powers they at present lacked. In these circumstances it was likely that they would be able to do it quickly, and without serious opposition from the country. It had been done in 1848. The refugees themselves always feared this, which was one reason why they so chastely desisted from intervening in Britain's internal politics. In retrospect their fears may appear exaggerated, but it is quite likely that they were not. One more Chartist rally, and a bad report from Sanders, and they might have seen the middle and upper classes of Britain rushing to their armoury again.

It could be said in fact that the whole political and social structure of liberal Britain in the mid nineteenth century, of stability through 'consent', which the contemporary establishment took such a great pride in, was only buttressed in this kind of way by the potentiality of repression. We have seen for example that it was the official view of the police authorities in 1851 that the Great Exhibition of that year had passed off as peacefully as it had for no other reason than that they had taken precautions against its not doing so. People were cowed into what seemed to be consent, but really was not; kept in order not by the license they were given but by the discipline, the sheer force, which they knew lay hidden in the wings against them. There is no way of testing this proposition empirically. The 1850s and 1860s were a time which was particularly free of subversion, unrest and rebellion in England, which appeared to justify the confidence which the Victorian middle classes reposed in their abnormally liberal and tolerant practices in many areas of life: but this may not have been the proper conclusion to draw. The liberalism and relative openness of their society may not have contributed at all to its stability. They may on the contrary have been a result of it, qualities which were only made possible by a pre-existing stability which had other roots entirely, among them a kind of covert repression.

But if this was so, then it was not knowingly or cynically done. If it was a confidence trick it fooled its practitioners too. The Victorians believed genuinely in the efficacy as well as in the morality of their particular brand of liberalism. If it had ever been proved to be less efficacious than it appeared to them to be – if it had turned out damaging to the stability of the state and therefore to those interests which were served by the state – then no doubt they would have revised their policies: but it would have been with the greatest regret, and the most disturbing implications for them. Liberalism in the mid nineteenth century drew a large part of its strength from its *belief* in its strength, in its natural resilience. Freedom, the loosening of restricting and frustrating bonds, giving free rein to the play of self-interest, risky though they might appear at first in some areas of political and economic activity, would create their own order of stability and security and progress. This was the natural way of development, the path of history. (Like present-day Marxists, it was important and, when things went wrong for the liberal cause somewhere in the world, consoling for British liberals in the nineteenth century to believe that they were on the side of history.) If freedom had in any particular instance been shown to be inconsistent with stability and security and progress it might have damaged the creed considerably, slowed it and eventually maybe stopped it in its steady progression towards utopia. Possibly this is what happened in the end. In the twentieth century things looked less simple, and liberal confidence cracked. In the 1850s and 1860s, however, that confidence was riding high. The refugee policy of those years was a manifestation of it. It was not, as we have seen, a quite spotlessly liberal policy in its origin or in its implementation. Nor should it be taken on its own to prove that the age which gave birth to it was in any general sense more essentially liberal than, or superior to, our own. It may have been more fragile than its long persistence suggests to hindsight. And it may have been naïve, founded on false assumptions, and more perilous than the Victorians knew. Nevertheless it came off, and while it persisted it afforded a special distinction to the polity of nineteenth-century Britain. It was unique in space and time, peculiar to the mid-Victorians, and offering a startling and revealing contrast to the world around them then. To the Victorians at the time it was an object of considerable pride. To their successors it might appear an object of admiration, or of envy.

Select Bibliography

There are hundreds of books, articles and manuscript collections which relate to refugees who lived in England in the nineteenth century. This list only includes those among them which have been found most relevant to the particular aspect of their exile which is the subject of this book.

Place of publication is London unless otherwise stated.

I. MANUSCRIPT SOURCES:

(a) Official:

Foreign Office Papers, Public Record Office, Kew.
Home Office Papers, Public Record Office, Kew.
Metropolitan Police Papers, Public Record Office, Kew.

(b) Private:

Aberdeen Papers, British Library.
Bloomfield Papers, Public Record Office, Kew.
Broughton Diaries, British Library.
Clarendon Papers, Bodleian Library, Oxford.
Cowen Papers, formerly in Newcastle Central Library, now in Tyne and Wear County Archives Dept., Newcastle.
Cowley Papers, Public Record Office, Kew.
Gladstone Papers, British Library.
Granville Papers, Public Record Office, Kew.
Malmesbury Papers, Hampshire Record Office, Winchester.
Palmerston Papers (Broadlands MSS.), Historical Manuscripts Commission, London, and British Library.
Royal Archives, Windsor.
Russell Papers, Public Record Office, Kew.

II. GOVERNMENT PUBLICATIONS:

Hansard's Parliamentary Debates, series 1–3.
The Statutes of the United Kingdom ('*Statutes at Large*'), 1786–.

Parliamentary papers:

A Return of the Annual Sums of Money issued towards the Relief of . . . Refugees emigrating to this Country . . . from the Year 1815 to the present Period: PP 1841 xiii.

Report from the Select Committee on the Laws affecting Aliens: PP 1843 v.
Return, showing the number of aliens who may have been directed under the provisions of the Act 11 & 12 Vict. c. 20, to depart the Realm: PP 1850 xxxiii.
Census of Great Britain 1851, vol. II: PP 1851 xliii.
Correspondence respecting the Foreign Refugees in London; and *Further correspondence respecting the foreign refugees in London*: PP 1852 liv.
Return of the Number of Aliens Naturalised under the Provisions of the Act of 7 & 8 Vict. c. 66 . . .: PP 1854 liii.
Paper Respecting Foreign Refugees; *Correspondence respecting Foreign Refugees in England*; *Despatch from Count Walewski to Count de Persigny*; and *Despatch from Her Majesty's Ambassador at Paris*: PP 1857–8 lx.
Census of England and Wales for the Year 1861: vol. II, *General Report*: PP 1863 liii.
Report from the Select Committee on Extradition: PP 1867–8 vii.
Report of the Royal Commissioners for Inquiring into the Laws of Naturalisation and Allegiance: PP 1868–9 xxv.
Correspondence respecting the Embarkation of Communist Prisoners from French Ports to England: PP 1872 lxx.
Correspondence between the British and Spanish Governments respecting the International Society: PP 1872 lxx.
Census of England and Wales for the Year 1871; vol. III: PP 1873 lxxii.
Statistical Tables relating to Emigration and Immigration . . . in the Year 1876: PP 1877 lxxxv.
Report of the Royal Commission on Extradition: PP 1878 xxiv.
Report from Select Committee on Emigration and Immigration (Foreigners): PP 1888 xi; PP 1889 x.

III. NEWSPAPERS AND PERIODICALS:

(a) *Newspapers*:

Daily News
Globe
John Bull
Manchester Guardian
Morning Advertiser
Morning Chronicle
Morning Herald
Morning Post
Northern Star and Star of Freedom
People's Paper
Press
Red Republican and Friend of the People
Reynolds's Newspaper
Standard
The Times
Weekly Dispatch

(b) *Periodical journals*:

Annual Register
Democratic Review
Fraser's Magazine
Household Words
Illustrated London News
Punch
Quarterly Review
Voix du Proscrit and Le Proscrit

IV. CONTEMPORARY PUBLISHED SOURCES:

All England Law Reports 1861–73 (Reprints, 1965, 1971).
[Anon.] 'Aliens', in *Chambers's Journal*, September 1867.

Bussy, Charles de, *Les Conspirateurs en Angleterre 1848–1858: Etude Historique* (Paris, 1858)

Cabinet Reports from Prime Ministers to the Crown, 1868–1916 (Harvester Press Microfilm, 1974)

Collins, Wilkie, *The Woman in White* (1860; new ed. 1975)

Elton, Sir Arthur Hallam, *The Case Against the Late Ministry Plainly Stated* (1858)

[Empson, William], ('An Alien'), 'On the Alien Bill', in *Edinburgh Review*, vol. 42 (1825).

Enfield, Viscountess (ed.), *Leaves from the Diary of Henry Greville*, vols. 1–2 (1883–4)

'Englishman out of office, An', *A Voice from England in answer to 'L 'Empereur Napoleon III et l'Angleterre'* (1858)

[Gallenga, Anthony] ('Anglomane'), 'Foscolo and English Hospitality', in *Fraser's Magazine*, vol. 31 (1845)

[Gladstone, W. E.], 'France and the late Ministry,' in *Quarterly Review*, vol. 103 (1858)

Greville, Charles C. F., *A Journal of the reigns of King George IV, King William IV and Queen Victoria ('The Greville Memoirs')*, new edn., ed. Henry Reeve (8 vols., 1896–8)

[Gueronnière, L. E. A. de la], *The Emperor Napoleon III and England* (Paris, 1858)

[Hamilton], [Mrs] C. G., *The Exiles of Italy* (Edinburgh, 1857).

Hardman, Frederick, 'The London Diary of a German Authoress', in *Blackwood's Magazine*, vol. 70 (August 1851).

Herzen, Alexander, *My Past and Thoughts* (English edition, 1968).

G. J. Holyoake, *Sixty Years of an Agitator's Life* (2 vols., 1892).

Bygones worth Remembering (2 vols., 1905).

'Homme du peuple, Un', *Les Assassins Politiques: deux mots à l'Angleterre* (Paris, 1858).

Hugo, Charles, *Les Hommes de l'Exil* (Paris, 1875).

Hugo, Victor, *Actes et Paroles pendant l'Exil*, vol. 1 (Paris, n.d.).

Kropotkin, P., *Memoirs of a Revolutionist* (2nd edn., 1906).

'Lancet', *Life of Dr. Bernard . . .* (n.d. [1858]).

Laughton, J. L. (ed.), *Memoirs of the Life and Correspondence of Henry Reeve* (1898).

Law Reports, Queen's Bench Division, vol. 7 (1872).

A. A. Ledru-Rollin, *The Decline of England* (2 vols., 1850).

Linton, W. J., *European Republicans. Recollections of Mazzini and his Friends* (1892).

Three Score and Ten years 1820–1890: Recollections (1894).

Literary Association of the Friends of Poland, *Annual Reports*, 1855, 1858, 1859.

Malmesbury, 3rd Earl, *Memoirs of an Ex-Minister* (1885 edn.).

[Marshall, Frederic], 'Alien Laws', in *Blackwood's Edinburgh Magazine*, vol. 116 (1874).

Martineau, Harriet, 'Representative men: Political agitators', in *Once a Week*, vol. 5 (1861).

Mazzini, G., *Epistolario di Giuseppe Mazzini*, 58 volumes, in *Scritti editi ed inediti di Giuseppe Mazzini* (Imola, 1909–41).

[Mednyánszky, Sándor], ('Miss A. M. Birkbeck'), 'Daguerreotype of an Exile's Fate', in *Sharpe's London Magazine*, n.s., vol. 4 (1853).

Parry, E. Jones (ed.), *The Correspondence of Lord Aberdeen and Princess Lieven 1832–1854* (2 vols., 1938, 1939).

Richards, E. F. (ed.), *Mazzini's Letters to an English Family 1844–72* (3 vols., n.d. [1920–2]).

[Sala, George A.], 'Perfidious Patmos', in *Household Words*, vol. 7 no. 155 (1853).

Savignac, Albert, *Attitude et Conduite de l'Angleterre envers la France et les autres nations* (Paris, 1858).

State Trials, n.s., vols. 7 and 8 (1896, 1898).

Strafford, Countess of (ed.), *Leaves from the Diary of Henry Greville*, 3rd series (1904).

Ulbach, Louis, *Nos Contemporains* (Paris, 1883).

The Letters of Queen Victoria, (11 vols., 1907–1932).

Waters, John, *The Refugees, and other Poems* (1862).

Wellesley, Col. the Hon. F.A. (ed.), *The Diary and Correspondence of Henry Wellesley, First Lord Cowley, 1790–1846* (n.d.).

(ed.), *The Paris Embassy during the Second Empire: Selections from the Papers of Henry Richard Charles Wellesley, 1st Earl Cowley* (1928).

[Wenckstern, Otto von], 'Lost in London', in *Household Words*, vol. 3 no. 68 (1851). 'The German Exile's New Year's Eve', in *Household Words*, vol. 4 no 92 (1851)

[Henry G. Wreford], 'Spy Police', in *Household Words*, vol. 1 no. 26 (1850).

v. SECONDARY WORKS:

Beales, Derek, *England and Italy 1859–60* (1961).

Bell, H. C. F., *Lord Palmerston* (2 vols., 1936).

Braunthal, Julius, *History of the International 1864–1914*, Part I, *The Forerunners* (1966).

Brock, Peter, 'Joseph Cowen and the Polish Exiles', in *Slavonic and East European Review*, vol. 32 (1953–4).

'Polish Democrats and English Radicals 1832–62', in *Journal of Modern History* vol. 25 (1953).

'Zeno Świętosławski, a Polish Forerunner of the *Narodniki*', in *American Slavic and East European Review*, vol. 13 (1954).

'The Polish Revolutionary Commune in London', in *Slavonic and East European Review*, vol. 35 (1956).

'Polish socialists in Early Victorian England: three documents', in *Polish Review*, vol. 6 no. 1/2 (1961).

'A Polish "Proscrit" in Jersey', in *Bulletin of the Société Jersiaise*, vol. xvi no. 2.

Bunyan, T., *The History and Practice of the Political Police in Britain* (1976).

Calman, Alvin R., *Ledru-Rollin après 1848 et les proscrits français en Angleterre* (Paris, 1921).

Carlton, Grace, *Friedrich Engels, the Shadow Prophet* (1965).

Carr, E. H., *The Romantic Exiles* (1933, new ed., Harmondsworth, 1968).

Cerutti, Toni, *Antonio Gallenga* (1974).

Connell, Brian, *Regina v. Palmerston* (1962).

Cunningham, W., *Alien Immigrants to England* (1897).

Dechène, H., 'Les Proscrits du Deux-Décembre à Jersey (1852–1855)', in *Etudes Religieuses*, vols. 151–2 (1917).

Deries, Léon, 'Policiers et Douaniers contre Victor Hugo', in *Grande Revue*, vol. LXXXV (1914).

Dessal, Marcel, *Un Révolutionnaire Jacobin: Charles Delescluze* (Paris, 1952).

Dictionary of National Biography (22 vols., 1921–2).

Florescu, Radu R. N., *The Struggle against Russia in the Roumanian Principalities* (Monachii, 1962).

Gainer, Bernard, *The Alien Invasion* (1972).

John A. Garrard, *The English and Immigration 1880–1910* (1971).

Gemkow, Heinrich *et al.*, *Karl Marx: a Biography* (Dresden, 1968).

Gilley, Sheriden, 'The Garibaldi Riots of 1862', in *Historical Journal*, vol. 16 no. 4 (1973).

Gleason, John H., *The Genesis of Russophobia in Great Britain* (Cambridge, Mass., 1950).

Gossman, N. J., 'British aid to Polish, Italian, and Hungarian exiles 1830–1870', in *South Atlantic Quarterly*, vol. 68 (1969).

Hales, E. E. Y., *Mazzini and the Secret Societies: the Making of a Myth* (1956).

Hall, Basil, 'Alessandro Gavazzi: a barnabite friar and the risorgimento', in D. Baker (ed.), *Studies in Church History*, vol. 12 (1975).

Hardcastle, Mrs (ed.), *Life of John, Lord Campbell* (2 vols., 1881).

Hearder, H., 'Napoleon III's Threat to break off Diplomatic Relations with England during the Crisis over the Orsini Attempt in 1858', in *English Historical Review*, vol. LXXII (1957).

Hollingsworth, Barry, 'The Society of Friends of Russian Freedom: English Liberals and Russian Socialists, 1890–1917', in *Oxford Slavonic Papers*, n.s. vol. 3 (Oxford, 1970).

Holmes, Colin (ed.), *Immigrants and Minorities in British Society* (1978).

Hooker, K. W., *The Fortunes of Victor Hugo in England* (New York, 1938, reprinted 1966).

Houghton, Walter E. (ed.), *The Wellesley Index to Victorian Periodicals* (2 vols., Toronto, 1966, 1972).

Hulse, James W., *Revolutionists in London: a Study of Five Unorthodox Socialists* (Oxford, 1970).

Imlah, Ann G., *Britain and Switzerland 1845–60* (1966).

Isser, Natalie, *The Second Empire and the Press* (The Hague, 1974).

Jánossy, Dénes A., *Great Britain and Kossuth* (Budapest, 1937).

Kimball, A., 'The Harassment of Russian Revolutionaries abroad', in *Oxford Slavonic Papers*, vol. 6 (Oxford, 1973).

Kutolowski, J. F., 'English Radicals and the Polish Insurrection of 1863–4', in *The Polish Review*, vol. XI (1966).

Lohrli, Anne (comp.), *Household Words . . . Table of Contents, List of Contributors and their Contributions* (Toronto, 1973).

Loubère, Leo A., *Louis Blanc* (Evanston, Ill., 1961).

McCabe, Joseph, *Life and Letters of George Jacob Holyoake* (1908).

McLellan, David, *Karl Marx, his life and thought* (1973).

Maxwell, Sir Herbert, *The Life and Letters of George William Frederick, Fourth Earl of Clarendon* (2 vols., 1913).

A. Müller-Lehning, 'The International Association (1855-9)', in *International Review for Social History*, vol. 3 (1938).

Nicolaevsky, B., 'Toward a History of "The Communist League" 1847–1852', in *International Review of Social History*, vol. 1 (1956).

Packe, Michael St. John, *The Bombs of Orsini* (1957).

Palm, Franklin J., *England and Napoleon III* (Durham, North Carolina, 1948).

Partridge, Monica, 'Alexander Herzen and the English Press', in *Slavonic and East European Review*, vol. 36 (1957–8).

    'Alexander Herzen and the younger Joseph Cowen, M. P.', in *Slavonic and East European Review*, vol. 41 (1962–3).

Payne, Howard C., *The Police State of Louis Napoleon Bonaparte 1851–1860* (Seattle, Wash., 1966).

Payne, Howard C. and Grosshans, H., 'The Exiled Revolutionaries and the French Political Police in the 1850s', in *American Historical Review*, vol. 68 (1963).

Payne, Robert, *Marx* (1968).

Renard, Edouard, *La vie et l'oeuvre de Louis Blanc* (Toulouse, 1922).

Ridley, Jasper, *Lord Palmerston* (1970).

Roberts, J. M., *The Mythology of the Secret Societies* (1972).

Roche, T. W. E., *The Key in the Lock* (1969).

Rothstein, Th., *From Chartism to Labourism* (1929).

Rudman, Harry W., *Italian Nationalism and English Letters* (1940).

Saville, John, *Ernest Jones: Chartist* (1952).

Schoyen, A. R., *The Chartist Challenge, A Portrait of George Julian Harney* (1958).

Seton-Watson, R. W., *Britain in Europe 1789–1914* (Cambridge, 1937).

Sibley, N. W. and A. Elias, *The Aliens Act and the Right of Asylum* (1906).

Smith, F. B., 'British Post Office Espionage, 1844', in *Historical Studies*, vol. 14 no. 54 (Melbourne, 1970).

    Radical Artisan: William James Linton, 1812–97 (1973).

Southgate, Donald, '*The Most English Minister . . .*': the policies and politics of Palmerston (1966).

Stevens, Austin, *The Dispossessed* (1975).

J. Tchernoff (ed.), *Associations et Sociétés Secrètes sous la deuxième République 1848–1851* (Paris, 1905).

Temperley, H. W. V. and L. M. Penson, *A century of diplomatic blue books, 1814–1914* (Cambridge, 1938).

Urban, Miriam B., *British opinion and policy on the unification of Italy 1856–1861* (New York 1938).

Vincent, E. R., *Gabriele Rossetti in England* (Oxford, 1936).

Weber, Günther, *Die Polnische Emigration im neunzehnten Jahrhundert* (Essen, 1937).

Weisser, Henry G., 'Polonophilism and the British Working Class, 1830 to 1845', in *The Polish Review*, vol. 12 (1967).

    British Working-class movements and Europe, 1815–48 (Manchester, 1975).

Wicks, Margaret C. W., *The Italian Exiles in London, 1816–1848* (1937).

Robert Woodall, 'Orsini and the Fall of Palmerston', in *History Today*, October 1976.

Zarek, Otto, *Kossuth* (1937).

Zévaès, Alexandre, 'Les Proscrits français en 1848 et 1851 à Londres', in *La Révolution de 1848*, vol. 20 (Paris, 1923–4).

Index

Aberdeen, 4th Earl, 105, 146, 148, 149, 179; coalition government (1852–5), 149
agents-provocateurs, 28–9, 38, 133, 155
Albert, Prince, 184
Alexander II, Tsar, 220
Alien Acts (1793–1836), 3, 8n., 9, 68, 70, 71, 73, 122n., 206; (1848), 3, 8n., 41, 57, 86, 142; (1905), 8n., 218, 222
Alien Bills, discussion of (1850–80), 119–20, 122, 142, 148, 167, 170, 175, 176, 177, 187, 196, 206, 222
aliens, disabilities of, 3–4; Select Committee on (1843), 5
alliance, Anglo-French (1854–6), see Crimean War alliance
Allsop, Mrs, 189n.
Allsop, Thomas, 190n., 196
ambassadors, see diplomats
America, see United States of America
amnesties, European, 16n., 17, 201, 202
anarchists, 207n., 209n., 220, 222
anglophilia among refugees, 69
anglophobia among refugees, 23–5
anti-catholicism, 39–40, 43, 79, 106–7 and n., 226
Argyll, 8th Duke, 172n., 184
aristocracy, 68, 72, 88–90, 91, 92, 97, 126, 146, 193, 221, 224; and foreign policy, 183–4, 222, 224–5
Art Journal, 6
Arundel, Earl of, 76, 93
Ashurst, William, 74
assassination, 33–7, 46, 61, 77, 102–3, 159, 207; *see also* conspiracies; Greco plot; murder; Orsini plot; Pianori plot; Tibaldi plot; tyrannicide
asylum, principle of, 1–3, 7–8, 111–12, 124, 143, 218
Auckland, Earl of, 90
Ausgleich (1867), 17
Austria, 10, 17, 32, 56, 59, 60, 61, 65, 66, 105, 131–2, 135–6, 140–1, 145, 146–7, 149, 159, 162, 173–4, 200–1, 215n., 223; emperor of, *see* Franz Joseph

Austrian army, 16, 29
Austrian Dungeons in Italy, The, 31
Austrian police, 137
Austrophilia, 105
Austrophobia, 71, 105, 111, 131

Baines, M. T., 176n.
Bakunin, Michael, 18
balance of power, 32, 131, 139–40, 225
banknotes, revolutionary, *see* bonds
banquets, 26, 31
Baranelli, Luigi, 43n.
Barclay and Perkins brewery, 108, 110
Baroche, P.-J., 58
Barthélemy, Emmanuel, 30, 43n., 76
Bauer, Heinrich, 14
Bavaria, 60
Bayonne plot (1852), 36, 159
beards, 76, 88
Beaufort, 7th Duke, 85n.
Beck, Baroness von, 28–9 and n., 31n.
begging, 20, 43 and n., 75, 81
Belgium, 1, 30, 46, 53, 57, 64
Beniowski, Major Bartłomiej, 40
Bentinck, Lord George, 182
Bernard, Martin, 190n.
Bernard, Simon, 79, 144, 146, 152n., 171, 190–6, 200, 210
Bernstorff, Count, 215n.
Bethell, Richard, 175
Bettera, Count, 8n.
Billault, A.-A.-M., 134
Birmingham, 120n., 170
Bismarck, Prince, 215
Blanc, Louis, 2, 14, 17, 23 and n., 27, 31n., 39n., 51, 84n., 87, 90
Blanquism, 27, 35
Blanquist rising (1839), 14
Blareau, Joseph, 151n.
Blas, Señor de, 215
Bloomfield, 2nd Baron, 114, 143, 152n., 162
Blue Books, 105–6, 149, 214
'Bomba', King, *see* Ferdinand II